ODYSSEY SERIES IN LITERATURE
ROBERT SHAFER, *General Editor*

TENNYSON

REPRESENTATIVE POEMS

ALFRED TENNYSON

*From the portrait in the National Portrait Gallery,
painted by Samuel Laurence about 1838*

TENNYSON

REPRESENTATIVE POEMS

Selected and Edited by
SAMUEL C. CHEW
Professor of English Literature, Bryn Mawr College

THE ODYSSEY PRESS
New York

PREFACE

The poems reprinted in the principal portion of this volume are arranged in eight groups within which the order is roughly chronological, though chronology is tempered with logic and convenience. The first group of three poems is intended to serve as a sort of preludium to the entire volume. Then follow the best of Tennyson's Songs, of which it may be safely said that no matter how much of his work is ultimately forgotten the world will not willingly let them die. "The Palace of Art" and "A Dream of Fair Women" are placed in a separate section as the most ambitious poems of Tennyson's early maturity. In the fourth group will be found the eight poems on classical subjects which range in date of composition over six decades. With them are the tributes to Catullus and Virgil and the lines to Milton, an experiment in classical metre. The fifth group contains poems on medieval themes, all but one drawn from Arthurian Legend. The reasons for the choice of the four *Idylls of the King* are indicated in the Introduction. The sixth section is something of a miscellany of which the chief item is *Maud*. Here will be found examples of the "domestic" poems, "Locksley Hall," "Enoch Arden," the ballad of "The Revenge," the powerful late dramatic monologue, "Rizpah," and "The Voyage of Maeldune." "The Charge of the Light Brigade" immediately follows *Maud* (though in date of composition it precedes it) because the monodrama closes with the outbreak of the Crimean War. The seventh section is devoted to elegiac poems, with the lines "In the Valley of Cauteretz" following *In Memoriam* because of the memories of Hallam recalled in them. The final group is made up of personal, autobiographical and "philosophical" poems. In Appendix I the Juvenilia include both some of the pieces which Tennyson retained in his Collected Works

v

in that category and also some pieces which he discarded. Appendix II ("Literary Squabbles"—the phrase is the poet's own) displays his sensitiveness to criticism and an ability as a satirist which he rarely exercised and once only with damaging effect. In Appendix III are reprinted a few representative pieces by Frederick Tennyson and Charles Tennyson-Turner. One of these poems, "The Phantom," is of too moving a loveliness to deserve the oblivion which has overtaken it; and the eight poems included in this Appendix will serve to associate the three brothers together once more in a single volume as they have not been for a hundred and fourteen years.

Save for an occasional doubt about punctuation, there is no "textual problem" for the editor of Tennyson's poems. The poems have been so fully commented upon by former editors that the task of the present commentator has been in the main one of selection and condensation. To his predecessors in this rich field, and especially to Professors Bradley, Mustard, and Van Dyke, he is under deep obligations.

Thanks are due to The Macmillan Company for permission to include "The Death of Œnone" and "The Silent Voices" from Tennyson's *Poetical Works,* Globe Edition, and to Professor William Ellery Leonard for permission to quote from his verse translation of Lucretius.

S. C. C.

CONTENTS

V. POEMS ON MEDIEVAL SUBJECTS

VI. MAUD AND MISCELLANEOUS POEMS

VII. IN MEMORIAM AND OTHER ELEGIES

VIII. PERSONAL AND MEDITATIVE POEMS

APPENDIX I. JUVENILIA

INTRODUCTION

I

"The poet's work is his life, and no one has the right to ask for more." There is this much of truth in Tennyson's dictum, that in his own case his biography (one soul-shaking event apart) is hardly more than the tale of his successive volumes of poetry which, with a few eddies and reverses, mark the slow broadening down of a great reputation till in his final decade he became, as it were, a national institution. What has to be said in this brief introduction will, therefore, concern the poetry more than the poet, and the poet only to the extent that his life and character must be taken into account in any estimate of his poetry.

So far as the records tell, the remoter forebears of Alfred Tennyson evinced no characteristics of temperament or talent which promised the stemming of a genius from the family tree; but the historians of literature who have said the same of the ancestry of many poets seem to forget that the wind of the spirit bloweth where it listeth. In 1809, a year of famous births, it chose to blow in various parts of England and America; and it blew strongly over a Lincolnshire wold where in the village of Somersby on August the fifth or sixth (testimony differs on this insignificant particular) the future Laureate was born. He was the fourth (the third to survive) of the twelve children of the Reverend Doctor George Clayton Tennyson, rector of Somersby. Dr. Tennyson came from a milieu that was well-to-do, but he had been disinherited by his father in favour of a younger brother. The mood of capricious impetuosity in which this action was taken was

characteristic of the Tennysons; and though the good old institution of pluralism provided the clergyman with a competence,
the loss of his inheritance may in part account for the tendency
to melancholia and hypersensitiveness which he passed on to
his darkly handsome children. The poet came naturally by
that formidable sternness of demeanour which awed the chance
acquaintances of later days, for his father had borne himself in
that manner. Dr. Tennyson's love and knowledge of classical
literature enabled him to supplement the training which his
sons obtained at a little school in nearby Louth. In the case
of his most famous son this devotion to the classics became a
chief part of his equipment as a poet. The father possessed to
a modest degree the gift of expressing himself in verse. Several of his children manifested at an early age a talent for
versification; in the two eldest boys this was marked; in the
third it quickly became pre-eminent in the family circle, so
that Frederick and Charles were overshadowed by the genius
of Alfred.

Biologists hold, or used to hold, that the unborn child passes
in the course of gestation through stages of earlier forms of
life; and just so, it may not too fancifully be held, the embryo
poet sometimes recaptures the modes of certain of his predecessors, discarding one for another as he develops towards his
individual style. This was the case with Keats, and even more
strikingly it was the case with Tennyson. The poet in whose
footsteps he first essayed to walk was James Thomson, the
author of *The Seasons;* and a Thomsonian delicacy in the description of natural objects, brought to a more discriminating
precision through love of his native region, remained a characteristic of his poetry. But a greater than Thomson was soon
to claim the homage of the boy's imitation; and before he was
ten years old he was writing hundreds of lines of heroic couplets, often cleverly antithetical, in the manner of Alexander
Pope. The earliest piece of his that has survived (printed
for the first time a few years ago by his grandson) is an expanded paraphrase of the opening lines of Claudian's *De Raptu
Proserpinae,* turned into couplets. To the theme of Proserpine

he was to return at the very end of his life, and in all the intervening years he was never unfaithful in his devotion to the poets of antiquity. The influence of Pope, on the other hand, endured for but a little while, and was succeeded, when he was about twelve, by that of Scott, in whose manner he composed (as he afterwards recalled) an epic of some six thousand lines, filled with battles set against a background of sea and mountains, and written "with Scott's regularity of octosyllables and his occasional varieties." This epic he afterwards destroyed; but he preserved the manuscript of a drama, written at the age of fourteen, which achieved posthumous publication and some celebrity more than a century after it was composed. This drama, *The Devil and the Lady,* is precociously clever and genuinely amusing even after all these years; to the family at Somersby it must have been an augury of genius, though what the solemn father made of it is not recorded. Examining it, we see that the boy had wandered or had been led into one of the blind alleys of romanticism which in the eighteen-twenties opened on either side of the highroad of poetry: on the one hand, the grotesque (which he here followed), and on the other, the pretty (which presently he was to follow for a time and into which he strayed back too frequently in later years). In *The Devil and the Lady* the young Tennyson was doing with a facility as obvious as his immaturity what Thomas Lovell Beddoes, unknown to him, was attempting to do. In other words, this little play and a fragmentary ballad "The Coach of Death" (written about the same time) show that he was affected by the vogue of grotesquerie and diablerie of which there are abundant examples among the drawings and engravings of the period. A touch of this macabre humour survives in an otherwise negligible poem "The Goose," for which Tennyson seems to have had a predilection, since he never discarded it from his collected works as he did so many poems of his nonage.

The three brothers collaborated in the preparation of a volume of poems for which they succeeded in finding at Louth a publisher so disinterested, or so much devoted to the inter-

ests of the Tennyson family, as to give them twenty pounds
for their verses. Since Frederick's part in the joint venture
was small and his nature retiring, the volume was entitled
Poems by Two Brothers. It appeared in the spring of 1827,
when Alfred was not yet eighteen. Naturally it attracted
almost no attention; but *The Gentleman's Magazine* commended it as "a graceful addition to our domestic poetry"
(whatever that may have meant) and one or two ephemeral
journals condescended to praise it more heartily than anyone
would today. A boyish exhibition of rather more than boyish
erudition is the most conspicuous characteristic of this now
rare and famous book. Greek literature is but seldom drawn
upon; but of Latin authors there is an ample display, and
there is a long array of English writers, with a sprinkling of
French and Spanish, who are quoted in the notes. In addition to poets, essayists, and historians, there is one writer
whose presence is perhaps surprising: Sir William Jones, the
orientalist. The influence of this great scholar's books en-
couraged the taste for oriental themes and imagery which the
young poets derived from their reading of Lord Byron and
Thomas Moore. This romantic vein outlasted the direct influence of Byron; and several years later, when Alfred Tennyson was no longer composing mere pastiche, he painted in a
style of his own a vision of "the golden prime" of the Baghdad
Caliphate; and in a poem where the aspiration comes as a
surprise he expressed his longing to see before his death "the
palms and temples of the South." The wish remained unful-
filled.

When in 1828 Tennyson with his brother Charles followed
Frederick to Cambridge, the Byronic influence, never very
strong, ceased abruptly, never to reappear. It was the moment
when the posthumous renown of Shelley was brightening and
the fire of Byron was beginning to pale into ineffectuality.
In the company of brilliant young men into which Tennyson
was now introduced — Arthur Henry Hallam, Richard C.
Trench, Richard Monckton Milnes (later Lord Houghton),
James Spedding, and others — he must have shared in many a

discussion of Shelley's genius. Presently there occurred the famous inter-university debate when Oxford championed Byron, the son of Cambridge, and Cambridge championed Shelley, the outcast son of Oxford. The cause of Byron won the verdict; but the fact of significance is that the question of relative greatness was debated at all. Tennyson may not wholly have sympathized with the enthusiasm of his fellow-collegians, for Shelley's genius remained alien from his own. There are not many Shelleyan echoes in his poetry; and the faintly Shelleyan quality of *The Lover's Tale,* which was privately printed in 1833, may account for Tennyson's dissatisfaction with it and for its long suppression.

In 1829 Tennyson won the chancellor's prize medal with "Timbuctoo," a poem in Miltonic blank verse in which along with further signs of promise in its wealth of imagery and occasional organ-music of diction there is still a good deal of fumbling immaturity in the design and in the expression of ideas. The influence of Milton here evident was probably shed upon him not so much directly as through the reading of Keats; for Keats, like Shelley, was now entering upon his posthumous renown. Certainly when the process of recapitulation was complete and Tennyson began to speak with his own voice, it was evident to the discerning that his immediate master in the art of poetry was Keats.

II

Meanwhile Tennyson had won the admiration of the Cambridge group, and particularly of Arthur Henry Hallam, who was now his closest friend, with a number of short poems for the most part in lyrical or quasi-lyrical form (though few, if any, possessed the true quality of song). These were gathered together and published early in 1830 in Tennyson's first independent volume, *Poems, Chiefly Lyrical.* They must be judged in the main for what they exhibit of promise rather than of performance. The young poet was experimenting in various directions and fingering his instrument uncertainly but with a determination to master it. Some essays in new metrical combinations resulted in irregular or even amorphous stanzas (such as those of "The Dying Swan") which occasioned Coleridge's comment that Tennyson had begun to write without understanding what metre is. In this volume begins the series of imaginary portraits of fair women which was to be expanded in 1832 and even so late as 1842, mawkish studies, as they seem to us, which have faded as have the contemporary pretty verses of Letitia Elizabeth Landon or the simpering or ecstatic beauties who look forth from the vignettes in the giftbooks and annuals which were fashionable at just this time. Tennyson never ceased to regard these "fancy figures" with complacency; and one feels, uncomfortably, that he never entirely outgrew the feminine ideal which they are intended to suggest. But they distressed some of his judicious friends, among them Edward FitzGerald who denounced "that stupid Gallery of Beauties" as "a nuisance." There is at least this to be said for them, that their delicate modulations of prosody were valuable as apprentice-work. Three or four poems stand out from the remainder of the slim collection. The "Recollections of the Arabian Nights" (already referred to) evokes with youthful enthusiasm rather than with passion a vision of oriental splendour. "Mariana," inspired by a few words of Shakespeare's, paints a world of dreams in the midst of which are set familiar objects painted with an Eyckian precision of detail. The "Ballad of Oriana" (a generation later much admired by the Pre-Raphaelites) is a bolder experiment in the direct delineation of passion than Tennyson often attempted in the poetry of his maturity. On a lower level, but not altogether negligible, is his first experiment in the way of a "philosophic" poem, the "Supposed Confessions of a Second-rate Sensitive Mind," which sounds a morbid note which was frequently to recur. Apart from all these must be set "The Poet," in which is audible a riper utterance, a note so well assured and so individual that it does not belong, properly speaking, among Tennyson's juvenilia, but is rather the first poem of his early maturity.

In the summer of 1830, after this volume was off his hands, Tennyson went with Hallam on a journey through France to the frontier of Spain, to volunteer, with an enthusiasm more characteristic of youth in general than of Tennyson in particular, in the army of certain Spanish insurgents. For a few weeks they marched about, and then they returned to England with no experience of actual warfare but with impressions of the Pyrenean landscape which Tennyson afterwards wove into the first version of "Œnone" and into other poems. A few months later Dr. Tennyson died, and the poet left Cambridge to live with his widowed mother in the Somersby rectory, which the new incumbent permitted her to occupy for the next six years. Hallam, who was now engaged to Tennyson's sister Emily, was a frequent guest at Somersby, and in this happy time Tennyson devoted himself wholly to the cultivation of his art.

Looking back long afterwards upon this formative period, Tennyson remarked: "I was a poet before I was an artist; I was nearer thirty than twenty before I was an artist." The two ages specified practically cover the period between the publication of *Poems Chiefly Lyrical* in 1830 and the period of final revision of the *Poems,* which were published in 1842. Towards the close of 1832 his second volume, bearing the simple title *Poems* and the date 1833, was published. It is usual to contrast the immature promise of the two collections of the early eighteen-thirties with the finished workmanship of 1842; but without denying that a development toward mastery and a greatly enlarged field of interests marked this decade, it may be held that the most wonderful period of growth was between 1830 and 1832. It is scarcely too much to say that with the exception of Keats's third and last book Tennyson's *Poems* of 1832 is the finest single volume of verse published during the nineteenth century. Here along with certain adolescent traits and turns of style and thought, such as the fastidious daintiness of some pieces and the sentimentalism of others, there are other features which indicate the path along which the poet was to progress from that time on. Already at Cambridge or even at an earlier time he had meditated upon a poem or perhaps a drama on the subject of King Arthur, and had thought to impose upon the old legend an allegorical interpretation which should enrich its meaning to the modern world. But of this intention there is no sign in "The Lady of Shalott," mysterious and vision-like, or in the lovely romantic fragment of "Sir Launcelot and Queen Guinevere." Here are the first poems on classical subjects other than the boyish experiments in the volume of 1827. "Œnone" and "The Lotos-Eaters" were later to be much revised and improved, but even in these first versions their beauty was of an order new to English poetry. "The Hesperides," that wonderful evocation of magic and wild mystery, Tennyson never again printed. Of "ethical" content there is nothing in that poem and no more than a suggestion of it in "The Lotos-Eaters"; but in "Œnone" there is discernible the tendency to infuse into old myth a moral purpose. The poems on classical themes, some nine in all, are perhaps that part of our heritage from Tennyson of most enduring value, and this is because (as the poet himself noted) he was not content with a mere retelling of an old story but took the tales rather as moulds into which to pour metal of his own fusing. Hence, consciously or unconsciously, he selected for treatment not the most famous stories of antiquity but comparatively unworked material, so that his own interpretation would not jar upon previously formed sympathies. In the case of "Œnone," the story of the Judgement of Paris had been handled by many poets of antiquity, but no English poet of consequence had hitherto chosen it. Tennyson's effort is to exalt the theme by centering the reader's sympathies upon the forsaken wife, through whose eyes and not through the eyes of the ardent Paris are seen the naked goddesses. Some critics of our more cynical age have scoffed at his treatment of the situation; but a hundred years ago the poet's colours seemed of a Titianesque radiance. The award goes to Aphrodite; but the speech of Pallas is made the central portion of the poem, and, departing from the usual classical tradition, Tennyson puts into her mouth the promise not of success in battle but of the gift of wisdom.

The conflict between Wisdom and Beauty is the theme of "The Palace of Art." Tennyson described this poem as "a sort of allegory," the allegory of the inadequacy of beauty alone to satisfy the longings of the human soul. One detects a deliberate effort at self-discipline, a rejection of the aestheticism to which the poet had been devoting his gift. But the theme does not quite carry conviction, for it is obvious that the young man's heart is with the beautiful objects which he so lovingly depicts and which at the close are put aside till the soul's guilt is purged. To say so much is only to say what has been remarked by many readers of *The Faerie Queene*.

In the poems already named and in "A Dream of Fair Women" and in many more there are abundant examples of Tennyson's infinitely painstaking skill in the exact rendering of details in imagery and accessories, so that the effect is of a velvety thickness of ornament. This characteristic of his art appealed later to the Pre-Raphaelites, and in their paintings there is often a Tennysonian richness of texture.

III

In literary circles in the middle eighteen-thirties Henry Taylor's Preface to his tragedy *Philip van Artevelde* provoked a good deal of discussion of the problem of moral values in poetry. Taylor was a convinced Wordsworthian and a hostile critic of the poetry not only of Byron but of Shelley. In the course of a correspondence suggested by this Preface, Edward FitzGerald found it necessary to defend his friend Tennyson from the accusation of refusing to turn his art to the direct service of morality. The following passage is worth quoting in view of the fact that the animus of much later criticism of Tennyson was that this service to morality was altogether too direct. "Wordsworth's is a natural bias that way," writes FitzGerald. "One must have labourers of different kinds in the vineyard of morality. . . . Tennyson does no little by raising and filling the brain with noble images and thoughts, which, if they do not direct us to our duty, purify and cleanse us from mean and vicious objects. . . . I think you will see Tennyson acquire all that at present you miss; when he has *felt* life, he will not die fruitless of instruction to men." If we would "place" Tennyson accurately in the history of literature, it will be well to remember that at the beginning of his career one of his closest friends found it necessary to defend him from the accusation of indifference to moral issues.

"When he has *felt* life" — these are FitzGerald's words in 1835. They seem to us strangely impercipient, for the poet had already, two years before, "felt life" with a sharper pang and in a deeper wound than he was ever to feel it again. In September, 1833, Arthur Hallam, who had been travelling with his father on the Continent, died suddenly in Vienna. For a time this crushing blow (as Tennyson told his son years afterwards) "blotted out all joy" from the poet's life. He was sustained only by the need to comfort the sister who had been betrothed to his friend. There were other causes of despondency, though light in the scale in comparison with this sorrow. The contemptuous reception accorded the *Poems* of 1832 by some of the influential reviews (notoriously by John W. Croker in the *Quarterly*) remains one of the scandals in English literary history. Then, there was the threat of failing eyesight and there were pecuniary difficulties as well, for though he was not in absolute penury the poet's means were narrow. The despondent quasi-philosophical poem "The Two Voices," originally entitled "Thoughts on Suicide," is one of the first pieces to show the effect of Hallam's death and throws light upon the dark period in which *In Memoriam* was begun. The state of mind which it disclosed gave his family and friends food for anxious thought.

He had now withdrawn more than ever from the world, and save for a visit to Westmorland in 1835 the next years were passed mainly at Somersby till in 1837 the family was turned out of the rectory. The distress occasioned by this ejection from his lifelong home, a place so charged with dear associations, is recorded in *In Memoriam,* as are the first impressions of High Beech, Epping Forest, the house to which the Tennysons moved. There were several other removals in subsequent years, but these we need not record. By this time he had become engaged to Emily Sellwood; but this happiness was overclouded, for the uncertainty of his prospects put marriage out of the question and for a long while the two lovers ceased to meet or even to correspond.

A lapse of about two years intervened between Hallam's death and a fresh vigorous flow of verse. The earliest jottings out of which *In Memoriam* was gradually to develop were set down in the dreary autumn of 1833; but we do not know the precise date of the composition of "Break, Break, Break" in which the sense of loss is poignantly quintessentialized; nor do we know just when the magnificent "Ulysses" was composed — that poem in which that same sense of loss is interwoven with an urge to go forward, albeit without "that strength which in old days moved earth and heaven." From 1835 and 1836 date many of the sections of *In Memoriam,* written down as "the spontaneous overflow of powerful feeling" without thought of publication and as yet not conceived as parts of a single poem. Only when the lapse of years enabled him to recollect emotion in comparative tranquillity did the process of fusing the separate "elegies" into one begin.

By 1837 the recovery of energy was complete; perhaps the removal from the sad associations of Somersby played its part in the process. There is something touching in the morose illgrace with which Tennyson at first refused and then consented to contribute a poem to a volume of miscellaneous pieces published for a charitable purpose. The volume was *The Tribute;* the poem was "O that 'twere possible," out of which *Maud* was to develop many years afterwards. In the same year and with a better grace Tennyson permitted the editor of *The Keepsake,* one of the fashionable satin-bound annuals, to publish "St. Agnes' Eve," a poem of delicate tenderness wrought out of mystical ideas rather than itself mystical, the first of his tributes to the asceticism of the Middle Ages. During an entire decade these two poems were all that he published; but he had been active in the revision of old work and in the composition of new during the latter half of this period.

In 1842 Tennyson emerged from the long twilight. His original intention seems to have been to issue a collection of new pieces only; but of the *Poems* in two volumes now published about half the contents had appeared ten or twelve years before. The revisions to which he subjected the old pieces have been carefully scrutinized by scholars; in fact, long before his death he expressed his annoyance with the bibliographers who were recording and comparing his *variae lectiones*. The study of these variants is, however, not merely a pedant's pastime, for much may be learned about the development and refinement of Tennyson's art by contrasting the earlier and later forms of famous poems. In every case the new version, whether in the precision in the rendering of mental states or in the delicacy of the visualization of outward objects, is, it is safe to say, better than the old. Occasionally something is lost, but invariably the sacrifice of a particular beauty has improved the effect of the whole. Thus, the opening stanzas of "A Dream of Fair Women," in which the poet is likened to a man soaring aloft in a free balloon, were wisely deleted. The speech of Pallas in "Œnone" was shortened and pointed up; and in the same poem the scenic background was altered so as to be less like a valley in the Pyrenees and more like what Tennyson imagined the Troad to be; and the whole poem was refurbished. "The Lady of Shalott" was subjected to drastic revision. A few poems were much expanded. "The Sleeping Beauty," for example, grew into "The Day-Dream." The section of the "Choric Song" of "The Lotos-Eaters" beginning "Dear is the memory of our wedded lives" was added, and in place of the original conclusion a new ending, with the magnificent Lucretian vision of the gods, was supplied. While we may hold that Tennyson was ill-advised in suppressing a few pieces (notably "The Hesperides"), on the whole there can be few regrets for the alterations wrought in the poems which he reprinted.

The new poems in this collection reveal an impressive expansion of interests and sympathies. The dramatic monologue (the form to which Emerson was presently to direct attention as the most characteristic of the period) is seen to perfection in "Ulysses." In the hero's words not only the stoic leader himself and the storm-beaten company of his followers but his son Telemachus and the subject people are set against a background of rocky twilit coast and glooming seas. Characters, scene, and situation are all evoked with incomparable power and with a magnificence of diction which is neither Miltonic nor Keatsian but purely Tennysonian. Of no other poem of the Victorian era may it more safely be said that it is part of the immortal heritage of English verse. In the same form and excellent in its kind but on a decidedly lower level of achievement is "St. Simeon Stylites," a study in psychopathology of a sort which Tennyson was to attempt more than once again and which impinges upon Browning's province.

In two poems there is shown a continuing interest in the great subject upon which Tennyson had been meditating for many years. "Sir Galahad" is quite off the line which might lead to epical narrative and is to be regarded as a sort of pendant to "St. Agnes' Eve." But the "Morte d'Arthur" points forward to the *Idylls of the King* of which it ultimately became, in revised and expanded form, the twelfth and concluding book. It is not without significance that as published in 1842 this rendering of the final episode in the Arthurian story is set within a somewhat longer poem called "The Epic." With a suggestion of the old device of the "frame-tale" Tennyson introduces to us a young poet (in whom we recognize a self-portrait) and a company of friends to whom he reads this the sole remaining fragment of an epic in twelve books of which the others have been destroyed. The destruction of the missing books is doubtless an imaginary incident, but it serves to show that Tennyson was thinking of something upon an ambitious scale.

The homely realism and touches of mild satire in the "frame" which surrounds the narrative of King Arthur's passing have something in common with the "domestic" poems which form a prominent group in the collection of 1842. Tennyson called these pieces "English Idyls" (spelled with one *l* to differentiate them from the Idylls of Arthur, as though there were less dignity in a single letter). In them there are faint reminiscences of Theocritus, and the line of descent from Wordsworth is also apparent; but they are more Victorian than either Theocritan or Wordsworthian — Victorian in the pejorative sense in which the adjective has been employed by later generations. Not so long ago "Dora," "The Gardener's Daughter," "The Lord of Burleigh," and other poems of later date written in the same mood and manner were perhaps (with the exception of the historical dramas) the most unreadable portion of Tennyson's work; but today the taste for nineteenth-century bric-à-brac may bring them into favour again for their quiet quaintness and dim prettiness. There are, moreover, lovely passages in them which illustrate Tennyson's kinship with the English school of landscape painters. It is doubtful whether any conceivable eddy of taste will ever again make tolerable the extremer examples of his work in this kind — the sickly sentimentality of "The May Queen," for instance. But there is less mawkishness in some of the others, and a representative selection from Tennyson's poems must include a couple of examples (or three, if we count the longer and later narrative, *Enoch Arden*), if only for the reason that the student of the history of English poetry should have before him a few of the pieces which alienated the sympathies of some of Tennyson's oldest friends (notably Edward FitzGerald) and which forced a younger generation into vociferous protest.

Related to these domestic pieces but fashioned out of more substantial stuff is "Locksley Hall." Properly to appreciate the reason for the enormous popularity of this poem among Tennyson's contemporaries the modern reader must attempt to throw his mind back into the period of Chartism, of railway expansion, of legislation for social and industrial reform, of Mrs. Browning's "Cry of the Children" and Thomas Hood's "Song of the Shirt." No other poem illustrates more clearly the accord between Tennyson and the time in which he lived. This is not to say that, like Lord Macaulay, he accepted unquestioningly and complacently the society of which he was a part. On the contrary, his criticism of various social and economic aspects of that society is itself characteristic of Victorianism. The oppression of social problems weighed upon the period and weighed upon Tennyson. Yet in "Locksley Hall," as in parts of *Maud* and in many later poems, we recognize with discomfort that he inclined, when writing on social problems, to imagine that a noisy but, somehow, hollow rhetoric was an acceptable substitute for deep-voiced indignation. The loud rhetoric of his verse rings falsely; one suspects uneasily that he is not so angry as he pretends to be. One has only to point the contrast to, for example, *Unto This Last* to distinguish between what carries conviction and what aims to carry conviction. The "rowdy or bullying element" which men so unlike each other as William Morris and Gerard Manly Hopkins found distasteful in Tennyson's poetry of this kind first becomes audible in "Locksley Hall." He was seldom to venture with success into the field of social criticism. On this point something further must be said when we come to *Maud*. For the moment it suffices to remark that though it is a false assumption that a great poet must necessarily be "a leader of thought" it must nevertheless be recognized that Tennyson was not such a leader. One of his most adverse critics, H. S. Salt, has described him as "an amateur aristocrat permitted to accompany the outlying portion of the campaign of progress"; and a more judicious critic, Professor Elton, has said: "He, the widest-known retailer of ideas in English verse, was all the while in a back-water where only the fainter wash of the larger currents reached him." In the eighteen-forties, when revolutionary sentiment was in the air and when events were moving towards the European outbreak of 1848, he was no leader of the advance, content (in Arnold's phrase) to fall by the walls, offering his body as a path for those who followed. His Shakespearean distrust of the "people" and his particular and repeated scorn of "the red fool-fury of the Seine" have their significance. Save in a few famous rhetorical outbursts, like the vision in "Locksley Hall" of the ghastly aerial warfare of the future or the more distant vision of "the parliament of man," he seldom seems to look far ahead. His sensitiveness was to the intellectual atmosphere of the world around him. The "simple faith" which he celebrated was yielding place to inquiry, analysis, theological discussion, "higher criticism," doubt. With doubt came discontent and introspection and the intrusion of a new morbidity into literature. The time was sicklied o'er with the pale cast of thought; and the "Virgilian cry" *Sunt lacrimae rerum et mentem mortalia tangunt* might be its epigraph. This "sense of tears in mortal things," this feeling for "the doubtful doom of human kind," is sounded constantly in Tennyson's verse. Like Virgil, he is "majestic in his sadness." There is little of spontaneous joy in his poetry.

The popular success of the volumes of 1842 did little to sustain the poet's spirits. He and his brothers and sisters lost their little patrimony in an unwise speculation which left him practically penniless. He became the victim of a profound hypochondria for which he sought a cure now in one and now in another health establishment whose methods would today savour of quackery. In 1845 friends bestirred themselves to interest Sir Robert Peel in his case with the consequence that the Prime Minister was prevailed upon to grant him a pension of two hundred pounds a year. This well-deserved recognition of his genius and much-needed practical aid prompted the jealous and acidulous Bulwer-Lytton to introduce a satiric fling at "School-Miss Alfred" into *The New Timon*, a poem now kept in remembrance only because it occasioned Tennyson's reply. The concentrated scorn of Tennyson's lines showed the world that there was more of a Timon in him than in "the padded man" who had so unwarrantably attacked him, and that however much of the "school-miss" there might be in some of Tennyson's poems there was nothing of her in his character.

In these years Tennyson drifted away from some of his old friends (notably from FitzGerald, who deplored his valetudinarianism) and associated much with Carlyle and Dickens. He also saw a good deal of Robert Browning. Here it may be remarked that though each of these two greatest poetical luminaries of the Victorian era said or wrote privately about the other's work things which he quite naturally would not have wished the other to see, their personal and public relationships were always creditable to them both. At this time also a friendship with Macready the actor may have implanted in Tennyson the ambition to write for the stage which caused him long afterwards to waste years of effort upon tasks with which his genius was not fitted to cope.

There is a familiar story, perhaps best told by David Alec Wilson, the biographer of Carlyle, that at a dinner-party some time in the eighteen-forties, Tennyson remarked: "I don't think that since Shakespeare there has been such a master of the English language as I"; and when his fellow-guests looked astonished, he added calmly — "To be sure, I've got nothing to say." The anecdote may be apocryphal, but it belongs in the category of the *ben trovati*. The date which Wilson assigns to it is in its favour, for it is about the time of the composition of *The Princess*. This poem was published in 1847. Tennyson, who, though often resentful of the criticism of "irresponsible, indolent reviewers," was a keen self-critic, could not have been unaware of the disproportion between manner and matter in this "medley." Friends who for long had looked to him for a poem of ambitious length which (in Wordsworth's phrase) would "deal boldly with substantial things" were disappointed. *The Princess* was not what they had hoped for. FitzGerald deplored "the wretched waste of power at a time of life when a man ought to be doing his best." But the general public thought otherwise, for the poem's mild liberalism and its "gentlemanly" patronage of the cause of female education suited the common taste and enormously widened Tennyson's audience. The solution of the problem of the social emancipation of women which was here offered was acceptable to the average Victorian household, and the words with which this solution was conveyed brought happy tears to countless eyes: "Lay thy

sweet hands in mine and trust in me." These words later on
were to provoke the grim comment of James Thomson (B. V.):
"The woman's hands may be grimy with work; she may have
learnt better than to trust in him." If it be objected that the
comment does not apply to the man and the woman of Tennyson's conception, that is but an indication of the limitations of
the poet's horizon.

The only way in which the theme of *The Princess* might
have been treated so as to keep it fresh in the affections of
posterity was to adopt the tone of intellectual comedy, the
Meredithian manner; but among Tennyson's endowments de-
bonair wit had no place. Nor was the blank verse, which was
so admirably adapted to other purposes, appropriate to this
versified novelette. There are amusing and sometimes beautiful episodic passages; there are two lyrics in blank verse
("Tears, Idle Tears" and "Come Down, O Maid") which, for-
tunately separable from their context, are of perennial loveliness; and there are the exquisite intercalary songs which were
added in the third edition in an effort to hold the poem more
firmly together, but whose gold shines the brighter when sep-
arated from the baser metal of the narrative. But the reason-
ing set forth in *The Princess* was inconclusive in the mid-nineteenth century; and it is negligible today. There were those
who began to suspect — what posterity knows — that Tennyson's architectonic skill was not sufficiently robust to construct
a closely articulated poem of more than medium length.

IV

In Memoriam is no exception to this statement. It was
published anonymously (but there was no effort to keep its
authorship a secret) in 1850, the year of Tennyson's marriage
to Emily Sellwood and of his succession to the laureateship.
It is significant that for a long while Tennyson was accustomed
to refer to this poem as "the elegies" (in the plural) rather than
as "the elegy." The poem, or poems, sprang from periods of
intermittent inspiration and desultory composition extending

over seventeen years. Not until most of the sections had been written did Tennyson begin to contemplate publication; and the task of welding the disparate parts into something approximating a unified whole was accomplished in the years immediately preceding publication. The epilogue celebrating the marriage of the poet's sister belongs to 1842; but the prologue is dated 1849; and we know that many of the sections were written in the later eighteen-forties in order to make the connection of thought and the progress of emotion clearer. As a result of this mode of composition the links between sections or groups of sections are often weak, and thoughts recur too frequently and are at times drawn out too tenuously. Though Tennyson made his customary excisions (sacrificing for the sake of greater compression some stanzas of poignant beauty), most readers feel that the poem is unnecessarily long, and (as Dr. Johnson said of *Paradise Lost*) no reader regrets that it is not longer. The employment of the same stanzaic form throughout (the iambic tetrameter quatrain with closed rhymes which Tennyson thought he had invented but which had actually been used in the seventeenth century) imposes an outward semblance of unity; but such inner unity as *In Memoriam* possesses comes from the drift of spiritual experience rather than from conscious artistic effort.

As pieced together, the structure of *In Memoriam* owes something, in a large indefinite way, to the tradition of the English elegy exemplified pre-eminently in *Lycidas* and *Adonais;* that is, the note of mourning modulates into a hymn of faith, though not with such triumphant abruptness as in Milton's poem and Shelley's. As in those elegies, so here the turning point in the mood is discernible (in Section LVII: "Peace, come away, the song of woe is after all an earthly song"); but the less definite structure leads to recurrences of earlier moods, so that the pattern is less precise. For this reason, among others, the poem is correspondingly more convincing as the expression of grief and personal loss and the alternate subsidence and upwelling of grief and finally renewed happiness. During a late period in its composition Tennyson

sought to impose upon the simple elegies a vague hint of
allegorical intent. He spoke of *In Memoriam* as "a Way of
the Soul" and described it as "a kind of *Divina Commedia*
ending with happiness." It is thus not the lyrical utterance
of a fresh grief only but the lyrical and meditative record of a
long series of changing moods and fluctuating thoughts.
"Many waters cannot quench love" — not even the waters of
death: this is the poem's high argument. In its progress there
is the gradual healing of personal grief (though the wound
breaks out again and again), with the continuance and widen-
ing of a love so spiritualized that it can exist without the
presence of the beloved.

In some sections Tennyson attempts to effect a harmony
between traditional religious faith and the new ideas of modern
science; yet in other sections he opposes faith to reason. In
section CXIV the contrast of Knowledge and Wisdom might have
come from Carlyle or even from Newman. There is, indeed,
a dichotomy in the poem which is part of its lasting attractive-
ness from both the poetical and the psychological points of
view, however much it weakens its force as a religious utterance. On the one hand there are concessions to the scientific
spirit in what seems a feeble attempt to save something from
the wreck of creeds. On the other hand there is a repudiation
of science and an anchoring upon faith. The first of these
moods is quintessentialized in the famous lines,

> O yet we trust that somehow good
> Will be the final goal of ill,

which, though often derided, summarize a characteristic Victorian state of mind. Less succinctly the mood is expressed in
the oft-quoted words of Henry Sidgwick, who said of *In
Memoriam* that it set forth "the indestructible and inalienable
minimum of faith which humanity cannot give up because it
is necessary for life." The contrasting mood comes and goes,
as do all mystical experiences, with the breath of the spirit; it
is revealed in passages of profound feeling and haunting beauty,

and especially in the incomparable ninety-fifth section, perhaps Tennyson's supreme utterance as a poet. These parts of *In Memoriam,* like similar parts of "The Holy Grail" (a poem of later date), are grounded upon certain trance-like experiences in Tennyson's life in which he seemed, like St. Paul, to be caught up into a region beyond earth.

The course of speculation is through doubt to the affirmation of belief in personal immortality ("I shall know him when we meet"). The final goal of being may be an absorption into the All ("Farewell! We vanish into Light"). But whether this be the tremendous consummation or whether the individual existence continue, the future life is looked upon as a continuation of the evolutionary process through development ever nearer and nearer to God. In the *Ode* in memory of the Duke of Wellington, written two years later, it is affirmed that in some higher sphere of existence there must be further tasks to be accomplished by the great departed; and in a poem in Tennyson's last volume, published posthumously, the truer name of Death is said to be "Onward." The thought, which is frequent in Browning's poetry, was one congenial to Tennyson's age. How sensitively aware Tennyson was to certain currents in contemporary thought is shown by the fact that some sections of the poem which draw upon evolutionary theory anticipate the publication of Robert Chambers's *Vestiges of the Natural History of Creation,* and that *In Memoriam* was published nine years before *The Origin of Species.*

It is not surprising that *In Memoriam* was received with approbation by leaders of various schools of thought. The natural scientists admired it not only because of the poet's meticulously accurate employment of natural phenomena in its imagery but also because of its echoes or reflections of tendencies in current speculation. Liberals accepted it because it attempted to compromise between religion and science. The orthodox made use of it in sermons and in tracts because it rescued (or they thought it rescued) faith from the clutches of an advancing materialism. Most modern readers may be inclined to brush aside these claims upon their attention. They may feel that to the extent that the poem appealed to the mid-nineteenth century it fails in appeal to the second third of the twentieth. But they will continue to read *In Memoriam* for its sustained beauty, its poignant feeling, its wealth of imagery, now tender and intimate, now gorgeous and elaborate. There are also those who are still conscious of an abiding appeal in Tennyson's expression of a mood which the world has not yet entirely put by: that wistful yearning after certainty which is more easily apprehended by the modern mind than is arrogant dogmatism. The very timidity and hesitation of the poet's faith render it the more moving. With an art and an emotion unparalleled in the writing of any other modern poet, Tennyson manages to suggest the inapprehensibility and intangibility of the life beyond the tomb — "a breath, a flame in the doorway, a feather in the wind."

V

The outward circumstances and events in Tennyson's life before the publication of his next considerable poem may be briefly summarized. During the summer after his marriage he and his wife made the tour of northern Italy which is memorialized in "The Daisy," one of the most exquisitely accomplished of his shorter pieces. In 1852 he spoke for the first time in his official capacity as Laureate, voicing with stately magnificence of style the national mourning for the Duke of Wellington. In 1853 he settled at Farringford in the Isle of Wight. In 1854 he achieved immense popular success with "The Charge of the Light Brigade." In 1855 he published *Maud*.

In the opinion of William Morris and his circle *Maud* came to be considered "the last of Tennyson's poems that mattered." But from the general public it not only failed to win acclaim, but occasioned an outcry against Tennyson which startled and wounded him. On the title-page the poem was described as a "Monodrama," that is, an extension of the form of the

dramatic monologue through a succession of episodes in which
the story is unfolded in soliloquies. Notwithstanding this
hint, there were those who tried to identify the protagonist
with the poet himself; and they were to this degree correct
that the sultry, moody side of Tennyson's temperament is at
least suggested in the character of his hero. But any serious
misunderstanding was inexcusable. In several earlier poems
of middling length Tennyson had successfully managed the
pathological soliloquy, the self-revelation of the character of a
speaker of abnormal mentality. He described the hero of
Maud as a kind of modern Hamlet — "a kind of Hamlet without the brains" is Professor Elton's modification of this interpretation. The somewhat hysterical tone of parts of the poem
may be due to conscious or unconscious imitation of the so-
called "spasmodic" poets, Sidney Dobell and Alexander Smith,
then in the midst of their short-lived vogue. There may also,
as has been suggested, have been a deliberate attempt to imitate
in verse the speeches of distraction or insanity which are a
feature of the romantic novels of the "School of Terror."
Tennyson's rendering of the phenomena of madness was much
admired at the time by people who claimed to speak with
authority; what the modern alienist would make of it is another question. At all events the tone is dramatically appropriate in the episode of the hero's madness. It is less excusable
when employed in the denunciation of the evils of modern
society. The hectoring manner upon which we have already
commented is very apparent at the close of *Maud* in the lines
on the glorification of war as a remedy for the irresponsibil-
ities of youth and for the lethargy of England. Tennyson
seems to have thought that the war in the Crimea would rouse
from their moral and intellectual stagnation those whom
Arthur Hugh Clough had a little earlier characterized as
"feeble and restless youth born to inglorious days"; but it is
difficult to see how a wholly needless struggle in a remote
province of Russia was to be made to serve as a remedy for
the economic ills and social inequalities against which the
poet fulminates.

Tennyson's weakness in architectonics — manifested whenever he was faced with the task of constructing a long poem —
was tacitly admitted by Tennyson himself when he left with
his son a sort of running commentary intended to make clear
the successive situations in *Maud*. The commonplace plot
was not beyond the inventive scope of a third-rate novelist of
the period, involving as it does such depressingly familiar lay-
figures as the beautiful heroine, the poor but proud hero, her
supercilious brother, the wealthy nobleman who is a rival for
her hand, and so forth. She prefers proud penury with love
to worldly affluence without it; and her choice involves her
lover in a duel in which her brother is slain. The tragedy
works itself out through the death of the heroine and the
hero's remorse, madness, and recovered sanity. The senti-
ments are old-fashioned and the psychology is for the most
part unsubtle. But the prosody is a triumph. The form
sustains and still vitalizes the subject. The poem is a succession of semi-lyrical episodes in which the varying moods and
situations are suggested rather than analyzed; and the skill
with which the metre is adapted to the mood and the mood
announced by the metre is beyond praise. Turn to whatever
sections you will and there will be observed synchronized variations of mood and metre. Misunderstood by Tennyson's
public, *Maud* soon won the admiration of younger poets; and
today it retains a freshness which much of his work, formerly
more popular, has lost.

VI

The ill-success of *Maud* opened the old wound of Tennyson's sensitiveness to hostile criticism, and there followed another period of withdrawal from the public eye. With
interruptions occasioned by holiday journeys to Norway and
Portugal, he was now engaged upon a long-contemplated task.
We have seen that from his youth he had meditated upon the
composition of an epic or dramatic poem on the subject of
King Arthur. That the theme was to have infused into it a

measure of ethical symbolism is evident from an early memo-
randum in which the King is made to represent Faith, and
the Round Table "liberal institutions." There is, however,
nothing of this allegorical intention in the romantic fragment
of "Sir Launcelot and Queen Guinevere" or in that brief
evocation of ascetic knighthood, "Sir Galahad"; nor is there
more than the faintest suggestion of it in the original "Morte
d'Arthur" of 1842. By 1848 Tennyson's friends were aware
of his choice of the subject for a *magnum opus;* and in that
year we find FitzGerald, though considering Arthur a worthy
subject, dubious as to the possibility of the "valetudinarian"
Tennyson accomplishing anything of consequence in heroic
poetry. In harmony as it was with the Gothic revival and
the general vogue of the Middle Ages, the Arthurian theme
was, so to speak, in the air of the mid-century. The young
Pre-Raphaelites and their friends chose it as the subject of
their famous and now lost frescoes in the Oxford Union. In
1849 Bulwer-Lytton published his pretentious epic, *King
Arthur.* William Morris's *Defence of Guenevere* preceded
the first group of Tennyson's *Idylls* by a year. About the
same time, Tennyson, vacationing in the West of England, was
on terms of congenial friendship with Robert Stephen Hawker,
a clergyman steeped in British lore, whose *Quest of the
Sangraal* is of later date (1863) than the first *Idylls,* but appeared several years before Tennyson's "Holy Grail."

Tennyson proceeded toward publication through the preliminary stages of two "trial issues" or privately printed
experimental volumes. Their titles shed light upon his conception. The earlier (1856) is called *Enid and Nimuë; or,
the True and the False.* A year later, when he had doubled
the number of the stories, he printed *The True and the False.
Four Idylls of the King.* After some further revision these
four poems were published as *Idylls of the King* in 1859. If
we would read these metrical tales as Tennyson's immediate
public read them, we must clear our minds of the interpretation which is reflected upon them from other *Idylls* of later
date into which allegory has been infused. The original four

are then seen to have a symmetry which is lacking in the
twelve parts of the entire work. Almost, if not quite, devoid
of allegorical implication, they are studies in two contrasted
types of womanhood: the "true" represented by Enid and
Elaine; the "false" by Vivien (her name changed from Nimuë)
and Guinevere. Judged as metrical tales and not as parts of
an intended longer work, they are not very different in technique from the "domestic" idyls on modern subjects. Vivien
is, indeed, Victorian rather than medieval in her waspishness;
and King Arthur (of whom it is customary to say that he is
not a man but a walking allegory) is really not so much an
unconvincing abstraction as an individual who carries all too
successfully the conviction of his priggishness. Though there
were readers who immediately missed the true medieval flavour
which, for all their fragility and faltering workmanship, was
suggested in Morris's early Arthurian pieces, and though
Matthew Arnold complained that Tennyson failed to give "the
peculiar charm and aroma of the Middle Age" and that "something magical" in the old stories had evaporated, it is but fair
to note that Tennyson, in subjecting the legends to a modern
treatment, was but employing the same process in the rendering of medieval tales that he had successfully used in his rendering of classical myths. He was pouring the new wine of
his own thought into the old bottles of legend. The difficulty
in the case of the *Idylls* was that the new wine was not potent
and the old bottles were too much loved for such liberties to
be taken lightly with them.

Of the four narratives "Enid" (later divided into two *Idylls,*
"The Marriage of Geraint" and "Geraint and Enid") adheres
most closely to the source (Lady Charlotte Guest's version of
the *Mabinogion*) and consequently retains something of the
lovely naïve medieval feeling which the others lack. But
"Guinevere," though sometimes judged a failure and certainly
not a complete success, is a finer poem, and is chosen, rather
than "Enid," for the present volume. In magnificence of
diction and richness of ornament it displays that "mystery of
music," that "noble full orbicular wholeness in complete pas-

sages" which Mrs. Browning had commended in some of Tennyson's earlier poetry. This largeness of utterance is heard, for example, in the episode of Arthur's arrival by night at the convent where Guinevere has taken refuge, when the Queen saw,

> Wet with the mists and smitten by the lights,
> The Dragon of the great Pendragonship
> Blaze, making all the night a steam of fire.

The emotional response to such passages — and there are many of them — is the reader's reward for the considerable effort without which the *Idylls* cannot be read today.

VII

To those who first read it on its publication in *Cornhill* in 1860 "Tithonus" may have suggested that Tennyson had reverted to an earlier manner and had recovered it with entire success. But actually the poem had been written so long before as 1842; why it was withheld from publication for nearly two decades has never been explained. In its humanization of an ancient myth it is much like "Ulysses," and its success is a triumph over even greater difficulties in that the poet has vitalized a character and situation alien from human experience by finding therein a theme common to humanity — the theme of mortality. Remarkable also is the setting — the background of "far-folded mists and gleaming halls of morn."

Tennyson's attention was now, however, diverted alike from classical antiquity and from the Middle Ages. In 1862 he finished *Enoch Arden,* which was published in 1864, in the volume to which it gives the title, together with "Aylmer's Field" and "The Northern Farmer," a vigorous experiment in the Lincolnshire dialect. *Enoch Arden* is included in the present selection not so much for its own merits (though the modulations of the verse are of lasting interest to students of technique and though the tropical scenery is of the utmost richness) as because it is an example on the most ambitious scale of the poetry of Tennyson's middle years, when he was read by countless thousands of admirers who had raised him to a pinnacle of popularity never reached by any other English poet before or since. As yet the general public was unaware of the fact that in the minds of the younger generation of writers his seat upon the poetic throne was beginning to be unstable. Swinburne had not yet spoken out as presently he was to speak. Meredith confided to a correspondent that he was "a little sick of Tennysonian green tea" and that he thought that *Enoch Arden* was "ill done" and "villanous weak." There are signs in "Lucretius" (published in *Macmillan's Magazine* in 1868) that Tennyson may have imitated, consciously or unconsciously, the style of Swinburne; but this is a detail which may be left to our commentary on the poem. Certainly there is nothing Swinburnian in the four *Idylls* that appeared in 1869 in the volume entitled *The Holy Grail and Other Poems*. In addition to the poem which gave its title to the book this contained three other *Idylls*. "The Coming of Arthur," though somewhat heavily burdened with detail and not so interesting as some of the other *Idylls,* is included in the present selection because as the introduction to the entire series it sets forth Tennyson's design as a whole. "Pelleas and Ettare" may be passed over without comment. "The Passing of Arthur" is a revised and expanded form of the original "Morte d'Arthur" of 1842, the "frame" omitted. With these four narratives Tennyson intended to complete the work; but in 1872 he added "Gareth and Lynette" and "The Last Tournament," the latter his rendering of the story of Tristram and Iseult in which he ill-advisedly followed the Malory version of the legend; and so late as 1888 he inserted "Balin and Balan" into the series.

The reception of *The Holy Grail,* though the sales were very large, was less enthusiastic on the part of the critics and men of letters of the younger generation than Tennyson had become accustomed to look for. In one of Meredith's letters there is a vigorous expression of what many people were thinking. The passage is worth quoting in part if only to show that the "reaction" against Tennyson which was characteristic of the early years of the present century had set in long before. Meredith writes:

The lines are satin lengths, the figures Sèvres china . . . To think! it's in these days that the foremost poet of the country goes on fluting of creatures that have not a breath of vital humanity in them, and doles us out his regular five-feet with the old trick of the vowel endings . . . Why, this stuff is not the Muse, it's Musery! . . . Isn't there a scent of damned hypocrisy in all this lisping and vowelled purity of the *Idylls*?

A little later came Swinburne's tremendous onslaught upon Tennyson's treatment of the Arthurian story in *Under the Microscope*. It is on record that Tennyson suspected that there existed a literary cabal determined to pull him down. When he visited FitzGerald in 1876 he complained of the treatment accorded him by the critics. FitzGerald's somewhat acidulous comment was: "I thought that if he had lived an active life as Scott and Shakespeare; or even ridden, shot, drunk, and played the Devil, as Byron, he would have done much more, and talked about it much less."

The fact is that about 1870 Tennyson's reputation was passing temporarily under a cloud. It was still assumed that he was the foremost poet of the age; he was honoured and revered by the great public; but the more critical and vocal part of that public was not so much interested in his new writings. He had to compete with Browning, who had just won belated popular recognition with the publication of *The Ring and the Book*, and with three younger poets: Swinburne, whose *Atalanta in Calydon* marked the rising of a new star and whose *Poems and Ballads* had taken the world by storm; Morris, whose *Earthly Paradise* had just appeared; and Rossetti, whose *Poems* of 1870 brought the new school of poetry to a climax. Within this shadow of something like indifference Tennyson remained for a decade. The eighteen-seventies are the years when he devoted himself to a series of tragedies in which he sought to illustrate the theme of "the Making of

England." The first of these, *Queen Mary*, appeared in 1875, *Harold* in 1877, and *Becket* in 1879. These and four other plays, *The Falcon* (1879), *The Cup* (1881), *The Promise of May* (1892), and *The Foresters* (also 1892), may be passed over with the remark that like every other great lyric and meditative poet of the nineteenth century, from Wordsworth to Swinburne, Tennyson nourished the ambition to achieve success in the theatre and, like them all, was disappointed. Through the loyal friendship of Sir Henry Irving and other actors several of his dramas reached the boards, but only *Becket* had a really successful run and that only after it had been condensed and heavily revised by Irving. Today these dramas, like almost all the "closet-plays" of the period, are dead beyond resurrection. We can only regret that Tennyson expended so much time and thought and energy upon them. During these same years he was much occupied with the building of Aldworth, his new home in a secluded spot on Blackdown in Sussex. The intrusion of admiring strangers upon his privacy at Farringford had for long been a torment to the shy and sensitive poet, and many are the stories of the gruff receptions accorded to those who sought to speak to him or perhaps shake his hand. Aldworth, being less accessible, was a refuge during parts of each year after about 1878.

As this somewhat unprofitable decade drew to a close Tennyson returned to fields in which he was a master. The abandonment of the historical dramas may have brought a relief which perhaps accounts in part for the astonishing rebirth of genius in his seventieth year. In 1878 was published the spirited ballad of "The Revenge." In 1880, at an age when it was generally assumed that he had passed into retirement, the magnificent volume *Ballads and Other Poems* appeared, ushering in the final decade of his glory. The fortunes of life and literature had, indeed, cleared the field for him once again, as in the middle of the century. Browning had passed into the penumbra of his latest volumes, the idol of the Browning Society but alien from the tastes and interests and to some degree from the understanding of the ordinary lover of poetry.

Socialism and the arts and crafts were claiming the abundant energies of William Morris. Swinburne had neither anything new to say nor a novel manner of saying the old things. No younger poet of promise or importance had as yet appeared. Small wonder, then, that Tennyson regained his eminence. After the *Ballads* of 1880, no less than four volumes of miscellaneous lyrical, narrative, and meditative verse were published: *Tiresias and Other Poems* (1885), *Locksley Hall Sixty Years After, Etc.* (1886), *Demeter and Other Poems* (1889), and *The Death of Œnone, Akbar's Dream, and Other Poems* (which appeared posthumously at the end of 1892). In range of moods, interests, and subjects these productions are as astonishing as in their quantity, coming as they did from a poet in his eighth decade. The narrative poems are sometimes quite objective, at other times tinged with symbolic meaning or with a faintly "mystical" intent. In the meditative pieces Tennyson sought again and again to summarize his thoughts on life. A good many poems are in memory of departed friends. The purely lyrical note is seldom sounded; even "Crossing the Bar" does not properly belong in the category of song.

From this ample body of work there is room here to select for comment only a few poems. "Tiresias," though not published till 1885, was partly written about the same time as "Ulysses" and "Tithonus." To discriminate between the early portions of this poem and those written much later is a valuable exercise in elementary literary connoisseurship. The scene of the prophet on the mountain, the vision of Pallas in the bath, and the final forecast of the prophet's death seem to be early work; the failure to realize the situation of the siege of Thebes and the undramatic length to which the discourse of Tiresias is spun out are signs of the old poet's loosening grasp upon his subject. The beautiful final paragraph, beginning

> But for me,
> I would that I were gather'd to my rest,
> And mingled with the famous kings of old,

Tennyson liked to quote as a specimen of his blank verse at its

best. He chose wisely. "Demeter and Persephone" was published when Tennyson was eighty years of age. There is no
hint in the *Memoir* or elsewhere that it incorporates work of
earlier years; yet in style, strength, and splendour of imagery
it seems to belong with the classical pieces of his prime; otherwise it is an example of his wonderful reserve of power. How
ample that reserve was had already been proved by the incomparable "Rizpah" (1880). Another poem which combines
strength and splendour is the address "To Virgil." The wide
reach of Tennyson's interests is further illustrated by the rendering of the Celtic tale of "The Voyage of Maeldune," by
the allegorical autobiography "Merlin and the Gleam," and
by such philosophical pieces as the symbolic narrative poem,
"The Voyage."

Of the events of these last years it is necessary to record but
few. In 1883 Tennyson voyaged with Gladstone to Copen-
hagen where the two great Englishmen were entertained by
the King of Denmark. In the following year Tennyson accepted a peerage. In 1892 his latest drama, *The Foresters,* was
produced in New York. So shortly before his death as the
summer of 1892 he visited the Channel Islands, and thereafter
he was engaged upon some of his latest poems. In August,
however, his strength began to fail, though till the end he
retained his faculties. The death-scene on the fourth of October, 1892, is one of the noble traditions of English literary
history: the moonlight flooding the bedroom at Aldworth
where lay the majestic figure clasping to his breast a volume of
Shakespeare. Six days later he was buried in Westminster
Abbey.

CHRONOLOGICAL OUTLINE

1807.   Birth of Frederick Tennyson.

1808.   Birth of Charles Tennyson (Tennyson-Turner).

1809.   Birth of Alfred Tennyson at Somersby, Lincolnshire, August 6.

1815–20.   Alfred Tennyson attended Grammar School at Louth.

1819–24.   Earliest poems written.

1827.   *Poems by Two Brothers* published.

1828.   Matriculated at Trinity College, Cambridge, February 20.

1829.   *Timbuctoo,* a poem which obtained the Chancellor's Medal, published.

1830.   *Poems, Chiefly Lyrical* published.

     Sonnets and Fugitive Pieces, by Charles Tennyson, published.

     Tennyson and Hallam in the Pyrenees as volunteers with Spanish insurgents.

1831.   Death of Tennyson's father.

     Hallam betrothed to Tennyson's sister.

1832.   *Poems* published, December (dated 1833).

1833.   Death of Hallam at Vienna, September 15.

     Earliest sections of *In Memoriam* written.

1835.   Visit to Westmorland; friendship with Hartley Coleridge.

1837.   Removal of Tennyson family from Somersby to High Beach in Epping Forest.

     Stanzas ("O that 'twere possible") published in *The Tribute.*

     "St. Agnes" (later called "St. Agnes' Eve") published in *The Keepsake.*

     Betrothal to Emily Sellwood.

1840.   Removal to Tunbridge Wells.

1841.   Removal to Boxley.

1842. *Poems* in two volumes published.
Beginning of wide fame.
New friendships: Carlyle, Dickens, Elizabeth Barrett, and others.
Hypochondria.

1845. Grant of pension by Sir Robert Peel.

1846. Restoration of health.
Visit to Switzerland.

1847. *The Princess* published.
Living at Cheltenham, but much in London.

1848. Tour of Cornwall; meeting with Robert Stephen Hawker.

1850. *In Memoriam* published, May.
Marriage to Emily Sellwood, June 13.
Appointed Poet Laureate, November 19.
Settles at Twickenham.

1851. Tour of Italy, summer.

1852. *Ode on the Death of the Duke of Wellington* published.
Birth of eldest son, Hallam (afterwards Second Lord Tennyson).

1853. Removal to Farringford, near Freshwater, Isle of Wight.

1854. Birth of second son, Lionel.
"The Charge of the Light Brigade" published.

1855. *Maud and Other Poems* published, July.
D. C. L. conferred at Oxford.

1857. Tour of Wales.

1858. Visit to Norway.

1859. Visit to Portugal.
Idylls of the King published.

1861. Tour of Auverge and thé Pyrenees with Arthur Hugh Clough.

1864. *Enoch Arden* published.

1865. Death of Tennyson's mother.

1866. Tour of Germany.

1867. Purchase of land on Blackdown near Haslemere and building of Aldworth.

1869. *The Holy Grail* published (dated 1870).
1872. *Gareth and Lynette* published.
       Swinburne's attack on Tennyson in *Under the Micro-
          scope.*
1873. Offer of baronetcy by Gladstone declined.
1874. Renewed offer by Disraeli declined.
1875. *Queen Mary* published.
1876. *Queen Mary* produced at Lyceum by Sir Henry Irving.
       Harold published (never produced).
1879. *Becket* written (published 1884; produced posthu-
          mously, 1893).
       The Lover's Tale published (privately printed, 1832).
1880. *Ballads and Other Poems* published.
1881–82. *The Cup* and *The Promise of May* produced.
1883. Visit with Gladstone to Norway and Denmark.
1884. Created Baron Tennyson of Aldworth and Farringford.
       The Cup and the Falcon published.
1885. *Tiresias and Other Poems* published.
1886. Lionel Tennyson's death.
       Locksley Hall Sixty Years After published.
1889. *Demeter and Other Poems* published.
1892. *The Foresters, Robin Hood and Maid Marian* pub-
          lished; produced in New York.
       Death of Tennyson at Aldworth, October 6.
       Burial in Westminster Abbey, October 12.
       *The Death of Œnone, Akbar's Dream, and Other
          Poems* published posthumously.
1896. Death of Lady Tennyson.
1897. *Alfred Lord Tennyson. A Memoir by His Son* pub-
          lished.

SELECTED BIBLIOGRAPHY

I. BIBLIOGRAPHIES

Cambridge Bibliography of English Literature, The. [The Tennyson section of this forthcoming work (announced by the Cambridge University Press) will supersede the bibliography in *The Cambridge History of English Literature,* XIII, 524–531.]

Ehrsam, T. G. and Deily, R. H., *Bibliographies of Twelve Victorian Authors.* New York: H. W. Wilson Company, 1936, pp. 299–362: "Tennyson." [The most nearly exhaustive list of books and articles of all periods and on all phases of Tennyson's life, character, and works; especially valuable for contemporary notices of his books, for parodies and the like, and for critical ephemera illustrating phases of taste. Unfortunately, slovenly in arrangement and not altogether free from inaccuracies.]

Wise, Thomas James, *A Bibliography of the Writings of Alfred Lord Tennyson.* London, 1908 (privately printed). [This supersedes earlier bibliographies (such as those of R. H. Shepherd and L. S. Livingston) of first editions, "trial issues," privately printed pieces, and the like. The collations are full and accurate, and there is a quantity of interesting subsidiary information. But the claims made for certain items must be controlled by reference to the damaging case against Mr. Wise made in John Carter and Graham Pollard, *An Enquiry into the Nature of Certain Nineteenth Century Pamphlets.* London: Constable, 1934, pp. 293–343.]

II. EDITIONS

The Life and Works of Alfred Lord Tennyson. 12 vols. London: Macmillan, 1898–9. [This *edition de luxe,* now out of print, contains the *Memoir* by Hallam Lord Tennyson (see below).]

The Works of Alfred Lord Tennyson. Edited by Hallam Lord Tennyson. Eversley Edition. 6 vols. London: Macmillan, 1908. [This edition includes annotations drawn from the poet's memoranda and conversations. The same material is included in a one-volume edition, 1913.]

Poetic and Dramatic Works of Alfred Lord Tennyson. Edited by W. J. Rolfe. Cambridge Edition. Boston: Houghton Mifflin Company, 1898. [This contains a biographical introduction and a commentary which includes information derived from personal interviews with the poet. The texts are not quite complete, a few poems still under copyright being omitted.]

Poems. London: Moxon, 1857. [This is the famous "Pre-Raphaelite Tennyson" with illustrations from designs by Rossetti, Millais, Holman Hunt, and other artists. These illustrations are reproduced in *Poems of Tennyson, 1830–1870,* Oxford, 1912.]

The Devil and the Lady. Edited by Charles Tennyson. New York: Macmillan, 1930. [A juvenile drama, precociously clever, hitherto unpublished and now edited by the poet's grandson.]

Unpublished Early Poems of Alfred Tennyson. Edited by Charles Tennyson. London: Macmillan, 1931.

Among numerous volumes of selections may be mentioned: (1) *Poems.* Edited by Henry Van Dyke and D. L. Chambers. Boston: Ginn, 1903 ("Athenæum Press Series"). (2) *Select Poems.* Edited by Archibald MacMechan. Boston: Heath, 1911 ("Belles-Lettres Series"). (3) *Poems, 1830–1865.* With an Introduction by T. Herbert Warren. Oxford, 1910 ("The World's Classics").

III. BIOGRAPHY AND CRITICISM

The first of the two following groups comprises the most important volumes devoted to the study and interpretation of Tennyson and his works. The second includes a representative selection of reviews, essays, lectures, and so forth. Of early publications those only are cited which still possess some value for their content or interest because of their authorship.

i.

Alden, Raymond M., *Tennyson: How to Know Him.* Indianapolis: Bobbs-Merrill, 1917. [A sound piece of conservative criticism, with some attention to biography and with an abundance of well-chosen illustrative excerpts from the poems.]

Baker, Arthur E., *A Concordance to the Poetical and Dramatic Works of Alfred Lord Tennyson.* London: Kegan Paul, 1914. [A supplementary concordance to *The Devil and the Lady* was issued by Mr. Baker in 1931 (London: Golden Vista Press).]

Baker, Arthur E., *A Tennyson Dictionary; the Characters and Place Names Contained in the Poetical and Dramatic Works.* London: Routledge, 1916.

Benson, Arthur Christopher, *Alfred Tennyson.* New York: Dutton, 1907. [A sketch of the poet's life, character, and ideals; an account of his view of the "poetic life"; and a study of the chief technical features of his art. In tone representative of the reverent attitude towards Tennyson characteristic of the more conservative section of the Late Victorian generation.]

Bradley, Andrew C., *A Commentary on Tennyson's "In Memoriam."* London: Macmillan, 1901 (revised ed., 1902). [The best commentary, superseding earlier similar works of which it incorporates the portions of lasting value.]

Brooke, Stopford A., *Tennyson: His Art and Relation to Modern Life.* London: Isbister, 1894. [For long an influential interpretation, especially in English non-conformist circles.]

Collins, J. Churton, *Illustrations of Tennyson.* London: Chatto and Windus, 1891. [An erudite source-study; in tone often of a disagreeable truculence as though the professor were catching the poet in the act of plagiarism. Analogues and unconscious reminiscences of earlier poets are sometimes misinterpreted as direct sources. But still of value, and not altogether superseded by Mustard's work (see below) since Collins ranges over a wider field.]

Dixon, W. Macneile, *A Primer of Tennyson.* London: Methuen, 1896. [Much information in compact form.]

Fausset, Hugh I'Anson, *Tennyson: a Modern Portrait.* London: Selwyn and Blount, 1923. [A very "modern portrait" indeed, by a disciple and imitator of Lytton Strachey. See C. H. Herford's masterly review of this book in *The Year's Work in English Studies: 1923,* pp. 217 f.]

Gatty, Alfred, *A Key to Tennyson's "In Memoriam."* London: Bogue, 1882. [For many years the standard guide. It embodies interpretations communicated by the poet. Still useful, though the most important parts have been incorporated in Bradley's *Commentary* (see above).]

Genung, J. F., *Tennyson's "In Memoriam": Its Purpose and Its Structure.* Boston: Houghton Mifflin, 1884. [For many years the most widely used commentary in America.]

Japikse, Cornelia G. H., *The Dramas of Alfred Lord Tennyson.* London: Macmillan, 1926. [This monograph by a Dutch scholar sets too high an estimate on the dramas, but it is clear and informative on such matters as sources, technique, and the contemporary reception of each play, and it contains interesting comments on the anachronistic nineteenth-century "colour" in characterization and ideas.]

Lang, Andrew, *Alfred Tennyson.* New York: Dodd, Mead, 1901. [In the "Modern English Writers" series. Mainly critical.]

Lounsbury, Thomas R., *The Life and Times of Tennyson.* New Haven: Yale University Press, 1915. [Not a formal biography, notwithstanding the title; but an exhaustive account of the reception of Tennyson's work by the critics and by the public, and of his reaction to criticism. Covers the period down to 1850.]

Luce, Morton, *A Handbook to the Works of Alfred Lord Tennyson.* London: Bell, 1906. [Much information, methodically arranged.]

Lyall, Sir Alfred C., *Tennyson.* London: Macmillan, 1902. [In the "English Men of Letters" series. Still the best of the short biographies.]

Mustard, Wilfred P., *Classical Echoes in Tennyson.* New York: Macmillan, 1904. [Very useful; and often drawn on in the commentary in the present volume.]

Napier, George C., *The Homes and Haunts of Alfred, Lord Tennyson*. Glasgow: MacLehose, 1892. [The most attractive of many books and articles on this subject.]

Nicolson, Harold, *Tennyson: Aspects of His Life, Character and Poetry*. London: Constable, 1923. ["Aspects" is a comfortable word, permitting the writer to dwell upon what is congenial to him and omit what is not (for example, any discussion of the *Idylls of the King*). The book is clever, perhaps too clever; but it is a more sympathetic portrait than might have been expected from this source. The abundant wit is more often exercised at the expense of Victorianism in general than of Tennyson in particular.]

Orsini, G. N. Giordano, *La Poesia di Alfred Tennyson*, Bari: Laterza, 1928. [A sober appreciation of Tennyson's achievement as a poet without the distraction of character-study. See the summary of Orsini's conclusions by H. V. Routh in *The Year's Work in English Studies, 1928*, pp. 307 f.]

Pyre, J. F. A., *The Formation of Tennyson's Style* (University of Wisconsin Studies in Language and Literature, Number 12), Madison, 1921. [The emphasis is upon versification rather than style in a broader sense. Especially it is a study of the processes whereby the promising imperfection of 1830–2 was converted into the mature perfection of 1842.]

Rawnsley, H. D., *Memories of the Tennysons*. Glasgow: MacLehose, 1900. [Canon Rawnsley was a close friend of Tennyson in the poet's later years.]

Salt, Henry S., *Tennyson as a Thinker*. London: Reeves and Turner, 1893. [An extremely hostile estimate by a Late Victorian rationalist.]

Tennyson, Hallam, Lord, *Alfred Lord Tennyson, A Memoir*. London: Macmillan, 1897. [The fundamental book for all Tennyson study, containing stores of material unrivalled in richness. A work of filial piety, reverent and reticent in tone and substance, eschewing controversy and literary gossip. It has been called "faultily faultless, icily regular, splendidly null"; but the unfair quotation suggests only what the poet's son left out of the portrait and fails to take account of what he included in it.]

Tennyson, Hallam, Lord, *Tennyson and His Friends*. London: Macmillan, 1911. [A supplement to the *Memoir*.

Reminiscences by various friends of the poet, with some appreciative criticism, the whole edited by the second Lord Tennyson.]

Van Dyke, Henry, *The Poetry of Tennyson*. New York: Scribner, 1889. [An influential study, repeatedly revised and enlarged in subsequent editions.]

Waugh, Arthur, *Alfred Lord Tennyson: A Study of His Life and Work*. London: Macmillan, 1896. [The revision of an earlier *Study* (London: Heineman, 1892) written immediately before, and published immediately after, Tennyson's death.]

ii.

Ainger, Alfred, "Tennyson, Alfred," in *The Dictionary of National Biography*, xix, 546 f. [For a less impersonal estimate by Canon Ainger see "The Death of Tennyson," *Macmillan's Magazine*, lxvii (November 1892), 76 f.; reprinted in *Lectures and Essays*, London: Macmillan, 1905, ii, 114 f.]

Austin, Alfred, "Tennyson," *Temple Bar*, xxviii (December 1869), 35 f.; reprinted in *The Poetry of the Period*. London: Bentley, 1870. [*The Poetry of the Period* roused Browning to satire and Swinburne to wrath; Tennyson, who was dealt with more respectfully than his *confrères*, made no public comment. As criticism, it is characteristic of Tennyson's unworthy successor in the laureateship, whom Wilfrid S. Blunt called "a pert little cocksparrow of a man." See also Austin's "A Vindication of Tennyson," in *The Bridling of Pegasus*, London: Macmillan, 1910, pp. 197 f. and his *Autobiography*, London: Macmillan, 1911, ii, 219 f.]

Bagehot, Walter, "Wordsworth, Tennyson, and Browning," *The National Review*, New Series, i (November 1864), 27 f.; reprinted in *Literary Studies*, London: Longmans, 1879, ii, 338 f. [The earliest criticism of Tennyson still possessing a value other than the merely historical or curious.]

Beach, Joseph Warren, *The Concept of Nature in Nineteenth-Century Poetry*. New York: Macmillan, 1936, Chapter xv: "Tennyson." [An invaluable survey of Tennyson's views of Science and Evolution and his religious beliefs.]

Boas, F. S., *"Idylls of the King* in 1921" (a lecture), in *Transactions of the Royal Society of Literature*, 1922, pp. 23 f. [A defence of the allegory — the conflict of Soul with Sense — as a mystic theme inspiring passages of great poetry; but grafted upon a medieval story of quite other origin.]

Bradley, Andrew C., "The Reaction against Tennyson," *English Association Pamphlets,* Number 39, Oxford, 1917; reprinted in *A Miscellany,* London: Macmillan, 1929, pp. 1 f.

Bush, Douglas, *Mythology and the Romantic Tradition in English Poetry.* Cambridge: Harvard University Press, 1937. [Chapter vi: "Tennyson." Tennyson's classical pieces are re-appraised in accordance with the general thesis that mythological poems are vital when the myths are re-created so that they carry modern implications, and are of a very inferior order, if not "dead," if myths are merely retold. See also Professor Bush's "The Personal Note in Tennyson's Classical Poems," *University of Toronto Quarterly,* iv (1935), 201 f.]

Dowden, Edward, "Mr. Tennyson and Mr. Browning," in *Studies in Literature, 1798–1877.* London: Kegan Paul, 1906, pp. 191 f. [A lecture delivered in Dublin in the eighteen-sixties. A comparison with Bagehot's essay (see above) is interesting.]

Elton, Oliver, *A Survey of English Literature, 1780–1880.* New York: Macmillan, 1920, iii, Chapter xiii: "Tennyson." [One of the best estimates within narrow compass. See also the same author's lecture on Tennyson (1902), in *Modern Studies,* London: Arnold, 1907, pp. 183 f.]

Granville-Barker, H. G., "Tennyson, Swinburne, Meredith and the Theatre," in *The Eighteen-seventies, Essays by Fellows of the Royal Society of Literature.* Cambridge, 1929. [The opinions of an expert on the theatre on the causes of Tennyson's failure as a dramatist.]

Grierson, H. J. C., "The Tennysons," in *The Cambridge History of English Literature.* New York: Putnam, xiii (1917), 25 f.

Hallam, Arthur Henry, *Poems . . . with His Essay on the Lyrical Poems of Alfred Tennyson.* Edited by Richard Le Gallienne. London: Mathews and Lane, 1893. [The essay is of historical interest because of its early date (1830) and because of the author's relations with Tennyson.]

Harrison, Frederick, "Tennyson," in *Tennyson, Ruskin, Mill, and Other Literary Estimates*. New York: Macmillan, 1900, pp. 1 f. [See also the same author's "The Burial of Tennyson," in *Memories and Thoughts*, New York: Macmillan, 1906, pp. 20 f., and "Studies in Tennyson," in *Among My Books*, New York: Macmillan, 1912, pp. 284 f.]

Henley, William Ernest, "Tennyson" (1892), in *Views and Reviews*, London: Nutt, 1908, i, 183 f. [An obituary notice, but (as would be expected of the writer) less of a conventional tribute than most such.]

Horne, Richard H., "Alfred Tennyson," in *A New Spirit of the Age*. London, 1844. [One of the very early estimates that still retain some interest.]

Hutton, Richard Holt, "Tennyson," *Macmillan's Magazine*, xxvii (December 1872), 143 f.; reprinted in *Literary Studies*. London: Macmillan, 1892, pp. 361 f. [Significant because of the critic's influential position as editor of *The Spectator*.]

Jebb, Sir Richard C., "On Mr. Tennyson's 'Lucretius,' " *Macmillan's Magazine*, xviii (June 1868), 97 f. [The earliest serious study of one of Tennyson's classical poems by a classical scholar. See also Jebb's article on Tennyson in Ward's *English Poets*. New York: Macmillan, 1907, iv, 755 f.]

Ker, William P., "Tennyson" (a lecture delivered in 1909), in *Collected Essays*, London: Macmillan, 1925, i, 258 f.

Lockhart, John Gibson, Review of the *Poems* of 1832 in *The Quarterly Review*, April 1833; reprinted in *Lockhart's Literary Criticism*. Edited by M. C. Hildyard. Oxford: Blackwell, 1931, pp. 132 f. [Though attributed to Lockhart, this is by John Wilson Croker.]

Lucas, F. L., "Tennyson," in *Eight Victorian Poets*. New York: Macmillan, 1930, pp. 3 f.

Mackail, J. W., "Tennyson," in *Studies of English Poets*. London: Longmans, 1926, pp. 227 f. [A lecture delivered from the Chair of Poetry at Oxford.]

Maynadier, Howard, *The Arthur of the English Poets*. Boston: Houghton Mifflin, 1907. [Chapter xxii: "Tennyson." For a more extended treatment of the same subject see M. W. MacCallum, *Tennyson's Idylls of the King and Arthurian Story from the Sixteenth Century*. Glasgow: MacLehose,

1894. Monographs and articles on the subject are very numerous.]

Meynell, Alice, "Some Thoughts of a Reader of Tennyson," in *Hearts of Controversy*. London: Burns and Oates, [1917], pp. 1 f. [On the element of "wildness" in Tennyson's poetry.]

More, Paul Elmer, "Tennyson," in *Shelburne Essays, Seventh Series*. New York: Putnam, 1910, pp. 64 f.

Nicoll, Sir William Robertson, and Wise, Thomas James, *Literary Anecdotes of the Nineteenth Century*. London: Hodder and Stoughton, 1896. [ii, 217 f.: "The Building of the *Idylls*"; ii, 419 f.: "Tennysoniana."]

Noyes, Alfred, "Tennyson and Some Recent Critics," in *Some Aspects of Modern Poetry*. London: Hodder and Stoughton, 1924, pp. 133 f.

Palmer, George Herbert, "Alfred Tennyson," in *Formative Types in English Poetry*. Boston: Houghton Mifflin, 1918, pp. 223 f.

Stedman, Edmund Clarence, "Alfred Tennyson," in *Victorian Poets*. Boston: Houghton Mifflin, 1896, pp. 150 f.

Stephen, Leslie, "Tennyson," in *Studies of a Biographer*. New York: Putnam, 1898, ii, 196 f.

Swinburne, Algernon Charles, *Under the Microscope*. London, 1872, pp. 36–45. [A fierce and ungenerous diatribe against Tennyson's treatment of the Arthurian story. Never reprinted by Swinburne, but included in his *Works*, Bonchurch Edition, London: Heinemann, 1925–7, xvi, 377 f. There are also several pirated reprints.]

Swinburne, Algernon Charles, "Tennyson and Musset," *The Fortnightly Review*, xxxv (February 1881), 129 f.; reprinted in *Miscellanies*, 1884. [A rhapsodic *amende* for earlier depreciation. See also Swinburne's letters, *passim*, and the "Birthday Ode" addressed to Tennyson in 1889.]

Walker, Hugh, *The Literature of the Victorian Era*. Cambridge, 1910, pp. 287–309; 374–410. [Supersedes, and in part incorporates material from, the same scholar's *The Greater Victorian Poets*, London, 1895, and *The Age of Tennyson*, London, 1897.]

Warren, Sir T. Herbert, *The Centenary of Tennyson.* Oxford, 1909. [A lecture by the Professor of Poetry.]

Watts-Dunton, Walter Theodore, "Alfred Lord Tennyson," in *Old Familiar Faces.* London: Jenkins, 1916. [In part a reprint of the obituary notice contributed to *The Athenaeum,* October 8 and 22, 1892; in part a reprint of reviews. A characteristic amalgam of personal impressions and critical opinions.]

IV. POETIC TRIBUTES: 1892

The quantity of elegies, threnodies, memorial verses and the like inspired by the death of Lord Tennyson is unexampled in the history of English literature since the death of Lord Byron, and the quality is much higher than that of the tributes to Byron. It seems worth while, therefore, to group together here references to about a score of these poems, selecting only those by writers famous or at least well known in their day, some of whom are still famous in ours.

Dobson, Austin, "Alfred, Lord Tennyson. Emigravit October VI, MDCCCXCII," *The Athenaeum,* October 8, 1892; reprinted in Dobson's *Poems on Several Occasions.* New York: Dodd, Mead, 1895.

Forman, H. Buxton, "Midnight: Lines on the Death of Alfred, Lord Tennyson," in Nicoll and Wise, *Literary Anecdotes* (see above), i, 29 f.

Garnett, Richard, "Alfred, Lord Tennyson," *The Illustrated London News,* October 15, 1892.

Gilder, Richard Watson, "The Silence of Tennyson," *The Critic* (New York), October 15, 1892; reprinted in Gilder's *Poems.* Boston: Houghton Mifflin, 1908, pp. 206-7.

Huxley, Thomas Henry, "Westminster Abbey, October 12, 1892," *The Nineteenth Century,* xxxii (November 1892), 831 f. [This is one of seven poems printed together under the general heading "To Tennyson: The Tributes of His Friends."]

Knowles, James, "Apotheosis: Westminster, October 1892," *ibid.*, pp. 843 f.

Lang, Andrew, "On the Death of Lord Tennyson," *Poetical Works*, London: Longmans, 1923, iii, 31. [The place of original publication is not recorded in this reprint.]

Miller, Joaquin, "The Passing of Tennyson," *The Critic* (New York), November 5, 1892.

Myers, Frederick W. H., "The Height and the Deep," *The Nineteenth Century, ut cit.*, pp. 833 f.

Noel, Roden, "The Death of Tennyson," *ibid.*, pp. 835 f.

Oliphant, Margaret O. W., "Alfred Tennyson," *The Spectator*, October 15, 1892.

Palgrave, Francis Turner, "In Pace," *The Nineteenth Century, ut cit.*, pp. 837 f.

Rawnsley, H. D., "The Laureate Dead," *The Academy*, October 15, 1892.

Swinburne, Algernon Charles, "Threnody. October 6, 1892," *The Nineteenth Century*, xxxiii (January 1893), 1 f.; reprinted in *Astrophel and Other Poems*, 1894, and in collected editions of Swinburne's works.

Tabb, John B. (Father Tabb), "Alfred Tennyson," *The Independent* (New York), October 27, 1892.

Todhunter, John, "In Westminster Abbey," *The Academy*, October 22, 1892.

Vere, Aubrey de, Three Sonnets, "The Land's Vigil," "In Westminster Abbey," and "The Poet," *The Nineteenth Century, ut cit.*, pp. 840 f.

Warren, T. Herbert, "In Memoriam: Alfred, Lord Tennyson," *The Spectator*, October 15, 1892.

Watson, William, "Lachrymae Musarum," *The Illustrated London News*, October 15, 1892; reprinted in book form and in collected editions of Sir William Watson's poems. [This is by far the finest of the elegies.]

Watts [-Dunton], Theodore, "In Westminster Abbey," *The Nineteenth Century, ut cit.*; reprinted in Watts-Dunton's *The Coming of Love and Other Poems*, London, 1898.

TENNYSON
REPRESENTATIVE POEMS

I

THE POET AND HIS LAND

THE POET[1]

THE poet in a golden clime was born,
    With golden stars above;
Dower'd with the hate of hate, the scorn of scorn,
    The love of love.

He saw thro' life and death, thro' good and ill,   5
    He saw thro' his own soul.
The marvel of the everlasting will,
    An open scroll,

Before him lay: with echoing feet he threaded
    The secretest walks of fame: 10
The viewless arrows of his thoughts were headed
    And wing'd with flame,

Like Indian reeds blown from his silver tongue,
    And of so fierce a flight,
From Calpe unto Caucasus they sung,   15
    Filling with light

And vagrant melodies the winds which bore
    Them earthward till they lit;
Then, like the arrow-seeds of the field flower,
    The fruitful wit   20

---

[1] Published in *Poems, Chiefly Lyrical*, 1830; reprinted, slightly revised,
in *Poems*, 1842.

13. *Indian reeds*, "blow pipes such as the South American Indians use
for shooting arrows" (Van Dyke).

15. *Calpe*, Gibraltar.

19. *the field flower*, the dandelion.

Cleaving, took root, and springing forth anew
    Where'er they fell, behold,
Like to the mother plant in semblance, grew
    A flower all gold,

And bravely furnish'd all abroad to fling   25
    The winged shafts of truth,
To throng with stately blooms the breathing spring
    Of Hope and Youth.

So many minds did gird their orbs with beams,
    Tho' one did fling the fire.   30
Heaven flow'd upon the soul in many dreams
    Of high desire.

Thus truth was multiplied on truth, the world
    Like one great garden show'd,
And thro' the wreaths of floating dark upcurl'd,   35
    Rare sunrise flow'd.

And Freedom rear'd in that august sunrise
    Her beautiful bold brow,
When rites and forms before his burning eyes
    Melted like snow.   40

There was no blood upon her maiden robes
    Sunn'd by those orient skies;
But round about the circles of the globes
    Of her keen eyes

And in her raiment's hem was traced in flame   45
    WISDOM, a name to shake
All evil dreams of power — a sacred name.
    And when she spake,

45–47. In 1830:

> And in the bordure of her robe was writ
> WISDOM, a name to shake
> Hoar anarchies, as with a thunderfit.

The rare word "thunderfit" is used by Coleridge (*The Ancient Mariner*, l. 69) and Shelley ("Lines written among the Euganean Hills," l. 182).

Her words did gather thunder as they ran,
    And as the lightning to the thunder 50
Which follows it, riving the spirit of man,
    Making earth wonder,

So was their meaning to her words. No sword
    Of wrath her right arm whirl'd,
But one poor poet's scroll, and with *his* word 55
    She shook the world.

"YOU ASK ME WHY"[1]

You ask me, why, tho' ill at ease,
    Within this region I subsist,
    Whose spirits falter in the mist,
And languish for the purple seas.

It is the land that freemen till, 5
    That sober-suited Freedom chose,
    The land, where girt with friends or foes
A man may speak the thing he will;

A land of settled government,
    A land of just and old renown, 10
    Where Freedom slowly broadens down
From precedent to precedent:

Where faction seldom gathers head,
    But by degrees to fullness wrought,
    The strength of some diffusive thought 15
Hath time and space to work and spread.

Should banded unions persecute
    Opinion, and induce a time
    When single thought is civil crime,
And individual freedom mute; 20

[1] Written in 1833; published in *Poems*, 1842.

Tho' Power should make from land to land
    The name of Britain trebly great —
    Tho' every channel of the State
Should fill and choke with golden sand —

Yet waft me from the harbour-mouth,   25
    Wild wind!   I seek a warmer sky,
    And I will see before I die
The palms and temples of the South.

"LOVE THOU THY LAND"[1]

Love thou thy land, with love far-brought
    From out the storied Past, and used
    Within the Present, but transfused
Thro' future time by power of thought.

True love turn'd round on fixed poles,   5
    Love, that endures not sordid ends,
    For English natures, freemen, friends,
Thy brothers and immortal souls.

But pamper not a hasty time,
    Nor feed with crude imaginings   10
    The herd, wild hearts and feeble wings
That every sophister can lime.

Deliver not the tasks of might
    To weakness, neither hide the ray
    From those, not blind, who wait for day,   15
Tho' sitting girt with doubtful light.

Make Knowledge circle with the winds;
    But let her herald, Reverence, fly
    Before her to whatever sky
Bear seed of men and growth of minds.   20

---

[1] Written about 1833; published in *Poems,* 1842.

Watch what main-currents draw the years:
  Cut Prejudice against the grain:
  But gentle words are always gain:
Regard the weakness of thy peers:

Nor toil for title, place, or touch   25
  Of pension, neither count on praise:
  It grows to guerdon after-days:
Nor deal in watch-words overmuch:

Not clinging to some ancient saw;
  Not master'd by some modern term;   30
  Not swift nor slow to change, but firm:
And in its season bring the law;

That from Discussion's lip may fall
  With Life, that, working strongly, binds —
  Set in all lights by many minds,   35
To close the interests of all.

For Nature also, cold and warm,
  And moist and dry, devising long,
  Thro' many agents making strong,
Matures the individual form.   40

Meet is it changes should control
  Our being, lest we rust in ease.
  We all are changed by still degrees,
All but the basis of the soul.

So let the change which comes be free   45
  To ingroove itself with that which flies,
  And work, a joint of state, that plies
Its office, moved with sympathy.

A saying, hard to shape in act;
  For all the past of Time reveals   50
  A bridal dawn of thunder-peals,
Wherever Thought hath wedded Fact.

Ev'n now we hear with inward strife
 A motion toiling in the gloom —
 The Spirit of the years to come   55
Yearning to mix himself with Life.

A slow-develop'd strength awaits
 Completion in a painful school;
 Phantoms of other forms of rule,
New Majesties of mighty States —   60

The warders of the growing hour,
 But vague in vapour, hard to mark;
 And round them sea and air are dark
With great contrivances of Power.

Of many changes, aptly join'd,   65
 Is bodied forth the second whole.
 Regard gradation, lest the soul
Of Discord race the rising wind;

A wind to puff your idol-fires,
 And heap their ashes on the head;   70
 To shame the boast so often made,
That we are wiser than our sires.

Oh yet, if Nature's evil star
 Drive men in manhood, as in youth,
 To follow flying steps of Truth   75
Across the brazen bridge of war —

If New and Old, disastrous feud,
 Must ever shock, like armed foes,
 And this be true, till Time shall close,
That Principles are rain'd in blood;   80

Not yet the wise of heart would cease
 To hold his hope thro' shame and guilt,
 But with his hand against the hilt,
Would pace the troubled land, like Peace;

Not less, tho' dogs of Faction bay,   85
   Would serve his kind in deed and word,
   Certain, if knowledge bring the sword
That knowledge takes the sword away —

Would love the gleams of good that broke
   From either side, nor veil his eyes: 90
   And if some dreadful need should rise
Would strike, and firmly, and one stroke:

To-morrow yet would reap to-day,
   As we bear blossom of the dead:
   Earn well the thrifty months, nor wed   95
Raw Haste, half-sister to Decay.

II

SONGS

"MOVE EASTWARD, HAPPY EARTH"[1]

Move eastward, happy earth, and leave
  Yon orange sunset waning slow:
From fringes of the faded eve,
  O, happy planet, eastward go;
Till over thy dark shoulder glow   5
  Thy silver sister-world, and rise
  To glass herself in dewy eyes
That watch me from the glen below.

Ah, bear me with thee, smoothly borne,
  Dip forward under starry light,   10
And move me to my marriage-morn,
  And round again to happy night.

A FAREWELL[1]

Flow down, cold rivulet, to the sea,
  Thy tribute wave deliver:
No more by thee my steps shall be,
  For ever and for ever.

Flow, softly flow, by lawn and lea,   5
  A rivulet, then a river:
No where by thee my steps shall be,
  For ever and for ever.

But here will sigh thine alder tree,
  And here thine aspen shiver;   10

---

[1] Published in *Poems,* 1842.

And here by thee will hum the bee,
   For ever and for ever.

A thousand suns will stream on thee,
   A thousand moons will quiver;
But not by thee my steps shall be,   15
   For ever and for ever.

"TEARS, IDLE TEARS" [1]

Tears, idle tears, I know not what they mean,
Tears from the depth of some divine despair
Rise in the heart, and gather to the eyes,
In looking on the happy Autumn-fields,
And thinking of the days that are no more.   5

Fresh as the first beam glittering on a sail,
That brings our friends up from the underworld,
Sad as the last which reddens over one
That sinks with all we love below the verge;
So sad, so fresh, the days that are no more.   10

Ah, sad and strange as in dark summer dawns
The earliest pipe of half-awaken'd birds
To dying ears, when unto dying eyes
The casement slowly grows a glimmering square;
So sad, so strange, the days that are no more.   15

Dear as remember'd kisses after death,
And sweet as those by hopeless fancy feign'd
On lips that are for others; deep as love,
Deep as first love, and wild with all regret;
O Death in Life, the days that are no more.   20

---

[1] Published in *The Princess: A Medley* (iv, 21 f.), 1847. Tennyson told James Knowles that the poem was written at Tintern Abbey "when the woods were all yellowing with autumn seen through the ruined windows."

"NOW SLEEPS THE CRIMSON PETAL"[1]

Now sleeps the crimson petal, now the white;
Nor waves the cypress in the palace walk;
Nor winks the gold fin in the porphyry font:
The fire-fly wakens: waken thou with me.

Now droops the milkwhite peacock like a ghost,   5
And like a ghost she glimmers on to me.

Now lies the Earth all Danaë to the stars,
And all thy heart lies open unto me.

Now slides the silent meteor on, and leaves
A shining furrow, as thy thoughts in me.   10

Now folds the lily all her sweetness up,
And slips into the bosom of the lake:
So fold thyself, my dearest, thou, and slip
Into my bosom and be lost in me.

"COME DOWN, O MAID"[1]

Come down, O maid, from yonder mountain height:
What pleasure lives in height (the shepherd sang)
In height and cold, the splendour of the hills?

---

[1] Published in *The Princess* (vii, 161 f.), 1847.

7. *Danaë* was the Argive princess to whom Zeus descended in the form of a golden shower.

10. The likening of a meteor's course to a furrow is Virgilian (*Aeneid*, ii, 697). Compare *The Princess*, iii, 1–2:

> Morn in the white wake of the morning star
> Came furrowing all the orient into gold.

---

[1] Published in *The Princess* (viii, 177 f.), 1847. Written in Switzerland, this song was suggested by the contrast between the bleak Alpine heights and the luxuriant valleys in the neighbourhood of Grindelwald. It is adapted and developed from the appeal of the Cyclops to Galatea in the eleventh *Idyl* of Theocritus. See W. P. Mustard, *Classical Echoes in Tennyson*, pp. 40 f.

But cease to move so near the Heavens, and cease
To glide a sunbeam by the blasted Pine,   5
To sit a star upon the sparkling spire;
And come, for Love is of the valley, come,
For Love is of the valley, come thou down
And find him; by the happy threshold, he,
Or hand in hand with Plenty in the maize,   10
Or red with spirted purple of the vats,
Or foxlike in the vine; nor cares to walk
With Death and Morning on the silver horns,
Nor wilt thou snare him in the white ravine,
Nor find him dropt upon the firths of ice,   15
That huddling slant in furrow-cloven falls
To roll the torrent out of dusky doors:
But follow; let the torrent dance thee down
To find him in the valley; let the wild
Lean-headed Eagles yelp alone, and leave   20
The monstrous ledges there to slope, and spill
Their thousand wreaths of dangling water-smoke,
That like a broken purpose waste in air:
So waste not thou; but come; for all the vales
Await thee; azure pillars of the hearth   25
Arise to thee; the children call, and I
Thy shepherd pipe, and sweet is every sound,
Sweeter thy voice, but every sound is sweet;
Myriads of rivulets hurrying thro' the lawn,
The moan of doves in immemorial elms,   30
And murmuring of innumerable bees.

12. Compare The Song of Solomon, ii, 15: "The little foxes that spoil the vines."

13. *horns,* peaks of the Bernese Oberland (Wetterhorn, Schreckhorn, Breithorn, etc.).

22. *water-smoke,* cataracts such as the Staubbach at Lauterbrunnen.

30. From Virgil, *Georgics,* iv, 19.

31. From Virgil, *Eclogues,* i, 59.

"AS THROUGH THE LAND AT EVE WE WENT" [1]

As THRO' the land at eve we went,
  And pluck'd the ripen'd ears,
We fell out, my wife and I,
O we fell out I know not why,
  And kiss'd again with tears.   5
And blessings on the falling out
  That all the more endears,
When we fall out with those we love
  And kiss again with tears!
For when we came where lies the child   10
  We lost in other years,
There above the little grave,
O there above the little grave,
  We kiss'd again with tears.

"SWEET AND LOW" [1]

SWEET and low, sweet and low,
  Wind of the western sea,
Low, low, breathe and blow,
  Wind of the western sea!
Over the rolling waters go,   5
Come from the dying moon, and blow,
  Blow him again to me;
While my little one, while my pretty one, sleeps.

Sleep and rest, sleep and rest,
  Father will come to thee soon;   10
Rest, rest, on mother's breast,
  Father will come to thee soon;
Father will come to his babe in the nest,
Silver sails all out of the west
  Under the silver moon: 15
Sleep, my little one, sleep, my pretty one, sleep.

---

[1] The intercalary songs in *The Princess* were added in the third edition, 1850, but had been part of Tennyson's original plan. This song is between cantos i and ii.

---

[1] Published in *The Princess*, third edition, 1850, between cantos ii and iii.

"THE SPLENDOUR FALLS" [1]

THE splendour falls on castle walls
    And snowy summits old in story:
The long light shakes across the lakes,
    And the wild cataract leaps in glory.
Blow, bugle, blow, set the wild echoes flying,   5
Blow, bugle; answer, echoes, dying, dying, dying.

O hark, O hear! how thin and clear,
    And thinner, clearer, farther going!
O sweet and far from cliff and scar
    The horns of Elfland faintly blowing!   10
Blow, let us hear the purple glens replying:
Blow, bugle; answer, echoes, dying, dying, dying.

O love, they die in yon rich sky,
    They faint on hill or field or river:
Our echoes roll from soul to soul,   15
    And grow for ever and for ever.
Blow, bugle, blow, set the wild echoes flying,
And answer, echoes, answer, dying, dying, dying.

"HOME THEY BROUGHT HER WARRIOR DEAD" [1]

HOME they brought her warrior dead:
    She nor swoon'd, nor utter'd cry:
All her maidens, watching, said,
    'She must weep or she will die.'

---

[1] Published in *The Princess,* third edition, 1850, between cantos iii and iv. This song was suggested to Tennyson by the echoes of a bugle on the Lakes of Killarney in Ireland in 1848. The "castle walls" are those of Ross Castle on Ross Island in the Lower Lake. The peaks of the district are not, however, "snowy summits."

---

[1] Published in *The Princess,* third edition, 1850, between cantos v and vi. Compare Sir Walter Scott, *The Lay of the Last Minstrel,* i, stanza ix, where, however, the bereaved mother takes comfort in the thought that her infant son will grow up to avenge his father's death.

Then they praised him, soft and low,   5
    Call'd him worthy to be loved,
Truest friend and noblest foe;
    Yet she neither spoke nor moved.

Stole a maiden from her place,
    Lightly to the warrior stept,   10
Took the face-cloth from the face;
    Yet she neither moved nor wept.

Rose a nurse of ninety years,
    Set his child upon her knee —
Like summer tempest came her tears —   15
    'Sweet my child, I live for thee.'

"ASK ME NO MORE"[1]

Ask me no more; the moon may draw the sea;
    The cloud may stoop from heaven and take the shape
    With fold to fold, of mountain or of cape;
But O too fond, when have I answer'd thee?
                  Ask me no more.   5

Ask me no more: what answer should I give?
    I love not hollow cheek or faded eye:
    Yet, O my friend, I will not have thee die!
Ask me no more, lest I should bid thee live;
                  Ask me no more.   10

Ask me no more: thy fate and mine are seal'd:
    I strove against the stream and all in vain:
    Let the great river take me to the main:
No more, dear love, for at a touch I yield;
                  Ask me no more.   15

---

    [1] Published in *The Princess*, third edition, 1850, between cantos vi and vii.

    12. Compare Shakespeare, *Venus and Adonis*, l. 772: "And all in vain you strive against the stream."

"TURN, FORTUNE, TURN THY WHEEL"[1]

Turn, Fortune, turn thy wheel and lower the proud;
Turn thy wild wheel thro' sunshine, storm, and cloud;
Thy wheel and thee we neither love nor hate.

Turn, Fortune, turn thy wheel with smile or frown;
With that wild wheel we go not up or down;   5
Our hoard is little, but our hearts are great.

Smile and we smile, the lords of many lands;
Frown and we smile, the lords of our own hands;
For man is man and master of his fate.

Turn, turn thy wheel above the staring crowd;   10
Thy wheel and thou are shadows in the cloud;
Thy wheel and thee we neither love nor hate.

---

[1] Enid's song in "The Marriage of Geraint" (ll. 347 f.), published in
Idylls of the King, 1859.

III

THE POET'S DREAMS

THE PALACE OF ART[1]

I BUILT my soul a lordly pleasure-house,
    Wherein at ease for aye to dwell.
I said, 'O Soul, make merry and carouse,
    Dear soul, for all is well.'

A huge crag-platform, smooth as burnish'd brass   5
    I chose. The ranged ramparts bright
From level meadow-bases of deep grass
    Suddenly scaled the light.

Thereon I built it firm. Of ledge or shelf
    The rock rose clear, or winding stair.   10

---

[1] Published in *Poems*, 1832; subjected to drastic alterations before re-printing in 1842, and to some further alterations in later editions. For the *variae lectiones* of the early editions consult *Works*, Cambridge edition, pp. 801 f. A few of these variants are recorded in the present commentary. To the poem Tennyson prefixed a dedication to an anonymous friend in which he interpreted the allegory as that of "a sinful soul," "a glorious devil," that loved Beauty for herself alone, not seeing that "Beauty, Good, and Knowledge are three sisters" that "never can be sunder'd without tears." There is a tradition that Tennyson in depicting the denizen of the Palace had William Beckford in mind. According to a recent view Tennyson was thinking of Cambridge as a home of sterile pedantry (A. C. Howell in *Studies in Philology*, xxxiii, 507 f.); but this intent, if present, is of secondary importance.

1. Various architectural details of the "pleasure-house" are collegiate; the poem was composed at Cambridge. Other details seem to have been suggested by Bacon's essay "Of Building."

3–4. Compare Luke, xii, 19: "I will say to my soul, Soul, thou hast much goods laid up for many years; take thine ease, eat, drink, and be merry."

My soul would live alone unto herself
   In her high palace there.

And 'While the world runs round and round,' I said,
   'Reign thou apart, a quiet king,
Still as, while Saturn whirls, his stedfast shade   15
   Sleeps on his luminous ring.'

To which my soul made answer readily:
   'Trust me, in bliss I shall abide
In this great mansion, that is built for me,
   So royal-rich and wide.'   20

     *   *   *   *
     *   *   *   *

Four courts I made, East, West and South and North,
   In each a squared lawn, wherefrom
The golden gorge of dragons spouted forth
   A flood of fountain-foam.

And round the cool green courts there ran a row   25
   Of cloisters, branch'd like mighty woods,
Echoing all night to that sonorous flow
   Of spouted fountain-floods.

And round the roofs a gilded gallery
   That lent broad verge to distant lands,
Far as the wild swan wings, to where the sky   30
   Dipt down to sea and sands.

From those four jets four currents in one swell
   Across the mountain stream'd below
In misty folds, that floating as they fell   35
   Lit up a torrent-bow.

And high on every peak a statue seem'd
   To hang on tiptoe, tossing up
A cloud of incense of all odour steam'd
   From out a golden cup.   40

15–16. The shadow which Saturn throws on its rings appears motion-less, though the planet revolves in ten and a half hours.

So that she thought, 'And who shall gaze upon
    My palace with unblinded eyes,
While this great bow will waver in the sun,
    And that sweet incense rise?'

For that sweet incense rose and never fail'd,   45
    And, while day sank or mounted higher,
The light aërial gallery, golden-rail'd,
    Burnt like a fringe of fire.

Likewise the deep-set windows, stain'd and traced,
    Would seem slow-flaming crimson fires   50
From shadow'd grots of arches interlaced,
    And tipt with frost-like spires.

*   *   *   *
*   *   *   *

Full of long-sounding corridors it was,
    That over-vaulted grateful gloom,
Thro' which the livelong day my soul did pass,   55
    Well-pleased, from room to room.

Full of great rooms and small the palace stood,
    All various, each a perfect whole
From living Nature, fit for every mood
    And change of my still soul.   60

For some were hung with arras green and blue,
    Showing a gaudy summer-morn,
Where with puff'd cheek the belted hunter blew
    His wreathed bugle-horn.

One seem'd all dark and red — a tract of sand,   65
    And some one pacing there alone,
Who paced for ever in a glimmering land,
    Lit with a low large moon.

One show'd an iron coast and angry waves.
    You seem'd to hear them climb and fall   70
And roar rock-thwarted under bellowing caves,
    Beneath the windy wall.

And one, a full-fed river winding slow
 By herds upon an endless plain,
The ragged rims of thunder brooding low,   75
 With shadow-streaks of rain.

And one, the reapers at their sultry toil.
 In front they bound the sheaves. Behind
Were realms of upland, prodigal in oil,
  And hoary to the wind.   80

And one a foreground black with stones and slags,
 Beyond, a line of heights, and higher
All barr'd with long white cloud the scornful crags,
  And highest, snow and fire.

And one, an English home — gray twilight pour'd 85
 On dewy pastures, dewy trees,
Softer than sleep — all things in order stored,
  A haunt of ancient Peace.

Nor these alone, but every landscape fair,
 As fit for every mood of mind,   90
Or gay, or grave, or sweet, or stern, was there
  Not less than truth design'd.

   * * * *
   * * * *

Or the maid-mother by a crucifix,
 In tracts of pasture sunny-warm,
Beneath branch-work of costly sardonyx 95
  Sat smiling, babe in arm.

Or in a clear-wall'd city on the sea,
 Near gilded organ-pipes, her hair
Wound with white roses, slept St. Cecily;
  An angel look'd at her.   100

---

99. Saint Cecilia, patron saint of music and traditionally the inventor of
the organ. Her music "drew an angel down" from heaven. See Dryden's
"Song for Saint Cecilia's Day."

Or thronging all one porch of Paradise
   A group of Houris bow'd to see
The dying Islamite, with hands and eyes
     That said, We wait for thee.

Or mythic Uther's deeply-wounded son   105
   In some fair space of sloping greens
Lay, dozing in the vale of Avalon,
     And watch'd by weeping queens.

Or hollowing one hand against his ear,
   To list a foot-fall, ere he saw   110
The wood-nymph, stay'd the Ausonian king to hear
     Of wisdom and of law.

Or over hills with peaky tops engrail'd,
   And many a tract of palm and rice,
The throne of Indian Cama slowly sail'd   115
     A summer fann'd with spice.

Or sweet Europa's mantle blew unclasp'd,
   From off her shoulder backward borne:
From one hand droop'd a crocus: one hand grasp'd
     The mild bull's golden horn.   120

Or else flush'd Ganymede, his rosy thigh
   Half-buried in the Eagle's down,
Sole as a flying star shot thro' the sky
     Above the pillar'd town.

---

105. King Arthur.

111. The *Ausonian* (Italian) *king* is Numa Pompilius, the legendary
lawgiver who, following the instructions of the nymph Egeria, decreed the
ceremonial observances of the religion of Rome. Compare Byron, *Childe
Harold's Pilgrimage,* iv, 1026 f.

115. *Cama,* Camdeo, or Kamadeva is the Eros of Hindu mythology.
Tennyson, who read of him in the writings of Sir William Jones the orientalist, had already described the god in "Love," in *Poems by Two Brothers.*

117. *Europa,* the Phœnician princess whom Zeus, in the form of a bull,
carried off to Crete.

121. *Ganymede,* the Trojan boy whom Zeus, in the form of an eagle,
carried up to Olýmpos.

Nor these alone: but every legend fair   125
   Which the supreme Caucasian mind
Carved out of Nature for itself, was there,
    Not less than life, design'd.

      *   *   *   *
      *   *   *   *

Then in the towers I placed great bells that swung,
   Moved of themselves, with silver sound;   130
And with choice paintings of wise men I hung
    The royal dais round.

For there was Milton like a seraph strong,
   Beside him Shakespeare bland and mild;
And there the world-worn Dante grasp'd his song,   135
    And somewhat grimly smiled.

And there the Ionian father of the rest;
   A million wrinkles carved his skin;
A hundred winters snow'd upon his breast,
    From cheek and throat and chin.   140

Above, the fair hall-ceiling stately-set
   Many an arch high up did lift,
And angels rising and descending met
    With interchange of gift.

Below was all mosaic choicely plann'd   145
   With cycles of the human tale
Of this wide world, the times of every land
    So wrought, they will not fail.

The people here, a beast of burden slow,
   Toil'd onward, prick'd with goads and stings;   150
Here play'd, a tiger, rolling to and fro
    The heads and crowns of kings;

---

137. The *Ionian father* of later poets is Homer.

143-4. See Genesis, xxviii, 12.

Here rose, an athlete, strong to break or bind
   All force in bonds that might endure,
And here once more like some sick man declined,   155
    And trusted any cure.

But over these she trod: and those great bells
   Began to chime. She took her throne:
She sat betwixt the shining oriels,
    To sing her songs alone.   160

And thro' the topmost oriels' coloured flame
   Two godlike faces gazed below;
Plato the wise, and large-brow'd Verulam,
    The first of those who know.

And all those names, that in their motion were   165
   Full-welling fountain-heads of change,
Betwixt the slender shafts were blazon'd fair
    In diverse raiment strange:

Thro' which the lights, rose, amber, emerald, blue,
   Flush'd in her temples and her eyes,   170
And from her lips, as morn from Memnon, drew
    Rivers of melodies.

No nightingale delighteth to prolong
   Her low preamble all alone,
More than my soul to hear her echo'd song   175
    Throb thro' the ribbed stone;

162-4. In the version of 1832 Plato is not mentioned, and Michael
Angelo and Luther are associated with Francis Bacon (Verulam). This
proves that the phrase "the first of those who know" is not intended to
apply (as Van Dyke and other commentators have asserted) to both Plato
and Bacon. In the original text the line was "The King of those who
know." Dante saw in Limbo Aristotle, "il maestro di color che sanno"
(*Inferno,* iv, 131).

171. The so-called Colossi of Memnon on the West Bank of the Nile
at Thebes are in reality statues of Amenophis III. The Northern Colossus
is the famous vocal statue of Memnon. See Baedeker's *Egypt,* ed. 1929,
pp. 345 f. Tennyson's imagination had already been touched by the
thought of "awful Memnonian countenances calm" of which he wrote in
some lines entitled "A Fragment," contributed to *The Gem, a Literary Annual* (1831).

Singing and murmuring in her feastful mirth,
   Joying to feel herself alive,
Lord over Nature, Lord of the visible earth,
    Lord of the senses five;   180

Communing with herself: 'All these are mine,
   And let the world have peace or wars,
'Tis one to me.' She — when young night divine
    Crown'd dying day with stars,

Making sweet close of his delicious toils —   185
   Lit light in wreaths and anadems,
And pure quintessences of precious oils
    In hollow'd moons of gems,

To mimic heaven; and clapt her hands and cried,
   'I marvel if my still delight   190
In this great house so royal-rich, and wide,
    Be flatter'd to the height.

'O all things fair to sate my various eyes!
   O shapes and hues that please me well!
O silent faces of the Great and Wise,
    My Gods, with whom I dwell!   195

'O God-like isolation which art mine,
   I can but count thee perfect gain,
What time I watch the darkening droves of swine
    That range on yonder plain.   200

'In filthy sloughs they roll a prurient skin,
   They graze and wallow, breed and sleep;
And oft some brainless devil enters in,
    And drives them to the deep.'

Then of the moral instinct would she prate   205
   And of the rising from the dead,
As hers by right of full-accomplish'd Fate;
    And at the last she said:

---

186. *anadems,* garlands, a word used by Shelley.
203–4. Luke, viii, 33.

'I take possession of man's mind and deed.
 I care not what the sects may brawl.   210
I sit as God holding no form of creed,
  But contemplating all.'

    * * * *
    * * * *

Full oft the riddle of the painful earth
 Flash'd thro' her as she sat alone,
Yet not the less held she her solemn mirth, 215
  And intellectual throne.

And so she throve and prosper'd: so three years
 She prosper'd: on the fourth she fell,
Like Herod, when the shout was in his ears,
  Struck thro' with pangs of hell.   220

Lest she should fail and perish utterly,
 God, before whom ever lie bare
The abysmal deeps of Personality,
  Plagued her with sore despair.

When she would think, where'er she turn'd her sight 225
 The airy hand confusion wrought,
Wrote, 'Mene, mene,' and divided quite
  The kingdom of her thought.

Deep dread and loathing of her solitude
 Fell on her, from which mood was born 230
Scorn of herself; again, from out that mood
  Laughter at her self-scorn.

'What! is not this my place of strength,' she said,
 'My spacious mansion built for me,
Whereof the strong foundation-stones were laid 235
  Since my first memory?'

---

  219. Acts, xii, 21 f.
  226. Daniel, v, 25.

But in dark corners of her palace stood
   Uncertain shapes; and unawares
On white-eyed phantasms weeping tears of blood,
    And horrible nightmares,   240

And hollow shades, enclosing hearts of flame,
   And, with dim fretted foreheads all,
On corpses three-months-old at noon she came,
    That stood against the wall.

A spot of dull stagnation, without light   245
   Or power of movement, seem'd my soul,
'Mid onward-sloping motions infinite
    Making for one sure goal.

A still salt pool, lock'd in with bars of sand,
   Left on the shore; that hears all night   250
The plunging seas draw backward from the land
    Their moon-led waters white.

A star that with the choral starry dance
   Join'd not, but stood, and standing saw
The hollow orb of moving Circumstance   255
    Roll'd round by one fix'd law.

Back on herself her serpent pride had curl'd.
   'No voice,' she shriek'd in that lone hall,
'No voice breaks thro' the stillness of this world:
    One deep, deep silence all!'   260

---

241. In *Vathek* William Beckford tells of the "vast multitude" of the
damned in the Hall of Eblis whose hearts are enveloped in flames. Compare also Byron, *The Giaour,* ll. 750 f.

242. *fretted,* worm-eaten. In a very early poem, "Supposed Confessions of a Second-rate Sensitive Mind," Tennyson had already meditated
somewhat morbidly upon

             the busy fret
    Of that sharp-headed worm . . .
    In the gross blackness underneath.

255. *Circumstance,* "the surrounding sphere of the heavens" (Palgrave).

She, mouldering with the dull earth's mouldering sod,
   Inwrapt tenfold in slothful shame,
Lay there exiled from eternal God,
    Lost to her place and name;

And death and life she hated equally,   265
   And nothing saw, for her despair,
But dreadful time, dreadful eternity,
    No comfort anywhere;

Remaining utterly confused with fears,
   And ever worse with growing time,   270
And ever unrelieved by dismal tears,
    And all alone in crime:

Shut up as in a crumbling tomb, girt round
   With blackness as a solid wall,
Far off she seem'd to hear the dully sound   275
    Of human footsteps fall.

As in strange lands a traveller walking slow,
   In doubt and great perplexity,
A little before moon-rise hears the low
    Moan of an unknown sea;   280

And knows not if it be thunder, or a sound
   Of rocks thrown down, or one deep cry
Of great wild beasts; then thinketh, 'I have found
    A new land, but I die.'

She howl'd aloud, 'I am on fire within.   285
   There comes no murmur of reply.
What is it that will take away my sin,
    And save me lest I die?'

So when four years were wholly finished,
   She threw her royal robes away.   290
'Make me a cottage in the vale,' she said,
    'Where I may mourn and pray.

'Yet pull not down my palace towers, that are
   So lightly, beautifully built:
Perchance I may return with others there   295
   When I have purged my guilt.'

A DREAM OF FAIR WOMEN[1]

I READ, before my eyelids dropt their shade,
   'The Legend of Good Women,' long ago
Sung by the morning star of song, who made
   His music heard below;

Dan Chaucer, the first warbler, whose sweet breath   5
   Preluded those melodious bursts that fill
The spacious times of great Elizabeth
   With sounds that echo still.

---

[1] Published in *Poems,* 1832; much altered in 1842; and retouched in
later editions. See the *variae lectiones* recorded in *Works,* Cambridge edition, pp. 805 f. The original version begins with the following stanzas:

> As when a man that sails in a balloon,
>   Down-looking, sees the solid shining ground
> Stream from beneath him in the broad blue noon,
>   Tilth, hamlet, mead and mound:
>
> And takes his flags and waves them to the mob,
>   That shout below, all faces turn'd to where
> Glows ruby-like the far-up crimson globe,
>   Fill'd with a finer air;
>
> So, lifted high, the poet at his will
>   Lets the great world flit from him, seeing all,
> Higher thro' secret splendours mounting still,
>   Self-poised, nor fears to fall,
>
> Hearing apart the echoes of his fame.
>   While I spoke thus, the seedsman, memory,
> Sow'd my deep-furrow'd thought with many a name,
>   Whose glory will not die.

To liken a poet to an aeronaut may have seemed less quaint in days when
balloon-ascensions were still a sensational novelty; but Tennyson was wise
to suppress the stanzas.

2. Of the women in Chaucer's *Legend* only Cleopatra reappears in Tennyson's *Dream*.

5. *Dan,* from Latin *dominus,* a title of honour. Compare Spenser, *The
Faerie Queene,* IV, ii, 32: "Dan Chaucer, well of English undefiled."

And, for a while, the knowledge of his art
   Held me above the subject, as strong gales   10
Hold swollen clouds from raining, tho' my heart,
   Brimful of those wild tales,

Charged both mine eyes with tears. In every land
   I saw, wherever light illumineth,
Beauty and anguish walking hand in hand   15
   The downward slope to death.

Those far-renowned brides of ancient song
   Peopled the hollow dark, like burning stars,
And I heard sounds of insult, shame, and wrong,
   And trumpets blown for wars;   20

And clattering flints batter'd with clanging hoofs;
   And I saw crowds in column'd sanctuaries;
And forms that pass'd at windows and on roofs
   Of marble palaces;

Corpses across the threshold; heroes tall   25
   Dislodging pinnacle and parapet
Upon the tortoise creeping to the wall;
   Lances in ambush set;

And high shrine-doors burst thro' with heated blasts
   That run before the fluttering tongues of fire;   30
White surf wind-scatter'd over sails and masts,
   And ever climbing higher;

Squadrons and squares of men in brazen plates,
   Scaffolds, still sheets of water, divers woes,
Ranges of glimmering vaults with iron grates,   35
   And hush'd seraglios.

So shape chased shape as swift as, when to land
   Bluster the winds and tides the self-same way,
Crisp foam-flakes scud along the level sand,
   Torn from the fringe of spray.   40

---

   27. *tortoise*, testudo, a Roman siege device.

I started once, or seem'd to start in pain,
  Resolved on noble things, and strove to speak,
As when a great thought strikes along the brain,
  And flushes all the cheek.

And once my arm was lifted to hew down   45
  A cavalier from off his saddle-bow,
That bore a lady from a leaguer'd town;
  And then, I know not how,

All those sharp fancies, by down-lapsing thought
  Stream'd onward, lost their edges, and did creep   50
Roll'd on each other, rounded, smooth'd, and brought
  Into the gulfs of sleep.

At last methought that I had wander'd far
  In an old wood: fresh-wash'd in coolest dew
The maiden splendours of the morning star   55
  Shook in the stedfast blue.

Enormous elm-tree-boles did stoop and lean
  Upon the dusky brushwood underneath
Their broad curved branches, fledged with clearest green,
  New from its silken sheath.   60

The dim red morn had died, her journey done,
  And with dead lips smiled at the twilight plain,
Half-fall'n across the threshold of the sun,
  Never to rise again.

There was no motion in the dumb dead air,   65
  Not any song of bird or sound of rill;
Gross darkness of the inner sepulchre
  Is not so deadly still

As that wide forest. Growths of jasmine turn'd
  Their humid arms festooning tree to tree,   70
And at the root thro' lush green grasses burn'd
  The red anemone.

I knew the flowers, I knew the leaves, I knew
  The tearful glimmer of the languid dawn
On those long, rank, dark wood-walks drench'd in dew,   75
  Leading from lawn to lawn.

The smell of violets, hidden in the green,
  Pour'd back into my empty soul and frame
The times when I remember to have been
  Joyful and free from blame.   80

And from within me a clear under-tone
  Thrill'd thro' mine ears in that unblissful clime,
'Pass freely thro': the wood is all thine own,
  Until the end of time.'

At length I saw a lady within call,   85
  Stiller than chisell'd marble, standing there;
A daughter of the gods, divinely tall,
  And most divinely fair.

Her loveliness with shame and with surprise
  Froze my swift speech: she turning on my face   90
The star-like sorrows of immortal eyes,
  Spoke slowly in her place.

'I had great beauty: ask thou not my name:
  No one can be more wise than destiny.
Many drew swords and died. Where'er I came   95
  I brought calamity.'

'No marvel, sovereign lady: in fair field
  Myself for such a face had boldly died,'
I answer'd free; and turning I appeal'd
  To one that stood beside.   100

But she, with sick and scornful looks averse,
  To her full height her stately stature draws;
'My youth,' she said, 'was blasted with a curse:
  This woman was the cause.

---

  85. Helen of Troy.
  100. Iphigenia, daughter of Agamemnon.

'I was cut off from hope in that sad place,   105
  Which men call'd Aulis in those iron years:
My father held his hand upon his face;
  I, blinded with my tears,

'Still strove to speak: my voice was thick with sighs
  As in a dream. Dimly I could descry   110
The stern black-bearded kings with wolfish eyes,
  Waiting to see me die.

'The high masts flicker'd as they lay afloat;
  The crowds, the temples, waver'd, and the shore;
The bright death quiver'd at the victim's throat;   115
  Touch'd; and I knew no more.'

Whereto the other with a downward brow:
  'I would the white cold heavy-plunging foam,
Whirl'd by the wind, had roll'd me deep below,
  Then when I left my home.'   120

Her slow full words sank thro' the silence drear,
  As thunder-drops fall on a sleeping sea:
Sudden I heard a voice that cried, 'Come here,
  That I may look on thee.'

I turning saw, throned on a flowery rise,   125
  One sitting on a crimson scarf unroll'd;
A queen, with swarthy cheeks and bold black eyes,
  Brow-bound with burning gold.

115–6. In the original version these lines read:
> One drew a sharp knife thro' my tender throat
> Slowly, — and nothing more.

Tennyson said that he altered the lines because he thought them "too ghastly realistic"; but Croker's ridicule in *The Quarterly Review*, April, 1833 ("What touching simplicity — what pathetic resignation — he cut my throat — *'nothing more!'* One might indeed ask, 'what more she would have?'") probably provided the original impulse to emend.

127. Cleopatra. Her cheeks are swarthy because, as in Shakespeare's *Antony and Cleopatra*, I, v, 28, she is "with Phoebus' amorous pinches black"; but the reference in l. 158 to "the polished argent of her breast" shows that Tennyson did not, as Thomas Love Peacock thought (see

She, flashing forth a haughty smile, began:
  'I govern'd men by change, and so I sway'd   130
All moods. 'Tis long since I have seen a man.
  Once, like the moon, I made

'The ever-shifting currents of the blood
  According to my humour ebb and flow.
I have no men to govern in this wood: 135
  That makes my only woe.

'Nay — yet it chafes me that I could not bend
  One will; nor tame and tutor with mine eye
That dull cold-blooded Cæsar. Prythee, friend,
  Where is Mark Antony?   140

'The man, my lover, with whom I rode sublime
  On Fortune's neck: we sat as God by God:
The Nilus would have risen before his time
  And flooded at our nod.

'We drank the Libyan Sun to sleep, and lit   145
  Lamps which out-burn'd Canopus. O my life
In Egypt! O the dalliance and the wit,
  The flattery and the strife,

'And the wild kiss, when fresh from war's alarms,
  My Hercules, my Roman Antony,   150
My mailed Bacchus leapt into my arms,
  Contented there to die!

'And there he died: and when I heard my name
  Sigh'd forth with life I would not brook my fear
Of the other: with a worm I balk'd his fame.   155
  What else was left? look here!'

Gryll Grange, chapter xxiii), forget that she was a Greek. Peacock was,
however, reasonable in his censure of Millais's illustration of the scene in
the Moxon *Tennyson* of 1857 where her portrait is of "a hideous grinning
Ethiop."
    139. Octavius.

(With that she tore her robe apart, and half
  The polish'd argent of her breast to sight
Laid bare. Thereto she pointed with a laugh,
  Showing the aspick's bite.)   160

'I died a Queen. The Roman soldier found
  Me lying dead, my crown about my brows,
A name for ever! — lying robed and crown'd,
  Worthy a Roman spouse.'

Her warbling voice, a lyre of widest range   165
  Struck by all passion, did fall down and glance
From tone to tone, and glided thro' all change
  Of liveliest utterance.

When she made pause I knew not for delight;
  Because with sudden motion from the ground   170
She raised her piercing orbs, and fill'd with light
  The interval of sound.

Still with their fires Love tipt his keenest darts;
  As once they drew into two burning rings
All beams of Love, melting the mighty hearts   175
  Of captains and of kings.

Slowly my sense undazzled. Then I heard
  A noise of some one coming thro' the lawn,
And singing clearer than the crested bird
  That claps his wings at dawn.   180

'The torrent brooks of hallow'd Israel
  From craggy hollows pouring, late and soon,
Sound all night long, in falling thro' the dell,
  Far-heard beneath the moon.

---

179. The commentators have disputed as to whether the "crested bird"
is the cock or the lark. The former interpretation seems the more natural; but Theocritus (*Idyls,* vii, 23) refers to the crested lark. Professor
Mustard, however, does not include this passage among Tennyson's
"echoes" of Theocritus.

'The balmy moon of blessed Israel   185
    Floods all the deep-blue gloom with beams divine:
All night the splinter'd crags that wall the dell
    With spires of silver shine.'

As one that museth where broad sunshine laves
    The lawn by some cathedral, thro' the door   190
Hearing the holy organ rolling waves
    Of sound on roof and floor

Within, and anthem sung, is charm'd and tied
    To where he stands,— so stood I, when that flow
Of music left the lips of her that died   195
    To save her father's vow;

The daughter of the warrier Gileadite,
    A maiden pure; as when she went along
From Mizpeh's tower'd gate with welcome light,
    With timbrel and with song.   200

My words leapt forth: 'Heaven heads the count of crimes
    With that wild oath.' She render'd answer high:
'Not so, nor once alone; a thousand times
    I would be born and die.

'Single I grew, like some green plant, whose root   205
    Creeps to the garden water-pipes beneath,
Feeding the flower; but ere my flower to fruit
    Changed, I was ripe for death.

'My God, my land, my father — these did move
    Me from my bliss of life, that Nature gave,   210
Lower'd softly with a threefold cord of love
    Down to a silent grave.

'And I went mourning, "No fair Hebrew boy
    Shall smile away my maiden blame among
The Hebrew mothers" — emptied of all joy,   215
    Leaving the dance and song,

195-6. The daughter of Jephtha; see Judges, xi, 26 f.

'Leaving the olive-gardens far below,
   Leaving the promise of my bridal bower,
The valleys of grape-loaded vines that glow
   Beneath the battled tower.   220

'The light white cloud swam over us. Anon
   We heard the lion roaring from his den;
We saw the large white stars rise one by one,
   Or, from the darken'd glen,

'Saw God divide the night with flying flame,   225
   And thunder on the everlasting hills.
I heard Him, for He spake, and grief became
   A solemn scorn of ills.

'When the next moon was roll'd into the sky,
   Strength came to me that equall'd my desire.   230
How beautiful a thing it was to die
   For God and for my sire!

'It comforts me in this one thought to dwell,
   That I subdued me to my father's will;
Because the kiss he gave me, ere I fell,   235
   Sweetens the spirit still.

'Moreover it is written that my race
   Hew'd Ammon, hip and thigh, from Aroer
On Arnon unto Minneth.' Here her face
   Glow'd, as I look'd at her.   240

She lock'd her lips: she left me where I stood:
   'Glory to God,' she sang, and past afar,
Thridding the sombre boskage of the wood,
   Toward the morning-star.

Losing her carol I stood pensively,   245
   As one that from a casement leans his head,
When midnight bells cease ringing suddenly,
   And the old year is dead.

'Alas! alas!' a low voice, full of care,
   Murmur'd beside me: 'Turn and look on me: 250
I am that Rosamond, whom men call fair,
   If what I was I be.

'Would I had been some maiden coarse and poor!
   O me, that I should ever see the light!
Those dragon eyes of anger'd Eleanor   255
   Do hunt me, day and night.'

She ceased in tears, fallen from hope and trust:
   To whom the Egyptian: 'Oh, you tamely died!
You should have clung to Fulvia's waist, and thrust
   The dagger thro' her side.'   260

With that sharp sound the white dawn's creeping beams,
   Stol'n to my brain, dissolved the mystery
Of folded sleep. The captain of my dreams
   Ruled in the eastern sky.

Morn broaden'd on the borders of the dark,   265
   Ere I saw her, who clasp'd in her last trance
Her murder'd father's head, or Joan of Arc,
   A light of ancient France;

Or her who knew that Love can vanquish Death,
   Who kneeling, with one arm about her king,   270

---

251. *Rosamond,* the mistress of Henry II. See Tennyson's *Becket* and Swinburne's *Rosamond.*

259. Cleopatra likens Queen Eleanor, Henry II's wife, to Fulvia, the wife of Antony.

263. Tennyson calls Venus, the morning star, the captain of his dreams because his dream was of fair women and appropriately inspired by the goddess of love and beauty.

266. Margaret Roper, the daughter of Sir Thomas More. Legend (but not history) has it that a month after More's execution in 1535 his daughter obtained permission to remove his head from where it was displayed on London Bridge, that she preserved it in spices, and that after her death it was buried with her.

269. Queen Eleanor, the wife of Edward I. The story, of dubious authenticity, is that when Edward was stabbed at the siege of Acre in 1272 the Queen, fearing lest the dagger had been poisoned, sucked the blood from the wound. See Sir Walter Scott, *The Talisman,* chapter xxi.

Drew forth the poison with her balmy breath,
  Sweet as new buds in Spring.

No memory labours longer from the deep
  Gold-mines of thought to lift the hidden ore
That glimpses, moving up, than I from sleep   275
  To gather and tell o'er

Each little sound and sight. With what dull pain
  Compass'd, how eagerly I sought to strike
Into that wondrous track of dreams again!
  But no two dreams are like.   280

As when a soul laments, which hath been blest,
  Desiring what is mingled with past years,
In yearnings that can never be exprest
  By sighs or groans or tears;

Because all words, tho' cull'd with choicest art,   285
  Failing to give the bitter of the sweet,
Wither beneath the palate, and the heart
  Faints, faded by its heat.

  285–8. The imagery of this final stanza is not clear. By what heat is
the heart faded? What connection is there between the words which fail
"to give the bitter of the sweet" and the heart's fainting?

POEMS ON CLASSICAL SUBJECTS

ŒNONE[1]

THERE lies a vale in Ida, lovelier
Than all the valleys of Ionian hills.
The swimming vapour slopes athwart the glen,
Puts forth an arm, and creeps from pine to pine,
And loiters, slowly drawn. On either hand   5
The lawns and meadow-ledges midway down
Hang rich in flowers, and far below them roars
The long brook falling thro' the clov'n ravine
In cataract after cataract to the sea.
Behind the valley topmost Gargarus   10
Stands up and takes the morning: but in front
The gorges, opening wide apart, reveal
Troas and Ilion's column'd citadel,
The crown of Troas.
              Hither came at noon
Mournful Œnone, wandering forlorn   15
Of Paris, once her playmate on the hills.
Her cheeks had lost the rose, and round her neck

---

[1] Published in *Poems*, 1832; much revised and in large part rewritten
before reprinting in 1842. For details of the alterations see *Works*, Cambridge edition, pp. 800 f. The story is taken from various classical sources
(Euripides, Ovid, Lucian, Apuleius) with a hint, perhaps, from William
Beattie's poem *The Judgment of Paris* and suggestions from familiar paintings of the subject. The Theocritan influence is strong; see Mustard, *op.
cit.*, pp. 35 f. The landscape is not that of the Troad but of the valley of
Cauteretz in the Pyrenees where, during a visit in 1830, much of the poem
was written.

10. *Gargarus,* Gargara or Gargaron, the highest peak of Mount Ida in
the Troad.

Floated her hair or seem'd to float in rest.
She, leaning on a fragment twined with vine,
Sang to the stillness, till the mountain-shade   20
Sloped downward to her seat from the upper cliff.

'O mother Ida, many-fountain'd Ida,
Dear mother Ida, harken ere I die.
For now the noonday quiet holds the hill:
The grasshopper is silent in the grass: 25
The lizard, with his shadow on the stone,
Rests like a shadow, and the winds are dead.
The purple flower droops: the golden bee
Is lily-cradled: I alone awake.
My eyes are full of tears, my heart of love,   30
My heart is breaking, and my eyes are dim,
And I am all aweary of my life.

'O mother Ida, many-fountain'd Ida,
Dear mother Ida, harken ere I die.
Hear me, O Earth, hear me, O Hills, O Caves   35
That house the cold crown'd snake! O mountain brooks,
I am the daughter of a River-God,
Hear me, for I will speak, and build up all
My sorrow with my song, as yonder walls
Rose slowly to a music slowly breathed,   40
A cloud that gather'd shape: for it may be
That, while I speak of it, a little while
My heart may wander from its deeper woe.

'O mother Ida, many-fountain'd Ida,
Dear mother Ida, harken ere I die.   45
I waited underneath the dawning hills,
Aloft the mountain lawn was dewy-dark,
And dewy-dark aloft the mountain pine:
Beautiful Paris, evil-hearted Paris,
Leading a jet-black goat white-horn'd, white-hooved,   50
Came up from reedy Simois all alone.

22–3. The refrain, which is Theocritan in effect, was singled out for
ridicule by Croker in his review of the *Poems* of 1832.

37. This detail is from Ovid, *Heroides,* v, 10.

39–40. Compare "Tithonus," ll. 62–3.

'O mother Ida, harken ere I die.
Far-off the torrent call'd me from the cleft:
Far up the solitary morning smote
The streaks of virgin snow. With down-dropt eyes   55
I sat alone: white-breasted like a star
Fronting the dawn he moved; a leopard skin
Droop'd from his shoulder, but his sunny hair
Cluster'd about his temples like a God's:
And his cheek brighten'd as the foam-bow brightens   60
When the wind blows the foam, and all my heart
Went forth to embrace him coming ere he came.

'Dear mother Ida, harken ere I die.
He smiled, and opening out his milk-white palm
Disclosed a fruit of pure Hesperian gold,   65
That smelt ambrosially, and while I look'd
And listen'd, the full-flowing river of speech
Came down upon my heart.
                              ' "My own Œnone,
Beautiful-brow'd Œnone, my own soul,
Behold this fruit, whose gleaming rind ingrav'n   70
'For the most fair,' would seem to award it thine,
As lovelier than whatever Oread haunt
The knolls of Ida, loveliest in all grace
Of movement, and the charm of married brows."

'Dear mother Ida, harken ere I die.   75
He prest the blossom of his lips to mine,
And added "This was cast upon the board,
When all the full-faced presence of the Gods
Ranged in the halls of Peleus; whereupon
Rose feud, with question unto whom 'twere due: 80
But light-foot Iris brought it yester-eve,
Delivering that to me, by common voice
Elected umpire, Herè comes to-day,
Pallas and Aphroditè, claiming each
This meed of fairest. Thou, within the cave   85
Behind yon whispering tuft of oldest pine,
Mayst well behold them unbeheld, unheard
Hear all, and see thy Paris judge of Gods."

---

79. *Peleus*, king of Thessaly, father of Achilles.

'Dear mother Ida, harken ere I die.
It was the deep midnoon: one silvery cloud   90
Had lost his way between the piney sides
Of this long glen.   Then to the bower they came,
Naked they came to that smooth-swarded bower,
And at their feet the crocus brake like fire,
Violet, armaracus and asphodel,   95
Lotos and lilies: and a wind arose,
And overhead the wandering ivy and vine,
This way and that, in many a wild festoon
Ran riot, garlanding the gnarled boughs
With bunch and berry and flower thro' and thro'   100

'O mother Ida, harken ere I die.
On the tree-tops a crested peacock lit,
And o'er him flow'd a golden cloud, and lean'd
Upon him, slowly dropping fragrant dew.
Then first I heard the voice of her, to whom   105
Coming thro' Heaven, like a light that grows
Larger and clearer, with one mind the Gods
Rise up for reverence.   She to Paris made
Proffer of royal power, ample rule
Unquestion'd, overflowing revenue   110
Wherewith to embellish state, "from many a vale
And river-sunder'd champaign clothed with corn,
Or labour'd mine undrainable of ore.
Honour," she said, "and homage, tax and toll,
From many an inland town and haven large,   115
Mast-throng'd beneath her shadowing citadel
In glassy bays among her tallest towers."

'O mother Ida, harken ere I die.
Still she spake on and still she spake of power,
"Which in all action is the end of all;   120
Power fitted to the season; wisdom-bred

---

95. *amaracus*, an aromatic plant, the dittany of Crete (Van Dyke).

102. *peacock*, the bird sacred to Herè.

108–31. With Herè's offer to Paris compare *Paradise Regained*, iii,
255 f.

And throned of wisdom — from all neighbour crowns
Alliance and allegiance, till thy hand
Fail from the sceptre-staff. Such boon from me,
From me, Heaven's Queen, Paris, to thee king-born,   125
A shepherd all thy life but yet king-born,
Should come most welcome, seeing men, in power
Only, are likest gods, who have attain'd
Rest in a happy place and quiet seats
Above the thunder, with undying bliss   130
In knowledge of their own supremacy."

   'Dear mother Ida, harken ere I die.
She ceased, and Paris held the costly fruit
Out at arm's length, so much the thought of power
Flatter'd his spirit; but Pallas where she stood   135
Somewhat apart, her clear and bared limbs
O'erthwarted with the brazen-headed spear
Upon her pearly shoulder leaning cold,
The while, above, her full and earnest eye
Over her snow-cold breast and angry cheek   140
Kept watch, waiting decision, made reply.

   ' "Self-reverence, self-knowledge, self-control
These three alone lead life to sovereign power.
Yet not for power (power of herself
   Would come uncall'd for) but to live by law,   145
Acting the law we live by without fear;
And because right is right, to follow right
Were wisdom in the scorn of consequence."

   128–31. Compare "The Lotos-Eaters," ll. 111 f.

   142–64. The speech of Pallas is much altered from the version of 1832
where it stood thus:

> Selfreverence, selfknowledge, selfcontrol
> Are the three hinges of the gates of Life,
> That open into power, everyway
> Without horizon, bound or shadow or cloud.
> Yet not for power (power of herself
> Will come uncalled-for) but to live by law,
> Acting the law we live by without fear,
> And because right is right to follow right
> Were wisdom, in the scorn of consequence
> (Dear mother Ida, hearken ere I die.)

'Dear mother Ida, harken ere I die.
Again she said: "I woo thee not with gifts.   150
Sequel of guerdon could not alter me
To fairer. Judge thou me by what I am,
So shalt thou find me fairest.
                      Yet, indeed
If gazing on divinity disrobed
Thy mortal eyes are frail to judge of fair,   155
Unbias'd by self-profit, oh! rest thee sure,
That I shall love thee well and cleave to thee,
So that my vigour, wedded to thy blood,
Shall strike within thy pulses like a God's,
To push thee forward thro' a life of shocks,   160
Dangers, and deeds, until endurance grow
Sinew'd with action, and the full-grown will,
Circled thro' all experiences, pure law,
Commeasure perfect freedom."
                 'Here she ceas'd,
And Paris ponder'd, and I cried, "O Paris,   165
Give it to Pallas!" but he heard me not,
Or hearing would not hear me, woe is me!

'O mother Ida, many-fountain'd Ida,
Dear mother Ida, harken ere I die.

    Not as men value gold because it tricks
    And blazons outward Life with ornament,
    But rather as the miser, for itself.
    Good for selfgood doth half destroy selfgood.
    The means and end, like two coiled snakes, infect
    Each other, bound in one with hateful love.
    So both into the fountain and the stream
    A drop of poison falls. Come hearken to me,
    And look upon me and consider me,
    So shalt thou find me fairest, so endurance,
    Like to an athlete's arm, shall still become
    Sinew'd with motion, till thine active will
    (As the dark body of the Sun robed round
    With his own ever-emanating lights)
    Be flooded o'er with her own effluences,
    And thereby grow to freedom.

  148. *wisdom*. The usual classical tradition was that Pallas offered victory in war; the offer of wisdom occurs in late forms of the story. See Douglas Bush, *Mythology and the Renaissance Tradition in English Poetry*, p. 17.

Idalian Aphroditè beautiful,   170
Fresh as the foam, new-bathed in Paphian wells,
With rosy slender fingers backward drew
From her warm brows and bosom her deep hair
Ambrosial, golden round her lucid throat
And shoulder: from the violets her light foot   175
Shone rosy-white, and o'er her rounded form
Between the shadows of the vine-bunches
Floated the glowing sunlights, as she moved.

   'Dear mother Ida, harken ere I die.
She with a subtle smile in her mild eyes,   180
The herald of her triumph, drawing nigh
Half-whisper'd in his ear, "I promise thee
The fairest and most loving wife in Greece."
She spoke and laugh'd: I shut my sight for fear:
But when I look'd, Paris had raised his arm,   185
And I beheld great Herè's angry eyes,
As she withdrew into the golden cloud,
And I was left alone within the bower;
And from that time to this I am alone,
And I shall be alone until I die.   190

   'Yet, mother Ida, harken ere I die.
Fairest — why fairest wife? am I not fair?
My love hath told me so a thousand times.
Methinks I must be fair, for yesterday,
When I past by, a wild and wanton pard,   195
Eyed like the evening star, with playful tail
Crouch'd fawning in the weed. Most loving is she?
Ah me, my mountain shepherd, that my arms
Were wound about thee, and my hot lips prest
Close, close to thine in that quick-falling dew   200
Of fruitful kisses, thick as Autumn rains
Flash in the pools of whirling Simois.

   'O mother, hear me yet before I die.
They came, they cut away my tallest pines,

171. *Paphian.* Paphos in Cyprus was the centre of the cult of Aphrodite.

My tall dark pines, that plumed the craggy ledge 205
High over the blue gorge, and all between
The snowy peak and snow-white cataract
Foster'd the callow eaglet — from beneath
Whose thick mysterious boughs in the dark morn
The panther's roar came muffled, while I sat 210
Low in the valley. Never, never more
Shall lone Œnone see the morning mist
Sweep thro' them; never see them overlaid
With narrow moon-lit slips of silver cloud,
Between the loud stream and the trembling stars. 215

'O mother, hear me yet before I die.
I wish that somewhere in the ruin'd folds,
Among the fragments tumbled from the glens,
Or the dry thickets, I could meet with her
The Abominable, that uninvited came 220
Into the fair Peleïan banquet-hall,
And cast the golden fruit upon the board,
And bred this change; that I might speak my mind,
And tell her to her face how much I hate
Her presence, hated both of Gods and men. 225

'O mother, hear me yet before I die.
Hath he not sworn his love a thousand times,
In this green valley, under this green hill,
Ev'n on this hand, and sitting on this stone?
Seal'd it with kisses? water'd it with tears? 230
O happy tears, and how unlike to these!
O happy Heaven, how canst thou see my face?
O happy earth, how canst thou bear my weight?
O death, death, death, thou ever-floating cloud,
There are enough unhappy on this earth; 235
Pass by the happy souls, that love to live:
I pray thee, pass before my light of life,
And shadow all my soul, that I may die.
Thou weighest heavy on the heart within,
Weigh heavy on my eyelids: let me die. 240

---

220. *The Abominable*, Eris, the goddess of Discord.

'O mother, hear me yet before I die.
I will not die alone, for fiery thoughts
Do shape themselves within me, more and more,
Whereof I catch the issue, as I hear
Dead sounds at night come from the inmost hills,   245
Like footsteps upon wool. I dimly see
My far-off doubtful purpose, as a mother
Conjectures of the features of her child
Ere it is born: her child! — a shudder comes
Across me: never child be born of me,   250
Unblest, to vex me with his father's eyes!

'O mother, hear me yet before I die.
Hear me, O earth. I will not die alone,
Lest their shrill happy laughter come to me
Walking the cold and starless road of Death   255
Uncomforted, leaving my ancient love
With the Greek woman. I will rise and go
Down into Troy, and ere the stars come forth
Talk with the wild Cassandra, for she says
A fire dances before her, and a sound   260
Rings ever in her eyes of armed men.
What this may be I know not, but I know
That, wheresoe'er I am by night and day,
All earth and air seem only burning fire.'

THE DEATH OF ŒNONE[1]

ŒNONE sat within the cave from out
Whose ivy-matted mouth she used to gaze
Down at the Troad; but the goodly view
Was now one blank, and all the serpent vines
Which on the touch of heavenly feet had risen,   5
And gliding thro' the branches over-bower'd
The naked Three, were wither'd long ago,
And thro' the sunless winter morning-mist
In silence wept upon the flowerless earth.
    And while she stared at those dead cords that ran   10

---

[1] We disregard chronology, to place next to "Œnone" the sequel, a
poem of Tennyson's old age. It was composed later than August 8, 1889,

Dark thro' the mist, and linking tree to tree,
But once were gayer than a dawning sky
With many a pendent bell and fragrant star,
Her Past became her Present, and she saw
Him, climbing toward her with the golden fruit,   15
Him, happy to be chosen Judge of Gods,
Her husband in the flush of youth and dawn,
Paris, himself as beauteous as a God.
   Anon from out the long ravine below,
She heard a wailing cry, that seem'd at first   20
Thin as the batlike shrillings of the Dead
When driven to Hades, but, in coming near,
Across the downward thunder of the brook
Sounded 'Œnone'; and on a sudden he,
Paris, no longer beauteous as a God,   25
Struck by a poison'd arrow in the fight,
Lame, crooked, reeling, livid, thro' the mist
Rose, like the wraith of his dead self, and moan'd
   'Œnone, *my* Œnone, while we dwelt
Together in this valley — happy then —   30

when Sir Richard Jebb supplied Tennyson with information as to the
source of the myth, and was first published in the posthumous volume,
The Death of Œnone, Akbar's Dream, and Other Poems, 1892. (It is reprinted here from Tennyson's *Poetical Works*, Globe Edition, by permission of The Macmillan Company.) In a dedication to the Master of Bal-
liol (Professor Jowett) Tennyson described it as

a Grecian tale re-told,
Which, cast in later Grecian mould,
Quintus Calaber
Somewhat lazily handled of old.

Quintus Smyrnaeus (that is, of Smyrna), called by scholars of the Renaissance Quintus Calaber merely because the manuscript by which his epic
became known to the modern world was discovered in Calabria, wrote
in the fifth century A.D. a sequel to the *Iliad*, carrying the story down to
the capture of Troy (*The Fall of Troy;* English version in the Loeb
Classical Library). In his tenth book occurs the episode of Œnone.
Paris, wounded by the poisoned arrow of Philoctetes, comes to Œnone to
plead for forgiveness. She spurns him, and he departs to die in the wilds
of Ida. She hears of his death; comes to his funeral pyre; and throws
herself into the flames. For details of Tennyson's indebtedness to Quintus
see Mustard, *op. cit.*, pp. 45 f.

   21. So the ghosts of the suitors slain by Odysseus gibber like bats as
Hermes leads them down to Hades (*Odyssey,* xxiv). Compare "The
Lotos-Eaters," l. 34, and "The Voyage of Maeldune," l. 83.

Too happy had I died within thine arms,
Before the feud of Gods had marr'd our peace,
And sunder'd each from each. I am dying now
Pierced by a poison'd dart. Save me. Thou knowest,
Taught by some God, whatever herb or balm   35
May clear the blood from poison, and thy fame
Is blown thro' all the Troad, and to thee
The shepherd brings his adder-bitten lamb,
The wounded warrior climbs from Troy to thee.
My life and death are in thy hand. The Gods   40
Avenge on stony hearts a fruitless prayer
For pity. Let me owe my life to thee.
I wrought thee bitter wrong, but thou forgive,
Forget it. Man is but the slave of Fate.
Œnone, by thy love which once was mine,   45
Help, heal me. I am poison'd to the heart.'
'And I to mine' she said 'Adulterer,
Go back to thine adulteress and die!'

   He groan'd, he turn'd, and in the mist at once
Became a shadow, sank and disappear'd,   50
But, ere the mountain rolls into the plain,
Fell headlong dead; and of the shepherds one
Their oldest, and the same who first had found
Paris, a naked babe, among the woods
Of Ida, following lighted on him there,   55
And shouted, and the shepherds heard and came.

   One raised the Prince, one sleek'd the squalid hair,
One kiss'd his hand, another closed his eyes,
And then, remembering the gay playmate rear'd
Among them, and forgetful of the man,   60
Whose crime had half unpeopled Ilion, these
All that day long labour'd, hewing the pines,
And built their shepherd-prince a funeral pile;
And, while the star of eve was drawing light
From the dead sun, kindled the pyre, and all   65
Stood round it, hush'd, or calling on his name.

   But when the white fog vanish'd like a ghost
Before the day, and every topmost pine
Spired into bluest heaven, still in her cave,
Amazed, and ever seeming stared upon   70

By ghastlier than the Gorgon head, a face, —
His face deform'd by lurid blotch and blain —
There, like a creature frozen to the heart
Beyond all hope of warmth, Œnone sat
Not moving, till in front of that ravine   75
Which drowsed in gloom, self-darken'd from the west,
The sunset blazed along the wall of Troy.

    Then her head sank, she slept, and thro' her dream
A ghostly murmur floated, 'Come to me,
Œnone! I can wrong thee now no more,   80
Œnone, my Œnone,' and the dream
Wail'd in her, when she woke beneath the stars.

    What star could burn so low? not Ilion yet.
What light was there? She rose and slowly down,
By the long torrent's ever-deepen'd roar,   85
Paced, following, as in trance, the silent cry.
She waked a bird of prey that scream'd and past;
She roused a snake that hissing writhed away;
A panther sprang across her path, she heard
The shriek of some lost life among the pines,   90
But when she gain'd the broader vale, and saw
The ring of faces redden'd by the flames
Enfolding that dark body which had lain
Of old in her embrace, paused — and then ask'd
Falteringly, 'Who lies on yonder pyre?'   95
But every man was mute for reverence.
Then moving quickly forward till the heat
Smote on her brow, she lifted up a voice
Of shrill command, "Who burns upon the pyre?'
Whereon their oldest and their boldest said,   100
'He, whom thou wouldst not heal!' and all at once
The morning light of happy marriage broke
Thro' all the clouded years of widowhood,
And muffling up her comely head, and crying
'Husband!' she leapt upon the funeral pile,   105
And mixt herself with *him* and past in fire.

---

    78 f. The episode of the dream is not in the narrative of Quintus
Smyrnaeus.

THE LOTOS–EATERS[1]

'COURAGE!' he said, and pointed toward the land,
'This mounting wave will roll us shoreward soon.'
In the afternoon they came unto a land
In which it seemed always afternoon.
All round the coast the languid air did swoon,   5
Breathing like one that hath a weary dream.
Full-faced above the valley stood the moon;
And like a downward smoke, the slender stream
Along the cliff to fall and pause and fall did seem.

A land of streams! some, like a downward smoke,   10
Slow-dropping veils of thinnest lawn, did go;
And some thro' wavering lights and shadows broke,
Rolling a slumbrous sheet of foam below.
They saw the gleaming river seaward flow
From the inner land: far off, three mountain-tops,   15
Three silent pinnacles of aged snow,
Stood sunset-flush'd: and, dew'd with showery drops,
Up-clomb the shadowy pine above the woven copse.

The charmed sunset linger'd low adown
In the red West: thro' mountain clefts the dale   20
Was seen far inland, and the yellow down

---

[1] Published in *Poems*, 1832. The sixth section of the "Choric Song"
was added and the eighth rewritten before republication in 1842; and there
were minor alterations. The source of the poem, scarcely more than a
suggestion, is Homer's brief story (*Odyssey*, ix, 83 f.) of the visit of Odysseus and his companions to the land of the lotos-eaters. "The Sea-Fairies,"
published in 1830 (see Appendix I), is a preliminary experiment in the
same field. The Spenserian stanzas of the opening narrative which introduces the "Choric Song" suggest a comparison with Spenser's descriptions
of the House of Morpheus (*The Faerie Queene*, I, i, 39–41) and the Idle
Lake (*ibid.*, II, vi, 11–25), and with the opening of James Thomson's
The Castle of Indolence.

3. *land*. The lack of rhyme is not due to an oversight. Tennyson said
that his first reading was "strand" but that the "no-rhyme" was "lazier."
This effect is reinforced by the repetition of "afternoon" in lines 3 and 4.

8. *downward smoke*. Compare "Come Down, O Maid," l. 22.

11. Tennyson said that the image "veils of thinnest lawn" suggested
itself to him when, during his visit to the Pyrenees in 1830, he saw a
water-fall in the Cirque de Gavarnie descending a thousand feet.

Border'd with palm, and many a winding vale
And meadow, set with slender galingale;
A land where all things always seem'd the same!
And round about the keel with faces pale,   25
Dark faces pale against that rosy flame,
The mild-eyed melancholy Lotos-eaters came.

Branches they bore of that enchanted stem,
Laden with flower and fruit, whereof they gave
To each, but whoso did receive of them,   30
And taste, to him the gushing of the wave
Far far away did seem to mourn and rave
On alien shores; and if his fellow spake,
His voice was thin, as voices from the grave;
And deep-asleep he seem'd, yet all awake,   35
And music in his ears his beating heart did make.

They sat them down upon the yellow sand,
Between the sun and moon upon the shore;
And sweet it was to dream of Fatherland,
Of child, and wife, and slave; but evermore   40
Most weary seem'd the sea, weary the oar,
Weary the wandering fields of barren foam.
Then some one said, 'We will return no more;'
And all at once they sang, 'Our island home
Is far beyond the wave; we will no longer roam.'   45

CHORIC SONG

I

There is sweet music here that softer falls
Than petals from blown roses on the grass,
Or night-dews on still waters between walls
Of shadowy granite, in a gleaming pass;
Music that gentlier on the spirit lies,   5
Than tir'd eyelids upon tir'd eyes;
Music that brings sweet sleep down from the blissful skies.

---

23. *galingale,* a kind of sedge (Palgrave).

Here are cool mosses deep,
And thro' the moss the ivies creep,
And in the stream the long-leaved flowers weep,   10
And from the craggy ledge the poppy hangs in sleep.

II

Why are we weigh'd upon with heaviness,
And utterly consumed with sharp distress,
While all things else have rest from weariness?
All things have rest: why should we toil alone,   15
We only toil, who are the first of things,
And make perpetual moan,
Still from one sorrow to another thrown:
Nor ever fold our wings,
And cease from wanderings,   20
Nor steep our brows in slumber's holy balm;
Nor harken what the inner spirit sings,
'There is no joy but calm!'
Why should we only toil, the roof and crown of things?

III

Lo! in the middle of the wood,   25
The folded leaf is woo'd from out the bud
With winds upon the branch, and there
Grows green and broad, and takes no care,
Sun-steep'd at noon, and in the moon
Nightly dew-fed; and turning yellow   30
Falls, and floats adown the air.
Lo! sweeten'd with the summer light,
The full-juiced apple, waxing over-mellow,
Drops in a silent autumn night.
All its allotted length of days,   35
The flower ripens in its place,
Ripens and fades, and falls, and hath no toil,
Fast-rooted in the fruitful soil.

IV

Hateful is the dark-blue sky,
Vaulted o'er the dark-blue sea.   40
Death is the end of life; ah, why
Should life all labour be?

Let us alone. Time driveth onward fast,
And in a little while our lips are dumb.
Let us alone.   What is it that will last?   45
All things are taken from us, and become
Portions and parcels of the dreadful Past.
Let us alone.   What pleasure can we have
To war with evil?   Is there any peace
In ever climbing up the climbing wave?   50
All things have rest, and ripen toward the grave
In silence; ripen, fall and cease:
Give us long rest or death, dark death, or dreamful ease.

V

How sweet it were, hearing the downward stream,
With half-shut eyes ever to seem   55
Falling asleep in a half-dream!
To dream and dream, like yonder amber light,
Which will not leave the myrrh-bush on the height;
To hear each other's whisper'd speech;
Eating the Lotos day by day,   60
To watch the crisping ripples on the beach,
And tender curving lines of creamy spray;
To lend our hearts and spirits wholly
To the influence of mild-minded melancholy;
To muse and brood and live again in memory,   65
With those old faces of our infancy
Heap'd over with a mound of grass,
Two handfuls of white dust, shut in an urn of brass!

VI

Dear is the memory of our wedded lives,
And dear the last embraces of our wives   70
And their warm tears: but all hath suffer'd change:
For surely now our household hearths are cold:
Our sons inherit us: our looks are strange:
And we should come like ghosts to trouble joy.
Or else the island princes over-bold   75
Have eat our substance, and the minstrel sings
Before them of the ten years' war in Troy,
And our great deeds, as half-forgotten things.
Is there confusion in the little isle?

Let what is broken so remain. 80
The Gods are hard to reconcile:
'Tis hard to settle order once again.
There *is* confusion worse than death,
Trouble on trouble, pain on pain,
Long labour unto aged breath, 85
Sore task to hearts worn out by many wars
And eyes grown dim with gazing on the pilot-stars.

VII

But, propt on beds of amaranth and moly,
How sweet (while warm airs lull us, blowing lowly)
With half-dropt eyelid still, 90
Beneath a heaven dark and holy,
To watch the long bright river drawing slowly
His waters from the purple hill —
To hear the dewy echoes calling
From cave to cave thro' the thick-twined vine — 95
To watch the emerald-colour'd water falling
Thro' many a wov'n acanthus-wreath divine!
Only to hear and see the far-off sparkling brine,
Only to hear were sweet, stretch'd out beneath the pine.

VIII

The Lotos blooms below the barren peak: 100
The Lotos blows by every winding creek:
All day the wind breathes low with mellower tone:
Thro' every hollow cave and alley lone
Round and round the spicy downs the yellow Lotos-dust is
    blown.
We have had enough of action, and of motion we, 105
Roll'd to starboard, roll'd to larboard, when the surge was
    seething free,
Where the wallowing monster spouted his foam-fountains in
    the sea.

---

88. *amaranth* (Greek "unfading"), mentioned by Pliny (*Historia naturalis*, xxi, 23) and by Milton (*Paradise Lost*, iii, 352 f.). *Moly* is the plant "that Hermes once to wise Ulysses gave" (Milton, *Comus*, l. 637); see *Odyssey*, x, 305.

100 f. For the original, far inferior, form of this final section see *Works*, Cambridge edition, pp. 804 f.

Let us swear an oath, and keep it with an equal mind,
In the hollow Lotos-land to live and lie reclined
On the hills like Gods together, careless of mankind.   110
For they lie beside their nectar, and the bolts are hurl'd
Far below them in the valleys, and the clouds are lightly curl'd
Round their golden houses, girdled with the gleaming world:
Where they smile in secret, looking over wasted lands,
Blight and famine, plague and earthquake, roaring deeps and
          fiery sands,   115
Clanging fights, and flaming towns, and sinking ships, and
          praying hands.
But they smile, they find a music centred in a doleful song
Steaming up, a lamentation and an ancient tale of wrong,
Like a tale of little meaning tho' the words are strong;
Chanted from an ill-used race of men that cleave the soil,   120
Sow the seed, and reap the harvest with enduring toil,
Storing yearly little dues of wheat, and wine and oil;
Till they perish and they suffer — some, 'tis whisper'd —down
          in hell
Suffer endless anguish, others in Elysian valleys dwell,
Resting weary limbs at last on beds of asphodel.   125
Surely, surely, slumber is more sweet than toil, the shore
Than labour in the deep mid-ocean, wind and wave and oar;
Oh rest ye, brother mariners, we will not wander more.

ULYSSES [1]

IT LITTLE profits that an idle king,
By this still hearth, among these barren crags,
Match'd with an aged wife, I mete and dole
Unequal laws into a savage race,
That hoard, and sleep, and feed, and know not me.   5

---

111 f. The conception of the life of the gods is Lucretian.

[1] Written soon after the death of Arthur Hallam (September 15, 1833);
published in *Poems,* 1842. Tennyson said that it expressed his feelings
"about the need of going forward and braving the struggle of life"
(*Memoir,* i, 196); and he told Sir James Knowles that "it was more written with the feeling of [Hallam's] loss upon me than many poems in *In
Memoriam*" (Knowles, "Aspects of Tennyson," *The Nineteenth Century,*
xxxiii, 182). In Homer the ghost of Tiresias prophesies to Odysseus that
after his return to Ithaca and the slaying of the suitors he will set out again

I cannot rest from travel: I will drink
Life to the lees: all times I have enjoy'd
Greatly, have suffer'd greatly, both with those
That loved me, and alone; on shore, and when
Thro' scudding drifts the rainy Hyades   10
Vext the dim sea: I am become a name;
For always roaming with a hungry heart
Much have I seen and known: cities of men,
And manners, climates, councils, governments,
Myself not least, but honour'd of them all;   15
And drunk delight of battle with my peers,
Far on the ringing plains of windy Troy.
I am a part of all that I have met;
Yet all experience is an arch wherethro'
Gleams that untravell'd world, whose margin fades   20

---

upon a new voyage (*Odyssey*, xi, 100 f.). Upon this hint post-Homeric
poets elaborated the story of the last voyage of Ulysses. Dante did not
know Homer, but he knew Claudian's and other allusions to the theme.
In the Eighth Chasm of Malebolge, where Evil Counsellors are enveloped in
flames, Dante and Virgil encounter a twin-forked fire within which are
Ulysses and Diomed. In response to Virgil's question Ulysses tells his story
(*Inferno*, xvi, 90 f.): "When I departed from Circe, . . . neither fondness
for my son, nor reverence for my aged father, nor the due love that should
have cheered Penelope, could conquer in me the ardour I had to become
experienced of the world and of human vices and valour. I put forth
upon the deep open sea, with but one ship and with that small company
which had not deserted me. . . . I and my companions were old and
slow when we came to that narrow pass where Hercules assigned his land-
marks to hinder men from venturing further. . . . 'O brothers,' I said,
'who through a hundred thousand perils have reached the West, refuse
not to this brief vigil of your senses that remains, experience of the unpeopled world behind the sun. Consider your origin; ye were not formed
to live like brutes, but to follow virtue and knowledge.' With this brief
speech I made my companions so eager for the voyage that I could hardly
then have restrained them; and, turning the poop towards morning, we
of our oars made wings."

10. *the rainy Hyades;* Virgil's "pluvias Hyades," *Aeneid*, i, 744; iii, 516.

16. *delight of battle.* The phrase is Homeric, but Tennyson may have
remembered that Sir Walter Scott had written of the "stern joy which
warriors feel" (*The Lady of the Lake*, v, 10) and of the "stern delight"
of battle (*The Lord of the Isles*, iv, 20).

17. *windy Troy.* "Windy" ('ηνεμόεσσα) is Homer's epithet for
Troy; see *Iliad*, xii, 115; xviii, 174 (Mustard, *op. cit.*, p. 6).

18. Compare Virgil, *Aeneid*, ii, 6: "Quorum pars magna fui."

For ever and for ever when I move.
How dull it is to pause, to make an end,
To rust unburnish'd, not to shine in use!
As tho' to breathe were life. Life piled on life
Were all too little, and of one to me   25
Little remains: but every hour is saved
From that eternal silence, something more,
A bringer of new things; and vile it were
For some three suns to store and hoard myself,
And this gray spirit yearning in desire   30
To follow knowledge like a sinking star,
Beyond the utmost bound of human thought.
    This is my son, mine own Telemachus,
To whom I leave the sceptre and the isle —
Well-loved of me, discerning to fulfil   35
This labour, by slow prudence to make mild
A rugged people, and thro' soft degrees
Subdue them to the useful and the good.
Most blameless is he, centred in the sphere
Of common duties, decent not to fail   40
In offices of tenderness, and pay
Meet adoration to my household gods,
When I am gone. He works his work, I mine.
    There lies the port; the vessel puffs her sail:
There gloom the dark broad seas. My mariners,   45
Souls that have toil'd, and wrought, and thought with me —
That ever with a frolic welcome took
The thunder and the sunshine, and opposed
Free hearts, free foreheads — you and I are old;
Old age hath yet his honour and his toil;   50
Death closes all: but something ere the end,

22-4. Tennyson may have had in mind the words of Shakespeare's
Ulysses (*Troilus and Cressida*, III, iii, 152 f.):

> To have done is to hang
> Quite out of fashion, like a rusty mail
> In monumental mockery.

45-9. Commentators have noted that Tennyson departs from Homer in
bringing the companions of Ulysses home with him from their wanderings after the fall of Troy. But the poet's son remarks: "The comrades
he addresses are of the same heroic mould as his old comrades" (*Works*,
Eversley edition, i, 726).

Some work of noble note, may yet be done,
Not unbecoming men that strove with Gods.
The lights begin to twinkle from the rocks:
The long day wanes: the slow moon climbs: the deep   55
Moans round with many voices. Come, my friends,
'Tis not too late to seek a newer world.
Push off, and sitting well in order smite
The sounding furrows; for my purpose holds
To sail beyond the sunset, and the baths   60
Of all the western stars, until I die.
It may be that the gulfs will wash us down:
It may be we shall touch the Happy Isles,
And see the great Achilles, whom we knew.
Tho' much is taken, much abides; and tho'   65
We are not now that strength which in old days
Moved earth and heaven; that which we are, we are;
One equal temper of heroic hearts,
Made weak by time and fate, but strong in will
To strive, to seek, to find, and not to yield.   70

TITHONUS [1]

THE woods decay, the woods decay and fall,
The vapours weep their burthen to the ground,
Man comes and tills the field and lies beneath,
And after many a summer dies the swan.
Me only cruel immortality   5
Consumes: I wither slowly in thine arms,

---

[1] Begun about 1835; resumed and completed in 1859; published in the *Cornhill Magazine,* February, 1860; reprinted with but two small alterations in *Enoch Arden, etc.,* 1864. — The story of how Eos, the goddess of the dawn, obtained from the gods for her husband, Tithonus, the boon of immortality but forgot to ask for eternal youth, so that he gradually withered away and was turned into a grasshopper, is told in the Homeric *Hymn to Aphrodite,* ll. 218 f. Tennyson suppresses the metamorphosis and adds the *motif* of the grief of the goddess. In an early poem, "The Grasshopper," published in *Poems, Chiefly Lyrical* (1830) and afterwards suppressed, he alludes to the myth:

> No Tithon thou as poets feign
> (Shame fall 'em, they are deaf and blind),
> But an insect lithe and strong.

Here at the quiet limit of the world,
A white-hair'd shadow roaming like a dream
The ever-silent spaces of the East,
Far-folded mists, and gleaming halls of morn.   10

Alas! for this gray shadow, once a man —
So glorious in his beauty and thy choice,
Who madest him thy chosen, that he seem'd
To his great heart none other than a God!
I ask'd thee, 'Give me immortality.'   15
Then didst thou grant mine asking with a smile,
Like wealthy men who care not how they give.
But thy strong Hours indignant work'd their wills,
And beat me down and marr'd and wasted me,
And tho' they could not end me, left me maim'd   20
To dwell in presence of immortal youth,
Immortal age beside immortal youth,
And all I was, in ashes. Can thy love,
Thy beauty, make amends, tho' even now,
Close over us, the silver star, thy guide,   25
Shines in those tremulous eyes that fill with tears
To hear me? Let me go: take back thy gift:
Why should a man desire in any way
To vary from the kindly race of men,
Or pass beyond the goal of ordinance   30
Where all should pause, as is most meet for all?

A soft air fans the cloud apart; there comes
A glimpse of that dark world where I was born.
Once more the old mysterious glimmer steals
From thy pure brows, and from thy shoulders pure,   35
And bosom beating with a heart renew'd.
Thy cheek begins to redden thro' the gloom,
Thy sweet eyes brighten slowly close to mine,
Ere yet they blind the stars, and the wild team
Which love thee, yearning for thy yoke, arise,   40
And shake the darkness from their loosen'd manes,
And beat the twilight into flakes of fire.

Lo! ever thus thou growest beautiful
In silence, then before thine answer given
Departest, and thy tears are on my cheek.   45

Why wilt thou ever scare me with thy tears,
And make me tremble lest a saying learnt,
In days far-off, on that dark earth, be true?
'The Gods themselves cannot recall their gifts.'

Ay me! ay me! with what another heart   50
In days far-off, and with what other eyes
I used to watch — if I be he that watch'd —
The lucid outline forming round thee; saw
The dim curls kindle into sunny rings;
Changed with thy mystic change, and felt my blood   55
Glow with the glow that slowly crimson'd all
Thy presence and thy portals, while I lay,
Mouth, forehead, eyelids, growing dewy-warm
With kisses balmier than half-opening buds
Of April, and could hear the lips that kiss'd   60
Whispering I knew not what of wild and sweet,
Like that strange song I heard Apollo sing,
While Ilion like a mist rose into towers.

Yet hold me not for ever in thine East:
How can my nature longer mix with thine?   65
Coldly thy rosy shadows bathe me, cold
Are all thy lights, and cold my wrinkled feet
Upon thy glimmering thresholds, when the steam
Floats up from those dim fields about the homes
Of happy men that have the power to die,   70
And grassy barrows of the happier dead.
Release me, and restore me to the ground;
Thou seëst all things, thou wilt see my grave:
Thou wilt renew thy beauty morn by morn;
I earth in earth forget these empty courts,   75
And thee returning on thy silver wheels.

62–3. For the myth that Apollo built the walls of Troy to the music of his lyre see Ovid, *Heroides*, xv, 179 f.; and compare "Œnone," ll. 39 f. and "Tiresias," l. 96. For other allusions to the myth in classical and English poets see Mustard, *op. cit.,* p. 118. So Camelot was builded to the music of the harps of fairies ("Gareth and Lynette," ll. 254 f.) and so Pandæmonium, "the high capital of Satan and his peers," rose "with the sound of dulcet symphonies" (*Paradise Lost,* i, 711 f.).

LUCRETIUS[1]

Lucilia, wedded to Lucretius, found
Her master cold; for when the morning flush
Of passion and the first embrace had died
Between them, tho' he lov'd her none the less,
Yet often when the woman heard his foot   5
Return from pacings in the field, and ran
To greet him with a kiss, the master took
Small notice, or austerely, for — his mind
Half buried in some weightier argument,
Or fancy-borne perhaps upon the rise   10
And long roll of the Hexameter — he past
To turn and ponder those three hundred scrolls
Left by the Teacher, whom he held divine.
She brook'd it not; but wrathful, petulant,
Dreaming some rival, sought and found a witch   15
Who brew'd the philtre which had power, they said,
To lead an errant passion home again.
And this, at times, she mingled with his drink,
And this destroy'd him; for the wicked broth
Confused the chemic labour of the blood,   20

---

[1] Published in *Macmillan's Magazine,* May, 1868, and in *Every Satur-
day* (New York), May 2, 1868; reprinted in *The Holy Grail and Other
Poems,* 1869 (dated 1870). — The tradition on which the poem is based
may have been current within a century of the death of Lucretius (55
B.C.); but Saint Gerome gave it literary form. In his addition to the
Eusebian Chronicle, under the date 94 B.C. is the following: "Titus
Lucretius the poet was born [in that year; actually *c.* 99 B.C.]. Later he
was driven mad by a love-philtre, after he had written several books in
the intervals of insanity . . . Lucretius died by his own hand in the
forty-fourth year of his age." Elsewhere in Gerome (*Epistolae,* xxxvi)
there is a reference to a certain Lucilia who slew her unnamed husband
because he did not love her. Tradition, followed by Tennyson, fused these
two stories. Compare John Lyly, *Euphues and His England* (*Works,* ed.
R. W. Bond, ii, 47): "Lucilia ministring an amorous potion unto her husband Lucretius, procured his death, whose life she onely desired." For a
demonstration of the fidelity with which Tennyson has reproduced the
spirit and tone of Lucretius see Mustard, *op. cit.,* chapter vi.

13. *The Teacher* is Epicurus. Compare the Proem to *De Rerum
Natura,* Book iii. At v, 8 f. Lucretius hails Epicurus as

a god,
Who first and chief found out that plan of life
Which now is called philosophy (W. E. Leonard's translation).

And tickling the brute brain within the man's
Made havock among those tender cells, and check'd
His power to shape: he loathed himself; and once
After a tempest woke upon a morn
That mock'd him with returning calm, and cried: 25

'Storm in the night! for thrice I heard the rain
Rushing; and once the flash of a thunderbolt —
Methought I never saw so fierce a fork —
Struck out the streaming mountain-side, and show'd
A riotous confluence of watercourses   30
Blanching and billowing in a hollow of it,
Where all but yester-eve was dusty-dry.

'Storm, and what dreams, ye holy Gods, what dreams!
For thrice I waken'd after dreams. Perchance
We do but recollect the dreams that come   35
Just ere the waking: terrible! for it seem'd
A void was made in Nature; all her bonds
Crack'd; and I saw the flaring atom-streams
And torrents of her myriad universe,
Ruining along the illimitable inane,   40
Fly on to clash together again, and make
Another and another frame of things
For ever: that was mine, my dream, I knew it —
Of and belonging to me, as the dog
With inward yelp and restless forefoot plies   45
His function of the woodland: but the next!
I thought that all the blood by Sylla shed
Came driving rainlike down again on earth,
And where it dash'd the reddening meadow, sprang
No dragon warriors from Cadmean teeth,   50
For these I thought my dream would show to me,

---

33. f. For the images of sleep that "terrify our intellects" see *De Rerum Natura*, iv, 33 f.

44 f. The simile of the dog was suggested by *De Rerum Natura*, iv, 991 f.

47 f. *Sylla,* Sulla. During the war with Marius and during his dictatorship (81–79 B.C.) Sulla caused the massacre of thousands. Lucretius had lived in his youth through the terrible days of the proscription.

But girls, Hetairai, curious in their art,
Hired animalisms, vile as those that made
The mulberry-faced Dictator's orgies worse
Than aught they fable of the quiet Gods.   55
And hands they mixt, and yell'd and round me drove
In narrowing circles till I yell'd again
Half-suffocated, and sprang up, and saw —
Was it the first beam of my latest day?

'Then, then, from utter gloom stood out the breasts,   60
The breasts of Helen, and hoveringly a sword
Now over and now under, now direct,
Pointed itself to pierce, but sank down shamed
At all that beauty; and as I stared, a fire,
The fire that left a roofless Ilion,   65
Shot out of them, and scorch'd me that I woke.

'Is this thy vengeance, holy Venus, thine,
Because I would not one of thine own doves,
Not ev'n a rose, were offer'd to thee? thine,
Forgetful how my rich prooemion makes   70
Thy glory fly along the Italian field,
In lays that will outlast thy Deity?

'Deity? nay, thy worshippers. My tongue
Trips, or I speak profanely. Which of these
Angers thee most, or angers thee at all?   75
Not if thou be'st of those who, far aloof
From envy, hate and pity, and spite and scorn,
Live the great life which all our greatest fain
Would follow, centr'd in eternal calm.

---

52. *Hetairai,* courtesans.

54. Plutarch records (*Life of Sulla,* ii) that in the Dictator's complexion "white was mixed with rough blotches of fiery red" and that an Athenian jester lampooned him as a mulberry sprinkled over with meal.

64–6. With the flames shooting out from the breasts of Helen compare the tradition current in Pre-Raphaelite circles (and recorded by Watts-Dunton) that a like awful vision was seen by Coleridge's Christabel when the Lady Geraldine disrobed.

70. *my rich prooemion,* the first forty-nine verses of *De Rerum Natura,* Book i, the address to Venus, the delight of gods and men.

'Nay, if thou canst, O Goddess, like ourselves   80
Touch, and be touch'd, then would I cry to thee
To kiss thy Mavors, roll thy tender arms
Round him, and keep him from the lust of blood
That makes a steaming slaughter-house of Rome.

'Ay, but I meant not thee; I meant not her,   85
Whom all the pines of Ida shook to see
Slide from that quiet heaven of hers, and tempt
The Trojan, while his neat-herds were abroad;
Nor her that o'er her wounded hunter wept
Her Deity, false in human-amorous tears;   90
Nor whom her beardless apple-arbiter
Decided fairest. Rather, O ye Gods,
Poet-like, as the great Sicilian called
Calliope to grace his golden verse —
Ay, and this Kypris also — did I take   95
That popular name of thine to shadow forth
The all-generating powers and genial heat
Of Nature, when she strikes thro' the thick blood
Of cattle, and light is large, and lambs are glad
Nosing the mother's udder, and the bird   100
Makes his heart voice amid the blaze of flowers:
Which things appear the work of mighty Gods.

'The Gods! and if I go *my* work is left
Unfinish'd — *if* I go. The Gods, who haunt
The lucid interspace of world and world,   105

---

82. *Mavors*, Mars.

88. *The Trojan*, Anchises.

89. *her wounded hunter*, Adonis.

93 f. *the great Sicilian*, Theocritus, according to Tennyson's son (*Works*, Eversley edition, i, 751), but Empedocles, according to Van Dyke and Mustard who quote the invocation of Calliope from one of his fragments. *Calliope*, the muse of epic poetry; *Kypris*, a name for Aphrodite ("the Cyprian").

104. *De Rerum Natura* is incomplete.

104–110. Compare Lucretius's vision of

> the majesty of gods,
> And their abodes of everlasting calm
> Which neither wind may shake nor rain-cloud splash,
> Nor snow, congealèd by sharp frosts, may harm;

Where never creeps a cloud, or moves a wind,
Nor ever falls the least white star of snow,
Nor ever lowest roll of thunder moans,
Nor sound of human sorrow mounts to mar
Their sacred everlasting calm! and such,   110
Not all so fine, nor so divine a calm,
Not such, nor all unlike it, man may gain
Letting his own life go. The Gods, the Gods!
If all be atoms, how then should the Gods
Being atomic not be dissoluble,   115
Not follow the great law? My master held
That Gods there are, for all men so believe.
I prest my footsteps into his, and meant
Surely to lead my Memmius in a train
Of flowery clauses onward to the proof   120
That Gods there are, and deathless. Meant? I meant?
I have forgotten what I meant: my mind
Stumbles, and all my faculties are lamed.

'Look where another of our Gods, the Sun,
Apollo, Delius, or of older use   125
All-seeing Hyperion — what you will —
Has mounted yonder; since he never sware,
Except his wrath were wreak'd on wretched man,
That he would only shine among the dead
Hereafter; tales! for never yet on earth   130

---

where nought "may ever pluck their peace of mind away" (*De Rerum Natura*, iii, 18 f.; Leonard's translation). The passage derives from *Odyssey*, vi, 42 f. Compare "The Lotos-Eaters," ll. 155 f.; "Œnone," ll. 128 f.; "The Passing of Arthur," ll. 424 f.

107. Tennyson remarked to a friend, "I improved on Homer, because I knew that snow crystallises into stars" (W. F. Rawnsley, "Personal Recollections of Tennyson," *The Nineteenth Century*, xcvii, 7).

116. *My master*, Epicurus. Compare *De Rerum Natura*, iii, 3; v, 55.

119. The *De Rerum Natura* is dedicated to Caius Memmius Gamellus.

120-1. For Lucretius's discussion of the grounds of belief in the gods see *De Rerum Natura*, v, 146 f., 1161 f.

126. *Hyperion*, a Titan, father of the sun-god Helios; but often used for Helios himself. The accent is properly, as here, on the penult; but Shakespeare has imposed upon English poetry (compare Keats) a wrong pronunciation.

Could dead flesh creep, or bits of roasting ox
Moan round the spit — nor knows he what he sees;
King of the East altho' he seem, and girt
With song and flame and fragrance, slowly lifts
His golden feet on those empurpled stairs   135
That climb into the windy halls of heaven:
And here he glances on an eye new-born,
And gets for greeting but a wail of pain;
And here he stays upon a freezing orb
That fain would gaze upon him to the last;   140
And here upon a yellow eyelid fall'n
And closed by those who mourn a friend in vain,
Not thankful that his troubles are no more.
And me, altho' his fire is on my face
Blinding, he sees not, nor at all can tell   145
Whether I mean this day to end myself,
Or lend an ear to Plato where he says,
That men like soldiers may not quit the post
Allotted by the Gods: but he that holds
The Gods are careless, wherefore need he care   150
Greatly for them, nor rather plunge at once,
Being troubled, wholly out of sight, and sink
Past earthquake — ay, and gout and stone, that break
Body toward death, and palsy, death-in-life,
And wretched age — and worst disease of all,   155
These prodigies of myriad nakednesses,
And twisted shapes of lust, unspeakable,
Abominable, strangers at my hearth
Not welcome, harpies miring every dish,
The phantom husks of something foully done   160
And fleeting thro' the boundless universe,

---

131. Compare *Odyssey*, xii, 382 f.

147-9. Tennyson follows the older interpretation of the *Phaedo*, 62 B:
"There is a doctrine whispered in secret, that we men are on a sort of
garrison duty, and that one should not free himself from it or run away."
See Mustard, *op. cit.*, p. 59.

160 and 165.   *husks* and *idols*.   These expressions "reflect the doctrine
of the idols or images (*simulacra*), iv, 30, which like small films constantly proceed from the surface of all things, and, to Epicurus or Lucretius,
account for all that we see or fancy" (Mustard, *op. cit.*, p. 75).

And blasting the long quiet of my breast
With animal heat and dire insanity?

'How should the mind, except it loved them, clasp
These idols to herself? or do they fly   165
Now thinner, and now thicker, like the flakes
In a fall of snow, and so press in, perforce
Of multitude, as crowds that in an hour
Of civic tumult jam the doors, and bear
The keepers down, and throng, their rags and they   170
The basest, far into that council-hall
Where sit the best and stateliest of the land?

'Can I not fling this horror off me again,
Seeing with how great ease Nature can smile,
Balmier and nobler from her bath of storm,   175
At random ravage? and how easily
The mountain there has cast his cloudy slough,
Now towering o'er him in serenest air,
A mountain o'er a mountain, — ay, and within
All hollow as the hopes and fears of men?   180

'But who was he, that in the garden snared
Picus and Faunus, rustic Gods? a tale
To laugh at — more to laugh at in myself —
For look! what is it? there? yon arbutus
Totters; a noiseless riot underneath   185
Strikes through the wood, sets all the tops quivering —
The mountain quickens into Nymph and Faun;
And here an Oread — how the sun delights

177–180. For the Lucretian elements in these images see Mustard, *op.
cit.*, p. 75.

181–3. Ovid (*Fasti,* iii, 289 f.) relates that King Numa captured on the
Aventine the gods Picus and Faunus, when they were drunk, in order
to compel them to reveal a way of averting the thunderbolts of Jove.

188–191. In the first published text (*Macmillan's Magazine,* May,
1868) these lines are compressed to —

       And here an Oread, and this way she runs.

"There are indications," says Mr. Harold Nicolson (*Tennyson,* p. 230),
"that the advent of Swinburne was leading the Laureate to consider
whether a little — a very little — wine might not with advantage be

To glance and shift about her slippery sides,
And rosy knees and supple roundedness,   190
And budded bosom-peaks — who this way runs
Before the rest — A satyr, a satyr, see,
Follows; but him I proved impossible;
Twy-natured is no nature: yet he draws
Nearer and nearer, and I scan him now   195
Beastlier than any phantom of his kind
That ever butted his rough brother-brute
For lust or lusty blood or provender:
I hate, abhor, spit, sicken at him; and she
Loathes him as well; such a precipitate heel,   200
Fledged as it were with Mercury's ankle-wing,
Whirls her to me: but will she fling herself,
Shameless upon me?   Catch her, goat-foot: nay,
Hide, hide them, million-myrtled wilderness,
And cavern-shadowing laurels, hide! do I wish —   205
What? — that the bush were leafless? or to whelm
All of them in one massacre? O ye Gods,
I know you careless, yet, behold, to you
From childly wont and ancient use I call —
I thought I lived securely as yourselves —   210

---

added to the limpid waters of Camelot. . . . Messrs. Macmillan were
appalled. They asked, they begged, the Laureate to suppress" the description of the Oread. Mr. Nicolson does not cite his authority for the
statement that Macmillan exercised a censorship; but the fact that the
omitted passage appeared in full in the American publication, *Every Sat-
urday,* and that it reappeared in all the collected editions makes it likely
that the suppression was due to an editor rather than to the poet. Fitz-
Gerald, however, had heard in 1867 that the poem was thought to be "too
free-spoken" in "amatory" tone for publication (*Letters,* ii, 226). There
is an anecdote, perhaps apocryphal, that Tennyson, after reading privately
to a little company his narrative of the love-frenzy of Lucretius, remarked
complacently, "Think what a mess little Swinburne would have made of
this!" (Samuel C. Chew, *Swinburne,* p. 262).

193–4. For the proof that "twy-natured" creatures are impossible and
that monsters half-man, half-brute, or beasts half of the sea, half of the
land, have never been begotten see *De Rerum Natura,* ii, 730 f.

207–8. Twice (*De Rerum Natura,* v, 82, and vi, 58) Lucretius affirms
in identical words ("securum agere aevum") that the gods lead a care-
free life.

210–218. A notably Lucretian passage; for its "echoes" of *De Rerum
Natura* see Mustard, *op. cit.,* p. 76.

No lewdness, narrowing envy, monkey spite,
No madness of ambition, avarice, none:
No larger feast than under plane or pine
With neighbours laid along the grass, to take
Only such cups as left us friendly-warm,   215
Affirming each his own philosophy —
Nothing to mar the sober majesties
Of settled, sweet, Epicurean life.
But now it seems some unseen monster lays
His vast and filthy hands upon my will,   220
Wrenching it backward into his; and spoils
My bliss in being; and it was not great;
For save when shutting reasons up in rhythm,
Or Heliconian honey in living words,
To make a truth less harsh, I often grew   225
Tired of so much within our little life,
Or of so little in our little life —
Poor little life that toddles half an hour
Crown'd with a flower or two, and there an end —
And since the nobler pleasure seems to fade,   230
Why should I, beastlike as I find myself,
Not manlike end myself? — our privilege —
What beast has heart to do it?   And what man,
What Roman would be dragg'd in triumph thus?
Not I; not he, who bears one name with her   235
Whose death-blow struck the dateless doom of kings,
When, brooking not the Tarquin in her veins,
She made her blood in sight of Collatine
And all his peers, flushing the guiltless air,
Spout from the maiden fountain in her heart.   240
And from it sprang the Commonwealth, which breaks
As I am breaking now!
                          'And therefore now
Let her, that is the womb and tomb of all,

---

235. *her,* Lucretia (Lucrece) who, having been ravished by Sextus
Tarquinius, stabbed herself, and so roused the Roman people against
the Tarquins.

241. At the time of Lucretius's death the Roman Republic was almost
extinct, power having been concentrated in the hands of the First Tri-
umvirate.

243. Compare *De Rerum Natura,* v, 258 f.:

Great Nature, take, and forcing far apart
Those blind beginnings that have made me man,   245
Dash them anew together at her will
Thro' all her cycles — into man once more,
Or beast or bird or fish, or opulent flower:
• But till this cosmic order everywhere
Shatter'd into one earthquake in one day   250
Cracks all to pieces, — and that hour perhaps
Is not so far when momentary man
Shall seem no more a something to himself,
But he, his hopes and hates, his homes and fanes,
And even his bones long laid within the grave,   255
The very sides of the grave itself shall pass,
Vanishing, atom and void, atom and void,
Into the unseen for ever, — till that hour,
My golden work in which I told a truth
That stays the rolling Ixionian wheel,   260
And numbs the Fury's ringlet-snake, and plucks
The mortal soul from out immortal hell,
Shall stand: ay, surely: then it falls at last
And perishes as I must; for O Thou,
Passionless bride, divine Tranquillity,   265
Yearn'd after by the wisest of the wise,

> Earth, the all-mother, is beheld to be
> Likewise the common sepulchre of things.
>   (Leonard's translation)

Compare also *Romeo and Juliet,* II, iii, 9: "The earth, that's Nature's
mother, is her tomb," and *Paradise Lost,* ii, 911: "The womb of Nature
and perhaps her grave."

250. Compare *De Rerum Natura,* v, 94 f.:

> The seas, the lands, the sky, . . .
> Three frames so vast, a single day shall give
> Unto annihilation! Then shall crash
> That massive form and fabric of the world
> Sustained so many aeons!
>   (Leonard's translation)

259. *My golden work,* the *De Rerum Natura.*

259–60. The "truth that stays" Ixion's wheel and has banished the
terrors of the torments of hell is the series of arguments by which Lucretius
seeks to show the mortality of the soul and the non-existence of a world
of the dead. See the long section in *De Rerum Natura* (iii, 828 f.) on the
folly of the fear of death.

Who fail to find thee, being as thou art
Without one pleasure and without one pain,
Howbeit I know thou surely must be mine
Or soon or late, yet out of season, thus   270
I woo thee roughly, for thou carest not
How roughly men may woo thee so they win —
Thus — thus: the soul flies out and dies in the air.'

With that he drove the knife into his side:
She heard him raging, heard him fall; ran in,   275
Beat breast, tore hair, cried out upon herself
As having fail'd in duty to him, shriek'd
That she but meant to win him back, fell on him,
Clasp'd, kiss'd him, wail'd: he answer'd, 'Care not thou!
Thy duty?   What is duty?   Fare thee well!'   280

TIRESIAS [1]

TO E. FITZGERALD [2]

Oᴌᴅ Fɪᴛᴢ, who from your suburb grange,
    Where once I tarried for a while,
Glance at the wheeling Orb of change,
    And greet it with a kindly smile;
Whom yet I see as there you sit   5
    Beneath your sheltering garden-tree,
And while your doves about you flit,
    And plant on shoulder, hand and knee,
Or on your head their rosy feet,
    As if they knew your diet spares   10
Whatever moved in that full sheet
    Let down to Peter at his prayers;
Who live on milk and meal and grass;
    And once for ten long weeks I tried

---

[1] Written in part about the same time as "Ulysses," but first published
in *Tiresias and Other Poems,* 1885.

[2] This dedicatory prelude was not seen by FitzGerald who died (1883)
before "Tiresias" was published. The visit to his home at Woodbridge
to which reference is made occurred in September, 1876.

10–12. See Acts, x, 11.

Your table of Pythagoras,   15
    And seem'd at first 'a thing enskied'
(As Shakespeare has it) airy-light
    To float above the ways of men,
Then fell from that half-spiritual height
    Chill'd, till I tasted flesh again   20
One night when earth was winter-black,
    And all the heavens flash'd in frost;
And on me, half-asleep, came back
    That wholesome heat the blood had lost,
And set me climbing icy capes   25
    And glaciers, over which there roll'd
To meet me long-arm'd vines with grapes
    Of Eshcol hugeness; for the cold
Without, and warmth within me, wrought
    To mould the dream; but none can say   30
That Lenten fare makes Lenten thought,
    Who reads your golden Eastern lay,
Than which I know no version done
    In English more divinely well;
A planet equal to the sun   35
    Which cast it, that large infidel
Your Omar; and your Omar drew
    Full-handed plaudits from our best
In modern letters, and from two,
    Old friends outvaluing all the rest,   40
Two voices heard on earth no more;
    But we old friends are still alive,
And I am nearing seventy-four,
    While you have touch'd at seventy-five,

---

15. The Pythagoreans were vegetarians. Compare *Twelfth Night,* IV,
ii, 54 f.

16. *Measure for Measure,* I, iv, 34.

20 f. For the dream to which allusion is here made see the *Memoir,*
ii, 317.

27–8. *grapes of Eshcol hugeness.* See Numbers, xiii, 23.

32–4. The English version of the "Eastern lay" is of course FitzGerald's
version of the *Rubáiyát* of Omar Khayyám (1859).

38 f. Rossetti and Swinburne were the first among "our best in modern letters" to give "full-handed plaudits" to the *Rubáiyát.* Who the two
old friends were is not apparent.

And so I send a birthday line   45
   Of greeting; and my son, who dipt
In some forgotten book of mine
   With sallow scraps of manuscript,
And dating many a year ago,
   Has hit on this, which you will take   50
My Fitz, and welcome, as I know
   Less for its own than for the sake
Of one recalling gracious times,
   When, in our younger London days,
You found some merit in my rhymes,   55
   And I more pleasure in your praise.

TIRESIAS [1]

I wish I were as in the years of old,
While yet the blessed daylight made itself
Ruddy thro' both the roofs of sight, and woke
These eyes, now dull, but then so keen to seek
The meanings ambush'd under all they saw,   5
The flight of birds, the flame of sacrifice,
What omens may foreshadow fate to man
And woman, and the secret of the Gods.
My son, the Gods, despite of human prayer,
Are slower to forgive than human kings.   10
The great God, Arês, burns in anger still
Against the guiltless heirs of him from Tyre,
Our Cadmus, out of whom thou art, who found
Beside the springs of Dircê, smote, and still'd
Thro' all its folds the multitudinous beast,   15
The dragon, which our trembling fathers call'd
The God's own son.

---

[1] The myth of Tiresias (Teiresias) is narrated or referred to by Homer, Pindar, Callimachus, Pausanias, Apollodorus, and other classical writers. Having seen Athena (or, in some forms of the story, Artemis) in her bath, he was stricken with blindness, in compensation for which he was granted the gift of prophecy; but his prophecies were not believed. (Compare Swinburne's "Tiresias" in *Songs before Sunrise*.) The self-sacrifice of Menœceus to save Thebes is from the *Phœnissae* of Euripides.

6. Pausanias records that at Thebes the "observatory" of Tiresias was pointed out, whence he watched for omens from birds.

13. Tiresias was a descendant of one of the men sprung from the dragon's teeth sown by Cadmus.

A tale, that told to me,
When but thine age, by age as winter-white
As mine is now, amazed, but made me yearn
For larger glimpses of that more than man   20
Which rolls the heavens, and lifts, and lays the deep,
Yet loves and hates with mortal hates and loves,
And moves unseen among the ways of men.

   Then, in my wanderings all the lands that lie
Subjected to the Heliconian ridge   25
Have heard this footstep fall, altho' my wont
Was more to scale the highest of the heights
With some strange hope to see the nearer God.

   One naked peak — the sister of the sun
Would climb from out the dark, and linger there   30
To silver all the valleys with her shafts —
There once, but long ago, five-fold thy term
Of years, I lay; the winds were dead for heat;
The noonday crag made the hand burn; and sick
For shadow — not one bush was near — I rose   35
Following a torrent till its myriad falls
Found silence in the hollows underneath.

   There in a secret olive-glade I saw
Pallas Athene climbing from the bath
In anger; yet one glittering foot disturb'd   40
The lucid well; one snowy knee was prest
Against the margin flowers; a dreadful light
Came from her golden hair, her golden helm
And all her golden armour on the grass,
And from her virgin breast, and virgin eyes   45
Remaining fixt on mine, till mine grew dark
For ever, and I heard a voice that said
'Henceforth be blind, for thou hast seen too much,
And speak the truth that no man may believe.'

   Son, in the hidden world of sight, that lives   50
Behind this darkness, I behold her still,
Beyond all work of those who carve the stone,
Beyond all dreams of Godlike womanhood,
Ineffable beauty, out of whom, at a glance,
And as it were, perforce, upon me flash'd   55
The power of prophesying — but to me
No power — so chain'd and coupled with the curse

Of blindness and their unbelief, who heard
And heard not, when I spake of famine, plague,
Shrine-shattering earthquake, fire, flood, thunderbolt,   60
And angers of the Gods for evil done
And expiation lack'd — no power on Fate,
Theirs, or mine own! for when the crowd would roar
For blood, for war, whose issue was their doom,
To cast wise words among the multitude   65
Was flinging fruit to lions; nor, in hours
Of civil outbreak, when I knew the twain
Would each waste each, and bring on both the yoke
Of stronger states, was mine the voice to curb
The madness of our cities and their kings.   70
    Who ever turn'd upon his heel to hear
My warning that the tyranny of one
Was prelude to the tyranny of all?
My counsel that the tyranny of all
Led backward to the tyranny of one?   75
    This power hath work'd no good to aught that lives,
And these blind hands were useless in their wars.
O therefore that the unfulfill'd desire,
The grief for ever born from griefs to be,
The boundless yearning of the Prophet's heart —   80
Could *that* stand forth, and, like a statue rear'd
To some great citizen, win all praise from all
Who past it, saying, 'That was he!'
                                        In vain!
Virtue must shape itself in deed, and those
Whom weakness or necessity have cramp'd   85
Within themselves, immerging, each, his urn
In his own well, draw solace as he may.
    Menœceus, thou hast eyes, and I can hear
Too plainly what full tides of onset sap
Our seven high gates, and what a weight of war   90
Rides on those ringing axles! jingle of bits,
Shouts, arrows, tramp of the hornfooted horse
That grind the glebe to powder!   Stony showers

92. *hornfooted horse.* Compare Virgil, *Aeneid,* vi, 590: "cornipedum
. . . equorum."
93. Compare Virgil, *Georgics,* i, 44 and 65.

Of that ear-stunning hail of Arês crash
Along the sounding walls. Above, below,   95
Shock after shock, the song-built towers and gates
Reel, bruised and butted with the shuddering
War-thunder of iron rams; and from within
The city comes a murmur void of joy,
Lest she be taken captive — maidens, wives,   100
And mothers with their babblers of the dawn,
And oldest age in shadow from the night,
Falling about their shrines before their Gods,
And wailing 'Save us.'
                        And they wail to thee!
These eyeless eyes, that cannot see thine own,   105
See this, that only in thy virtue lies
The saving of our Thebes; for, yesternight,
To me, the great God Arês, whose one bliss
Is war, and human sacrifice — himself
Blood-red from battle, spear and helmet tipt   110
With stormy light as on a mast at sea,
Stood out before a darkness, crying 'Thebes,
Thy Thebes shall fall and perish, for I loathe
The seed of Cadmus — yet if one of these
By his own hand — if one of these ——'
                                My son,   115
No sound is breathed so potent to coerce,
And to conciliate, as their names who dare
For that sweet mother land which gave them birth
Nobly to do, nobly to die. Their names,
Graven on memorial columns, are a song   120
Heard in the future; few, but more than wall
And rampart, their examples reach a hand
Far thro' all years, and everywhere they meet
And kindle generous purpose, and the strength
To mould it into action pure as theirs.   125
    Fairer thy fate than mine, if life's best end
Be to end well! and thou refusing this,
Unvenerable will thy memory be
While men shall move the lips: but if thou dare —
Thou, one of these, the race of Cadmus — then   130

_____

96. See note on "Tithonus," ll. 62–3.

No stone is fitted in yon marble girth
Whose echo shall not tongue thy glorious doom,
Nor in this pavement but shall ring thy name
To every hoof that clangs it, and the springs
Of Dircê laving yonder battle-plain,   135
Heard from the roofs by night, will murmur thee
To thine own Thebes, while Thebes thro' thee shall stand
Firm-based with all her Gods.
                                   The Dragon's cave
Half-hid, they tell me, now in flowing vines —
Where once he dwelt and whence he roll'd himself   140
At dead of night — thou knowest, and that smooth rock
Before it, altar-fashion'd, where of late
The woman-breasted Sphinx, with wings drawn back,
Folded her lion paws, and look'd to Thebes.
There blanch the bones of whom she slew, and these   145
Mixt with her own, because the fierce beast found
A wiser than herself, and dash'd herself
Dead in her rage: but thou art wise enough,
Tho' young, to love thy wiser, blunt the curse
Of Pallas, hear, and tho' I speak the truth   150
Believe I speak it, let thine own hand strike
Thy youthful pulses into rest and quench
The red God's anger, fearing not to plunge
Thy torch of life in darkness, rather — thou
Rejoicing that the sun, the moon, the stars   155
Send no such light upon the ways of men
As one great deed.
                        Thither, my son, and there
Thou, that hast never known the embrace of love,
Offer thy maiden life.
                        This useless hand!
I felt one warm tear fall upon it. Gone!   160
He will achieve his greatness.
                                    But for me,
I would that I were gather'd to my rest,
And mingled with the famous kings of old,
On whom about their ocean-islets flash

161–177. Tennyson's son records (*Memoir,* ii, 318) that his father
liked to quote this passage as a sample of his blank verse.

The faces of the Gods — the wise man's word,   165
Here trampled by the populace underfoot,
There crown'd with worship — and these eyes will find
The men I knew, and watch the chariot whirl
About the goal again, and hunters race
The shadowy lion, and the warrior-kings,   170
In height and prowess more than human, strive
Again for glory, while the golden lyre
Is ever sounding in heroic ears
Heroic hymns, and every way the vales
Wind, clouded with the grateful incense-fume   175
Of those who mix all odour to the Gods
On one far height in one far-shining fire.

EPILOGUE [1]

'One height and one far-shining fire,'
    And while I fancied that my friend
For this brief idyll would require
    A less diffuse and opulent end,
And would defend his judgment well,   5
    If I should deem it over nice —
The tolling of his funeral bell
    Broke on my Pagan Paradise,
And mixt the dream of classic times
    And all the phantoms of the dream,   10
With present grief, and made the rhymes,
    That miss'd his living welcome, seem
Like would-be guests an hour too late,
    Who down the highway moving on
With easy laughter find the gate   15
    Is bolted, and the master gone.
Gone into darkness, that full light
    Of friendship! past, in sleep, away
By night, into the deeper night!
    The deeper night? A clearer day   20

167–177. These lines are a paraphrase of Fragment x, No. i of the
Θρῆνοι of Pindar. See Mustard, *op. cit.,* p. 28, and *Works,* Eversley edition, iv, 563.

[1] The poet gave no title to these concluding lines, but they are called
the "Epilogue" in *Tennyson and His Friends,* edited by Hallam, Lord
Tennyson, p. 138.

Than our poor twilight dawn on earth —
   If night, what barren toil to be!
What life, so maim'd by night, were worth
   Our living out?   Not mine to me
Remembering all the golden hours   25
   Now silent, and so many dead,
And him the last; and laying flowers,
   This wreath, above his honour'd head,
And praying that, when I from hence
   Shall fade with him into the unknown,   30
My close of earth's experience
   May prove as peaceful as his own.

DEMETER AND PERSEPHONE

(IN ENNA) [1]

FAINT as a climate-changing bird that flies
All night across the darkness, and at dawn
Falls on the threshold of her native land,
And can no more, thou camest, O my child,
Led upward by the God of ghosts and dreams,   5
Who laid thee at Eleusis, dazed and dumb
With passing thro' at once from state to state,
Until I brought thee hither, that the day,
When here thy hands let fall the gather'd flower,
Might break thro' clouded memories once again   10

---

[1] Written in 1887; published in *Demeter and Other Poems,* 1889. The rape of Persephone (Proserpine) by Dis (Pluto) from the fields of Enna in Sicily (in some versions from Eleusis) is narrated in the Homeric *Hymn to Demeter,* in Hesiod, *Theogony,* ll. 912 f., in Ovid, *Metamorphoses,* v, 341 f. and *Fasti,* iv, 419 f., and in Claudian, *De Raptu Proserpinae.* Compare also George Meredith's poem "The Day of the Daughter of Hades"; and *Paradise Lost,* iv, 268 f.:

                    That fair field
Of Enna, where Proserpin gath'ring flow'rs
Herself a fairer Flow'r by gloomy Dis
Was gather'd, which cost Ceres all that pain
To seek her through the world.

In Tennyson's dramatic monologue Demeter (Ceres) addresses her daughter.

   5. *the God of ghosts and dreams,* Hermes.   Compare ll. 25 f.

On thy lost self. A sudden nightingale
Saw thee, and flash'd into a frolic of song
And welcome; and a gleam as of the moon,
When first she peers along the tremulous deep,
Fled wavering o'er thy face, and chased away   15
That shadow of a likeness to the king
Of shadows, thy dark mate. Persephone!
Queen of the dead no more — my child!   Thine eyes
Again were human-godlike, and the Sun
Burst from a swimming fleece of winter gray,   20
And robed thee in his day from head to feet —
'Mother!' and I was folded in thine arms.

    Child, those imperial, disimpassion'd eyes
Awed even me at first, thy mother — eyes
That oft had seen the serpent-wanded power   25
Draw downward into Hades with his drift
Of flickering spectres, lighted from below
By the red race of fiery Phlegethon;
But when before have Gods or men beheld
The Life that had descended re-arise,   30
And lighted from above him by the Sun?
So mighty was the mother's childless cry,
A cry that rang thro' Hades, Earth, and Heaven!

    So in this pleasant vale we stand again,
The field of Enna, now once more ablaze   35
With flowers that brighten as thy footstep falls,
All flowers — but for one black blur of earth
Left by that closing chasm, thro' which the car
Of dark Aïdoneus rising rapt thee hence.
And here, my child, tho' folded in thine arms,   40
I feel the deathless heart of motherhood
Within me shudder, lest the naked glebe
Should yawn once more into the gulf, and thence
The shrilly whinnyings of the team of Hell,
Ascending, pierce the glad and songful air,   45
And all at once their arch'd necks, midnight-maned,

---

39. *Aïdoneus,* Dis.

Jet upward thro' the mid-day blossom. No!
For, see, thy foot has touch'd it; all the space
Of blank earth-baldness clothes itself afresh,
And breaks into the crocus-purple hour   50
That saw thee vanish.

              Child, when thou wert gone,
I envied human wives, and nestled birds,
Yea, the cubb'd lioness; went in search of thee
Thro' many a palace, many a cot, and gave
Thy breast to ailing infants in the night,   55
And set the mother waking in amaze
To find her sick one whole; and forth again
Among the wail of midnight winds, and cried,
'Where is my loved one?   Wherefore do ye wail?'
And out from all the night an answer shrill'd,   60
'We know not, and we know not why we wail.'
I climb'd on all the cliffs of all the seas,
And ask'd the waves that moan about the world,
'Where? do ye make your moaning for my child?'
And round from all the world the voices came,   65
'We know not, and we know not why we moan.'
'Where?' and I stared from every eagle-peak,
I thridded the black heart of all the woods,
I peer'd thro' tomb and cave, and in the storms
Of Autumn swept across the city, and heard   70
The murmur of their temples chanting me,
Me, me, the desolate Mother! 'Where?' — and turn'd,
And fled by many a waste, forlorn of man,
And griev'd for man thro' all my grief for thee, —
The jungle rooted in his shatter'd hearth,   75
The serpent coil'd about his broken shaft,
The scorpion crawling over naked skulls; —
I saw the tiger in the ruin'd fane
Spring from his fallen God, but trace of thee
I saw not; and far on, and, following out   80
A league of labyrinthine darkness, came
On three gray heads beneath a gleaming rift.

---

82. *three gray heads,* the Fates.

'Where?' and I heard one voice from all the three,
'We know not, for we spin the lives of men,
And not of Gods, and know not why we spin!   85
There is a Fate beyond us.'   Nothing knew.

   Last, as the likeness of a dying man,
Without his knowledge, from him flits to warn
A far-off friendship that he comes no more,
So he, the God of dreams, who heard my cry,   90
Drew from thyself the likeness of thyself
Without thy knowledge, and thy shadow past
Before me, crying, 'The Bright one in the highest
Is brother of the Dark one in the lowest,
And Bright and Dark have sworn that I, the child   95
Of thee, the great Earth-Mother, thee, the Power
That lifts her buried life from gloom to bloom,
Should be for ever and for evermore
The Bride of Darkness.'

                 So the Shadow wail'd.
Then I, Earth-Goddess, cursed the Gods of Heaven.   100
I would not mingle with their feasts; to me
Their nectar smack'd of hemlock on the lips,
Their rich ambrosia tasted aconite.
The man, that only lives and loves an hour,
Seem'd nobler than their hard Eternities.   105
My quick tears kill'd the flower, my ravings hush'd
The bird, and lost in utter grief I fail'd
To send my life thro' olive-yard and vine
And golden grain, my gift to helpless man.
Rain-rotten died the wheat, the barley-spears   110
Were hollow-husk'd, the leaf fell, and the sun,
Pale at my grief, drew down before his time
Sickening, and Ætna kept her winter snow.
   Then He, the brother of this Darkness, He
Who still is highest, glancing from his height   115

----

114. *He,* Zeus, the brother of Dis.

On earth a fruitless fallow, when he miss'd
The wonted steam of sacrifice, the praise
And prayer of men, decreed that thou should'st dwell
For nine white moons of each whole year with me,
Three dark ones in the shadow with thy King.   120

    Once more the reaper in the gleam of dawn
Will see me by the landmark far away,
Blessing his field, or seated in the dusk
Of even, by the lonely threshing-floor,
Rejoicing in the harvest and the grange.   125
    Yet I, Earth-Goddess, am but ill-content
With them, who still are highest. Those gray heads,
What meant they by their 'Fate beyond the Fates'
But younger kindlier Gods to bear us down,
As we bore down the Gods before us? Gods,   130
To quench, not hurl the thunderbolt, to stay,
Not spread the plague, the famine; Gods indeed,
To send the noon into the night and break
The sunless halls of Hades into Heaven?
Till thy dark lord accept and love the Sun,   135
And all the Shadow die into the Light,
When thou shalt dwell the whole bright year with me,
And souls of men, who grew beyond their race,
And made themselves as Gods against the fear
Of Death and Hell; and thou that hast from men,   140
As Queen of Death, that worship which is Fear,
Henceforth, as having risen from out the dead,
Shalt ever send thy life along with mine
From buried grain thro' springing blade, and bless
Their garner'd Autumn also, reap with me,   145
Earth-mother, in the harvest hymns of Earth

---

119. In some versions of the myth Persephone is compelled to pass
half the year in Hades.

126–136. Tennyson was wont to point to this passage as an example
of the modern "frame" into which he put old legends. See *Memoir*,
ii, 364.

129. The theme of Keats's *Hyperion*. In Tennyson's line there is an
echo of *Odyssey*, xi, 538.

The worship which is Love, and see no more
The Stone, the Wheel, the dimly-glimmering lawns
Of that Elysium, all the hateful fires
Of torment, and the shadowy warrior glide   150
Along the silent field of Asphodel.

'FRATER AVE ATQUE VALE'[1]

Row us out from Desenzano, to your Sirmione row!
So they row'd, and there we landed — 'O venusta Sirmio!'
There to me thro' all the groves of olive in the summer glow,
There beneath the Roman ruin where the purple flowers grow,
Came that 'Ave atque Vale' of the Poet's hopeless woe,   5
Tenderest of Roman poets nineteen hundred years ago,
'Frater Ave atque Vale,' — as we wander'd to and fro,
Gazing at the Lydian laughter of the Garda Lake below,
Sweet Catullus's all-but-island, olive-silvery Sirmio!

---

148. The stone of Sisyphus; the wheel of Ixion.

[1] In the summer of 1880 Tennyson visited northern Italy with his son.
From Desenzano on the southern shore of Lake Garda they were rowed
to Sirmione (the Sirmio of antiquity) near the northern end of the narrow
peninsula which juts more than two miles into the lake. Here is the
so-called "Grotto of Catullus" and the remains of a late Roman building which tradition holds to have been the country-house of the poet.
Here Tennyson composed his beautiful tribute. It was published in *The
Nineteenth Century*, March, 1883, and reprinted in *Tiresias and Other
Poems*, 1885. Tennyson had said many years earlier to Thackeray, "I
love Catullus for his perfection in form and for his tenderness: he is the
tenderest of Roman poets" (*Memoir*, i, 266).

2. "O lovely Sirmio!" Catullus, xxxi, 12. This is the poem in which
Catullus expressed his delight in his home-coming after a year's absence
in Bithynia.

4. Amid the ruins near Sirmione Tennyson noticed a deep purple iris
growing (*Works*, Eversley edition, iv, 577).

5. "Hail and farewell!" the invocation offered by Catullus at the tomb
of his brother (ci).

8. The Etruscans, who were thought to be of Lydian origin, settled
near Lake Garda. Hence Catullus: "O Lydiae lacus undae, ridete" —
"Laugh, O lake of Lydian waves" (xxxi, 13).

9. *all-but-island*, peninsula; Catullus: "paene insularum Sirmio"
(xxxi, 1).

TO VIRGIL

WRITTEN AT THE REQUEST OF THE MANTUANS FOR THE
NINETEENTH CENTENARY OF VIRGIL'S DEATH [1]

I

ROMAN VIRGIL, thou that singest Ilion's lofty temples robed
   in fire,
Ilion falling, Rome arising, wars, and filial faith, and Dido's
   pyre;

II

Landscape-lover, lord of language more than he that sang the
   Works and Days,
All the chosen coin of fancy flashing out from many a golden
   phrase;

III

Thou that singest wheat and woodland, tilth and vineyard, hive
   and horse and herd;   5
All the charm of all the Muses often flowering in a lonely word;

IV

Poet of the happy Tityrus piping underneath his beechen
   bowers;
Poet of the poet-satyr whom the laughing shepherd bound
   with flowers;

V

Chanter of the Pollio, glorying in the blissful years again to be,
Summers of the snakeless meadow, unlaborious earth and
   oarless sea;   10

---

[1] Mantua, the city near which Virgil was born, observed the nineteenth
centenary of his death on September 21, 1882. Tennyson's tribute was
published in *The Nineteenth Century*, September, 1882, and reprinted in
Tiresias and Other Poems, 1885.

1–2. The chief themes of the *Aeneid*.

3. Hesiod, the author of the *Works and Days*.

5. Virgil sings of wheat and cultivation (tilth) in the first book of
the *Georgics*, of woodland and vineyard in the second, of horse and herd
in the third, and of the hive in the fourth.

7. See the opening lines of Virgil's first *Eclogue*.

8. *Eclogues*, vi, 13 f.

9–10. *Eclogues*, iv (the Pollio).

VI

Thou that seëst Universal Nature moved by Universal Mind;
Thou majestic in thy sadness at the doubtful doom of human
    kind;

VII

Light among the vanish'd ages; star that gildest yet this
    phantom shore;
Golden branch amid the shadows, kings and realms that pass
    to rise no more;

VIII

Now thy Forum roars no longer, fallen every purple Cæsar's
    dome —   15
Tho' thine ocean-roll of rhythm sound for ever of Imperial
    Rome —

IX

Now the Rome of slaves hath perish'd, and the Rome of free-
    men holds her place,
I, from out the Northern Island sunder'd once from all the
    human race,

X

I salute thee, Mantovano, I that loved thee since my day began,
Wielder of the stateliest measure ever moulded by the lips of
    man.   20

---

11. Compare *Aeneid*, vi, 727.

12. The allusion is especially to the famous line "Sunt lacrimae rerum
et mentem mortalia tangunt" (Aeneid, i, 462).

14. The poet who opens to us the world of ancient Rome is likened
to the "golden bough" plucked by Aeneas which gave him entrance to
the world of shades (*Aeneid*, vi, 208).

15. *purple Cæsar*. Compare Horace, *Odes*, i, 35, 12: "purpurei
tyranni."

17. *the Rome of freemen*, an allusion to the lately accomplished libera-
tion and unification of Italy (1871).

18. Tennyson translates Virgil's description of Britain: "penitus toto
divisos orbe Britannos" (*Eclogue*, i, 67).

19. *Mantovano*, Mantuan.

MILTON

ALCAICS [1]

O MIGHTY-MOUTH'D inventor of harmonies,
O skill'd to sing of Time or Eternity,
   God-gifted organ-voice of England,
     Milton, a name to resound for ages;
Whose Titan angels, Gabriel, Abdiel,   5
Starr'd from Jehovah's gorgeous armouries,
   Tower, as the deep-domed empyrëan
     Rings to the roar of an angel onset —
Me rather all that bowery loneliness,
The brooks of Eden mazily murmuring,   10
   And bloom profuse and cedar arches
     Charm, as a wanderer out in ocean,
Where some refulgent sunset of India
Streams o'er a rich ambrosial ocean isle,
   And crimson-hued the stately palm-woods   15
     Whisper in odorous heights of even.

---

[1] This is one of three experiments in classical quantitative metres published in the *Cornhill Magazine,* December, 1863. It was reprinted in *Enoch Arden, etc.,* 1864. Tennyson's intention was not to imitate the Alcaics of Horace but the "freer and lighter movement" of the Greek Alcaic (*Memoir,* ii, 11).

POEMS OF MEDIEVAL SUBJECTS

ST. AGNES' EVE [1]

DEEP on the convent-roof the snows
　　Are sparkling to the moon:
My breath to heaven like vapour goes:
　　May my soul follow soon!
The shadows of the convent-towers　　　　5
　　Slant down the snowy sward,
Still creeping with the creeping hours
　　That lead me to my Lord:
Make Thou my spirit pure and clear
　　As are the frosty skies,　　　　　　10
Or this first snowdrop of the year
　　That in my bosom lies.

As these white robes are soil'd and dark,
　　To yonder shining ground;
As this pale taper's earthly spark,　　　15
　　To yonder argent round;

---

[1] The precise date of composition is unknown, but this poem was written by 1834 when Tennyson mentions it in a letter to James Spedding (*Memoir*, i, 142). With the title "St. Agnes" it was published in *The Keepsake* (a literary annual) in 1837; reprinted in *Poems*, 1842. In the collected edition of 1857 the title was changed to "St. Agnes' Eve." The speaker is not the virgin-martyr of Diocletian's persecution but a medieval nun. According to a famous superstition, it was thought possible for a girl, on the eve of St. Agnes's Day (January 21), to obtain by divination a vision of her future husband. Upon this belief Keats founded his "Eve of St. Agnes." Tennyson, with Keats's poem in mind, substitutes for its sensuous amorousness a mystical devotion which enables the nun to have sight of the Heavenly Bridegroom. He probably remembered that the Gospel for St. Agnes's Day is Matthew, xxvi, 1–13, the parable of the wise and foolish virgins who await the coming of the Bridegroom.

So shows my soul before the Lamb,
  My spirit before Thee;
So in mine earthly house I am,
  To that I hope to be.   20
Break up the heavens, O Lord! and far,
  Thro' all yon starlight keen,
Draw me, thy bride, a glittering star,
  In raiment white and clean.

He lifts me to the golden doors;   25
  The flashes come and go;
All heaven bursts her starry floors,
  And strows her lights below,
And deepens on and up! the gates
  Roll back, and far within   30
For me the Heavenly Bridegroom waits,
  To make me pure of sin.
The sabbaths of Eternity,
  One sabbath deep and wide —
A light upon the shining sea —   35
  The Bridegroom with his bride!

SIR GALAHAD [1]

MY GOOD blade carves the casques of men,
  My tough lance thrusteth sure,
My strength is as the strength of ten,
  Because my heart is pure.
The shattering trumpet shrilleth high,   5
  The hard brands shiver on the steel,
The splinter'd spear-shafts crack and fly,
  The horse and rider reel:
They reel, they roll in clanging lists,
  And when the tide of combat stands,   10
Perfume and flowers fall in showers,
  That lightly rain from ladies' hands.

---

[1] The precise date of composition is unknown, but the poem was new
to Spedding in September, 1834 (*Memoir*, i, 139).   It was first published
in *Poems*, 1842. Tennyson told Spedding that Galahad "was intended
for something of a male counterpart to St. Agnes" (*ibid.*, i, 142).

How sweet are looks that ladies bend
   On whom their favours fall!
For them I battle till the end,   15
   To save from shame and thrall:
But all my heart is drawn above,
   My knees are bow'd in crypt and shrine:
I never felt the kiss of love,
   Nor maiden's hand in mine.   20
More bounteous aspects on me beam,
   Me mightier transports move and thrill;
So keep I fair thro' faith and prayer
   A virgin heart in work and will.

When down the stormy crescent goes,   25
   A light before me swims,
Between dark stems the forest glows,
   I hear a noise of hymns:
Then by some secret shrine I ride;
   I hear a voice but none are there;   30
The stalls are void, the doors are wide,
   The tapers burning fair.
Fair gleams the snowy altar-cloth,
   The silver vessels sparkle clean,
The shrill bell rings, the censer swings,   35
   And solemn chaunts resound between.

Sometimes on lonely mountain-meres
   I find a magic bark;
I leap on board: no helmsman steers:
   I float till all is dark.   40
A gentle sound, an awful light!
   Three angels bear the holy Grail:
With folded feet, in stoles of white,
   On sleeping wings they sail.
Ah, blessed vision! blood of God!   45
   My spirit beats her mortal bars,
As down dark tides the glory slides,
   And star-like mingles with the stars.

---

38. The magic bark is one of various details from Malory's *Le Morte
Darthur* (xvi, 17, etc.).

When on my goodly charger borne
    Thro' dreaming towns I go,   50
The cock crows ere the Christmas morn,
    The streets are dumb with snow.
The tempest crackles on the leads,
    And, ringing, springs from brand and mail;
But o'er the dark a glory spreads,   55
    And gilds the driving hail.
I leave the plain, I climb the height;
    No branchy thicket shelter yields;
But blessed forms in whistling storms
    Fly o'er waste fens and windy fields.   60

A maiden knight — to me is given
    Such hope, I know not fear;
I yearn to breathe the airs of heaven
    That often meet me here.
I muse on joy that will not cease,   65
    Pure spaces clothed in living beams,
Pure lilies of eternal peace,
    Whose odours haunt my dreams;
And, stricken by an angel's hand,
    This mortal armour that I wear,   70
This weight and size, this heart and eyes,
    Are touch'd, are turn'd to finest air.

The clouds are broken in the sky,
    And thro' the mountain-walls
A rolling organ-harmony   75
    Swells up, and shakes and falls.
Then move the trees, the copses nod,
    Wings flutter, voices hover clear:
'O just and faithful knight of God!
    Ride on! the prize is near.'   80
So pass I hostel, hall, and grange;
    By bridge and ford, by park and pale,
All-arm'd I ride, whate'er betide,
    Until I find the holy Grail.

----

51. For the superstition that the cock crows all night on Christmas
Eve compare *Hamlet*, I, i, 158 f.

SIR LAUNCELOT AND QUEEN GUINEVERE

A FRAGMENT [1]

LIKE souls that balance joy and pain,
With tears and smiles from heaven again
The maiden Spring upon the plain
Came in a sun-lit fall of rain.
    In crystal vapour everywhere   5
Blue isles of heaven laugh'd between,
And far, in forest-deeps unseen,
The topmost elm-tree gather'd green
    From draughts of balmy air.

Sometimes the linnet piped his song: 10
Sometimes the throstle whistled strong:
Sometimes the sparhawk, wheel'd along,
Hush'd all the groves from fear of wrong:
    By grassy capes with fuller sound
In curves the yellowing river ran,   15
And drooping chestnut-buds began
To spread into the perfect fan,
    Above the teeming ground.

Then, in the boyhood of the year,
Sir Launcelot and Queen Guinevere   20
Rode thro' the coverts of the deer,
With blissful treble ringing clear.
    She seem'd a part of joyous Spring
A gown of grass-green silk she wore,
Buckled with golden clasps before;   25
A light-green tuft of plumes she bore
    Closed in a golden ring.

---

[1] Though not published till 1842, this poem was "partly if not wholly written in 1830" (*Memoir*, ii, 122). Edward FitzGerald preserved an eight-line lyric ("Life of the Life within my blood") which was among some verses of the poem "handed about at Cambridge" among Tennyson's contemporaries (*ibid.*, i, 59). One's guess is that the Fragment is of slightly earlier date than "The Lady of Shalott" which is obviously a companion piece. — In Malory (*Le Morte Darthur*, iii, 1) Merlin, not Lancelot, is the envoy sent to escort Guinevere to her wedding to King Arthur. Compare "The Coming of Arthur," ll. 446 f. and "Guinevere," ll. 377 f. The incident is referred to elsewhere in the *Idylls of the King*.

Now on some twisted ivy-net,
Now by some tinkling rivulet,
In mosses mixt with violet   30
Her cream-white mule his pastern set:
    And fleeter now she skimm'd the plains
Than she whose elfin prancer springs
By night to eery warblings,
When all the glimmering moorland rings   35
    With jingling bridle-reins.

As fast she fled thro' sun and shade,
The happy winds upon her play'd,
Blowing the ringlet from the braid:
She look'd so lovely, as she sway'd   40
    The rein with dainty finger-tips,
A man had given all other bliss,
And all his worldly worth for this,
To waste his whole heart in one kiss
    Upon her perfect lips.   45

THE LADY OF SHALOTT [1]

PART I

ON EITHER side the river lie
Long fields of barley and of rye,
That clothe the wold and meet the sky;
And thro' the field the road runs by
    To many-tower'd Camelot;   5
And up and down the people go,
Gazing where the lilies blow
Round an island there below,
    The island of Shalott.

---

[1] Published in *Poems*, 1832; much revised before reprinting in 1842. For variant readings see *Works*, Cambridge edition, pp. 796 f. The source, according to Palgrave, was "an Italian romance upon the Donna di Scalotta" — undoubtedly novella lxxxi of the *Cento Novelle Antiche* which Tennyson may have known in Thomas Roscoe's translation (*Italian Novelists*, 1825, i, 45 f.) and about which he could have read in Dunlop's *History of Fiction*, 1814. Several details in the poem seem to be drawn directly from the Italian story. Compare "Lancelot and Elaine" in the *Idylls of the King*.

Willows whiten, aspens quiver,   10
Little breezes dusk and shiver
Thro' the wave that runs for ever
By the island in the river
     Flowing down to Camelot.
Four gray walls, and four gray towers,   15
Overlook a space of flowers,
And the silent isle imbowers
     The Lady of Shalott.

By the margin, willow-veil'd
Slide the heavy barges trail'd   20
By slow horses; and unhail'd
The shallop flitteth silken-sail'd
     Skimming down to Camelot:
But who hath seen her wave her hand?
Or at the casement seen her stand?   25
Or is she known in all the land,
     The Lady of Shalott?

Only reapers, reaping early
In among the bearded barley,
Hear a song that echoes cheerly   30
From the river winding clearly,
     Down to tower'd Camelot:
And by the moon the reaper weary,
Piling sheaves in uplands airy,
Listening, whispers ' 'Tis the fairy   35
     Lady of Shalott.'

PART II

There she weaves by night and day
A magic web with colours gay.
She has heard a whisper say,
A curse is on her if she stay   40
     To look down to Camelot.
She knows not what the curse may be,
And so she weaveth steadily,
And little other care hath she,
     The Lady of Shalott.   45

And moving thro' a mirror clear
That hangs before her all the year,
Shadows of the world appear.
There she sees the highway near
        Winding down to Camelot: 50
There the river eddy whirls,
And there the surly village-churls,
And the red cloaks of market girls,
        Pass onward from Shalott.

Sometimes a troop of damsels glad,   55
An abbot on an ambling pad,
Sometimes a curly shepherd-lad,
Or long-hair'd page in crimson clad,
        Goes by to tower'd Camelot:
And sometimes thro' the mirror blue   60
The knights come riding two and two:
She hath no loyal knight and true,
        The Lady of Shalott.

But in her web she still delights
To weave the mirror's magic sights,   65
For often thro' the silent nights
A funeral, with plumes and lights
        And music, went to Camelot:
Or when the moon was overhead,
Came two young lovers lately wed;   70
'I am half sick of shadows,' said
        The Lady of Shalott.

PART III

A bow-shot from her bower-eaves,
He rode between the barley-sheaves,
The sun came dazzling thro' the leaves,   75
And flamed upon the brazen greaves
        Of bold Sir Lancelot.

69–71. According to the *Memoir* (i, 116), these lines are the "key" to
this tale of magic "symbolism." Tennyson gave to Canon Ainger (*ibid.*,
i, 117) the following interpretation: "The new-born love for something,
for some one in the wide world from which she has been so long secluded,
takes her out of the region of shadows into that of realities."

A red-cross knight for ever kneel'd
To a lady in his shield,
That sparkled on the yellow field,   80
    Beside remote Shalott.

The gemmy bridle glitter'd free,
Like to some branch of stars we see
Hung in the golden Galaxy.
The bridle bells rang merrily   85
    As he rode down to Camelot:
And from his blazon'd baldric slung
A mighty silver bugle hung,
And as he rode his armour rung,
    Beside remote Shalott.   90

All in the blue unclouded weather
Thick-jewell'd shone the saddle-leather,
The helmet and the helmet-feather
Burn'd like one burning flame together,
    As he rode down to Camelot.   95
As often thro' the purple night,
Below the starry clusters bright,
Some bearded meteor, trailing light,
    Moves over still Shalott.

His broad clear brow in sunlight glow'd;   100
On burnish'd hooves his war-horse trode;
From underneath his helmet flow'd
His coal-black curls as on he rode,
    As he rode down to Camelot.
From the bank and from the river   105
He flash'd into the crystal mirror,
'Tirra lirra,' by the river
    Sang Sir Lancelot.

She left the web, she left the loom,
She made three paces thro' the room,   110
She saw the water-lily bloom,
She saw the helmet and the plume,
    She look'd down to Camelot.

---

78. *A red-cross knight.* An echo of *The Faerie Queene;* the old romances give no warrant for such a description of Lancelot.

Out flew the web and floated wide;
The mirror crack'd from side to side;   115
'The curse is come upon me,' cried
  The Lady of Shalott.

    PART IV

In the stormy east-wind straining,
The pale yellow woods were waning,
The broad stream in his banks complaining,   120
Heavily the low sky raining
  Over tower'd Camelot;
Down she came and found a boat
Beneath a willow left afloat,
And round about the prow she wrote   125
  The Lady of Shalott.

And down the river's dim expanse
Like some bold seër in a trance,
Seeing all his own mischance —
With a glassy countenance   130
  Did she look to Camelot.
And at the closing of the day
She loosed the chain, and down she lay;
The broad stream bore her far away,
  The Lady of Shalott.   135

Lying, robed in snowy white
That loosely flew to left and right —
The leaves upon her falling light —
Thro' the noises of the night
  She floated down to Camelot: 140
And as the boat-head wound along
The willowy hills and fields among,
They heard her singing her last song,
  The Lady of Shalott.

Heard a carol, mournful, holy,   145
Chanted loudly, chanted lowly,
Till her blood was frozen slowly,
And her eyes were darken'd wholly,
  Turn'd to tower'd Camelot.
For ere she reach'd upon the tide   150

The first house by the water-side,
Singing in her song she died,
    The Lady of Shalott.

Under tower and balcony,
By garden-wall and gallery,   155
A gleaming shape she floated by,
Dead-pale between the houses high,
    Silent into Camelot.
Out upon the wharfs they came,
Knight and burgher, lord and dame,   160
And round the prow they read her name,
    The Lady of Shalott.

Who is this? and what is here?
And in the lighted palace near
Died the sound of royal cheer;   165
And they cross'd themselves for fear,
    All the knights at Camelot:
But Lancelot mused a little space;
He said, 'She has a lovely face;
God in his mercy lend her grace,   170
    The Lady of Shalott.'

---

163 f. In 1832 this final stanza was as follows:

    They crossed themselves, their stars they blest,
    Knight, minstrel, abbot, squire and guest.
    There lay a parchment on her breast,
    That puzzled more than all the rest,
        The wellfed wits at Camelot.
    'The web was woven curiously,
    The charm is broken utterly,
    Draw near and fear not — this is I,
        The Lady of Shalott.'

SELECTIONS FROM THE

IDYLLS OF THE KING

'Flos Regum Arthurus.' — JOSEPH OF EXETER.

Editor's Note. — Much has been written about the "growth" of the *Idylls*. The facts may be briefly summarized. The first poetic fruits of the love of Arthurian story which Tennyson had from boyhood are the "Sir Launcelot and Queen Guinevere" and "The Lady of Shalott." Some time before 1840 Tennyson drew up the rough draft of a scenario of a "musical masque" on portions of the legend (See *Memoir*, ii, 124 f.). "Morte d'Arthur," set in a frame with the more general title "The Epic," was begun in 1834, published in 1842, and ultimately, revised, expanded, and with the frame removed, took its place among the *Idylls* as "The Passing of Arthur." The final shape of the poem was determined about 1855. The first instalment to appear consisted of four narratives: "Enid" (afterwards divided into "The Marriage of Geraint" and "Geraint and Enid"); "Vivien" (afterwards called "Merlin and Vivien"); "Elaine" (afterwards called "Lancelot and Elaine"); and "Guinevere." In 1869 (dated 1870) appeared *The Holy Grail and Other Poems* which, in addition to the title-poem, contained "The Coming of Arthur," "Pelleas and Ettarre," and the revised "Passing of Arthur." "The Last Tournament" was privately printed in 1871, published in *The Contemporary Review*, December, 1871, and reprinted with another *Idyll* in the volume entitled *Gareth and Lynette* in 1872. The series, which was now thought to be complete, was for the first time arranged in the correct order in the Library edition of Tennyson's *Works*, 1872–3, volumes v and vi. However, in 1885 "Balin and Balan" was published in *Tiresias and Other Poems*. It was first incorporated with the other *Idylls* in the collected edition of 1888.

DEDICATION [1]

THESE to His Memory — since he held them dear,
Perchance as finding there unconsciously
Some image of himself — I dedicate,
I dedicate, I consecrate with tears —
These Idylls.   5

        And indeed He seems to me
Scarce other than my king's ideal knight,
'Who reverenced his conscience as his king;
Whose glory was, redressing human wrong;
Who spake no slander, no, nor listen'd to it;
Who loved one only and who clave to her —'   10
Her — over all whose realms to their last isle,
Commingled with the gloom of imminent war,
The shadow of His loss drew like eclipse,
Darkening the world. We have lost him: he is gone:
We know him now: all narrow jealousies   15
Are silent; and we see him as he moved,
How modest, kindly, all-accomplish'd, wise,
With what sublime repression of himself,
And in what limits, and how tenderly;
Not swaying to this faction or to that;   20
Not making his high place the lawless perch
Of wing'd ambitions, nor a vantage-ground
For pleasure; but thro' all this tract of years
Wearing the white flower of a blameless life,
Before a thousand peering littlenesses,   25
In that fierce light which beats upon a throne,
And blackens every blot: for where is he,
Who dares foreshadow for an only son
A lovelier life, a more unstain'd than his?
Or how should England dreaming of *his* sons   30
Hope more for these than some inheritance
Of such a life, a heart, a mind as thine,
Thou noble Father of her Kings to be,

---

[1] To the memory of the Prince Consort. The Dedication was added in
the edition of 1862, shortly after the death of Prince Albert.

7 f. See "Guinevere," ll. 465 f.

12. An allusion to the *Trent* affair (1861).

Laborious for her people and her poor —
Voice in the rich dawn of an ampler day —   35
Far-sighted summoner of War and Waste
To fruitful strifes and rivalries of peace —
Sweet nature gilded by the gracious gleam
Of letters, dear to Science, dear to Art,
Dear to thy land and ours, a Prince indeed,   40
Beyond all titles, and a household name,
Hereafter, thro' all times, Albert the Good.

Break not, O woman's-heart, but still endure;
Break not, for thou art Royal, but endure,
Remembering all the beauty of that star   45
Which shone so close beside Thee that ye made
One light together, but has past and leaves
The Crown a lonely splendour.

                                        May all love,
His love, unseen but felt, o'ershadow Thee,
The love of all Thy sons encompass Thee,   50
The love of all Thy daughters cherish Thee,
The love of all Thy people comfort Thee,
Till God's love set Thee at his side again!

THE COMING OF ARTHUR[1]

LEODOGRAN, the King of Cameliard,
Had one fair daughter, and none other child;
And she was fairest of all flesh on earth,
Guinevere, and in her his one delight.

For many a petty king ere Arthur came   5
Ruled in this isle, and ever waging war
Each upon other, wasted all the land;
And still from time to time the heathen host
Swarm'd overseas, and harried what was left.

35-6. The Prince Consort had a large share in the organization of the International Exhibition of 1851 and was engaged upon plans for the similar Exhibition of 1862 at the time of his death.

40. *thy land*, Saxe-Coburg Gotha.

[1] The matter of this first *Idyll* is drawn from Malory, especially Book i;

And so there grew great tracts of wilderness,   10
Wherein the beast was ever more and more,
But man was less and less, till Arthur came.
For first Aurelius lived and fought and died,
And after him King Uther fought and died,
But either fail'd to make the kingdom one.   15
And after these King Arthur for a space,
And thro' the puissance of his Table Round,
Drew all their petty princedoms under him,
Their king and head, and made a realm, and reign'd.

And thus the land of Cameliard was waste,   20
Thick with wet woods, and many a beast therein,
And none or few to scare or chase the beast;
So that wild dog, and wolf and boar and bear
Came night and day, and rooted in the fields,
And wallow'd in the gardens of the King.   25
And ever and anon the wolf would steal
The children and devour, but now and then,
Her own brood lost or dead, lent her fierce teat
To human sucklings; and the children, housed
In her foul den, there at their meat would growl,   30
And mock their foster-mother on four feet,
Till, straighten'd, they grew up to wolf-like men,
Worse than the wolves.   And King Leodogran
Groan'd for the Roman legions here again,
And Cæsar's eagle: then his brother king,   35
Urien, assail'd him: last a heathen horde,
Reddening the sun with smoke and earth with blood,
And on the spike that split the mother's heart
Spitting the child, brake on him, till, amazed,
He knew not whither he should turn for aid.   40

___

from Geoffrey of Monmouth; and from the later romances; with additions
and modifications of Tennyson's own. Limitations of space forbid the
discussion of Tennyson's sources and *a fortiori* of the Arthurian problem.
For the latest view of the historicity of Arthur see R. G. Collingwood and
J. N. L. Myres, *Roman Britain and the English Settlements* (*Oxford History
of England,* volume i), second edition, 1937, pp. 320 f.

13. *Aurelius,* Ambrosius Aurelianus, on whom see *ibid.,* especially
pp. 381 f.

26 f. Compare the story of Romulus and Remus.

But — for he heard of Arthur newly crown'd,
Tho' not without an uproar made by those
Who cried, 'He is not Uther's son' — the King
Sent to him, saying, 'Arise, and help us thou!
For here between the man and beast we die.'   45

And Arthur yet had done no deed of arms,
But heard the call, and came: and Guinevere
Stood by the castle walls to watch him pass;
But since he neither wore on helm or shield
The golden symbol of his kinglihood,   50
But rode a simple knight among his knights,
And many of these in richer arms than he,
She saw him not, or mark'd not, if she saw,
One among many, tho' his face was bare.
But Arthur, looking downward as he past,   55
Felt the light of her eyes into his life
Smite on the sudden, yet rode on, and pitch'd
His tents beside the forest. Then he drave
The heathen; after, slew the beast, and fell'd
The forest, letting in the sun, and made   60
Broad pathways for the hunter and the knight
And so return'd.

          For while he linger'd there,
A doubt that ever smoulder'd in the hearts
Of those great Lords and Barons of his realm
Flash'd forth and into war: for most of these,   65
Colleaguing with a score of petty kings,
Made head against him, crying, 'Who is he
That he should rule us? who hath proven him
King Uther's son? for lo! we look at him,
And find nor face nor bearing, limbs nor voice,   70
Are like to those of Uther whom we knew.
This is the son of Gorloïs, not the King;
This is the son of Anton, not the King.'

And Arthur, passing thence to battle, felt
Travail, and throes and agonies of the life,   75
Desiring to be join'd with Guinevere;
And thinking as he rode, 'Her father said

That there between the man and beast they die.
Shall I not lift her from this land of beasts
Up to my throne, and side by side with me?   80
What happiness to reign a lonely king,
Vext — O ye stars that shudder over me,
O earth that soundest hollow under me,
Vext with waste dreams? for saving I be join'd
To her that is the fairest under heaven,   85
I seem as nothing in the mighty world,
And cannot will my will, nor work my work
Wholly, nor make myself in mine own realm
Victor and lord.   But were I join'd with her,
Then might we live together as one life,   90
And reigning with one will in everything
Have power on this dark land to lighten it,
And power on this dead world to make it live.'

     Thereafter — as he speaks who tells the tale —
When Arthur reach'd a field-of-battle bright   95
With pitch'd pavilions of his foe, the world
Was all so clear about him, that he saw
The smallest rock far on the faintest hill,
And even in high day the morning star.
So when the King had set his banner broad,   100
At once from either side, with trumpet-blast,
And shouts, and clarions shrilling unto blood,
The long-lanced battle let their horses run.
And now the Barons and the kings prevail'd,
And now the King, as here and there that war   105
Went swaying; but the Powers who walk the world
Made lightnings and great thunders over him,
And dazed all eyes, till Arthur by main might,
And mightier of his hands with every blow,
And leading all his knighthood threw the kings   110
Carádos, Urien, Cradlemont of Wales,
Claudius, and Clariance of Northumberland,
The King Brandagoras of Latangor,
With Anguisant of Erin, Morganore,
And Lot of Orkney.   Then, before a voice   115

94–133. This passage is not in the original version of 1869.

As dreadful as the shout of one who sees
To one who sins, and deems himself alone
And all the world asleep, they swerved and brake
Flying, and Arthur call'd to stay the brands
That hack'd among the flyers, 'Ho! they yield!'   120
So like a painted battle the war stood
Silenced, the living quiet as the dead,
And in the heart of Arthur joy was lord.
He laugh'd upon his warrior whom he loved
And honour'd most. 'Thou dost not doubt me King,   125
So well thine arm hath wrought for me to-day.'
'Sir and my liege,' he cried, 'the fire of God
Descends upon thee in the battle-field:
I know thee for my King!' Whereat the two,
For each had warded either in the fight,   130
Sware on the field of death a deathless love.
And Arthur said, 'Man's word is God in man:
Let chance what will, I trust thee to the death.'

Then quickly from the foughten field he sent
Ulfius, and Brastias, and Bedivere,   135
His new-made knights, to King Leodogran,
Saying, 'If I in aught have served thee well,
Give me thy daughter Guinevere to wife.'

Whom when he heard, Leodogran in heart
Debating — 'How should I that am a king,   140
However much he holp me at my need,
Give me my one daughter saving to a king,
And a king's son?' — lifted his voice, and called
A hoary man, his chamberlain, to whom
He trusted all things, and of him required   145
His counsel: 'Knowest thou aught of Arthur's birth?'

Then spake the hoary chamberlain and said,
'Sir King, there be but two old men that know:
And each is twice as old as I; and one
Is Merlin, the wise man that ever served   150
King Uther thro' his magic art; and one
Is Merlin's master (so they call him) Bleys,

Who taught him magic; but the scholar ran
Before the master, and so far, that Bleys
Laid magic by, and sat him down, and wrote   155
All things and whatsoever Merlin did
In one great annal-book, where after-years
Will learn the secret of our Arthur's birth.'

   To whom the King Leodogran replied,
'O friend, had I been holpen half as well   160
By this King Arthur as by thee to-day,
Then beast and man had had their share of me:
But summon here before us yet once more
Ulfius, and Brastias, and Bedivere.'

   Then, when they came before him, the King said,   165
'I have seen the cuckoo chased by lesser fowl,
And reason in the chase: but wherefore now
Do these your lords stir up the heat of war,
Some calling Arthur born of Gorloïs,
Others of Anton?   Tell me, ye yourselves,   170
Hold ye this Arthur for King Uther's son?'

   And Ulfius and Brastias answer'd, 'Ay.'
Then Bedivere, the first of all his knights
Knighted by Arthur at his crowning, spake —
For bold in heart and act and word was he,   175
Whenever slander breathed against the King —

   'Sir, there be many rumours on this head:
For there be those who hate him in their hearts,
Call him baseborn, and since his ways are sweet,
And theirs are bestial, hold him less than man: 180
And there be those who deem him more than man,
And dream he dropt from heaven: but my belief
In all this matter — so ye care to learn —
Sir, for ye know that in King Uther's time
The prince and warrior Gorloïs, he that held   185
Tintagil castle by the Cornish sea,
Was wedded with a winsome wife, Ygerne:
And daughters had she borne him, — one whereof,
Lot's wife, the Queen of Orkney, Bellicent,

Hath ever like a loyal sister cleaved   190
To Arthur, — but a son she had not borne.
And Uther cast upon her eyes of love:
But she, a stainless wife to Gorloïs,
So loathed the bright dishonour of his love,
That Gorloïs and King Uther went to war: 195
And overthrown was Gorloïs and slain.
Then Uther in his wrath and heat besieged
Ygerne within Tintagil, where her men,
Seeing the mighty swarm about their walls,
Left her and fled, and Uther enter'd in,   200
And there was none to call to but himself.
So, compass'd by the power of the King,
Enforced she was to wed him in her tears,
And with a shameful swiftness: afterward,
Not many moons, King Uther died himself,   205
Moaning and wailing for an heir to rule
After him, lest the realm should go to wrack.
And that same night, the night of the new year,
By reason of the bitterness and grief
That vext his mother, all before his time   210
Was Arthur born, and all as soon as born
Deliver'd at a secret postern-gate
To Merlin, to be holden far apart
Until his hour should come; because the lords
Of that fierce day were as the lords of this,   215
Wild beasts, and surely would have torn the child
Piecemeal among them, had they known; for each
But sought to rule for his own self and hand,
And many hated Uther for the sake
Of Gorloïs. Wherefore Merlin took the child,   220
And gave him to Sir Anton, an old knight
And ancient friend of Uther; and his wife
Nursed the young prince, and rear'd him with her own;
And no man knew. And ever since the lords
Have foughten like wild beasts among themselves,   225
So that the realm has gone to wrack: but now,
This year, when Merlin (for his hour had come)
Brought Arthur forth, and set him in the hall,
Proclaiming, "Here is Uther's heir, your king,"
A hundred voices cried, "Away with him!   230

No king of ours! a son of Gorloïs he,
Or else the child of Anton, and no king,
Or else baseborn." Yet Merlin thro' his craft,
And while the people clamour'd for a king,
Had Arthur crown'd; but after, the great lords   235
Banded, and so brake out in open war.'

    Then while the King debated with himself
If Arthur were the child of shamefulness,
Or born the son of Gorloïs, after death,
Or Uther's son, and born before his time,   240
Or whether there were truth in anything
Said by these three, there came to Cameliard,
With Gawain and young Modred, her two sons,
Lot's wife, the Queen of Orkney, Bellicent;
Whom as he could, not as he would, the King   245
Made feast for, saying, as they sat at meat,

    'A doubtful throne is ice on summer seas.
Ye come from Arthur's court. Victor his men
Report him! Yea, but ye — think ye this king —
So many those that hate him, and so strong,   250
So few his knights, however brave they be —
Hath body enow to hold his foemen down?'

    'O King,' she cried, 'and I will tell thee: few,
Few, but all grave, all of one mind with him;
For I was near him when the savage yells   255
Of Uther's peerage died, and Arthur sat
Crown'd on the daïs, and his warriors cried,
"Be thou the king, and we will work thy will
Who love thee." Then the King in low deep tones,
And simple words of great authority,   260
Bound them by so strait vows to his own self,
That when they rose, knighted from kneeling, some
Were pale as at the passing of a ghost,
Some flush'd and others dazed, as one who wakes
Half-blinded at the coming of a light.   265

    'But when he spake and cheer'd his Table Round
With large, divine, and comfortable words,

Beyond my tongue to tell thee — I beheld
From eye to eye thro' all their Order flash
A momentary likeness of the King: 270
And ere it left their faces, thro' the cross
And those around it and the Crucified,
Down from the casement over Arthur, smote
Flame-colour, vert and azure in three rays,
One falling upon each of three fair queens,   275
Who stood in silence near his throne, the friends
Of Arthur, gazing on him, tall, with bright
Sweet faces, who will help him at his need.

'And there I saw mage Merlin, whose vast wit
And hundred winters are but as the hands   280
Of loyal vassals toiling for their liege.

'And near him stood the Lady of the Lake,
Who knows a subtler magic than his own —
Clothed in white samite, mystic, wonderful.
She gave the King his huge cross-hilted sword,   285
Whereby to drive the heathen out: a mist
Of incense curl'd about her, and her face
Wellnigh was hidden in the minster gloom;
But there was heard among the holy hymns
A voice as of the waters, for she dwells   290
Down in a deep; calm, whatsoever storms
May shake the world, and when the surface rolls,
Hath power to walk the waters like our Lord.

'There likewise I beheld Excalibur
Before him at his crowning borne, the sword   295
That rose from out the bosom of the lake,
And Arthur row'd across and took it — rich

---

275. Upon the commentators who interpreted the three queens as
Faith, Hope, and Charity the poet commented: "They are right, and they
are not right. They mean that and they do not. . . . They are . . .
those three Graces, but they are much more. . . . The thought within
the image is much more than any one interpretation" (*Memoir*, ii, 127).

282. Tennyson admitted that in a general way the Lady of the Lake
symbolized Religion.

With jewels, elfin Urim, on the hilt,
Bewildering heart and eye — the blade so bright
That men are blinded by it — on one side,   300
Graven in the oldest tongue of all this world,
"Take me," but turn the blade and ye shall see,
And written in the speech ye speak yourself,
"Cast me away!"   And sad was Arthur's face
Taking it, but old Merlin counsell'd him,   305
"Take thou and strike! the time to cast away
Is yet far-off."   So this great brand the king
Took, and by this will beat his foemen down.'

   Thereat Leodogran rejoiced, but thought
To sift his doubtings to the last, and ask'd,   310
Fixing full eyes of question on her face,
'The swallow and the swift are near akin,
But thou art closer to this noble prince,
Being his own dear sister;' and she said,
'Daughter of Gorloïs and Ygerne am I;'   315
'And therefore Arthur's sister?' ask'd the King.
She answer'd, 'These be secret things,' and sign'd
To those two sons to pass, and let them be.
And Gawain went, and breaking into song
Sprang out, and follow'd by his flying hair   320
Ran like a colt, and leapt at all he saw:
But Modred laid his ear beside the doors,
And there half-heard; the same that afterward
Struck for the throne, and striking found his doom.

   And then the Queen made answer, 'What know I?   325
For dark my mother was in eyes and hair,
And dark in hair and eyes am I; and dark
Was Gorloïs, yea and dark was Uther too,
Wellnigh to blackness; but this King is fair
Beyond the race of Britons and of men.   330
Moreover, always in my mind I hear
A cry from out the dawning of my life,
A mother weeping, and I hear her say,

---

298. *Urim.*   See Exodus, xxviii, 30; Numbers, xxvii, 21.

"O that ye had some brother, pretty one,
To guard thee on the rough ways of the world." '   335

   'Ay,' said the King, 'and hear ye such a cry?
But when did Arthur chance upon thee first?'

   'O King!' she cried, 'and I will tell thee true:
He found me first when yet a little maid:
Beaten had I been for a little fault   340
Whereof I was not guilty; and out I ran
And flung myself down on a bank of heath,
And hated this fair world and all therein,
And wept, and wish'd that I were dead; and he —
I know not whether of himself he came,   345
Or brought by Merlin, who, they say, can walk
Unseen at pleasure — he was at my side,
And spake sweet words, and comforted my heart,
And dried my tears, being a child with me.
And many a time he came, and evermore   350
As I grew greater grew with me; and sad
At times he seem'd, and sad with him was I,
Stern too at times, and then I loved him not,
But sweet again, and then I loved him well.
And now of late I see him less and less,   355
But those first days had golden hours for me,
For then I surely thought he would be king.

   'But let me tell thee now another tale:
For Bleys, our Merlin's master, as they say,
Died but of late, and sent his cry to me,   360
To hear him speak before he left his life.
Shrunk like a fairy changeling lay the mage;
And when I enter'd told me that himself
And Merlin ever served about the King,
Uther, before he died; and on the night   365
When Uther in Tintagil past away
Moaning and wailing for an heir, the two
Left the still King, and passing forth to breathe,
Then from the castle gateway by the chasm
Descending thro' the dismal night — a night   370

In which the bounds of heaven and earth were lost —
Behold, so high upon the dreary deeps
It seem'd in heaven, a ship, the shape thereof
A dragon wing'd, and all from stem to stern
Bright with a shining people on the decks,   375
And gone as soon as seen.   And then the two
Dropt to the cove, and watch'd the great sea fall,
Wave after wave, each mightier than the last,
Till last, a ninth one, gathering half the deep
And full of voices, slowly rose and plunged   380
Roaring, and all the wave was in a flame:
And down the wave and in the flame was borne
A naked babe, and rode to Merlin's feet,
Who stoopt and caught the babe, and cried "The King!
Here is an heir for Uther!"   And the fringe   385
Of that great breaker, sweeping up the strand,
Lash'd at the wizard as he spake the word,
And all at once all round him rose in fire,
So that the child and he were clothed in fire.
And presently thereafter follow'd calm,   390
Free sky and stars: "And this same child," he said,
"Is he who reigns; nor could I part in peace
Till this were told."   And saying this the seer
Went thro' the strait and dreadful pass of death,
Nor ever to be question'd any more   395
Save on the further side; but when I met
Merlin, and ask'd him if these things were truth —
The shining dragon and the naked child
Descending in the glory of the seas —
He laugh'd as is his wont, and answer'd me   400
In riddling triplets of old time, and said:

   ' "Rain, rain, and sun! a rainbow in the sky!
A young man will be wiser by and by;
An old man's wit may wander ere he die.
   Rain, rain, and sun! a rainbow on the lea!   405
And truth is this to me, and that to thee;

---

401. *riddling triplets.* What follows is an imitation or "echo" of the
old Welsh triads.

And truth or clothed or naked let it be.
  Rain, sun, and rain! and the free blossom blows:
Sun, rain, and sun! and where is he who knows?
From the great deep to the great deep he goes."   410
  'So Merlin riddling anger'd me; but thou
Fear not to give this King thine only child,
Guinevere: so great bards of him will sing
Hereafter; and dark sayings from of old
Ranging and ringing thro' the minds of men,   415
And echo'd by old folk beside their fires
For comfort after their wage-work is done,
Speak of the King; and Merlin in our time
Hath spoken also, not in jest, and sworn
Tho' men may wound him that he will not die,   420
But pass, again to come; and then or now
Utterly smite the heathen underfoot,
Till these and all men hail him for their king.'

  She spake and King Leodogran rejoiced,
But musing 'Shall I answer yea or nay?'   425
Doubted, and drowsed, nodded and slept, and saw,
Dreaming, a slope of land that ever grew,
Field after field, up to a height, the peak
Haze-hidden, and thereon a phantom king,
Now looming, and now lost; and on the slope   430
The sword rose, the hind fell, the herd was driven,
Fire glimpsed; and all the land from roof and rick,
In drifts of smoke before a rolling wind,
Stream'd to the peak, and mingled with the haze
And made it thicker; while the phantom king   435
Sent out at times a voice; and here or there
Stood one who pointed toward the voice, the rest
Slew on and burnt, crying, 'No king of ours,
No son of Uther, and no king of ours;'
Till with a wink his dream was changed, the haze   440
Descended, and the solid earth became
As nothing, but the King stood out in heaven,
Crown'd. And Leodogran awoke, and sent
Ulfius, and Brastias and Bedivere,
Back to the court of Arthur answering yea.   445

Then Arthur charged his warrior whom he loved
And honour'd most, Sir Lancelot, to ride forth
And bring the Queen; — and watch'd him from the gates:
And Lancelot past away among the flowers,
(For then was latter April) and return'd   450
Among the flowers, in May, with Guinevere.
To whom arrived, by Dubric the high saint,
Chief of the church in Britain, and before
The stateliest of her altar-shrines, the King
That morn was married, while in stainless white,   455
The fair beginners of a nobler time,
And glorying in their vows and him, his knights
Stood round him, and rejoicing in his joy.
Far shone the fields of May thro' open door,
The sacred altar blossom'd white with May,   460
The Sun of May descended on their King,
They gazed on all earth's beauty in their Queen,
Roll'd incense, and there past along the hymns
A voice as of the waters, while the two
Sware at the shrine of Christ a deathless love: 465
And Arthur said, 'Behold, thy doom is mine.
Let chance what will, I love thee to the death!'
To whom the Queen replied with drooping eyes,
'King and my lord, I love thee to the death!'
And holy Dubric spread his hands and spake,   470
'Reign ye, and live and love, and make the world
Other, and may thy Queen be one with thee,
And all this Order of thy Table Round
Fulfil the boundless purpose of their King!'

So Dubric said; but when they left the shrine   475
Great Lords from Rome before the portal stood,
In scornful stillness gazing as they past;
Then while they paced a city all on fire
With sun and cloth of gold, the trumpets blew,
And Arthur's knighthood sang before the King: —   480

'Blow trumpet, for the world is white with May;
Blow trumpet, the long night hath roll'd away!
Blow thro' the living world — "Let the King reign."

'Shall Rome or Heathen rule in Arthur's realm?
Flash brand and lance, fall battleaxe upon helm,   485
Fall battleaxe, and flash brand!   Let the King reign.

'Strike for the King and live! his knights have heard
That God hath told the King a secret word.
Fall battleaxe and flash brand!   Let the King reign.

'Blow trumpet; he will lift us from the dust.   490
Blow trumpet! live the strength and die the lust!
Clang battleaxe, and clash brand!   Let the King reign.

'Strike for the King and die! and if thou diest,
The King is King, and ever wills the highest.
Clang battleaxe, and clash brand!   Let the King reign.   495

'Blow, for our Sun is mighty in his May!
Blow, for our Sun is mightier day by day!
Clang battleaxe, and clash brand!   Let the King reign.

'The King will follow Christ, and we the King
In whom high God hath breathed a secret thing.   500
Fall battleaxe, and flash brand!   Let the King reign.'

So sang the knighthood, moving to their hall.
There at the banquet those great Lords from Rome,
The slowly-fading mistress of the world,
Strode in, and claim'd their tribute as of yore.   505
But Arthur spake, 'Behold, for these have sworn
To wage my wars, and worship me their King;
The old order changeth, yielding place to new;
And we that fight for our fair father Christ,
Seeing that ye be grown too weak and old   510
To drive the heathen from your Roman wall,
No tribute will we pay:' so those great lords
Drew back in wrath, and Arthur strove with Rome.

And Arthur and his knighthood for a space
Were all one will, and thro' that strength the King   515
Drew in the petty princedoms under him,
Fought, and in twelve great battles overcame
The heathen hordes, and made a realm and reign'd.

THE HOLY GRAIL [1]

FROM noiseful arms, and acts of prowess done
In tournament or tilt, Sir Percivale,
Whom Arthur and his knighthood call'd The Pure,
Had pass'd into the silent life of prayer,
Praise, fast, and alms; and leaving for the cowl   5
The helmet in an abbey far away
From Camelot, there, and not long after, died.

   And one, a fellow-monk among the rest,
Ambrosius, loved him much beyond the rest,
And honour'd him, and wrought into his heart   10
A way by love that waken'd love within,
To answer that which came: and as they sat
Beneath a world-old yew-tree, darkening half
The cloisters, on a gustful April morn
That puff'd the swaying branches into smoke   15
Above them, ere the summer when he died,
The monk Ambrosius question'd Percivale:

   'O brother, I have seen this yew-tree smoke,
Spring after spring, for half a hundred years:
For never have I known the world without,   20
Nor ever stray'd beyond the pale: but thee,
When first thou camest — such a courtesy
Spake thro' the limbs and in the voice — I knew
For one of those who eat in Arthur's hall;
For good ye are and bad, and like to coins,   25
Some true, some light, but every one of you
Stamp'd with the image of the King; and now

---

[1] Tennyson began "The Holy Grail" about September 9, 1868, and had
finished it by September 23. "It came like a breath of inspiration"
(*Memoir*, ii, 57). He considered it "one of the most imaginative" of his
poems. "I have expressed there my strong feeling as to the Reality of the
Unseen" (*ibid.*, ii, 90). His son's opinion was that of all the *Idylls* it
seemed "to express most my father's highest self" (*ibid.*, ii, 92). — The
story follows, with omissions and variations, Malory, *Le Morte Darthur*,
Books ix to xvii.

15. The pollen blown by the yew resembles smoke. Compare *In
Memoriam*, xxxix.

Tell me, what drove thee from the Table Round,
My brother? was it earthly passion crost?'

'Nay,' said the knight; 'for no such passion mine.   30
But the sweet vision of the Holy Grail
Drove me from all vainglories, rivalries,
And earthly heats that spring and sparkle out
Among us in the jousts, while women watch
Who wins, who falls; and waste the spiritual strength   35
Within us, better offer'd up to Heaven.'

To whom the monk: 'The Holy Grail! — I trust
We are green in Heaven's eyes; but here too much
We moulder — as to things without I mean —
Yet one of your own knights, a guest of ours,   40
Told us of this in our refectory,
But spake with such a sadness and so low
We heard not half of what he said. What is it?
The phantom of a cup that comes and goes?'

'Nay, monk! what phantom?' answer'd Percivale.   45
'The cup, the cup itself, from which our Lord
Drank at the last sad supper with his own.
This, from the blessed land of Aromat —
After the day of darkness, when the dead
Went wandering o'er Moriah — the good saint   50
Arimathæan Joseph, journeying brought
To Glastonbury, where the winter thorn
Blossoms at Christmas, mindful of our Lord.
And there awhile it bode; and if a man
Could touch or see it, he was heal'd at once,   55
By faith, of all his ills. But then the times
Grew to such evil that the holy cup
Was caught away to Heaven, and disappear'd.'

To whom the monk: 'From our old books I know
That Joseph came of old to Glastonbury,   60

---

48. *Aromat,* Arimathea, the home of Joseph. The change of name,
unwarranted by history or geography, is intended to suggest eastern
spicery and balms.

49–50. See Matthew, xxvii, 50 f.

And there the heathen Prince, Arviragus,
Gave him an isle of marsh whereon to build;
And there he built with wattles from the marsh
A little lonely church in days of yore,
For so they say, these books of ours, but seem   65
Mute of this miracle, far as I have read.
But who first saw the holy thing to-day?'

   'A woman,' answer'd Percivale, 'a nun,
And one no further off in blood from me
Than sister; and if ever holy maid   70
With knees of adoration wore the stone,
A holy maid; tho' never maiden glow'd,
But that was in her earlier maidenhood,
With such a fervent flame of human love,
Which being rudely blunted, glanced and shot   75
Only to holy things; to prayer and praise
She gave herself, to fast and alms. And yet,
Nun as she was, the scandal of the Court,
Sin against Arthur and the Table Round,
And the strange sound of an adulterous race,   80
Across the iron grating of her cell
Beat, and she pray'd and fasted all the more.

   'And he to whom she told her sins, or what
Her all but utter whiteness held for sin,
A man wellnigh a hundred winters old,   85
Spake often with her of the Holy Grail,
A legend handed down thro' five or six,
And each of these a hundred winters old,
From our Lord's time. And when King Arthur made
His Table Round, and all men's hearts became   90
Clean for a season, surely he had thought
That now the Holy Grail would come again;
But sin broke out. Ah, Christ, that it would come,
And heal the world of all their wickedness!
"O Father!" ask'd the maiden, "might it come   95
To me by prayer and fasting?" "Nay," said he,
"I know not, for thy heart is pure as snow."
And so she pray'd and fasted, till the sun

Shone, and the wind blew, thro' her, and I thought
She might have risen and floated when I saw her.   100

'For on a day she sent to speak with me.
And when she came to speak, behold her eyes
Beyond my knowing of them, beautiful,
Beyond all knowing of them, wonderful,
Beautiful in the light of holiness.   105
And "O my brother Percivale," she said,
"Sweet brother, I have seen the Holy Grail:
For, waked at dead of night, I heard a sound
As of a silver horn from o'er the hills
Blown, and I thought, 'It is not Arthur's use   110
To hunt by moonlight;' and the slender sound
As from a distance beyond distance grew
Coming upon me — O never harp nor horn,
Nor aught we blow with breath, or touch with hand,
Was like that music as it came; and then   115
Stream'd thro' my cell a cold and silver beam,
And down the long beam stole the Holy Grail,
Rose-red with beatings in it, as if alive,
Till all the white walls of my cell were dyed
With rosy colours leaping on the wall;   120
And then the music faded, and the Grail
Past, and the beam decay'd, and from the walls
The rosy quiverings died into the night.
So now the Holy Thing is here again
Among us, brother, fast thou too and pray,   125
And tell thy brother knights to fast and pray,
That so perchance the vision may be seen
By thee and those, and all the world be heal'd."

'Then leaving the pale nun, I spake of this
To all men; and myself fasted and pray'd   130
Always, and many among us many a week

---

107. Tennyson was wont to point out the difference between the
visions of the Grail as seen by the Nun, Sir Galahad, Sir Percivale, Sir
Lancelot, and Sir Bors, "according to their different, their own peculiar
natures and circumstances, and the perfection or imperfection of their
Christianity" (*Memoir,* ii, 63).

Fasted and pray'd even to the uttermost,
Expectant of the wonder that would be.

'And one there was among us, ever moved
Among us in white armour, Galahad.   135
"God make thee good as thou art beautiful,"
Said Arthur, when he dubb'd him knight; and none
In so young youth, was ever made a knight
Till Galahad; and this Galahad, when he heard
My sister's vision, fill'd me with amaze;   140
His eyes became so like her own, they seem'd
Hers, and himself her brother more than I.

'Sister or brother none had he; but some
Call'd him a son of Lancelot, and some said
Begotten by enchantment — chatterers they,   145
Like birds of passage piping up and down,
That gape for flies — we know not whence they come;
For when was Lancelot wanderingly lewd?

'But she, the wan sweet maiden, shore away
Clean from her forehead all that wealth of hair   150
Which made a silken mat-work for her feet;
And out of this she plaited broad and long
A strong sword-belt, and wove with silver thread
And crimson in the belt a strange device,
A crimson grail within a silver beam;   155
And saw the bright boy-knight, and bound it on him,
Saying, "My knight, my love, my knight of heaven,
O thou, my love, whose love is one with mine,
I, maiden, round thee, maiden, bind my belt.
Go forth, for thou shalt see what I have seen,   160
And break thro' all, till one will crown thee king
Far in the spiritual city:" and as she spake
She sent the deathless passion in her eyes
Thro' him, and made him hers, and laid her mind
On him, and he believed in her belief.   165

'Then came a year of miracle: O brother,
In our great hall there stood a vacant chair,
Fashion'd by Merlin ere he past away,

And carven with strange figures; and in and out
The figures, like a serpent, ran a scroll   170
Of letters in a tongue no man could read.
And Merlin call'd it "The Siege perilous,"
Perilous for good and ill; "for there," he said,
"No man could sit but he should lose himself:"
And once by misadvertence Merlin sat   175
In his own chair, and so was lost; but he,
Galahad, when he heard of Merlin's doom,
Cried, "If I lose myself, I save myself!"

'Then on a summer night it came to pass,
While the great banquet lay along the hall,   180
That Galahad would sit down in Merlin's chair.

'And all at once, as there we sat, we heard
A cracking and a riving of the roofs,
And rending, and a blast, and overhead
Thunder, and in the thunder was a cry.   185
And in the blast there smote along the hall
A beam of light seven times more clear than day:
And down the long beam stole the Holy Grail
All over cover'd with a luminous cloud,
And none might see who bare it, and it past.   190
But every knight beheld his fellow's face
As in a glory, and all the knights arose,
And staring each at other like dumb men
Stood, till I found a voice and sware a vow.

'I sware a vow before them all, that I,   195
Because I had not seen the Grail, would ride
A twelvemonth and a day in quest of it,
Until I found and saw it, as the nun
My sister saw it; and Galahad sware the vow,
And good Sir Bors, our Lancelot's cousin, sware,   200
And Lancelot sware, and many among the knights,
And Gawain sware, and louder than the rest.'

---

172. *The Siege perilous.* Tennyson explained that the perilous seat
stands for the spiritual imagination (*Works,* Eversley edition, iii, 492).
182 f. Compare Malory, xiii, 7.

Then spake the monk Ambrosius, asking him,
'What said the King?   Did Arthur take the vow?'

'Nay, for my lord,' said Percivale, 'the King,   205
Was not in hall: for early that same day,
Scaped thro' a cavern from a bandit hold,
An outraged maiden sprang into the hall
Crying on help: for all her shining hair
Was smear'd with earth, and either milky arm   210
Red-rent with hooks of bramble, and all she wore
Torn as a sail that leaves the rope is torn
In tempest: so the King arose and went
To smoke the scandalous hive of those wild bees
That made such honey in his realm.   Howbeit   215
Some little of this marvel he too saw,
Returning o'er the plain that then began
To darken under Camelot; whence the King
Look'd up, calling aloud, "Lo, there! the roofs
Of our great hall are roll'd in thunder-smoke!   220
Pray Heaven, they be not smitten by the bolt."
For dear to Arthur was that hall of ours,
As having there so oft with all his knights
Feasted, and as the stateliest under heaven.

'O brother, had you known our mighty hall,   225
Which Merlin built for Arthur long ago!
For all the sacred mount of Camelot,
And all the dim rich city, roof by roof,
Tower after tower, spire beyond spire,
By grove, and garden-lawn, and rushing brook,   230
Climbs to the mighty hall that Merlin built.
And four great zones of sculpture, set betwixt
With many a mystic symbol, gird the hall:
And in the lowest beasts are slaying men,
And in the second men are slaying beasts,   235
And on the third are warriors, perfect men,

_____

232 f. Tennyson's son interpreted the four zones as representative of
human progress: human society in the savage state; the stage when man
lords it over the beasts; the full development of man; and the progress
toward spiritual ideals.

And on the fourth are men with growing wings,
And over all one statue in the mould
Of Arthur, made by Merlin, with a crown,
And peak'd wings pointed to the Northern Star.   240
And eastward fronts the statue, and the crown
And both the wings are made of gold, and flame
At sunrise till the people in far fields,
Wasted so often by the heathen hordes,
Behold it, crying, "We have still a King."   245

'And, brother, had you known our hall within,
Broader and higher than any in all the lands!
Where twelve great windows blazon Arthur's wars,
And all the light that falls upon the board
Streams thro' the twelve great battles of our King.   250
Nay, one there is, and at the eastern end,
Wealthy with wandering lines of mount and mere,
Where Arthur finds the brand Excalibur.
And also one to the west, and counter to it,
And blank: and who shall blazon it? when and how? —   255
O there, perchance, when all our wars are done,
The brand Excalibur will be cast away.

'So to this hall full quickly rode the King,
In horror lest the work by Merlin wrought,
Dreamlike, should on the sudden vanish, wrapt   260
In unremorseful folds of rolling fire.
And in he rode, and up I glanced, and saw
The golden dragon sparkling over all:
And many of those who burnt the hold, their arms
Hack'd, and their foreheads grimed with smoke, and sear'd, 265
Follow'd, and in among bright faces, ours,
Full of the vision, prest: and then the King
Spake to me, being nearest, "Percivale"
(Because the hall was all in tumult — some
Vowing, and some protesting), "what is this?"   270

'O brother, when I told him what had chanced,
My sister's vision, and the rest, his face
Darken'd, as I have seen it more than once,
When some brave deed seem'd to be done in vain,

Darken; and "Woe is me, my knights," he cried,   275
"Had I been here, ye had not sworn the vow."
Bold was mine answer, "Had thyself been here,
My King, thou wouldst have sworn." "Yea, yea," said he,
"Art thou so bold and hast not seen the Grail?"

    ' "Nay, lord, I heard the sound, I saw the light,   280
But since I did not see the Holy Thing,
I sware a vow to follow it till I saw."

    'Then when he ask'd us, knight by knight, if any
Had seen it, all their answers were as one:
"Nay, lord, and therefore have we sworn our vows."   285

    ' "Lo now," said Arthur, "have ye seen a cloud?
What go ye into the wilderness to see?"

    'Then Galahad on the sudden, and in a voice
Shrilling along the hall to Arthur, call'd,
"But I, Sir Arthur, saw the Holy Grail,   290
I saw the Holy Grail and heard a cry —
'O Galahad, and O Galahad, follow me.' "

    ' "Ah, Galahad, Galahad," said the King, "for such
As thou art is the vision, not for these.
Thy holy nun and thou have seen a sign —   295
Holier is none, my Percivale, than she —
A sign to maim this Order which I made.
But ye, that follow but the leader's bell"
(Brother, the King was hard upon his knights),
"Taliessin is our fullest throat of song,   300
And one hath sung and all the dumb will sing.
Lancelot is Lancelot, and hath overborne
Five knights at once, and every younger knight,
Unproven, holds himself as Lancelot,
Till overborne by one, he learns — and ye,   305
What are ye? Galahads? — no, nor Percivales"
(For thus it pleased the King to range me close

---

300. *Taliessin*, the greatest British singer of the seventh century, is
referred to by Thomas Gray in "The Bard," l. 121.

After Sir Galahad); "nay," said he, "but men
With strength and will to right the wrong'd, of power
To lay the sudden heads of violence flat,   310
Knights that in twelve great battles splash'd and dyed
The strong White Horse in his own heathen blood —
But one hath seen, and all the blind will see.
Go, since your vows are sacred, being made:
Yet — for ye know the cries of all my realm   315
Pass thro' this hall — how often, O my knights,
Your places being vacant at my side,
This chance of noble deeds will come and go
Unchallenged, while ye follow wandering fires
Lost in the quagmire! Many of you, yea most,   320
Return no more: ye think I show myself
Too dark a prophet: come now, let us meet
The morrow morn once more in one full field
Of gracious pastime, that once more the King,
Before ye leave him for this Quest, may count   325
The yet-unbroken strength of all his knights,
Rejoicing in that Order which he made."

'So when the sun broke next from under ground,
All the great table of our Arthur closed
And clash'd in such a tourney and so full,   330
So many lances broken — never yet
Had Camelot seen the like, since Arthur came;
And I myself and Galahad, for a strength
Was in us from the vision, overthrew
So many knights that all the people cried,   335
And almost burst the barriers in their heat,
Shouting, "Sir Galahad and Sir Percivale!"

'But when the next day brake from under ground —
O brother, had you known our Camelot,
Built by old kings, age after age, so old   340
The King himself had fears that it would fall,
So strange, and rich, and dim; for where the roofs
Totter'd toward each other in the sky,
Met foreheads all along the street of those

---
312. The White Horse was the banner of Hengist.

Who watch'd us pass; and lower, and where the long   345
Rich galleries, lady-laden, weigh'd the necks
Of dragons clinging to the crazy walls,
Thicker than drops from thunder, showers of flowers
Fell as we past; and men and boys astride
On wyvern, lion, dragon, griffin, swan,   350
At all the corners, named us each by name,
Calling "God speed!" but in the ways below
The knights and ladies wept, and rich and poor
Wept, and the King himself could hardly speak
For grief, and all in middle street the Queen,   355
Who rode by Lancelot, wail'd and shriek'd aloud,
"This madness has come on us for our sins."
So to the Gate of the three Queens we came,
Where Arthur's wars are render'd mystically,
And thence departed every one his way.   360

'And I was lifted up in heart, and thought
Of all my late-shown prowess in the lists,
How my strong lance had beaten down the knights,
So many and famous names; and never yet
Had heaven appear'd so blue, nor earth so green,   365
For all my blood danced in me, and I knew
That I should light upon the Holy Grail.

'Thereafter, the dark warning of our King,
That most of us would follow wandering fires,
Came like a driving gloom across my mind.   370
Then every evil word I had spoken once,
And every evil thought I had thought of old,
And every evil deed I ever did,
Awoke and cried, "This Quest is not for thee."
And lifting up mine eyes, I found myself   375
Alone, and in a land of sand and thorns,
And I was thirsty even unto death;
And I, too, cried, "This Quest is not for thee."

---

350. *wyvern,* a two-legged dragon. This and the other creatures are
heraldic devices.

'And on I rode, and when I thought my thirst
Would slay me, saw deep lawns, and then a brook,   380
With one sharp rapid, where the crisping white
Play'd ever back upon the sloping wave,
And took both ear and eye; and o'er the brook
Were apple-trees, and apples by the brook
Fallen, and on the lawns. "I will rest here,"   385
I said, "I am not worthy of the Quest;"
But even while I drank the brook, and ate
The goodly apples, all these things at once
Fell into dust, and I was left alone,
And thirsting, in a land of sand and thorns.   390

'And then behold a woman at a door
Spinning; and fair the house whereby she sat,
And kind the woman's eyes and innocent,
And all her bearing gracious; and she rose
Opening her arms to meet me, as who should say,   395
"Rest here;" but when I touch'd her, lo! she, too,
Fell into dust and nothing, and the house
Became no better than a broken shed,
And in it a dead babe; and also this
Fell into dust, and I was left alone.   400

'And on I rode, and greater was my thirst.
Then flash'd a yellow gleam across the world,
And where it smote the plowshare in the field,
The plowman left his plowing, and fell down
Before it; where it glitter'd on her pail,   405
The milkmaid left her milking, and fell down
Before it, and I knew not why, but thought
"The sun is rising," tho' the sun had risen.
Then was I ware of one that on me moved
In golden armour with a crown of gold   410
About a casque all jewels; and his horse
In golden armour jewell'd everywhere:
And on the splendour came, flashing me blind;

379–439. Tennyson pointed out that neither the gratification of sensual
desire, nor the love of wife or family, nor wealth, nor glory, nor fame,
brings content to Percivale.

And seem'd to me the Lord of all the world,
Being so huge. But when I thought he meant   415
To crush me, moving on me, lo! he, too,
Open'd his arms to embrace me as he came,
And up I went and touch'd him, and he, too,
Fell into dust, and I was left alone
And wearying in a land of sand and thorns.   420

'And I rode on and found a mighty hill,
And on the top, a city wall'd: the spires
Prick'd with incredible pinnacles into heaven.
And by the gateway stirr'd a crowd; and these
Cried to me climbing, "Welcome, Percivale!   425
Thou mightiest and thou purest among men!"
And glad was I and clomb, but found at top
No man, nor any voice. And thence I past
Far thro' a ruinous city, and I saw
That man had once dwelt there; but there I found   430
Only one man of an exceeding age.
"Where is that goodly company," said I,
"That so cried out upon me?" and he had
Scarce any voice to answer, and yet gasp'd,
"Whence and what art thou?" and even as he spoke   435
Fell into dust, and disappear'd, and I
Was left alone once more, and cried in grief,
"Lo, if I find the Holy Grail itself
And touch it, it will crumble into dust."

'And thence I dropt into a lowly vale   440
Low as the hill was high, and where the vale
Was lowest, found a chapel, and thereby
A holy hermit in a hermitage,
To whom I told my phantoms, and he said:

' "O son, thou hast not true humility,   445
The highest virtue, mother of them all;
For when the Lord of all things made Himself
Naked of glory for His mortal change,
'Take thou my robe,' she said, 'for all is thine,'

435. Compare *Paradise Lost,* ii, 681: "Whence and what art thou, execrable shape?"

And all her form shone forth with sudden light   450
So that the angels were amazed, and she
Follow'd Him down, and like a flying star
Led on the gray-hair'd wisdom of the east;
But her thou hast not known: for what is this
Thou thoughtest of thy prowess and thy sins?   455
Thou hast not lost thyself to save thyself
As Galahad." When the hermit made an end,
In silver armour suddenly Galahad shone
Before us, and against the chapel door
Laid lance, and enter'd, and we knelt in prayer.   460
And there the hermit slaked my burning thirst,
And at the sacring of the mass I saw
The holy elements alone; but he,
"Saw ye no more? I, Galahad, saw the Grail,
The Holy Grail, descend upon the shrine: 465
I saw the fiery face as of a child
That smote itself into the bread, and went;
And hither am I come; and never yet
Hath what thy sister taught me first to see,
This Holy Thing, fail'd from my side, nor come   470
Cover'd, but moving with me night and day,
Fainter by day, but always in the night
Blood-red, and sliding down the blacken'd marsh
Blood-red, and on the naked mountain top
Blood-red, and in the sleeping mere below   475
Blood-red. And in the strength of this I rode,
Shattering all evil customs everywhere,
And past thro' Pagan realms, and made them mine,
And clash'd with Pagan hordes, and bore them down,
And broke thro' all, and in the strength of this   480
Come victor. But my time is hard at hand,
And hence I go; and one will crown me king
Far in the spiritual city; and come thou, too,
For thou shalt see the vision when I go."

'While thus he spake, his eye, dwelling on mine,   485
Drew me, with power upon me, till I grew

---

453. The Magi.
466 f. Compare Malory, xvii, 20.

One with him, to believe as he believed.
Then, when the day began to wane, we went.

'There rose a hill that none but man could climb,
Scarr'd with a hundred wintry watercourses —   490
Storm at the top, and when we gain'd it, storm
Round us and death; for every moment glanced
His silver arms and gloom'd: so quick and thick
The lightnings here and there to left and right
Struck, till the dry old trunks about us, dead,   495
Yea, rotten with a hundred years of death,
Sprang into fire: and at the base we found
On either hand, as far as eye could see,
A great black swamp and of an evil smell,
Part black, part whiten'd with the bones of men,   500
Not to be crost, save that some ancient king
Had built a way, where, link'd with many a bridge,
A thousand piers ran into the great Sea.
And Galahad fled along them bridge by bridge,
And every bridge as quickly as he crost   505
Sprang into fire and vanish'd, tho' I yearn'd
To follow; and thrice above him all the heavens
Open'd and blazed with thunder such as seem'd
Shoutings of all the sons of God: and first
At once I saw him far on the great Sea,   510
In silver-shining armour starry-clear;
And o'er his head the Holy Vessel hung
Clothed in white samite or a luminous cloud.
And with exceeding swiftness ran the boat,
If boat it were — I saw not whence it came.   515
And when the heavens open'd and blazed again
Roaring, I saw him like a silver star —
And had he set the sail, or had the boat
Become a living creature clad with wings?
And o'er his head the Holy Vessel hung   520
Redder than any rose, a joy to me,
For now I knew the veil had been withdrawn.
Then in a moment when they blazed again
Opening, I saw the least of little stars
Down on the waste, and straight beyond the star   525
I saw the spiritual city and all her spires

And gateways in a glory like one pearl —
No larger, tho' the goal of all the saints —
Strike from the sea; and from the star there shot
A rose-red sparkle to the city, and there   530
Dwelt, and I knew it was the Holy Grail,
Which never eyes on earth again shall see.
Then fell the floods of heaven drowning the deep.
And how my feet recrost the deathful ridge
No memory in me lives; but that I touch'd   535
The chapel-doors at dawn I know; and thence
Taking my war-horse from the holy man,
Glad that no phantom vext me more, return'd
To whence I came, the gate of Arthur's wars.'

'O brother,' ask'd Ambrosius, — 'for in sooth   540
These ancient books — and they would win thee — teem,
Only I find not there this Holy Grail,
With miracles and marvels like to these,
Not all unlike; which oftentime I read,
Who read but on my breviary with ease,   545
Till my head swims; and then go forth and pass
Down to the little thorpe that lies so close,
And almost plaster'd like a martin's nest
To these old walls — and mingle with our folk;
And knowing every honest face of theirs   550
As well as ever shepherd knew his sheep,
And every homely secret in their hearts,
Delight myself with gossip and old wives,
And ills and aches, and teethings, lyings-in,
And mirthful sayings, children of the place,   555
That have no meaning half a league away:
Or lulling random squabbles when they rise,
Chafferings and chatterings at the market-cross,
Rejoice, small man, in this small world of mine,
Yea, even in their hens and in their eggs —   560
O brother, saving this Sir Galahad,
Came ye on none but phantoms in your quest,
No man, no woman?'

Then Sir Percivale:
'All men, to one so bound by such a vow,

And women were as phantoms. O my brother,   565
Why wilt thou shame me to confess to thee
How far I falter'd from my quest and vow?
For after I had lain so many nights,
A bedmate of the snail and eft and snake,
In grass and burdock, I was changed to wan   570
And meagre, and the vision had not come;
And then I chanced upon a goodly town
With one great dwelling in the middle of it;
Thither I made, and there was I disarm'd
By maidens each as fair as any flower: 575
But when they led me into hall, behold,
The Princess of that castle was the one,
Brother, and that one only, who had ever
Made my heart leap; for when I moved of old
A slender page about her father's hall,   580
And she a slender maiden, all my heart
Went after her with longing: yet we twain
Had never kiss'd a kiss, or vow'd a vow.
And now I came upon her once again,
And one had wedded her, and he was dead,   585
And all his land and wealth and state were hers.
And while I tarried, every day she set
A banquet richer than the day before
By me; for all her longing and her will
Was toward me as of old; till one fair morn,   590
I walking to and fro beside a stream
That flash'd across her orchard underneath
Her castle-walls, she stole upon my walk,
And calling me the greatest of all knights,
Embraced me, and so kiss'd me the first time,   595
And gave herself and all her wealth to me.
Then I remember'd Arthur's warning word,
That most of us would follow wandering fires,
And the Quest faded in my heart. Anon,
The heads of all her people drew to me,   600
With supplication both of knees and tongue:
"We have heard of thee: thou art our greatest knight,
Our Lady says it, and we well believe:
Wed thou our Lady, and rule over us,
And thou shalt be as Arthur in our land."   605

O me, my brother! but one night my vow
Burnt me within, so that I rose and fled,
But wail'd and wept, and hated mine own self,
And ev'n the Holy Quest, and all but her;
Then after I was join'd with Galahad   610
Cared not for her, nor anything upon earth.'

   Then said the monk, 'Poor men, when yule is cold,
Must be content to sit by little fires.
And this am I, so that ye care for me
Ever so little; yea, and blest be Heaven   615
That brought thee here to this poor house of ours
Where all the brethren are so hard, to warm
My cold heart with a friend: but O the pity
To find thine own first love once more — to hold,
Hold her a wealthy bride within thine arms,   620
Or all but hold, and then — cast her aside,
Foregoing all her sweetness, like a weed.
For we that want the warmth of double life,
We that are plagued with dreams of something sweet
Beyond all sweetness in a life so rich, —   625
Ah, blessed Lord, I speak too earthly-wise,
Seeing I never stray'd beyond the cell,
But live like an old badger in his earth,
With earth about him everywhere, despite
All fast and penance. Saw ye none beside,   630
None of your knights?'

                    'Yea so,' said Percivale:
'One night my pathway swerving east, I saw
The pelican on the casque of our Sir Bors
All in the middle of the rising moon:
And toward him spurr'd, and hail'd him, and he me,   635
And each made joy of either; then he ask'd,
"Where is he? hast thou seen him — Lancelot? — Once,"
Said good Sir Bors, "he dash'd across me — mad,
And maddening what he rode: and when I cried,
'Ridest thou then so hotly on a quest   640
So holy,' Lancelot shouted, 'Stay me not!
I have been the sluggard, and I ride apace,

For now there is a lion in the way.'
So vanish'd."

        'Then Sir Bors had ridden on
Softly, and sorrowing for our Lancelot,   645
Because his former madness, once the talk
And scandal of our table, had return'd;
For Lancelot's kith and kin so worship him
That ill to him is ill to them; to Bors
Beyond the rest: he well had been content   650
Not to have seen, so Lancelot might have seen,
The Holy Cup of healing; and, indeed,
Being so clouded with his grief and love,
Small heart was his after the Holy Quest:
If God would send the vision, well: if not,   655
The Quest and he were in the hands of Heaven.

    'And then, with small adventure met, Sir Bors
Rode to the lonest tract of all the realm,
And found a people there among their crags,
Our race and blood, a remnant that were left   660
Paynim amid their circles, and the stones
They pitch up straight to heaven: and their wise men
Were strong in that old magic which can trace
The wandering of the stars, and scoff'd at him
And this high Quest as at a simple thing: 665
Told him he follow'd — almost Arthur's words —
A mocking fire: "What other fire than he,
Whereby the blood beats, and the blossom blows,
And the sea rolls, and all the world is warm'd?"
And when his answer chafed them, the rough crowd,   670
Hearing he had a difference with their priests,
Seized him, and bound and plunged him into a cell
Of great piled stones; and lying bounden there
In darkness thro' innumerable hours
He heard the hollow-ringing heavens sweep   675
Over him till by miracle — what else? —
Heavy as it was, a great stone slipt and fell,
Such as no wind could move: and thro' the gap
Glimmer'd the streaming scud: then came a night

Still as the day was loud; and thro' the gap   680
The seven clear stars of Arthur's Table Round —
For, brother, so one night, because they roll
Thro' such a round in heaven, we named the stars,
Rejoicing in ourselves and in our King —
And these, like bright eyes of familiar friends,   685
In on him shone: "And then to me, to me,"
Said good Sir Bors, "beyond all hopes of mine,
Who scarce had pray'd or ask'd it for myself —
Across the seven clear stars — O grace to me —
In colour like the fingers of a hand   690
Before a burning taper, the sweet Grail
Glided and past, and close upon it peal'd
A sharp quick thunder."   Afterwards, a maid,
Who kept our holy faith among her kin
In secret, entering, loosed and let him go.'   695

   To whom the monk: 'And I remember now
That pelican on the casque: Sir Bors it was
Who spake so low and sadly at our board;
And mighty reverent at our grace was he:
A square-set man and honest; and his eyes,   700
An out-door sign of all the warmth within,
Smiled with his lips — a smile beneath a cloud,
But heaven had meant it for a sunny one:
Ay, ay, Sir Bors, who else?   But when ye reach'd
The city, found ye all your knights return'd,   705
Or was there sooth in Arthur's prophecy,
Tell me, and what said each, and what the King?'

   Then answer'd Percivale: 'And that can I,
Brother, and truly; since the living words
Of so great men as Lancelot and our King   710
Pass not from door to door and out again,
But sit within the house. O, when we reach'd
The city, our horses stumbling as they trode

---

681. The seven stars of the constellation of the Great Bear. For the
connection between the name Arthur and Ursus, the Bear, see Collingwood and Myres, *op. cit.*, pp. 320 f.

On heaps of ruin, hornless unicorns,
Crack'd basilisks, and splinter'd cockatrices,   715
And shatter'd talbots, which had left the stones
Raw, that they fell from, brought us to the hall.

'And there sat Arthur on the daïs-throne,
And those that had gone out upon the Quest,
Wasted and worn, and but a tithe of them,   720
And those that had not, stood before the King,
Who, when he saw me, rose, and bade me hail,
Saying, "A welfare in thine eye reproves
Our fear of some disastrous chance for thee
On hill, or plain, at sea, or flooding ford.   725
So fierce a gale made havoc here of late
Among the strange devices of our kings;
Yea, shook this newer, stronger hall of ours,
And from the statue Merlin moulded for us
Half-wrench'd a golden wing; but now — the Quest,   730
This vision — hast thou seen the Holy Cup,
That Joseph brought of old to Glastonbury?"

'So when I told him all thyself hast heard,
Ambrosius, and my fresh but fixt resolve
To pass away into the quiet life,   735
He answer'd not, but, sharply turning, ask'd
Of Gawain, "Gawain, was this Quest for thee?"

' "Nay, lord," said Gawain, "not for such as I.
Therefore I communed with a saintly man,
Who made me sure the Quest was not for me;   740
For I was much awearied of the Quest:
But found a silk pavilion in a field,
And merry maidens in it; and then this gale
Tore my pavilion from the tenting-pin,
And blew my merry maidens all about   745
With all discomfort; yea, and but for this,
My twelvemonth and a day were pleasant to me."

---

714 f. Fantastic creatures of heraldry. The basilisk, a serpent whose
look slew the beholder; the cockatrice, half-snake, half-cock; the talbot,
a sort of dog.

'He ceased; and Arthur turn'd to whom at first
He saw not, for Sir Bors, on entering, push'd
Athwart the throng to Lancelot, caught his hand,   750
Held it, and there, half-hidden by him, stood,
Until the King espied him, saying to him,
"Hail, Bors! if ever loyal man and true
Could see it, thou hast seen the Grail;" and Bors,
"Ask me not, for I may not speak of it: 755
I saw it;" and the tears were in his eyes.

'Then there remain'd but Lancelot, for the rest
Spake but of sundry perils in the storm;
Perhaps, like him of Cana in Holy Writ,
Our Arthur kept his best until the last;   760
"Thou, too, my Lancelot," ask'd the King, "my friend,
Our mightiest, hath this Quest avail'd for thee?"

' "Our mightiest!" answer'd Lancelot, with a groan;
"O King!" — and when he paused, methought I spied
A dying fire of madness in his eyes —   765
"O King, my friend, if friend of thine I be,
Happier are those that welter in their sin,
Swine in the mud, that cannot see for slime,
Slime of the ditch: but in me lived a sin
So strange, of such a kind, that all of pure,   770
Noble, and knightly in me twined and clung
Round that one sin, until the wholesome flower
And poisonous grew together, each as each,
Not to be pluck'd asunder; and when thy knights
Sware, I sware with them only in the hope   775
That could I touch or see the Holy Grail
They might be pluck'd asunder. Then I spake
To one most holy saint, who wept and said,
That save they could be pluck'd asunder, all
My quest were but in vain; to whom I vow'd   780
That I would work according as he will'd.
And forth I went, and while I yearn'd and strove
To tear the twain asunder in my heart,
My madness came upon me as of old,
And whipt me into waste fields far away;   785
There was I beaten down by little men,

Mean knights, to whom the moving of my sword
And shadow of my spear had been enow
To scare them from me once; and then I came
All in my folly to the naked shore,   790
Wide flats, where nothing but coarse grasses grew;
But such a blast, my King, began to blow,
So loud a blast along the shore and sea,
Ye could not hear the waters for the blast,
Tho' heapt in mounds and ridges all the sea   795
Drove like a cataract, and all the sand
Swept like a river, and the clouded heavens
Were shaken with the motion and the sound.
And blackening in the sea-foam sway'd a boat,
Half-swallow'd in it, anchor'd with a chain;   800
And in my madness to myself I said,
'I will embark and I will lose myself,
And in the great sea wash away my sin.'
I burst the chain, I sprang into the boat.
Seven days I drove along the dreary deep,   805
And with me drove the moon and all the stars;
And the wind fell, and on the seventh night
I heard the shingle grinding in the surge,
And felt the boat shock earth, and looking up,
Behold, the enchanted towers of Carbonek,   810
A castle like a rock upon a rock,
With chasm-like portals open to the sea,
And steps that met the breaker! there was none
Stood near it but a lion on each side
That kept the entry, and the moon was full.   815
Then from the boat I leapt, and up the stairs.
There drew my sword. With sudden-flaring manes
Those two great beasts rose upright like a man,
Each gript a shoulder, and I stood between;
And, when I would have smitten them, heard a voice,   820
'Doubt not, go forward; if thou doubt, the beasts
Will tear thee piecemeal.' Then with violence
The sword was dash'd from out my hand, and fell.
And up into the sounding hall I past;

792 f. Compare Malory, xvii, 14.
810. *Carbonek.* See Malory, xvii, 16.

But nothing in the sounding hall I saw,   825
No bench nor table, painting on the wall
Or shield of knight; only the rounded moon
Thro' the tall oriel on the rolling sea.
But always in the quiet house I heard,
Clear as a lark, high o'er me as a lark,   830
A sweet voice singing in the topmost tower
To the eastward: up I climb'd a thousand steps
With pain: as in a dream I seem'd to climb
For ever: at the last I reach'd a door,
A light was in the crannies, and I heard,   835
'Glory and joy and honour to our Lord
And to the Holy Vessel of the Grail.'
Then in my madness I essay'd the door;
It gave; and thro' a stormy glare, a heat
As from a seventimes-heated furnace, I,   840
Blasted and burnt, and blinded as I was,
With such a fierceness that I swoon'd away —
O, yet methought I saw the Holy Grail,
All pall'd in crimson samite, and around
Great angels, awful shapes, and wings and eyes.   845
And but for all my madness and my sin,
And then my swooning, I had sworn I saw
That which I saw; but what I saw was veil'd
And cover'd; and this Quest was not for me."

'So speaking, and here ceasing, Lancelot left   850
The hall long silent, till Sir Gawain — nay,
Brother, I need not tell thee foolish words, —
A reckless and irreverent knight was he,
Now bolden'd by the silence of his King, —
Well, I will tell thee: "O King, my liege," he said,   855
"Hath Gawain fail'd in any quest of thine?
When have I stinted stroke in foughten field?
But as for thine, my good friend Percivale,
Thy holy nun and thou have driven men mad,
Yea, made our mightiest madder than our least.   860
But by mine eyes and by mine ears I swear,

827–8. Tennyson "was fond of quoting these lines for the beauty of
the sound" (*Works,* Eversley edition, iii, 497).

I will be deafer than the blue-eyed cat,
And thrice as blind as any noonday owl,
To holy virgins in their ecstasies,
Henceforward."

   ' "Deafer," said the blameless King,   865
"Gawain, and blinder unto holy things
Hope not to make thyself by idle vows,
Being too blind to have desire to see.
But if indeed there came a sign from heaven,
Blessed are Bors, Lancelot and Percivale,   870
For these have seen according to their sight.
For every fiery prophet in old times,
And all the sacred madness of the bard,
When God made music thro' them, could but speak
His music by the framework and the chord;   875
And as ye saw it ye have spoken truth.

   ' "Nay — but thou errest, Lancelot: never yet
Could all of true and noble in knight and man
Twine round one sin, whatever it might be,
With such a closeness, but apart there grew,   880
Save that he were the swine thou spakest of,
Some root of knighthood and pure nobleness;
Whereto see thou, that it may bear its flower.

   ' "And spake I not too truly, O my knights?
Was I too dark a prophet when I said   885
To those who went upon the Holy Quest,
That most of them would follow wandering fires,
Lost in the quagmire? — lost to me and gone,
And left me gazing at a barren board,
And a lean Order — scarce return'd a tithe —   890
And out of those to whom the vision came
My greatest hardly will believe he saw;
Another hath beheld it afar off,
And leaving human wrongs to right themselves,

---

   862. The unexpected simile is an amusing example of the imagery
which Tennyson drew from his reading of modern scientific literature.
Darwin had written: "Cats which are entirely white and have blue eyes
are generally deaf" (*The Origin of Species,* chapter i).

Cares but to pass into the silent life.   895
And one hath had the vision face to face,
And now his chair desires him here in vain,
However they may crown him otherwise.

  ' "And some among you held, that if the King
Had seen the sight he would have sworn the vow: 900
Not easily, seeing that the King must guard
That which he rules, and is but as the hind
To whom a space of land is given to plow.
Who may not wander from the allotted field
Before his work be done; but, being done,   905
Let visions of the night or of the day
Come, as they will; and many a time they come,
Until this earth he walks on seems not earth,
This light that strikes his eyeball is not light,
This air that smites his forehead is not air   910
But vision — yea, his very hand and foot —
In moments when he feels he cannot die,
And knows himself no vision to himself,
Nor the high God a vision, nor that One
Who rose again: ye have seen what ye have seen."   915

  'So spake the King: I knew not all he meant.'

GUINEVERE [1]

QUEEN GUINEVERE had fled the court, and sat
There in the holy house at Almesbury
Weeping, none with her save a little maid,
A novice: one low light betwixt them burn'd
Blurr'd by the creeping mist, for all abroad,   5

912–14. Tennyson said that these three lines are "the (spiritually)
central lines of the *Idylls*" (*Memoir*, ii, 90).
  [1] According to the *Memoir* (i, 419, 424), "Guinevere" was written between July, 1857, and March, 1858; but elsewhere (*Works*, Eversley edition, iii, 506) the poet's son records that it was written in "about a fortnight." Tennyson departs widely and radically from the story in Malory
(Books xx and xxi), where after Arthur's discovery of the love of Lancelot and Guinevere she is condemned to be burnt alive. Lancelot rescues
her and carries her off to his castle, Joyeuse Gard, to which Arthur lays

Beneath a moon unseen albeit at full,
The white mist, like a face-cloth to the face,
Clung to the dead earth, and the land was still.

For hither had she fled, her cause of flight
Sir Modred; he that like a subtle beast   10
Lay couchant with his eyes upon the throne,
Ready to spring, waiting a chance: for this
He chill'd the popular praises of the King
With silent smiles of slow disparagement;
And tamper'd with the Lords of the White Horse,   15
Heathen, the brood by Hengist left; and sought
To make disruption in the Table Round
Of Arthur, and to splinter it into feuds
Serving his traitorous end; and all his aims
Were sharpen'd by strong hate for Lancelot.   20

For thus it chanced one morn when all the court,
Green-suited, but with plumes that mock'd the may,
Had been, their wont, a-maying and return'd,
That Modred still in green, all ear and eye,
Climb'd to the high top of the garden-wall   25
To spy some secret scandal if he might,
And saw the Queen who sat betwixt her best
Enid, and lissome Vivien, of her court
The wiliest and the worst; and more than this
He saw not, for Sir Lancelot passing by   30

siege. By command of the Pope, Lancelot surrenders her to the King.
Lancelot retires to his lands beyond the sea whither Arthur follows him
to wage further war. During his absence Mordred usurps the throne.
There follows the fatal battle in the West which Tennyson relates in
"The Passing of Arthur." After the King's death — not before, as in
Tennyson's version — the Queen becomes a nun at Almesbury. There
she has the final meeting with Lancelot of which Tennyson says nothing
but which (with a change of locality) is the theme of William Morris's
"King Arthur's Tomb" in *The Defence of Guenevere* (1858).

2. *Almesbury,* Amesbury or Ambresbury, eight miles north of Salis-
bury. The Norman abbey-church is, traditionally, a relic of the "holy
house" in which Guinevere sought refuge.

10. In Malory and many other old versions Modred (or Mordred) is
the incestuous son of Arthur and his half-sister. Tennyson rejects this
relationship. Compare l. 570, below.

22. *the may,* hawthorne.

Spied where he couch'd, and as the gardener's hand
Picks from the colewort a green caterpillar,
So from the high wall and the flowering grove
Of grasses Lancelot pluck'd him by the heel,
And cast him as a worm upon the way;   35
But when he knew the Prince tho' marr'd with dust,
He, reverencing king's blood in a bad man,
Made such excuses as he might, and these
Full knightly without scorn; for in those days
No knight of Arthur's noblest dealt in scorn;   40
But, if a man were halt or hunch'd, in him
By those whom God had made full-limb'd and tall,
Scorn was allow'd as part of his defect,
And he was answer'd softly by the King
And all his Table. So Sir Lancelot holp   45
To raise the Prince, who rising twice or thrice
Full sharply smote his knees, and smiled, and went:
But, ever after, the small violence done
Rankled in him and ruffled all his heart,
As the sharp wind that ruffles all day long   50
A little bitter pool about a stone
On the bare coast.

                    But when Sir Lancelot told
This matter to the Queen, at first she laugh'd
Lightly, to think of Modred's dusty fall,
Then shudder'd, as the village wife who cries   55
'I shudder, some one steps across my grave;'
Then laugh'd again, but faintlier, for indeed
She half-foresaw that he, the subtle beast,
Would track her guilt until he found, and hers
Would be for evermore a name of scorn.   60
Henceforward rarely could she front in hall,
Or elsewhere, Modred's narrow foxy face,
Heart-hiding smile, and gray persistent eye:
Henceforward too, the Powers that tend the soul,
To help it from the death that cannot die,   65
And save it even in extremes, began
To vex and plague her. Many a time for hours,
Beside the placid breathings of the King,
In the dead night, grim faces came and went

Before her, or a vague spiritual fear —   70
Like to some doubtful noise of creaking doors,
Heard by the watcher in a haunted house,
That keeps the rust of murder on the walls —
Held her awake: or if she slept, she dream'd
An awful dream; for then she seem'd to stand   75
On some vast plain before a setting sun,
And from the sun there swiftly made at her
A ghastly something, and its shadow flew
Before it, till it touch'd her, and she turn'd —
When lo! her own, that broadening from her feet,   80
And blackening, swallow'd all the land, and in it
Far cities burnt, and with a cry she woke.
And all this trouble did not pass but grew;
Till ev'n the clear face of the guileless King,
And trustful courtesies of household life,   85
Became her bane; and at the last she said,
'O Lancelot, get thee hence to thine own land,
For if thou tarry we shall meet again,
And if we meet again, some evil chance
Will make the smouldering scandal break and blaze   90
Before the people, and our lord the King.'
And Lancelot ever promised, but remain'd,
And still they met and met. Again she said,
'O Lancelot, if thou love me get thee hence.'
And then they were agreed upon a night   95
(When the good King should not be there) to meet
And part for ever. Vivien, lurking, heard.
She told Sir Modred. Passion-pale they met
And greeted. Hands in hands, and eye to eye
Low on the border of her couch they sat   100
Stammering and staring. It was their last hour,
A madness of farewells. And Modred brought
His creatures to the basement of the tower
For testimony; and crying with full voice
'Traitor, come out, ye are trapt at last,' aroused   105
Lancelot, who rushing outward lionlike
Leapt on him, and hurl'd him headlong, and he fell
Stunn'd, and his creatures took and bare him off,
And all was still: then she, 'The end is come,
And I am shamed for ever;' and he said,   110

'Mine be the shame; mine was the sin: but rise,
And fly to my strong castle overseas:
There will I hide thee, till my life shall end,
There hold thee with my life against the world.'
She answer'd, 'Lancelot, wilt thou hold me so?   115
Nay, friend, for we have taken our farewells.
Would God that thou couldst hide me from myself!
Mine is the shame, for I was wife, and thou
Unwedded: yet rise now, and let us fly,
For I will draw me into sanctuary,   120
And bide my doom.' So Lancelot got her horse,
Set her thereon, and mounted on his own,
And then they rode to the divided way,
There kiss'd, and parted weeping: for he past,
Love-loyal to the least wish of the Queen,   125
Back to his land; but she to Almesbury
Fled all night long by glimmering waste and weald,
And heard the Spirits of the waste and weald
Moan as she fled, or thought she heard them moan:
And in herself she moan'd, 'Too late, too late!'   130
Till in the cold wind that foreruns the morn,
A blot in heaven, the Raven, flying high,
Croak'd, and she thought, 'He spies a field of death;
For now the Heathen of the Northern Sea,
Lured by the crimes and frailties of the court,   135
Begin to slay the folk, and spoil the land.'

    And when she came to Almesbury she spake
There to the nuns, and said, 'Mine enemies
Pursue me, but, O peaceful Sisterhood,
Receive, and yield me sanctuary, nor ask   140
Her name to whom ye yield it, till her time
To tell you:' and her beauty, grace and power,
Wrought as a charm upon them, and they spared
To ask it.

---

132. The raven in folklore has the faculty of "smelling death." Compare *Macbeth*, I, v, 37 f.:

> The raven himself is hoarse
> That croaks the fatal entrance of Duncan
> Under my battlements.

So the stately Queen abode
For many a week, unknown, among the nuns;   145
Nor with them mix'd, nor told her name, nor sought,
Wrapt in her grief, for housel or for shrift,
But communed only with the little maid,
Who pleased her with a babbling heedlessness
Which often lured her from herself; but now,   150
This night, a rumour wildly blown about
Came, that Sir Modred had usurp'd the realm,
And leagued him with the heathen, while the King
Was waging war on Lancelot: then she thought,
'With what a hate the people and the King   155
Must hate me,' and bow'd down upon her hands
Silent, until the little maid, who brook'd
No silence, brake it, uttering, 'Late! so late!
What hour, I wonder, now?' and when she drew
No answer, by and by began to hum   160
An air the nuns had taught her, 'Late, so late!'
Which when she heard, the Queen look'd up, and said,
'O maiden, if indeed ye list to sing,
Sing, and unbind my heart that I may weep.'
Whereat full willingly sang the little maid.   165

    'Late, late, so late! and dark the night and chill!
Late, late, so late! but we can enter still.
Too late, too late! ye cannot enter now.

    'No light had we: for that we do repent;
And learning this, the bridegroom will relent.   170
Too late, too late! ye cannot enter now.

    'No light: so late! and dark and chill the night!
O let us in, that we may find the light!
Too late, too late: ye cannot enter now.

    'Have we not heard the bridegroom is so sweet?   175
O let us in, tho' late, to kiss his feet!
No, no, too late! ye cannot enter now.'

---

147. *housel,* the Eucharist; *shrift,* confession.
166 f. Compare Matthew, xxv, 1 f

So sang the novice, while full passionately,
Her head upon her hands, remembering
Her thought when first she came, wept the sad Queen. 180
Then said the little novice prattling to her,

'O pray you, noble lady, weep no more;
But let my words, the words of one so small,
Who knowing nothing knows but to obey,
And if I do not there is penance given — 185
Comfort your sorrows; for they do not flow
From evil done; right sure am I of that,
Who see your tender grace and stateliness.
But weigh your sorrows with our lord the King's,
And weighing find them less; for gone is he 190
To wage grim war against Sir Lancelot there,
Round that strong castle where he holds the Queen;
And Modred whom he left in charge of all,
The traitor — Ah sweet lady, the King's grief
For his own self, and his own Queen, and realm, 195
Must needs be thrice as great as any of ours.
For me, I thank the saints, I am not great.
For if there ever come a grief to me
I cry my cry in silence, and have done.
None knows it, and my tears have brought me good: 200
But even were the griefs of little ones
As great as those of great ones, yet this grief
Is added to the griefs the great must bear,
That howsoever much they may desire
Silence, they cannot weep behind a cloud: 205
As even here they talk at Almesbury
About the good King and his wicked Queen,
And were I such a King with such a Queen,
Well might I wish to veil her wickedness,
But were I such a King, it could not be.' 210

Then to her own sad heart mutter'd the Queen,
'Will the child kill me with her innocent talk?'
But openly she answer'd, 'Must not I,
If this false traitor have displaced his lord,
Grieve with the common grief of all the realm?' 215

'Yea,' said the maid, 'this is all woman's grief,
That *she* is woman, whose disloyal life
Hath wrought confusion in the Table Round
Which good King Arthur founded, years ago,
With signs and miracles and wonders, there   220
At Camelot, ere the coming of the Queen.'

Then thought the Queen within herself again,
'Will the child kill me with her foolish prate?'
But openly she spake and said to her,
'O little maid, shut in by nunnery walls,   225
What canst thou know of Kings and Tables Round,
Or what of signs and wonders, but the signs
And simple miracles of thy nunnery?'

To whom the little novice garrulously,
'Yea, but I know: the land was full of signs   230
And wonders ere the coming of the Queen.
So said my father, and himself was knight
Of the great Table — at the founding of it;
And rode thereto from Lyonesse, and he said
That as he rode, an hour or maybe twain   235
After the sunset, down the coast, he heard
Strange music, and he paused, and turning — there,
All down the lonely coast of Lyonesse,
Each with a beacon-star upon his head,
And with a wild sea-light about his feet,   240
He saw them — headland after headland flame
Far on into the rich heart of the west:
And in the light the white mermaiden swam,
And strong man-breasted things stood from the sea,
And sent a deep sea-voice thro' all the land,   245
To which the little elves of chasm and cleft
Made answer, sounding like a distant horn.

_____

234. *Lyonesse*, the legendary land beyond Cornwall which sank beneath the sea. Compare the close of Swinburne's *Tristram of Lyonesse*.

236 f. The supernatural beings whom Lancelot saw "in the old days
of the King Arthur" remind one of the opening·lines of Chaucer's 'Prologue' to *The Wife of Bath's Tale*, which Tennyson may have had in
mind.

So said my father — yea, and furthermore,
Next morning, while he passed the dimlit woods,
Himself beheld three spirits mad with joy   250
Come dashing down on a tall wayside flower,
That shook beneath them, as the thistle shakes
When three gray linnets wrangle for the seed:
And still at evenings on before his horse
The flickering fairy-circle wheel'd and broke   255
Flying, and link'd again, and wheel'd and broke
Flying, for all the land was full of life.
And when at last he came to Camelot,
A wreath of airy dancers hand-in-hand
Swung round the lighted lantern of the hall;   260
And in the hall itself was such a feast
As never man had dream'd; for every knight
Had whatsoever meat he long'd for served
By hands unseen; and even as he said
Down in the cellars merry bloated things   265
Shoulder'd the spigot, straddling on the butts
While the wine ran: so glad were spirits and men
Before the coming of the sinful Queen.'

    Then spake the Queen and somewhat bitterly,
'Were they so glad? ill prophets were they all,   270
Spirits and men: could none of them foresee,
Not even thy wise father with his signs
And wonders, what has fall'n upon the realm?'

    To whom the novice garrulously again,
'Yea, one, a bard; of whom my father said,   275
Full many a noble war-song had he sung,
Ev'n in the presence of an enemy's fleet,
Between the steep cliff and the coming wave;

261 f. In the Old French *Roman de Merlin* the Round Table has the
property of providing delicious food in abundance and variety. Malory
(xiii, 7) attributes this property to the Holy Grail.

265 f. Tennyson took this incident, as J. Churton Collins notes (*Illustrations of Tennyson*, p. 152), from Crofton Croker, *Fairy Legends of the South of Ireland* (ed. 1862, p. 79): "On advancing into the cellar, he perceived a little figure, about six inches in height, astride upon the pipe of the oldest port, and bearing a spigot upon his shoulder."

And many a mystic lay of life and death
Had chanted on the smoky mountain-tops,   280
When round him bent the spirits of the hills
With all their dewy hair blown back like flame:
So said my father — and that night the bard
Sang Arthur's glorious wars, and sang the King
As wellnigh more than man, and rail'd at those   285
Who call'd him the false son of Gorloïs:
For there was no man knew from whence he came;
But after tempest, when the long wave broke
All down the thundering shores of Bude and Bos,
There came a day as still as heaven, and then   290
They found a naked child upon the sands
Of dark Tintagil by the Cornish sea;
And that was Arthur; and they foster'd him
Till he by miracle was approven King:
And that his grave should be a mystery   295
From all men, like his birth; and could he find
A woman in her womanhood as great
As he was in his manhood, then, he sang,
The twain together well might change the world.
But even in the middle of his song   300
He falter'd, and his hand fell from the harp,
And pale he turn'd, and reel'd, and would have fall'n,
But that they stay'd him up; nor would he tell
His vision; but what doubt that he foresaw
This evil work of Lancelot and the Queen?'   305

Then thought the Queen, 'Lo! they have set her on,
Our simple-seeming Abbess and her nuns,
To play upon me,' and bow'd her head nor spake.
Whereat the novice crying, with clasp'd hands,
Shame on her own garrulity garrulously,   310
Said the good nuns would check her gadding tongue
Full often, 'and, sweet lady, if I seem
To vex an ear too sad to listen to me,
Unmannerly, with prattling and the tales

---

286. See "The Coming of Arthur," ll. 184 f.

288. *Bude and Bos* (Boscastle) are towns on the Cornish coast north-east of Tintagil.

Which my good father told me, check me too   315
Nor let me shame my father's memory, one
Of noblest manners, tho' himself would say
Sir Lancelot had the noblest; and he died,
Kill'd in a tilt, come next, five summers back,
And left me; but of others who remain,   320
And of the two first-famed for courtesy —
And pray you check me if I ask amiss —
But pray you, which had noblest, while you moved
Among them, Lancelot or our lord the King?'

    Then the pale Queen look'd up and answer'd her,   325
'Sir Lancelot, as became a noble knight,
Was gracious to all ladies, and the same
In open battle or the tilting-field
Forbore his own advantage, and the King
In open battle or the tilting-field   330
Forbore his own advantage, and these two
Were the most nobly-manner'd men of all;
For manners are not idle, but the fruit
Of loyal nature, and of noble mind.'

    'Yea,' said the maid, 'be manners such fair fruit?   335
Then Lancelot's needs must be a thousand-fold
Less noble, being, as all rumour runs,
The most disloyal friend in all the world.'

    To which a mournful answer made the Queen:
'O closed about by narrowing nunnery-walls,   340
What knowest thou of the world, and all its lights
And shadows, all the wealth and all the woe?
If ever Lancelot, that most noble knight,
Were for one hour less noble than himself,
Pray for him that he scape the doom of fire,   345
And weep for her who drew him to his doom.'

    'Yea,' said the little novice, 'I pray for both;
But I should all as soon believe that his,
Sir Lancelot's, were as noble as the King's,
As I could think, sweet lady, yours would be   350
Such as they are, were you the sinful Queen.'

So she, like many another babbler, hurt
Whom she would soothe, and harm'd where she would heal;
For here a sudden flush of wrathful heat
Fired all the pale face of the Queen, who cried,   355
'Such as thou art be never maiden more
For ever! thou their tool, set on to plague
And play upon, and harry me, petty spy
And traitress.'   When that storm of anger brake
From Guinevere, aghast the maiden rose,   360
White as her veil, and stood before the Queen
As tremulously as foam upon the beach
Stands in a wind, ready to break and fly,
And when the Queen had added 'Get thee hence,'
Fled frighted.   Then that other left alone   365
Sigh'd, and began to gather heart again,
Saying in herself, 'The simple, fearful child
Meant nothing, but my own too-fearful guilt,
Simpler than any child, betrays itself.
But help me, heaven, for surely I repent.   370
For what is true repentance but in thought —
Not ev'n in inmost thought to think again
The sins that made the past so pleasant to us:
And I have sworn never to see him more,
To see him more.'

               And ev'n in saying this,   375
Her memory from old habit of the mind
Went slipping back upon the golden days
In which she saw him first, when Lancelot came,
Reputed the best knight and goodliest man,
Ambassador, to lead her to his lord   380
Arthur, and led her forth, and far ahead
Of his and her retinue moving, they,
Rapt in sweet talk or lively, all on love
And sport and tilts and pleasure (for the time
Was maytime, and as yet no sin was dream'd),   385
Rode under groves that look'd a paradise
Of blossom, over sheets of hyacinth

---

382. *retinue.* The accent is Shakespearean and Miltonic.
385 f. Compare "Sir Launcelot and Queen Guinevere."

That seem'd the heavens upbreaking thro' the earth,
And on from hill to hill, and every day
Beheld at noon in some delicious dale   390
The silk pavilions of King Arthur raised
For brief repast or afternoon repose
By couriers gone before; and on again,
Till yet once more ere set of sun they saw
The Dragon of the great Pendragonship,   395
That crown'd the state pavilion of the King,
Blaze by the rushing brook or silent well.

But when the Queen immersed in such a trance,
And moving thro' the past unconsciously,
Came to that point where first she saw the King   400
Ride toward her from the city, sigh'd to find
Her journey done, glanced at him, thought him cold,
High, self-contain'd, and passionless, not like him,
'Not like my Lancelot' — while she brooded thus
And grew half-guilty in her thoughts again,   405
There rode an armed warrior to the doors.
A murmuring whisper thro' the nunnery ran,
Then on a sudden a cry, 'The King.'   She sat
Stiff-stricken, listening; but when armed feet
Thro' the long gallery from the outer doors   410
Rang coming, prone from off her seat she fell,
And grovell'd with her face against the floor:
There with her milkwhite arms and shadowy hair
She made her face a darkness from the King:
And in the darkness heard his armed feet   415
Pause by her; then came silence, then a voice,
Monotonous and hollow like a Ghost's
Denouncing judgment, but tho' changed, the King's:

'Liest thou here so low, the child of one
I honour'd, happy, dead before thy shame?   420
Well is it that no child is born of thee.
The children born of thee are sword and fire,
Red ruin, and the breaking up of laws,
The craft of kindred and the Godless hosts

---

395. *Pendragonship.* *Pen* in Welsh is "chief"; *Dragon*, "war-leader."

Of heathen swarming o'er the Northern Sea;   425
Whom I, while yet Sir Lancelot, my right arm,
The mightiest of my knights, abode with me,
Have everywhere about this land of Christ
In twelve great battles ruining overthrown.
And knowest thou now from whence I come — from him, 430
From waging bitter war with him: and he,
That did not shun to smite me in worse way,
Had yet that grace of courtesy in him left,
He spared to lift his hand against the King
Who made him knight: but many a knight was slain; 435
And many more, and all his kith and kin
Clave to him, and abode in his own land
And many more when Modred raised revolt,
Forgetful of their troth and fealty, clave
To Modred, and a remnant stays with me.   440
And of this remnant will I leave a part,
True men who love me still, for whom I live,
To guard thee in the wild hour coming on,
Lest but a hair of this low head be harm'd.
Fear not: thou shalt be guarded till my death.   445
Howbeit I know, if ancient prophecies
Have err'd not, that I march to meet my doom.
Thou hast not made my life so sweet to me,
That I the King should greatly care to live;
For thou hast spoilt the purpose of my life.   450
Bear with me for the last time while I show,
Ev'n for thy sake, the sin which thou hast sinn'd.
For when the Roman left us, and their law
Relax'd its hold upon us, and the ways
Were fill'd with rapine, here and there a deed   455
Of prowess done redress'd a random wrong.
But I was first of all the kings who drew
The Knighthood-errant of this realm and all
The realms together under me, their Head,
In that fair Order of my Table Round,   460
A glorious company, the flower of men,
To serve as model for the mighty world,
And be the fair beginning of a time.
I made them lay their hands in mine and swear
To reverence the King, as if he were   465

Their conscience, and their conscience as their King,
To break the heathen and uphold the Christ,
To ride abroad redressing human wrongs,
To speak no slander, no, nor listen to it,
To honour his own word as if his God's,   470
To lead sweet lives in purest chastity,
To love one maiden only, cleave to her,
And worship her by years of noble deeds,
Until they won her; for indeed I knew
Of no more subtle master under heaven   475
Than is the maiden passion for a maid,
Not only to keep down the base in man,
But teach high thought, and amiable words
And courtliness, and the desire of fame,
And love of truth, and all that makes a man.   480
And all this throve before I wedded thee
Believing, "lo mine helpmate, one to feel
My purpose and rejoicing in my joy."
Then came thy shameful sin with Lancelot;
Then came the sin of Tristram and Isolt;   485
Then others, following these my mightiest knights,
And drawing foul ensample from fair names,
Sinn'd also, till the loathsome opposite
Of all my heart had destined did obtain,
And all thro' thee! so that this life of mine   490
I guard as God's high gift from scathe and wrong,
Not greatly care to lose; but rather think
How sad it were for Arthur, should he live,
To sit once more within his lonely hall,
And miss the wonted number of my knights,   495
And miss to hear high talk of noble deeds
As in the golden days before thy sin.
For which of us, who might be left, could speak
Of the pure heart, nor seem to glance at thee?
And in thy bowers of Camelot or of Usk   500

---

485. Told by Tennyson, who follows Malory closely, in "The Last
Tournament." Contrast, among the many versions, Swinburne's *Tristram
of Lyonesse* and Thomas Hardy's *The Queen of Cornwall*.

500. *Usk*, a river of western Britain. Caerleon, where Arthur held
court, lay upon it.

Thy shadow still would glide from room to room,
And I should evermore be vext with thee
In hanging robe or vacant ornament,
Or ghostly footfall echoing on the stair.
For think not, tho' thou wouldst not love thy lord,   505
Thy lord has wholly lost his love for thee.
I am not made of so slight elements.
Yet must I leave thee, woman, to thy shame.
I hold that man the worst of public foes
Who either for his own or children's sake,   510
To save his blood from scandal, lets the wife
Whom he knows false, abide and rule the house:
For being thro' his cowardice allow'd
Her station, taken everywhere for pure,
She like a new disease, unknown to men,   515
Creeps, no precaution used, among the crowd,
Makes wicked lightnings of her eyes, and saps
The fealty of our friends, and stirs the pulse
With devil's leaps, and poisons half the young.
Worst of the worst were that man he that reigns!   520
Better the King's waste hearth and aching heart
Than thou reseated in thy place of light,
The mockery of my people, and their bane.'

  He paused, and in the pause she crept an inch
Nearer, and laid her hands about his feet.   525
Far off a solitary trumpet blew.
Then waiting by the doors the warhorse neigh'd
As at a friend's voice, and he spake again:

  'Yet think not that I come to urge thy crimes,
I did not come to curse thee, Guinevere,   530
I, whose vast pity almost makes me die
To see thee, laying there thy golden head,
My pride in happier summers, at my feet.
The wrath which forced my thoughts on that fierce law,
The doom of treason and the flaming death   535
(When first I learnt thee hidden here), is past.

---

535. *the flaming death,* death at the stake, to which in many old versions Guinevere is condemned.

The pang — which while I weigh'd thy heart with one
Too wholly true to dream untruth in thee,
Made my tears burn — is also past — in part.
And all is past, the sin is sinn'd and I,   540
Lo! I forgive thee, as Eternal God
Forgives: do thou for thine own soul the rest.
But how to take last leave of all I loved?
O golden hair, with which I used to play
Not knowing! O imperial-moulded form,   545
And beauty such as never woman wore,
Until it came a kingdom's curse with thee —
I cannot touch thy lips, they are not mine,
But Lancelot's: nay, they never were the King's.
I cannot take thy hand; that too is flesh,   550
And in the flesh thou hast sinn'd; and mine own flesh,
Here looking down on thine polluted, cries
"I loathe thee:" yet not less, O Guinevere,
For I was ever virgin save for thee,
My love thro' flesh hath wrought into my life   555
So far, that my doom is, I love thee still.
Let no man dream but that I love thee still.
Perchance, and so thou purify thy soul,
And so thou lean on our fair father Christ,
Hereafter in that world where all are pure   560
We two may meet before high God, and thou
Wilt spring to me, and claim me thine, and know
I am thine husband — not a smaller soul,
Nor Lancelot, nor another. Leave me that,
I charge thee, my last hope. Now must I hence.   565
Thro' the thick night I hear the trumpet blow:
They summon me their King to lead mine hosts
Far down to that great battle in the west,
Where I must strike against the man they call
My sister's son — no kin of mine, who leagues   570
With Lords of the White Horse, heathen, and knights,

---

569 f. In the original edition (1859) these lines read:
> Where I must strike against my sister's son,
> Leagued with the lords of the White Horse and knights
> Once mine, and strike him dead, etc.

The denial of the relationship was an after-thought of Tennyson's.

Traitors — and strike him dead, and meet myself
Death, or I know not what mysterious doom.
And thou remaining here wilt learn the event;
But hither shall I never come again,   575
Never lie by thy side; see thee no more —
Farewell!'

          And while she grovell'd at his feet,
She felt the King's breath wander o'er her neck,
And in the darkness o'er her fallen head,
Perceived the waving of his hands that blest.   580

   Then, listening till those armed steps were gone,
Rose the pale Queen, and in her anguish found
The casement: 'peradventure,' so she thought,
'If I might see his face, and not be seen.'
And lo, he sat on horseback at the door!   585
And near him the sad nuns with each a light
Stood, and he gave them charge about the Queen,
To guard and foster her for evermore.
And while he spake to these his helm was lower'd,
To which for crest the golden dragon clung   590
Of Britain; so she did not see the face,
Which then was as an angel's, but she saw,
Wet with the mists and smitten by the lights,
The Dragon of the great Pendragonship
Blaze, making all the night a steam of fire.   595
And even then he turn'd; and more and more
The moony vapour rolling round the King,
Who seem'd the phantom of a Giant in it,
Enwound him fold by fold, and made him gray
And grayer, till himself became as mist   600
Before her, moving ghostlike to his doom.

   Then she stretch'd out her arms and cried aloud
'O Arthur!' there her voice brake suddenly,
Then — as a stream that spouting from a cliff
Fails in mid-air, but gathering at the base   605
Re-makes itself, and flashes down the vale —
Went on in passionate utterance:

'Gone — my lord!
Gone thro' my sin to slay and to be slain!
And he forgave me, and I could not speak.
Farewell? I should have answer'd his farewell.   610
His mercy choked me. Gone, my lord the King,
My own true lord! how dare I call him mine?
The shadow of another cleaves to me,
And makes me one pollution: he, the King,
Call'd me polluted: shall I kill myself?   615
What help in that? I cannot kill my sin,
If soul be soul; nor can I kill my shame;
No, nor by living can I live it down.
The days will grow to weeks, the weeks to months,
The months will add themselves and make the years,   620
The years will roll into the centuries,
And mine will ever be a name of scorn.
I must not dwell on that defeat of fame.
Let the world be; that is but of the world —
What else? what hope? I think there was a hope,   625
Except he mock'd me when he spake of hope;
His hope he call'd it; but he never mocks,
For mockery is the fume of little hearts.
And blessed be the King, who hath forgiven
My wickedness to him, and left me hope   630
That in mine own heart I can live down sin
And be his mate hereafter in the heavens
Before high God. Ah great and gentle lord,
Who wast, as is the conscience of a saint
Among his warring senses, to thy knights —   635
To whom my false voluptuous pride, that took
Full easily all impressions from below,
Would not look up, or half-despised the height
To which I would not or I could not climb —
I thought I could not breathe in that fine air   640
That pure severity of perfect light —
I yearn'd for warmth and colour which I found
In Lancelot — now I see thee what thou art,
Thou art the highest and most human too,
Not Lancelot, nor another. Is there none   645
Will tell the King I love him tho' so late?
Now — ere he goes to the great Battle? none:

Myself must tell him in that purer life,
But now it were too daring. Ah my God,
What might I not have made of thy fair world,   650
Had I but loved thy highest creature here?
It was my duty to have loved the highest:
It surely was my profit had I known:
It would have been my pleasure had I seen.
We needs must love the highest when we see it,   655
Not Lancelot, nor another.'

                    Here her hand
Grasp'd, made her vail her eyes: she look'd and saw
The novice, weeping, suppliant, and said to her,
'Yea, little maid, for am *I* not forgiven?'
Then, glancing up beheld the holy nuns   660
All round her, weeping; and her heart was loosed
Within her, and she wept with these and said,

    'Ye know me then, that wicked one, who broke
The vast design and purpose of the King.
O shut me round with narrowing nunnery-walls,   665
Meek maidens, from the voices crying "shame."
I must not scorn myself: he loves me still.
Let no one dream but that he loves me still.
So let me, if you do not shudder at me,
Nor shun to call me sister, dwell with you;   670
Wear black and white, and be a nun like you,
Fast with your fasts, not feasting with your feasts;
Grieve with your griefs, not grieving at your joys,
But not rejoicing; mingle with your rites;
Pray and be pray'd for; lie before your shrines;   675
Do each low office of your holy house;
Walk your dim cloister, and distribute dole
To poor sick people, richer in His eyes
Who ransom'd us, and haler too than I;
And treat their loathsome hurts and heal mine own;   680
And so wear out in almsdeed and in prayer
The sombre close of that voluptuous day,
Which wrought the ruin of my lord the King.'

_____

    657. *Vail,* lower.

She said: they took her to themselves; and she
Still hoping, fearing 'is it yet too late?'   685
Dwelt with them, till in time their Abbess died.
Then she, for her good deeds and her pure life,
And for the power of ministration in her,
And likewise for the high rank she had borne,
Was chosen Abbess, there, an Abbess, lived   690
For three brief years, and there, an Abbess, past
To where beyond these voices there is peace.

THE PASSING OF ARTHUR [1]

THAT story which the bold Sir Bedivere,
First made and latest left of all the knights,
Told, when the man was no more than a voice
In the white winter of his age, to those
With whom he dwelt, new faces, other minds.   5

For on their march to westward, Bedivere,
Who slowly paced among the slumbering host,
Heard in his tent the moanings of the King:

'I found Him in the shining of the stars,
I mark'd Him in the flowering of His fields,   10
But in His ways with men I find Him not.
I waged His wars, and now I pass and die.
O me! for why is all around us here
As if some lesser god had made the world,
But had not force to shape it as he would,   15
Till the High God behold it from beyond,
And enter it, and make it beautiful?
Or else as if the world were wholly fair,
But that these eyes of men are dense and dim,
And have not power to see it as it is: 20
Perchance, because we see not to the close; —

---

[1] To the "Morte d'Arthur" of 1834 (published in *Poems,* 1842) 176
lines were added about 1868 to form this last of the twelve *Idylls.* It was
published in 1869. In later editions 23 more lines were added and there
were a few verbal changes. See next note.

6–28. This passage is not in the edition of 1869.

For I, being simple, thought to work His will,
And have but stricken with the sword in vain;
And all whereon I lean'd in wife and friend
Is traitor to my peace, and all my realm   25
Reels back into the beast, and is no more.
My God, thou hast forgotten me in my death:
Nay — God my Christ — I pass but shall not die.'

Then, ere that last weird battle in the west,
There came on Arthur sleeping, Gawain kill'd   30
In Lancelot's war, the ghost of Gawain blown
Along a wandering wind, and past his ear
Went shrilling, 'Hollow, hollow all delight!
Hail, King! to-morrow thou shalt pass away.
Farewell! there is an isle of rest for thee.   35
And I am blown along a wandering wind,
And hollow, hollow, hollow all delight.'
And fainter onward, like wild birds that change
Their season in the night and wail their way
From cloud to cloud, down the long wind the dream   40
Shrill'd; but in going mingled with dim cries
Far in the moonlit haze among the hills,
As of some lonely city sack'd by night,
When all is lost, and wife and child with wail
Pass to new lords; and Arthur woke and call'd,   45
'Who spake? A dream. O light upon the wind,
Thine, Gawain, was the voice — are these dim cries
Thine? or doth all that haunts the waste and wild
Mourn, knowing it will go along with me?'

This heard the bold Sir Bedivere and spake: 50
'O me, my King, let pass whatever will,
Elves, and the harmless glamour of the field;
But in their stead thy name and glory cling
To all high places like a golden cloud
For ever: but as yet thou shalt not pass.   55
Light was Gawain in life, and light in death

---

29. The story of the last battle and of Arthur's passing is from Malory,
xxi, 5. For the historical substratum of the tradition of the battle of
Camlann see Collingwood and Myres, *op. cit.*, p. 324.

Is Gawain, for the ghost is as the man;
And care not thou for dreams from him, but rise —
I hear the steps of Modred in the west,
And with him many of thy people, and knights   60
Once thine, whom thou hast loved, but grosser grown
Than heathen, spitting at their vows and thee.
Right well in heart they know thee for the King.
Arise, go forth and conquer as of old.'

    Then spake King Arthur to Sir Bedivere: 65
'Far other is this battle in the west
Whereto we move, than when we strove in youth,
And brake the petty kings, and fought with Rome,
Or thrust the heathen from the Roman wall,
And shook him thro' the north. Ill doom is mine   70
To war against my people and my knights.
The king who fights his people fights himself.
And they my knights, who loved me once, the stroke
That strikes them dead is as my death to me.
Yet let us hence, and find or feel a way   75
Thro' this blind haze, which ever since I saw
One lying in the dust at Almesbury,
Hath folded in the passes of the world.'

    Then rose the King and moved his host by night,
And ever push'd Sir Modred, league by league,   80
Back to the sunset bound of Lyonesse —
A land of old upheaven from the abyss
By fire, to sink into the abyss again;
Where fragments of forgotten peoples dwelt,
And the long mountains ended in a coast   85
Of ever-shifting sand, and far away
The phantom circle of a moaning sea.
There the pursuer could pursue no more,
And he that fled no further fly the King;
And there, that day when the great light of heaven   90
Burn'd at his lowest in the rolling year,
On the waste sand by the waste sea they closed.
Nor ever yet had Arthur fought a fight
Like this last, dim, weird battle of the west.
A deathwhite mist slept over sand and sea: 95

Whereof the chill, to him who breathed it, drew
Down with his blood, till all his heart was cold
With formless fear; and ev'n on Arthur fell
Confusion, since he saw not whom he fought.
For friend and foe were shadows in the mist,   100
And friend slew friend not knowing whom he slew;
And some had visions out of golden youth,
And some beheld the faces of old ghosts
Look in upon the battle; and in the mist
Was many a noble deed, many a base,   105
And chance and craft and strength in single fights,
And ever and anon with host to host
Shocks, and the splintering spear, the hard mail hewn,
Shield-breakings, and the clash of brands, the crash
Of battleaxes on shatter'd helms, and shrieks   110
After the Christ, of those who falling down
Look'd up for heaven, and only saw the mist;
And shouts of heathen and the traitor knights,
Oaths, insult, filth, and monstrous blasphemies,
Sweat, writhings, anguish, labouring of the lungs   115
In that close mist, and cryings for the light,
Moans of the dying, and voices of the dead.

    Last, as by some one deathbed after wail
Of suffering, silence follows, or thro' death
Or deathlike swoon, thus over all that shore,   120
Save for some whisper of the seething seas,
A dead hush fell; but when the dolorous day
Grew drearier toward twilight falling, came
A bitter wind, clear from the North, and blew
The mist aside, and with that wind the tide   125
Rose, and the pale King glanced across the field
Of battle: but no man was moving there;
Nor any cry of Christian heard thereon,
Nor yet of heathen; only the wan wave
Brake in among dead faces, to and fro   130
Swaying the helpless hands, and up and down
Tumbling the hollow helmets of the fallen,
And shiver'd brands that once had fought with Rome,
And rolling far along the gloomy shores
The voice of days of old and days to be.   135

Then spake King Arthur to Sir Bedivere,
And whiter than the mist that all day long
Had held the field of battle was the King:

'Hearest thou this great voice that shakes the world,
And wastes the narrow realm whereon we move,   140
And beats upon the faces of the dead,
My dead, as tho' they had not died for me? —
O Bedivere, for on my heart hath fall'n
Confusion, till I know not what I am,
Nor whence I am, nor whether I be King,   145
Behold, I seem but King among the dead.'

Then spake the bold Sir Bedivere: 'My King,
King everywhere! and so the dead have kings,
There also will I worship thee as King.
Yet still thy life is whole, and still I live   150
Who love thee; but who hates thee, he that brought
The heathen back among us, yonder stands,
Modred unharm'd, the traitor of thine house.'

Then spake the King: 'My house hath been my doom.
But call not thou this traitor of my house   155
Who hath but dwelt beneath one roof with me.
My house are rather they who sware my vows,
Yea, even while they brake them, own'd me King.
And well for thee, saying in my dark hour,
When all the purport of my throne hath fail'd,   160
That quick or dead thou holdest me for King.
King am I, whatsoever be their cry;
And one last act of kinghood shalt thou see
Yet, ere I pass.' And uttering this the King
Made at the man: then Modred smote his liege   165
Hard on that helm which many a heathen sword
Had beaten thin; while Arthur at one blow,
Striking the last stroke with Excalibur,
Slew him, and all but slain himself, he fell.

So all day long the noise of battle roll'd   170
Among the mountains by the winter sea;

_____

170. At this point the early "Morte d'Arthur" begins.

Until King Arthur's Table, man by man,
Had fall'n in Lyonesse about their lord,
King Arthur. Then, because his wound was deep,
The bold Sir Bedivere uplifted him,   175
And bore him to a chapel nigh the field,
A broken chancel with a broken cross,
That stood on a dark strait of barren land:
On one side lay the Ocean, and on one
Lay a great water, and the moon was full.   180

    Then spake King Arthur to Sir Bedivere:
'The sequel of to-day unsolders all
The goodliest fellowship of famous knights
Whereof this world holds record. Such a sleep
They sleep — the men I loved. I think that we   185
Shall never more, at any future time,
Delight our souls with talk of knightly deeds,
Walking about the gardens and the halls
Of Camelot, as in the days that were.
I perish by this people which I made, —   190
Tho' Merlin sware that I should come again
To rule once more; but, let what will be, be,
I am so deeply smitten thro' the helm
That without help I cannot last till morn.
Thou therefore take my brand Excalibur,   195
Which was my pride: for thou rememberest how
In those old days, one summer noon, an arm
Rose up from out the bosom of the lake,
Clothed in white samite, mystic, wonderful,
Holding the sword — and how I row'd across   200
And took it, and have worn it, like a king;
And, wheresoever I am sung or told
In aftertime, this also shall be known:
But now delay not: take Excalibur,
And fling him far into the middle mere: 205
Watch what thou seëst, and lightly bring me word.'

    To him replied the bold Sir Bedivere:
'It is not meet, Sir King, to leave thee thus,
Aidless, alone, and smitten thro' the helm —
A little thing may harm a wounded man;   210

Yet I thy hest will all perform at full,
Watch what I see, and lightly bring thee word.'

So saying, from the ruin'd shrine he stept,
And in the moon athwart the place of tombs,
Where lay the mighty bones of ancient men,   215
Old knights, and over them the sea-wind sang
Shrill, chill, with flakes of foam. He, stepping down
By zigzag paths, and juts of pointed rock,
Came on the shining levels of the lake.

There drew he forth the brand Excalibur,   220
And o'er him, drawing it, the winter moon,
Brightening the skirts of a long cloud, ran forth
And sparkled keen with frost against the hilt:
For all the haft twinkled with diamond sparks,
Myriads of topaz-lights, and jacinth-work   225
Of subtlest jewellery. He gazed so long
That both his eyes were dazzled as he stood,
This way and that dividing the swift mind,
In act to throw: but at the last it seem'd
Better to leave Excalibur conceal'd   230
There in the many-knotted waterflags,
That whistled stiff and dry about the marge.
So strode he back slow to the wounded King.

Then spake King Arthur to Sir Bedivere:
'Hast thou perform'd my mission which I gave?   235
What is it thou has seen? or what hast heard?'

And answer made the bold Sir Bedivere:
'I heard the ripple washing in the reeds,
And the wild water lapping on the crag.'

To whom replied King Arthur, faint and pale: 240
'Thou hast betray'd thy nature and thy name,
Not rendering true answer, as beseem'd
Thy fëalty, nor like a noble knight:

_____

228. Compare Virgil, *Aeneid,* iv, 285 and viii, 20: "atque animum
nunc huc celerem, nunc dividit illuc."

For surer sign had follow'd, either hand,
Or voice, or else a motion of the mere.   245
This is a shameful thing for men to lie.
Yet now, I charge thee, quickly go again,
As thou art lief and dear, and do the thing
I bade thee, watch, and lightly bring me word.'

Then went Sir Bedivere the second time   250
Across the ridge, and paced beside the mere,
Counting the dewy pebbles, fix'd in thought;
But when he saw the wonder of the hilt,
How curiously and strangely chased, he smote
His palms together, and he cried aloud: 255

'And if indeed I cast the brand away,
Surely a precious thing, one worthy note,
Should thus be lost for ever from the earth,
Which might have pleased the eyes of many men.
What good should follow this, if this were done?   260
What harm, undone?   Deep harm to disobey,
Seeing obedience is the bond of rule.
Were it well to obey then, if a king demand
An act unprofitable, against himself?
The King is sick, and knows not what he does.   265
What record, or what relic of my lord
Should be to aftertime, but empty breath
And rumours of a doubt?   But were this kept,
Stored in some treasure-house of mighty kings,
Some one might show it at a joust of arms,   270
Saying, "King Arthur's sword, Excalibur,
Wrought by the lonely maiden of the Lake.
Nine years she wrought it, sitting in the deeps
Upon the hidden bases of the hills."
So might some old man speak in the aftertime   275
To all the people, winning reverence.
But now much honour and much fame were lost.'

So spake he, clouded with his own conceit,
And hid Excalibur the second time,
And so strode back slow to the wounded King.   280

---

248. *lief,* beloved.

Then spoke King Arthur, breathing heavily:
'What is it thou hast seen? or what hast heard?'

And answer made the bold Sir Bedivere:
'I heard the water lapping on the crag,
And the long ripple washing in the reeds.'   285

To whom replied King Arthur, much in wrath:
'Ah, miserable and unkind, untrue,
Unknightly, traitor-hearted!   Woe is me!
Authority forgets a dying king,
Laid widow'd of the power in his eye   290
That bow'd the will.   I see thee what thou art,
For thou, the latest-left of all my knights,
In whom should meet the offices of all,
Thou wouldst betray me for the precious hilt;
Either from lust of gold, or like a girl   295
Valuing the giddy pleasure of the eyes.
Yet, for a man may fail in duty twice,
And the third time may prosper, get thee hence:
But, if thou spare to fling Excalibur,
I will arise and slay thee with my hands.'   300

Then quickly rose Sir Bedivere, and ran,
And, leaping down the ridges lightly, plunged
Among the bulrush beds, and clutch'd the sword,
And strongly wheel'd and threw it.   The great brand
Made lightnings in the splendour of the moon,   305
And flashing round and round, and whirl'd in an arch,
Shot like a streamer of the northern morn,
Seen where the moving isles of winter shock
By night, with noises of the Northern Sea.
So flash'd and fell the brand Excalibur: 310
But ere he dipt the surface, rose an arm
Clothed in white samite, mystic, wonderful,
And caught him by the hilt, and brandish'd him
Three times, and drew him under in the mere.
And lightly went the other to the King.   315

---

307. The aurora borealis.   Compare Scott, *The Lady of the Lake,* iv, 9:
"The red streamers of the north."

Then spoke King Arthur, drawing thicker breath:
'Now see I by thine eyes that this is done.
Speak out: what is it thou hast heard, or seen?'

And answer made the bold Sir Bedivere:
'Sir King, I closed mine eyelids, lest the gems   320
Should blind my purpose, for I never saw,
Nor shall see, here or elsewhere, till I die,
Not tho' I live three lives of mortal men,
So great a miracle as yonder hilt.
Then with both hands I flung him, wheeling him;   325
But when I look'd again, behold an arm,
Clothed in white samite, mystic, wonderful,
That caught him by the hilt, and brandish'd him
Three times, and drew him under in the mere.'

And answer made King Arthur, breathing hard: 330
'My end draws nigh; 'tis time that I were gone.
Make broad thy shoulders to receive my weight,
And bear me to the margin; yet I fear
My wound hath taken cold, and I shall die.'

So saying, from the pavement he half rose,   335
Slowly, with pain, reclining on his arm,
And looking wistfully with wide blue eyes
As in a picture. Him Sir Bedivere
Remorsefully regarded thro' his tears,
And would have spoken, but he found not words;   340
Then took with care, and kneeling on one knee,
O'er both his shoulders drew the languid hands,
And rising bore him thro' the place of tombs.

But, as he walk'd, King Arthur panted hard,
Like one that feels a nightmare on his bed   345
When all the house is mute. So sigh'd the King,
Muttering and murmuring at his ear, 'Quick, quick!
I fear it is too late, and I shall die.'
But the other swiftly strode from ridge to ridge,
Clothed with his breath, and looking, as he walk'd,   350
Larger than human on the frozen hills.
He heard the deep behind him, and a cry

Before. His own thought drove him like a goad.
Dry clash'd his harness in the icy caves
And barren chasms, and all to left and right   355
The bare black cliff clang'd round him, as he based
His feet on juts of slippery crag that rang
Sharp-smitten with the dint of armed heels —
And on a sudden, lo! the level lake,
And the long glories of the winter moon.   360

  Then saw they how there hove a dusky barge,
Dark as a funeral scarf from stem to stern,
Beneath them; and descending they were ware
That all the decks were dense with stately forms,
Black-stoled, black-hooded, like a dream — by these   365
Three Queens with crowns of gold: and from them rose
A cry that shiver'd to the tingling stars,
And, as it were one voice, an agony
Of lamentation, like a wind that shrills
All night in a waste land, where no one comes,   370
Or hath come, since the making of the world.

  Then murmur'd Arthur, 'Place me in the barge.'
So to the barge they came. There those three Queens
Put forth their hands, and took the King, and wept.
But she, that rose the tallest of them all   375
And fairest, laid his head upon her lap,
And loosed the shatter'd casque, and chafed his hands,
And call'd him by his name, complaining loud,
And dropping bitter tears against a brow
Striped with dark blood: for all his face was white   380
And colourless, and like the wither'd moon
Smote by the fresh beam of the springing east;
And all his greaves and cuisses dash'd with drops
Of onset; and the light and lustrous curls —
That made his forehead like a rising sun   385
High from the daïs-throne — were parch'd with dust;
Or clotted into points and hanging loose,
Mix'd with the knightly growth that fringed his lips.
So like a shatter'd column lay the King;

---

366. *Three Queens.* See "The Coming of Arthur," ll. 275 f.

Not like that Arthur who, with lance in rest,   390
From spur to plume a star of tournament,
Shot thro' the lists at Camelot, and charged
Before the eyes of ladies and of kings.

    Then loudly cried the bold Sir Bedivere:
'Ah! my Lord Arthur, whither shall I go?   395
Where shall I hide my forehead and my eyes?
For now I see the true old times are dead,
When every morning brought a noble chance,
And every chance brought out a noble knight.
Such times have been not since the light that led   400
The holy Elders with the gift of myrrh.
But now the whole Round Table is dissolved
Which was an image of the mighty world,
And I, the last, go forth companionless,
And the days darken round me, and the years,   405
Among new men, strange faces, other minds.'

    And slowly answer'd Arthur from the barge:
'The old order changeth, yielding place to new,
And God fulfils himself in many ways,
Lest one good custom should corrupt the world.   410
Comfort thyself: what comfort is in me?
I have lived my life, and that which I have done
May He within himself make pure! but thou,
If thou shouldst never see my face again,
Pray for my soul. More things are wrought by prayer   415
Than this world dreams of. Wherefore, let thy voice
Rise like a fountain for me night and day.
For what are men better than sheep or goats
That nourish a blind life within the brain,
If, knowing God, they lift not hands of prayer   420
Both for themselves and those who call them friend?
For so the whole round earth is every way

---

    408. Mustard (*op. cit.,* p. 82) suggests that this line may be a para-
phrase of Lucretius, *De Rerum Natura,* iii, 964: "Cedit enim rerum novitate
extrusa vetustas."

    410. Tennyson said that he referred specifically to the custom of
chivalry.

Bound by gold chains about the feet of God.
But now farewell. I am going a long way
With these thou seëst — if indeed I go   425
(For all my mind is clouded with a doubt) —
To the island-valley of Avilion;
Where falls not hail, or rain, or any snow,
Nor ever wind blows loudly; but it lies
Deep-meadow'd, happy, fair with orchard lawns   430
And bowery hollows crown'd with summer sea,
Where I will heal me of my grievous wound.'

    So said he, and the barge with oar and sail
Moved from the brink, like some full-breasted swan
That, fluting a wild carol ere her death,   435
Ruffles her pure cold plume, and takes the flood
With swarthy webs. Long stood Sir Bedivere
Revolving many memories, till the hull
Look'd one black dot against the verge of dawn,
And on the mere the wailing died away.   440

    But when that moan had past for evermore,
The stillness of the dead world's winter dawn
Amazed him, and he groan'd, 'The King is gone.'
And therewithal came on him the weird rhyme,
'From the great deep to the great deep he goes.'   445

    Whereat he slowly turn'd and slowly clomb
The last hard footstep of that iron crag;
Thence mark'd the black hull moving yet, and cried,
'He passes to be King among the dead,
And after healing of his grievous wound   450
He comes again; but — if he come no more —
O me, be yon dark Queens in yon black boat,
Who shriek'd and wail'd, the three whereat we gazed
On that high day, when, clothed with living light,
They stood before his throne in silence, friends   455
Of Arthur, who should help him at his need?'

---

427 f. Compare "Lucretius," ll. 104 f. and the note.
434 f. Compare the early poem, "The Dying Swan" (1830).
440. With this line the original "Morte d'Arthur" ends.

Then from the dawn it seem'd there came, but faint
As from beyond the limit of the world,
Like the last echo born of a great cry,
Sounds, as if some fair city were one voice   460
Around a king returning from his wars.

Thereat once more he moved about, and clomb
Ev'n to the highest he could climb, and saw,
Straining his eyes beneath an arch of hand,
Or thought he saw, the speck that bare the King,   465
Down that long water opening on the deep
Somewhere far off, pass on and on, and go
From less to less and vanish into light.
And the new sun rose bringing the new year.

TO THE QUEEN[1]

O LOYAL to the royal in thyself,
And loyal to the land, as this to thee —
Bear witness, that rememberable day,
When, pale as yet, and fever-worn, the Prince
Who scarce had pluck'd his flickering life again   5
From halfway down the shadow of the grave,
Past with thee thro' thy people and their love,
And London roll'd one tide of joy thro' all
Her trebled millions, and loud leagues of man
And welcome! witness, too, the silent cry,   10
The prayer of many a race and creed, and clime —
Thunderless lightnings striking under sea
From sunset and sunrise of all thy realm,
And that true North, whereof we lately heard
A strain to shame us 'keep you to yourselves;   15

[1] This epilogue to the *Idylls of the King* was first published in the Library edition of the *Works,* 1872–3. It is important for its indication (ll. 36 f.) of the allegory with which Tennyson overshadows the legend.

3. *rememberable day,* the day of the service of thanksgiving at St. Paul's cathedral for the recovery of the Prince of Wales from a dangerous illness (February, 1872).

14. *that true North,* Canada. This passage was written in reply to the argument that the connection of Canada with the mother-country should be severed because the dominion was "too costly" to be maintained.

So loyal is too costly! friends — your love
Is but a burthen: loose the bond, and go.'
Is this the tone of empire? here the faith
That made us rulers? this, indeed, her voice
And meaning, whom the roar of Hougoumont   20
Left mightiest of all peoples under heaven?
What shock has fool'd her since, that she should speak
So feebly? wealthier — wealthier — hour by hour!
The voice of Britain, or a sinking land,
Some third-rate isle half-lost among her seas?   25
There rang her voice, when the full city peal'd
Thee and thy Prince! The loyal to their crown
Are loyal to their own far sons, who love
Our ocean-empire with her boundless homes
For ever-broadening England, and her throne   30
In our vast Orient, and one isle, one isle,
That knows not her own greatness: if she knows
And dreads it we are fall'n. — But thou, my Queen
Not for itself, but thro' thy living love
For one to whom I made it o'er his grave   35
Sacred, accept this old imperfect tale,
New-old, and shadowing Sense at war with Soul
Ideal manhood closed in real man
Rather than that gray king, whose name, a ghost,
Streams like a cloud, man-shaped, from mountain peak,   40
And cleaves to cairn and cromlech still; or him
Of Geoffrey's book, or him of Malleor's, one
Touch'd by the adulterous finger of a time
That hover'd between war and wantonness,
And crownings and dethronements: take withal   45
Thy poet's blessing, and his trust that Heaven
Will blow the tempest in the distance back
From thine and ours: for some are scared, who mark,
Or wisely or unwisely, signs of storm,
Waverings of every vane with every wind,   50

---

20. *Hougoumont*, Waterloo.

35. A reference to the Dedication of the *Idylls* to the memory of the
Prince Consort.

39–41. These magnificent lines refer to the legendary Arthur.

42. *Geoffrey*, Geoffrey of Monmouth; *Malleor*, Sir Thomas Malory.

And wordy trucklings to the transient hour,
And fierce or careless looseners of the faith,
And Softness breeding scorn of simple life,
Or Cowardice, the child of lust for gold,
Or Labour, with a groan and not a voice,   55
Or Art with poisonous honey stol'n from France,
And that which knows, but careful for itself,
And that which knows not, ruling that which knows
To its own harm: the goal of this great world
Lies beyond sight: yet — if our slowly-grown   60
And crown'd Republic's crowning common-sense,
That saved her many times, not fail — their fears
Are morning shadows huger than the shapes
That cast them, not those gloomier which forego
The darkness of that battle in the West,   65
Where all of high and holy dies away.

_____

56. Compare the epigram "Art for Art's Sake," never published by
Tennyson but printed in the *Memoir*. In this oft-quoted line Tennyson
is almost certainly referring to Swinburne's *Poems and Ballads*, 1866, and
Rossetti's *Poems*, 1870.

VI

"MAUD" AND MISCELLANEOUS POEMS

THE GARDENER'S DAUGHTER;

OR, THE PICTURES[1]

THIS morning is the morning of the day,
When I and Eustace from the city went
To see the gardener's daughter; I and he,
Brothers in Art; a friendship so complete
Portion'd in halves between us, that we grew   5
The fable of the city where we dwelt.
  My Eustace might have sat for Hercules;
So muscular he spread, so broad of breast.
He, by some law that holds in love, and draws
The greater to the lesser, long desired   10
A certain miracle of symmetry,
A miniature of loveliness, all grace
Summ'd up and closed in little; — Juliet, she
So light of foot, so light of spirit — oh, she
To me myself, for some three careless moons,   15
The summer pilot of an empty heart
Unto the shores of nothing! Know you not
Such touches are but embassies of love,
To tamper with the feelings, ere he found
Empire for life? but Eustace painted her,   20
And said to me, she sitting with us then,

---

[1] Written, at least in part, by 1833 when it is mentioned in a letter (*Memoir*, i, 130); published in *Poems*, 1842; unchanged since then save for the alteration of one word (see note on l. 230). For the Theocritan imitations and "echoes" in this "English Idyl" see Mustard, *op. cit.*, pp. 33 f. The poem is a dramatic monologue; the speaker an old man. It has been compared, not very aptly, to Browning's "My Last Duchess."

'When will *you* paint like this?' and I replied,
(My words were half in earnest, half in jest,)
' 'Tis not your work, but Love's. Love unperceived,
A more ideal Artist he than all,   25
Came, drew your pencil from you, made those eyes
Darker than darkest pansies, and that hair
More black than ashbuds in the front of March.'
And Juliet answer'd laughing, 'Go and see
The gardener's daughter: trust me, after that,   30
You scarce can fail to match his masterpiece.'
And up we rose, and on the spur we went.
    Not wholly in the busy world, nor quite
Beyond it, blooms the garden that I love.
News from the humming city comes to it   35
In sound of funeral or of marriage bells;
And, sitting muffled in dark leaves, you hear
The windy clanging of the minster clock;
Although between it and the garden lies
A league of grass, wash'd by a slow broad stream,   40
That, stirr'd with languid pulses of the oar,
Waves all its lazy lilies, and creeps on,
Barge-laden, to three arches of a bridge
Crown'd with the minster-towers.
                            The fields between
Are dewy-fresh, browsed by deep-udder'd kine,   45
And all about the large lime feathers low,
The lime a summer home of murmurous wings.
    In that still place she, hoarded in herself,
Grew, seldom seen; not less among us lived
Her fame from lip to lip. Who had not heard   50
Of Rose, the gardener's daughter? Where was he,
So blunt in memory, so old at heart,
At such a distance from his youth in grief,
That, having seen, forgot? The common mouth,
So gross to express delight, in praise of her   55
Grew oratory. Such a lord is Love,
And Beauty such a mistress of the world.
    And if I said that Fancy, led by Love,

---

    35. The city is Lincoln.
    40. The stream is the Witham.

Would play with flying forms and images,
Yet this is also true, that, long before   60
I look'd upon her, when I heard her name
My heart was like a prophet to my heart,
And told me I should love.   A crowd of hopes,
That sought to sow themselves like winged seeds,
Born out of everything I heard and saw,   65
Flutter'd about my senses and my soul;
And vague desires, like fitful blasts of balm
To one that travels quickly, made the air
Of Life delicious, and all kinds of thought,
That verged upon them, sweeter than the dream   70
Dream'd by a happy man, when the dark East,
Unseen, is brightening to his bridal morn.
    And sure this orbit of the memory folds
For ever in itself the day we went
To see her.   All the land in flowery squares,   75
Beneath a broad and equal-blowing wind,
Smelt of the coming summer, as one large cloud
Drew downward: but all else of heaven was pure
Up to the Sun, and May from verge to verge,
And May with me from head to heel.   And now,   80
As tho' 'twere yesterday, as tho' it were
The hour just flown, that morn with all its sound,
(For those old Mays had thrice the life of these,)
Rings in mine ears.   The steer forgot to graze,
And, where the hedge-row cuts the pathway, stood,   85
Leaning his horns into the neighbour field,
And lowing to his fellows.   From the woods
Came voices of the well-contented doves.
The lark could scarce get out his notes for joy,
But shook his song together as he near'd   90
His happy home, the ground.   To left and right,
The cuckoo told his name to all the hills;
The mellow ouzel fluted in the elm;
The redcap whistled; and the nightingale
Sang loud, as tho' he were the bird of day.   95
    And Eustace turn'd, and smiling said to me,
'Hear how the bushes echo! by my life,
These birds have joyful thoughts.   Think you they sing
Like poets, from the vanity of song?

Or have they any sense of why they sing?   100
And would they praise the heavens for what they have?'
And I made answer, 'Were there nothing else
For which to praise the heavens but only love,
That only love were cause enough for praise.'

 Lightly he laugh'd, as one that read my thought,   105
And on we went; but ere an hour had pass'd,
We reach'd a meadow slanting to the North;
Down which a well-worn pathway courted us
To one green wicket in a privet hedge;
This, yielding, gave into a grassy walk   110
Thro' crowded lilac-ambush trimly pruned;
And one warm gust, full-fed with perfume, blew
Beyond us, as we enter'd in the cool.
The garden stretches southward. In the midst
A cedar spread his dark-green layers of shade.   115
The garden-glasses glanced, and momently
The twinkling laurel scatter'd silver lights.

 'Eustace,' I said, 'this wonder keeps the house.'
He nodded, but a moment afterwards
He cried, 'Look! look!' Before he ceased I turn'd,   120
And, ere a star can wink, beheld her there.

 For up the porch there grew an Eastern rose,
That, flowering high, the last night's gale had caught,
And blown across the walk. One arm aloft —
Gown'd in pure white, that fitted to the shape —   125
Holding the bush, to fix it back, she stood,
A single stream of all her soft brown hair
Pour'd on one side: the shadow of the flowers
Stole all the golden gloss, and, wavering
Lovingly lower, trembled on her waist —   130
Ah, happy shade — and still went wavering down,
But, ere it touch'd a foot, that might have danced
The greensward into greener circles, dipt,
And mix'd with shadows of the common ground!
But the full day dwelt on her brows, and sunn'd   135

---

 133. *greener circles,* made, according to the folk belief, by fairies in
their dances. Compare *The Tempest,* V, i, 36 f.:
     You demi-puppets that
  By moonshine do the green sour ringlets make.

Her violet eyes, and all her Hebe bloom,
And doubled his own warmth against her lips,
And on the bounteous wave of such a breast
As never pencil drew.   Half light, half shade,
She stood, a sight to make an old man young.   140
    So rapt, we near'd the house; but she, a Rose
In roses, mingled with her fragrant toil,
Nor heard us come, nor from her tendance turn'd
Into the world without; till close at hand,
And almost ere I knew mine own intent,   145
This murmur broke the stillness of that air
Which brooded round about her:
                                        'Ah, one rose,
One rose, but one, by those fair fingers cull'd,
Were worth a hundred kisses press'd on lips
Less exquisite than thine.'
                              She look'd: but all   150
Suffused with blushes — neither self-possess'd
Nor startled, but betwixt this mood and that,
Divided in a graceful quiet — paused,
And dropt the branch she held, and turning, wound
Her looser hair in braid, and stirr'd her lips   155
For some sweet answer, tho' no answer came,
Nor yet refused the rose, but granted it,
And moved away, and left me, statue-like,
In act to render thanks.
                          I, that whole day,
Saw her no more, altho' I linger'd there   160
Till every daisy slept, and Love's white star
Beam'd thro' the thicken'd cedar in the dusk.
    So home we went, and all the livelong way
With solemn gibe did Eustace banter me.
'Now,' said he, 'will you climb the top of Art.   165
You cannot fail but work in hues to dim
The Titianic Flora. Will you match
My Juliet? you, not you, — the Master, Love,
A more ideal Artist he than all.'
    So home I went, but could not sleep for joy,   170
Reading her perfect features in the gloom,

---

167. The "Flora" of Titian in the Uffizi Gallery in Florence.

Kissing the rose she gave me o'er and o'er,
And shaping faithful record of the glance
That graced the giving — such a noise of life
Swarm'd in the golden present, such a voice   175
Call'd to me from the years to come, and such
A length of bright horizon rimm'd the dark.
And all that night I heard the watchman peal
The sliding season: all that night I heard
The heavy clocks knolling the drowsy hours.   180
The drowsy hours. dispensers of all good,
O'er the mute city stole with folded wings,
Distilling odors on me as they went
To greet their fairer sisters of the East.

   Love at first sight, first-born, and heir to all,   185
Made this night thus.   Henceforward squall nor storm
Could keep me from that Eden where she dwelt.
Light pretexts drew me; sometimes a Dutch love
For tulips: then for roses, moss or musk,
To grace my city rooms; or fruits and cream   190
Served in the weeping elm; and more and more
A word could bring the colour to my cheek;
A thought would fill my eyes with happy dew;
Love trebled life within me, and with each
The year increased.

            The daughters of the year,   195
One after one, thro' that still garden pass'd;
Each garlanded with her peculiar flower
Danced into light, and died into the shade;
And each in passing touch'd with some new grace
Or seem'd to touch her, so that day by day,   200
Like one that never can be wholly known,
Her beauty grew; till Autumn brought an hour
For Eustace, when I heard his deep 'I will,'
Breathed, like the covenant of a God, to hold
From thence thro' all the worlds: but I rose up   205
Full of his bliss, and following her dark eyes
Felt earth as air beneath me, till I reach'd
The wicket-gate, and found her standing there.

   There sat we down upon a garden mound,
Two mutually enfolded; Love, the third,   210
Between us, in the circle of his arms

Enwound us both; and over many a range
Of waning lime the gray cathedral towers,
Across a hazy glimmer of the west,
Reveal'd their shining windows: from them clash'd   215
The bells; we listen'd; with the time we play'd,
We spoke of other things; we coursed about
The subject most at heart, more near and near,
Like doves about a dovecote, wheeling round
The central wish, until we settled there.   220
   Then, in that time and place, I spoke to her,
Requiring, tho' I knew it was mine own,
Yet for the pleasure that I took to hear,
Requiring at her hand the greatest gift,
A woman's heart, the heart of her I loved;   225
And in that time and place she answer'd me,
And in the compass of three little words,
More musical than ever came in one,
The silver fragments of a broken voice,
Made me most happy, faltering, 'I am thine.'   230
   Shall I cease here?   Is this enough to say
That my desire, like all strongest hopes,
By its own energy fulfill'd itself,
Merged in completion?   Would you learn at full
How passion rose thro' circumstantial grades   235
Beyond all grades develop'd? and indeed
I had not staid so long to tell you all,
But while I mused came Memory with sad eyes,
Holding the folded annals of my youth;
And while I mused, Love with knit brows went by,   240
And with a flying finger swept my lips,
And spake, 'Be wise: not easily forgiven
Are those who, setting wide the doors that bar
The secret bridal chambers of the heart,
Let in the day.'   Here, then, my words have end.   245
   Yet might I tell of meetings, of farewells —
Of that which came between, more sweet than each,
In whispers, like the whispers of the leaves
That tremble round a nightingale — in sighs
Which perfect Joy, perplex'd for utterance,   250

---

230. *faltering,* 1842: "lisping."

Stole from her sister Sorrow.   Might I not tell
Of difference, reconcilement, pledges given,
And vows, where there was never need of vows,
And kisses, where the heart on one wild leap
Hung tranced from all pulsation, as above   255
The heavens between their fairy fleeces pale
Sow'd all their mystic gulfs with fleeting stars;
Or while the balmy glooming, crescent-lit,
Spread the light haze along the river-shores,
And in the hollows; or as once we met   260
Unheedful, tho' beneath a whispering rain
Night slid down one long stream of sighing wind,
And in her bosom bore the baby, Sleep.
    But this whole hour your eyes have been intent
On that veil'd picture — veil'd, for what it holds   265
May not be dwelt on by the common day.
This prelude has prepared thee.   Raise thy soul;
Make thine heart ready with thine eyes: the time
Is come to raise the veil.
                          Behold her there,
As I beheld her ere she knew my heart,   270
My first, last love; the idol of my youth,
The darling of my manhood, and, alas!
Now the most blessed memory of mine age.

DORA [1]

WITH farmer Allan at the farm abode
William and Dora.   William was his son,
And she his niece.   He often look'd at them,
And often thought, 'I'll make them man and wife.'
Now Dora felt her uncle's will in all,   5

---

263. Compare Shelley, *Queen Mab*, i, 40 f.:

> On their lids . . .
> The baby Sleep is pillowed.

[1] Written by 1835 (*Memoir*, i, 151); published in *Poems*, 1842. This
"Idyl" was partly suggested (as Tennyson acknowledged in a note in the
original edition) by the story "Dora Creswell" in Miss Mitford's *Our Village*. J. Churton Collins's accusation (*Illustrations of Tennyson*, p. 55)
that "Tennyson, like Gray, leaves his commentators to track him to his raw
material" is quite groundless.   Nor is it true, as Collins asserts, that "the

And yearn'd toward William; but the youth, because
He had been always with her in the house,
Thought not of Dora.
                          Then there came a day
When Allan call'd his son, and said, 'My son:
I married late, but I would wish to see   10
My grandchild on my knees before I die:
And I have set my heart upon a match.
Now therefore look to Dora; she is well
To look to; thrifty too beyond her age.
She is my brother's daughter: he and I   15
Had once hard words, and parted, and he died
In foreign lands; but for his sake I bred
His daughter Dora: take her for your wife;
For I have wish'd this marriage, night and day,
For many years.' But William answer'd short: 20
'I cannot marry Dora; by my life,
I will not marry Dora.' Then the old man
Was wroth, and doubled up his hands, and said:
'You will not, boy! you dare to answer thus!
But in my time a father's word was law,   25
And so it shall be now for me. Look to it;
Consider, William: take a month to think,
And let me have an answer to my wish;
Or, by the Lord that made me, you shall pack,
And never more darken my doors again.'   30
But William answer'd madly; bit his lips,
And broke away. The more he look'd at her
The less he liked her; and his ways were harsh;
But Dora bore them meekly. Then before
The month was out he left his father's house,   35
And hired himself to work within the fields;
And half in love, half spite, he woo'd and wed

---

whole plot . . . to the minutest detail" is taken from Miss Mitford's story.
In the original, Dora is a child; and the conclusion is managed differently.
In its bareness of style and lack of poetic imagery it is the most Words-
worthian of Tennyson's poems; James Spedding remarked that "this was
the poem which Wordsworth always intended to have written" (*Works*,
Eversley edition, i, 720); and Wordsworth himself said magnanimously:
"Mr. Tennyson, I have been endeavouring all my life to write a pastoral
like your 'Dora' and have not succeeded" (*Memoir*, i, 265).

A labourer's daughter, Mary Morrison.
   Then, when the bells were ringing, Allan call'd
His niece and said: 'My girl, I love you well;   40
But if you speak with him that was my son,
Or change a word with her he calls his wife,
My home is none of yours. My will is law.'
And Dora promised, being meek. She thought,
'It cannot be: my uncle's mind will change!'   45
   And days went on, and there was born a boy
To William; then distresses came on him;
And day by day he pass'd his father's gate,
Heart-broken, and his father help'd him not.
But Dora stored what little she could save,   50
And sent it them by stealth, nor did they know
Who sent it; till at last a fever seized
On William, and in harvest time he died.
   Then Dora went to Mary. Mary sat
And look'd with tears upon her boy, and thought   55
Hard things of Dora. Dora came and said:
   'I have obey'd my uncle until now,
And I have sinn'd, for it was all thro' me
This evil came on William at the first.
But, Mary, for the sake of him that's gone,   60
And for your sake, the woman that he chose,
And for this orphan, I am come to you:
You know there has not been for these five years
So full a harvest: let me take the boy,
And I will set him in my uncle's eye   65
Among the wheat; that when his heart is glad
Of the full harvest, he may see the boy,
And bless him for the sake of him that's gone.'
   And Dora took the child, and went her way
Across the wheat, and sat upon a mound   70
That was unsown, where many poppies grew.
Far off the farmer came into the field
And spied her not; for none of all his men
Dare tell him Dora waited with the child;
And Dora would have risen and gone to him,   75
But her heart fail'd her; and the reapers reap'd,
And the sun fell, and all the land was dark.
   But when the morrow came, she rose and took

The child once more, and sat upon the mound;
And made a little wreath of all the flowers   80
That grew about, and tied it round his hat
To make him pleasing in her uncle's eye.
Then when the farmer pass'd into the field
He spied her, and he left his men at work,
And came and said: 'Where were you yesterday?   85
Whose child is that?   What are you doing here?'
So Dora cast her eyes upon the ground,
And answer'd softly, 'This is William's child!'
'And did I not,' said Allan, 'did I not
Forbid you, Dora?' Dora said again: 90
'Do with me as you will, but take the child,
And bless him for the sake of him that's gone!'
And Allan said, 'I see it is a trick
Got up betwixt you and the woman there.
I must be taught my duty, and by you!   95
You knew my word was law, and yet you dared
To slight it.   Well — for I will take the boy;
But go you hence, and never see me more.'
    So saying, he took the boy, that cried aloud
And struggled hard. The wreath of flowers fell   100
At Dora's feet. She bowed upon her hands,
And the boy's cry came to her from the field,
More and more distant. She bow'd down her head,
Remembering the day when first she came,
And all the things that had been. She bow'd down   105
And wept in secret; and the reapers reap'd,
And the sun fell, and all the land was dark.
    Then Dora went to Mary's house, and stood
Upon the threshold. Mary saw the boy
Was not with Dora. She broke out in praise   110
To God, that help'd her in her widowhood.
And Dora said, 'My uncle took the boy;
But, Mary, let me live and work with you:
He says that he will never see me more.'
Then answer'd Mary, 'This shall never be,   115
That thou shouldst take my trouble on thyself:
And, now I think, he shall not have the boy,
For he will teach him hardness, and to slight
His mother; therefore thou and I will go,

And I will have my boy, and bring him home;   120
And I will beg of him to take thee back:
But if he will not take thee back again,
Then thou and I will live within one house,
And work for William's child, until he grows
Of age to help us.'   125
          So the women kiss'd
Each other, and set out, and reach'd the farm.
The door was off the latch: they peep'd, and saw
The boy set up betwixt his grandsire's knees,
Who thrust him in the hollows of his arm,
And clapt him on the hands and on the cheeks,   130
Like one that loved him: and the lad stretch'd out
And babbled for the golden seal, that hung
From Allan's watch, and sparkled by the fire.
Then they came in: but when the boy beheld
His mother, he cried out to come to her: 135
And Allan set him down, and Mary said:
   'O Father! — if you let me call you so —
I never came a-begging for myself,
Or William, or this child; but now I come
For Dora: take her back; she loves you well.   140
O Sir, when William died, he died at peace
With all men; for I ask'd him, and he said
He could not ever rue his marrying me —
I had been a patient wife: but, Sir, he said
That he was wrong to cross his father thus: 145
"God bless him!" he said, "and may he never know
The troubles I have gone thro'!" Then he turn'd
His face and pass'd — unhappy that I am!
But now, Sir, let me have my boy, for you
Will make him hard, and he will learn to slight   150
His father's memory; and take Dora back,
And let all this be as it was before.'
   So Mary said, and Dora hid her face
By Mary. There was silence in the room;
And all at once the old man burst in sobs: —   155
   'I have been to blame — to blame. I have kill'd my son.
I have kill'd him — but I loved him — my dear son.
May God forgive me! — I have been to blame.
Kiss me, my children.'

Then they clung about
The old man's neck, and kiss'd him many times.   160
And all the man was broken with remorse;
And all his love came back a hundred-fold;
And for three hours he sobb'd o'er William's child
Thinking of William.
                         So those four abode
Within one house together; and as years   165
Went forward, Mary took another mate;
But Dora lived unmarried till her death.

LOCKSLEY HALL[1]

COMRADES, leave me here a little, while as yet 'tis early morn:
Leave me here, and when you want me, sound upon the bugle-
        horn.

'Tis the place, and all around it, as of old, the curlews call,
Dreary gleams about the moorland flying over Locksley Hall;

---

[1] The date of composition is uncertain, though at least one line (182; see
note) is as early as 1830. The poem was published in *Poems,* 1842, and
was subjected to but little revision in later editions. Tennyson said
(*Memoir,* i, 195) that the idea of the poem was given him by Sir William
Jones's translation the *Mu'allaqāt,* the famous seven "suspended" Odes of
pre-Islamic Arabia (so-called because, according to legend, they were inscribed in golden letters and suspended on the walls of the Ka'bah at
Mecca). See Sir William Jones, *Works,* London, 1799, iv, 245 f. There
is a translation into English verse by Lady Anne and Wilfrid Scawen Blunt:
The Seven Golden Odes of Pagan Arabia, London, 1903. See also P. K.
Hitti, *History of the Arabs,* New York, 1937, pp. 93 f. The Odes are on
various themes, but they have this in common, that they all begin with sad
meditations upon deserted dwellings, plighted vows, and broken faith.
This was the germinating theme of "Locksley Hall." It has been suggested (see Sir Alfred Lyall, *Tennyson,* p. 50; Emil Koeppel, "Tennysoniana," *Englische Studien,* xxviii, 404 f.) that Tennyson may have imitated the metre of the Arabic originals; but the resemblances noted are probably due to coincidence, for the poet said (*Memoir,* i, 195) that he chose
the trochaic metre because Henry Hallam told him that English people
liked it. The poem is a dramatic monologue. Its enormous contemporary
popularity was due in part to an identification of the poet with the speaker.
The disrepute into which it has fallen is due in part to association with
"Locksley Hall Sixty Years After," that "long, ranting and pathetic diatribe" (as Mr. Harold Nicolson calls it) which Tennyson composed towards
the end of his life.

4. Locksley Hall is an imaginary building, but the landscape is that of
the Lincolnshire coast.

Locksley Hall, that in the distance overlooks the sandy tracts, 5
And the hollow ocean-ridges roaring into cataracts.

Many a night from yonder ivied casement, ere I went to rest,
Did I look on great Orion sloping slowly to the West.

Many a night I saw the Pleiads, rising thro' the mellow shade,
Glitter like a swarm of fire-flies tangled in a silver braid.   10

Here about the beach I wander'd, nourishing a youth sublime
With the fairy tales of science, and the long result of Time;

When the centuries behind me like a fruitful land reposed;
When I clung to all the present for the promise that it closed:

When I dipt into the future far as human eye could see;   15
Saw the Vision of the world, and all the wonder that would
    be. —

In the Spring a fuller crimson comes upon the robin's breast;
In the Spring the wanton lapwing gets himself another crest;

In the Spring a livelier iris changes on the burnish'd dove;
In the Spring a young man's fancy lightly turns to thoughts
    of love.   20

Then her cheek was pale and thinner than should be for one
    so young,
And her eyes on all my motions with a mute observance hung.

And I said, 'My cousin Amy, speak, and speak the truth to me,
Trust me, cousin, all the current of my being sets to thee.'

On her pallid cheek and forehead came a color and a light,   25
As I have seen the rosy red flushing in the northern night.

And she turn'd — her bosom shaken with a sudden storm of
    sighs —
All the spirit deeply dawning in the dark of hazel eyes —

9–10. This famous couplet affords the closest parallel (not very close)
to the *Mu'allaqāt:*

> What time in the eastern heavens the Pleiades clomb the sky
> Like the jewelled clasps of a girdle aslant on a woman's waist.

Saying, 'I have hid my feelings, fearing they should do me
        wrong;'
Saying, 'Dost thou love me, cousin?' weeping, 'I have loved
        thee long.'   30

Love took up the glass of Time, and turn'd it in his glowing
        hands;
Every moment, lightly shaken, ran itself in golden sands.

Love took up the harp of Life, and smote on all the chords
        with might;
Smote the chord of Self, that, trembling, pass'd in music out
        of sight.

Many a morning on the moorland did we hear the copses
        ring,   35
And her whisper throng'd my pulses with the fullness of the
        Spring.

Many an evening by the waters did we watch the stately ships,
And our spirits rush'd together at the touching of the lips.

O my cousin, shallow-hearted!   O my Amy, mine no more!
O the dreary, dreary moorland!   O the barren, barren shore! 40

Falser than all fancy fathoms, falser than all songs have sung,
Puppet to a father's threat, and servile to a shrewish tongue!

Is it well to wish thee happy? — having known me — to
        decline
On a range of lower feelings and a narrower heart than mine!

Yet it shall be: thou shalt lower to his level day by day,   45
What is fine within thee growing coarse to sympathise with
        clay.

43–4. Compare *Hamlet,* I, v, 50 f.:
                        To decline
                Upon a wretch whose natural gifts were poor
                To those of mine;
and *In Memoriam* lxii, 5.

As the husband is, the wife is: thou art mated with a clown,
And the grossness of his nature will have weight to drag thee
    down.

He will hold thee, when his passion shall have spent its novel
    force,
Something better than his dog, a little dearer than his horse. 50

What is this? his eyes are heavy: think not they are glazed
    with wine.
Go to him: it is thy duty: kiss him: take his hand in thine.

It may be my lord is weary, that his brain is overwrought:
Soothe him with thy finer fancies, touch him with thy lighter
    thought.

He will answer to the purpose, easy things to understand — 55
Better thou wert dead before me, tho' I slew thee with my
    hand!

Better thou and I were lying, hidden from the heart's disgrace,
Roll'd in one another's arms, and silent in a last embrace.

Cursed be the social wants that sin against the strength of
    youth!
Cursed be the social lies that warp us from the living truth! 60

Cursed be the sickly forms that err from honest Nature's rule!
Cursed be the gold that gilds the straiten'd forehead of the
    fool!

Well — 'tis well that I should bluster! — Hadst thou less un-
    worthy proved —
Would to God — for I had loved thee more than ever wife
    was loved.

Am I mad, that I should cherish that which bears but bitter
    fruit?   65
I will pluck it from my bosom, tho' my heart be at the root.

Never, tho' my mortal summers to such length of years should
come
As the many-winter'd crow that leads the clanging rookery
home.

Where is comfort? in division of the records of the mind?
Can I part her from herself, and love her, as I knew her,
kind? 70

I remember one that perish'd: sweetly did she speak and move:
Such a one do I remember, whom to look at was to love.

Can I think of her as dead, and love her for the love she bore?
No — she never loved me truly: love is love for evermore.

Comfort? comfort scorn'd of devils! this is truth the poet
sings, 75
That a sorrow's crown of sorrow is remembering happier
things.

Drug thy memories, lest thou learn it, lest thy heart be put to
proof,
In the dead unhappy night, and when the rain is on the roof.

Like a dog, he hunts in dreams, and thou art staring at the wall,
Where the dying night-lamp flickers, and the shadows rise and
fall. 80

_____

68. *the many-winter'd crow.* Tennyson doubtless had in mind
Horace's "annosa cornix" (*Odes,* iii, 17, 13) and perhaps Shakespeare's
"treble-dated crow" ("The Phœnix and the Turtle"); but, as he noted,
"rooks are called crows in the Northern Counties."

75–6. The parallels cited by some commentators (*e.g.,* J. Churton Collins, *op. cit.,* p. 63) from Pindar, Thucydides, Boethius, Chaucer, Hoccleve,
and Marini are all beside the mark; for "the poet" is Dante and "the truth"
is:

Nessun maggior dolore
che ricordarsi del tempo felice
nella miseria

(*Inferno,* v, 121 f.). For the opposite sentiment see the fine sonnet in
Esther by W. S. Blunt beginning:

He who has once been happy is for aye
Out of destruction's reach.

79. Compare "Lucretius," ll. 43 f.

Then a hand shall pass before thee, pointing to his drunken
    sleep,
To thy widow'd marriage-pillows, to the tears that thou wilt
    weep.

Thou shalt hear the 'Never, never,' whisper'd by the phantom
    years,
And a song from out the distance in the ringing of thine ears;

And an eye shall vex thee, looking ancient kindness on thy
    pain. 85
Turn thee, turn thee on thy pillow: get thee to thy rest again.

Nay, but Nature brings thee solace; for a tender voice will cry.
'Tis a purer life than thine; a lip to drain thy trouble dry.

Baby lips will laugh me down: my latest rival brings thee rest.
Baby fingers, waxen touches, press me from the mother's
    breast. 90

O, the child too clothes the father with a dearness not his due.
Half is thine and half is his: it will be worthy of the two.

O, I see thee old and formal, fitted to thy petty part,
With a little hoard of maxims preaching down a daughter's
    heart.

'They were dangerous guides the feelings — she herself was
    not exempt — 95
Truly, she herself had suffer'd' — Perish in thy self-contempt!

Overlive it — lower yet — be happy! wherefore should I care?
I myself must mix with action, lest I wither by despair.

What is that which I should turn to, lighting upon days like
    these?
Every door is barr'd with gold, and opens but to golden
    keys. 100

Every gate is throng'd with suitors, all the markets overflow.
I have but an angry fancy: what is that which I should do?

I had been content to perish, falling on the foeman's ground,
When the ranks are roll'd in vapour, and the winds are laid
with sound.

But the jingling of the guinea helps the hurt that Honour
feels,   105
And the nations do but murmur, snarling at each other's heels.

Can I but relive in sadness?   I will turn that earlier page.
Hide me from my deep emotion, O thou wondrous Mother-
Age!

Make me feel the wild pulsation that I felt before the strife,
When I heard my days before me, and the tumult of my
life;   110

Yearning for the large excitement that the coming years would
yield,
Eager-hearted as a boy when first he leaves his father's field,

And at night along the dusky highway near and nearer drawn,
Sees in heaven the light of London flaring like a dreary dawn;

And his spirit leaps within him to be gone before him then, 115
Underneath the light he looks at, in among the throngs of
men:

Men, my brothers, men the workers, ever reaping something
new:
That which they have done but earnest of the things that they
shall do:

For I dipt into the future, far as human eye could see,
Saw the Vision of the world, and all the wonder that would
be;   120

Saw the heavens fill with commerce, argosies of magic sails,
Pilots of the purple twilight, dropping down with costly bales;

113-4. Tennyson said that this simile was "drawn from old times and
the top of the mail-coach.   They that go by trains seldom see this" (*Works,*
Eversley edition, i, 730).

Heard the heavens fill with shouting, and there rain'd a
    ghastly dew
From the nations' airy navies grappling in the central blue;

Far along the world-wide whisper of the south-wind rushing
    warm,   125
With the standards of the peoples plunging thro' the thunder-
    storm;

Till the war-drum throbb'd no longer, and the battle-flags were
    furl'd
In the Parliament of man, the Federation of the world.

There the common sense of most shall hold a fretful realm in
    awe,
And the kindly earth shall slumber, lapt in universal law.   130

So I triumph'd ere my passion sweeping thro' me left me dry,
Left me with the palsied heart, and left me with the jaundiced
    eye;

Eye, to which all order festers, all things here are out of joint:
Science moves, but slowly slowly, creeping on from point to
    point:

Slowly comes a hungry people, as a lion creeping nigher,   135
Glares at one that nods and winks behind a slowly-dying fire.

Yet I doubt not thro' the ages one increasing purpose runs,
And the thoughts of men are widen'd with the process of the
    suns.

What is that to him that reaps not harvest of his youthful joys,
Tho' the deep heart of existence beat for ever like a boy's?   140

Knowledge comes, but wisdom lingers, and I linger on the
    shore,
And the individual withers, and the world is more and more.

135–6. The simile of the lion was drawn from Thomas Pringle's *Narrative of a Residence in South Africa*, 1834, p. 39, a book which Tennyson
read in 1837. See *Works*, Eversley edition, i, 730.

141. Compare *In Memoriam*, cxiv.

Knowledge comes, but wisdom lingers, and he bears a laden
    breast,
Full of sad experience, moving toward the stillness of his rest.

Hark, my merry comrades call me, sounding on the bugle-
    horn,   145
They to whom my foolish passion were a target for their scorn:

Shall it not be scorn to me to harp on such a moulder'd string?
I am shamed thro' all my nature to have loved so slight a thing.

Weakness to be wroth with weakness! woman's pleasure,
    woman's pain —
Nature made them blinder motions bounded in a shallower
    brain: 150

Woman is the lesser man, and all thy passions, match'd with
    mine,
Are as moonlight unto sunlight, and as water unto wine —

Here at least, where nature sickens, nothing. Ah, for some
    retreat
Deep in yonder shining Orient, where my life began to beat;

Where in wild Mahratta-battle fell my father evil-starr'd; — 155
I was left a trampled orphan, and a selfish uncle's ward.

Or to burst all links of habit — there to wander far away,
On from island unto island at the gateways of the day.

Larger constellations burning, mellow moons and happy skies,
Breadths of tropic shade and palms in cluster, knots of Para-
    dise.   160

Never comes the trader, never floats an European flag,
Slides the bird o'er lustrous woodland, swings the trailer from
    the crag;

---

155. The Mahrattas, a people of central India, fought three wars with
the English. The reference is probably to the campaign of 1803 in which
Sir Arthur Wellesley commanded the English.

Droops the heavy-blossom'd bower, hangs the heavy-fruited
    tree —
Summer isles of Eden lying in dark-purple spheres of sea.

There methinks would be enjoyment more than in this march
    of mind,   165
In the steamship, in the railway, in the thoughts that shake
    mankind.

There the passions cramp'd no longer shall have scope and
    breathing space;
I will take some savage woman, she shall rear my dusky race.

Iron-jointed, supple-sinew'd, they shall dive, and they shall run,
Catch the wild goat by the hair, and hurl their lances in the
    sun;   170

Whistle back the parrot's call, and leap the rainbows of the
    brooks,
Not with blinded eyesight poring over miserable books —

Fool, again the dream, the fancy! but I *know* my words are
    wild,
But I count the gray barbarian lower than the Christian child.

I, to herd with narrow foreheads, vacant of our glorious
    gains,   175
Like a beast with lower pleasures, like a beast with lower pains!

Mated with a squalid savage — what to me were sun or clime?
I the heir of all the ages, in the foremost files of time —

I that rather held it better men should perish one by one,
Than that earth should stand at gaze like Joshua's moon in
    Ajalon!   180

Not in vain the distance beacons. Forward, forward let us
    range,
Let the great world spin for ever down the ringing grooves of
    change.

Thro' the shadow of the globe we sweep into the younger day:
Better fifty years of Europe than a cycle of Cathay.

Mother-Age (for mine I knew not) help me as when life
    begun: 185
Rift the hills, and roll the waters, flash the lightnings, weigh
    the Sun.

O, I see the crescent promise of my spirit hath not set.
Ancient founts of inspiration well thro' all my fancy yet.

Howsoever these things be, a long farewell to Locksley Hall!
Now for me the woods may wither, now for me the roof-tree
    fall.   190

Comes a vapour from the margin, blackening over heath and
    holt,
Cramming all the blast before it, in its breast a thunderbolt.

Let it fall on Locksley Hall, with rain or hail, or fire or snow;
For the mighty wind arises, roaring seaward, and I go.

MAUD; A MONODRAMA

Editor's Note. — In 1836 the Marquis of Northampton interested himself in compiling "a charity book of poetry" for the
benefit of the destitute family of the Rev. Edward Smedley, an
obscure man of letters lately deceased. Richard Monckton
Milnes undertook to secure a contribution from Tennyson.
The poet at first refused, remarking: "To write for people with
prefixes to their names is to milk he-goats; there is neither honour nor profit." But presently, realizing that he should not be
"backward in doing a really charitable deed," he sent the lyric
"Oh! that 'twere possible" (written in 1834) which, under the

---

182. *the great world;* 1842: "the peoples." The alteration is a notable
improvement. Tennyson said (*Memoir,* i, 195): "When I went by the first
train from Liverpool to Manchester (1830), I thought that the wheels ran
in a groove. It was a black night and there was such a vast crowd round
the train at the station that I could not see the wheels. Then I made this
line."

simple heading "Stanzas by Alfred Tennyson, Esq.," appeared in *The Tribute: a Collection of Miscellaneous Unpublished Poems by Various Authors*, 1837, pp. 244 f. In 1854 Tennyson was visiting his friend Sir John Simeon at Swainston in the Isle of Wight (about ten miles from Farringford). Simeon suggested that to render "Oh! that 'twere possible" fully intelligible a preceding poem was necessary; and when that poem (which it was is not on record) had been written, it was obvious that it, too, required a predecessor. Thus *Maud* came to be composed backwards, as it were. Much of it was written at Swainston, and the landscape is in many places suggestive of the Isle of Wight. The poem was published in 1855, and in a second edition (1856) was altered and enlarged. — A monodrama, though an expansion of a characteristic Victorian poetic genre, the dramatic monologue, was a novelty which led to misunderstandings, the thoughts and feelings of the morbid and for a time insane protagonist being attributed to the author. Consequently there was a considerable outcry against Tennyson. *Anti-Maud. By a Poet of the People* (1855) won sufficient attention to go into a second edition (1856). The gravamen was Tennyson's supposed glorification of war (for the poem was written during the excitement at the beginning of the Crimean conflict). A certain Dr. R. J. Mann published *Tennyson's "Maud" Vindicated* (1856) and earned the poet's gratitude (*Memoir,* i, 405). The additions to the enlarged version of 1856 were partly intended to make the story clearer. Even so, Tennyson thought it worth while to leave to his son a series of headings and notes to guard the reader from misunderstandings. These are quoted or condensed in the present commentary. Many years before, when the unnamed hero and Maud were children, the father of the hero was killed in what may have been an accident, though circumstances pointed to suicide or to foul play. He had lately been ruined through an unfortunate speculation. Through this same financial transaction an old friend of his family, the father of Maud, became very rich. He maintained his residence in the Hall, though he and his daughter lived abroad. Meanwhile the

mother of the hero died, and the young man lived in narrow
circumstances (with only one man-servant and one maid-
servant — an amusingly Victorian criterion of such circumstances) in his native village. The poem opens just before
the return of Maud, now a young lady of seventeen, from the
Continent. With her are her father and her brother. The
only other mute in the monodrama is the young lord who is
her suitor. — In the original edition the poem is not divided
into parts but into twenty-six sections.

PART I

I [1]

I

I HATE the dreadful hollow behind the little wood,
Its lips in the field above are dappled with blood-red heath,
The red-ribb'd ledges drip with a silent horror of blood,
And Echo there, whatever is ask'd her, answers 'Death.'

II

For there in the ghastly pit long since a body was found,   5
His who had given me life — O father! O God! was it well? —
Mangled, and flatten'd, and crush'd, and dinted into the
    ground:
There yet lies the rock that fell with him when he fell.

III

Did he fling himself down? who knows? for a vast speculation
    had fail'd,
And ever he mutter'd and madden'd, and ever wann'd with
    despair,   10

---

[1] Before the arrival of Maud.

2. When reading the poem aloud (it was Tennyson's favourite choice
for such performances), he was careful to note that the epithet "blood-red"
applied to the heath should have shown the critics that the hero who indulged in such an extravagant fancy was on the road to madness.

9. *a vast speculation.* In 1843–4 Tennyson had invested all his small
capital as well as part of his mother's and brother's in a scheme for carving
wood by machinery. This project collapsed with the loss of the poet's
patrimony. See *Memoir*, i, 220 f.

And out he walk'd when the wind like a broken worldling
    wail'd,
And the flying gold of the ruin'd woodlands drove thro' the air.

IV

I remember the time, for the roots of my hair were stirr'd
By a shuffled step, by a dead weight trail'd, by a whisper'd
    fright,
And my pulses closed their gates with a shock on my heart as
    I heard   15
The shrill-edged shriek of a mother divide the shuddering
    night.

V

Villainy somewhere! whose?   One says, we are villains all.
Not he; his honest fame should at least by me be maintained:
But that old man, now lord of the broad estate and the Hall,
Dropt off gorged from a scheme that had left us flaccid and
    drain'd.   20

VI

Why do they prate of the blessings of Peace? we have made
    them a curse,
Pickpockets, each hand lusting for all that is not its own;
And lust of gain, in the spirit of Cain, is it better or worse
Than the heart of the citizen hissing in war on his own hearth-
    stone?

VII

But these are the days of advance, the works of the men of
    mind,   25
When who but a fool would have faith in a tradesman's ware
    or his word?
Is it peace or war?   Civil war, as I think, and that of a kind
The viler, as underhand, not openly bearing the sword.

VIII

Sooner or later I too may passively take the print
Of the golden age — why not?   I have neither hope nor
    trust;   30

---

   21 f. The passage of Carlyle-like invective which follows is one of the
sections of the poem which critics censured in 1855.

May make my heart as a millstone, set my face as a flint,
Cheat and be cheated, and die: who knows? we are ashes and
    dust.

IX

Peace sitting under her olive, and slurring the days gone by,
When the poor are hovell'd and hustled together, each sex, like
    swine.
When only the ledger lives, and when only not all men lie;   35
Peace in her vineyard — yes! — but a company forges the wine.

X

And the vitriol madness flushes up in the ruffian's head,
Till the filthy by-lane rings to the yell of the trampled wife,
And chalk and alum and plaster are sold to the poor for bread,
And the spirit of murder works in the very means of life,   40

XI

And Sleep must lie down arm'd, for the villainous centre-bits
Grind on the wakeful ear in the hush of the moonless nights,
While another is cheating the sick of a few last gasps, as he sits
To pestle a poison'd poison behind his crimson lights.

XII

When a Mammonite mother kills her babe for a burial fee,   45
And Timour-Mammon grins on a pile of children's bones,
Is it peace or war? better, war! loud war by land and by sea,
War with a thousand battles, and shaking a hundred thrones.

XIII

For I trust if an enemy's fleet came yonder round by the hill,
And the rushing battle-boat sang from the three-decker out of
    the foam,   50
That the smooth-faced snubnosed rogue would leap from his
    counter and till,
And strike, if he could, were it but with his cheating yardwand,
    home. ——

XIV

What! am I raging alone as my father raged in his mood?
Must *I* too creep to the hollow and dash myself down and die

---

53–64. These three stanzas were added in the second edition, 1856.

Rather than hold by the law that I made, nevermore to
brood   55
On a horror of shatter'd limbs and a wretched swindler's lie?

XV

Would there be sorrow for *me?* there was *love* in the passionate shriek,
Love for the silent thing that had made false haste to the
grave —
Wrapt in a cloak, as I saw him, and thought he would rise
and speak
And rave at the lie and the liar, ah God, as he used to rave. 60

XVI

I am sick of the Hall and the hill, I am sick of the moor and
the main.
Why should I stay? can a sweeter chance ever come to me
here?
O, having the nerves of motion as well as the nerves of pain,
Were it not wise if I fled from the place and the pit and the
fear?

XVII

Workmen up at the Hall! — they are coming back from
abroad;   65
The dark old place will be gilt by the touch of a millionaire:
I have heard, I know not whence, of the singular beauty of
Maud;
I play'd with the girl when a child; she promised then to be
fair.

XVIII

Maud with her venturous climbings and tumbles and childish
escapes,
Maud the delight of the village, the ringing joy of the Hall, 70
Maud with her sweet purse-mouth when my father dangled
the grapes,
Maud the beloved of my mother, the moon-faced darling of
all, —

XIX

What is she now?   My dreams are bad.   She may bring me a
    curse.
No, there is fatter game on the moor: she will let me alone.
Thanks, for the fiend best knows whether woman or man be
    the worse.   75
I will bury myself in myself, and the Devil may pipe to his own.

II [1]

Long have I sigh'd for a calm: God grant I may find it at last!
It will never be broken by Maud, she has neither savour nor
    salt,
But a cold and clear-cut face, as I found when her carriage past,
Perfectly beautiful: let it be granted her: where is the fault?
All that I saw (for her eyes were downcast, not to be seen)   5
Faultily faultless, icily regular, splendidly null,
Dead perfection, no more; nothing more, if it had not been
For a chance of travel, a paleness, an hour's defect of the rose,
Or an underlip, you may call it a little too ripe, too full,
Or the least little delicate aquiline curve in a sensitive nose,   10
From which I escaped heart-free, with the least little touch of
    spleen.

III [2]

Cold and clear-cut face, why come you so cruelly meek,
Breaking a slumber in which all spleenful folly was drown'd,
Pale with the golden beam of an eyelash dead on the cheek,
Passionless, pale, cold face, star-sweet on a gloom profound;
Womanlike, taking revenge too deep for a transient wrong   5
Done but in thought to your beauty, and ever as pale as before
Growing and fading and growing upon me without a sound,
Luminous, gemlike, ghostlike, deathlike, half the night long
Growing and fading and growing, till I could bear it no more,
But arose, and all by myself in my own dark garden ground,   10

---

76. *I will bury myself in myself.*   The original edition reads: "I will
bury myself in my books"; but the final reading is a restoration of that in
the first manuscript draft of the poem (*Works,* Eversley edition, ii, 506).

[1] The first sight of Maud.

[2] The hero has not escaped quite heart-free, for Maud's beautiful face
comes to him in visions of the night.

Listening now to the tide in its broad-flung shipwrecking roar,
Now to the scream of a madden'd beach dragg'd down by the
    wave,
Walk'd in a wintry wind by a ghastly glimmer, and found
The shining daffodil dead, and Orion low in his grave.

IV [1]

I

A million emeralds break from the ruby-budded lime
In the little grove where I sit — ah, wherefore cannot I be
Like things of the season gay, like the bountiful season bland,
When the far-off sail is blown by the breeze of a softer clime,
Half-lost in the liquid azure bloom of a crescent of sea,   5
The silent sapphire-spangled marriage ring of the land?

II

Below me, there, is the village, and looks how quiet and small!
And yet bubbles o'er like a city, with gossip, scandal, and spite;
And Jack on his ale-house bench has as many lies as a Czar;
And here on the landward side, by a red rock, glimmers the
    Hall;   10
And up in the high Hall-garden I see her pass like a light;
But sorrow seize me if ever that light be my leading star!

III

When have I bow'd to her father, the wrinkled head of the
    race?
I met her to-day with her brother, but not to her brother I
    bow'd:
I bow'd to his lady-sister as she rode by on the moor;   15
But the fire of a foolish pride flash'd over her beautiful face.
O child, you wrong your beauty, believe it, in being so proud;
Your father has wealth well-gotten, and I am nameless and
    poor.

IV

I keep but a man and a maid, ever ready to slander and steal;
I know it, and smile a hard-set smile, like a stoic, or like   20

III. 11. Tennyson noted that the roar of the tide can be heard nine miles inland on the Isle of Wight.

[1] "Mood of bitterness after fancied disdain" (Tennyson).

A wiser epicurean, and let the world have its way:
For nature is one with rapine, a harm no preacher can heal;
The Mayfly is torn by the swallow, the sparrow spear'd by the
    shrike,
And the whole little wood where I sit is a world of plunder and
    prey.

v

We are puppets, Man in his pride, and Beauty fair in her
    flower;   25
Do we move ourselves, or are moved by an unseen hand at a
    game
That pushes us off from the board, and others ever succeed?
Ah yet, we cannot be kind to each other here for an hour;
We whisper, and hint, and chuckle, and grin at a brother's
    shame;
However we brave it out, we men are a little breed.   30

VI

A monstrous eft was of old the Lord and Master of Earth,
For him did his high sun flame, and his river billowing ran,
And he felt himself in his force to be Nature's crowning
    race.
As nine months go to the shaping an infant ripe for his birth,
So many a million of ages have gone to the making of man: 35
He now is first, but is he the last? is he not too base?

VII

The man of science himself is fonder of glory, and vain,
An eye well-practised in nature, a spirit bounded and poor;
The passionate heart of the poet is whirl'd into folly and vice.
I would not marvel at either, but keep a temperate brain;   40
For not to desire or admire, if a man could learn it, were
    more
Than to walk all day like the sultan of old in a garden of spice.

    IV. 31. *A monstrous eft,* "the great old lizards of geology" (Tennyson). Compare *In Memoriam,* lvi, 22 f.
    41. *not to desire or admire.* The "Nil admirari" of Horace, *Epodes,* i, 6.

VIII

For the drift of the Maker is dark, an Isis hid by the veil.
Who knows the ways of the world, how God will bring them
    about?
Our planet is one, the suns are many, the world is wide.   45
Shall I weep if a Poland fall? shall I shriek if a Hungary fail?
Or an infant civilisation be ruled with rod or with knout?
I have not made the world, and He that made it will guide.

IX

Be mine a philosopher's life in the quiet woodland ways,
Where if I cannot be gay let a passionless peace be my lot,   50
Far-off from the clamour of liars belied in the hubbub of lies;
From the long-neck'd geese of the world that are ever hissing
    dispraise
Because their natures are little, and, whether he heed it or not,
Where each man walks with his head in a cloud of poisonous
    flies.

X

And most of all would I flee from the cruel madness of
    love,   55
The honey of poison-flowers and all the measureless ill.
Ah Maud, you milkwhite fawn, you are all unmeet for a wife.
Your mother is mute in her grave as her image in marble
    above;
Your father is ever in London, you wander about at your will;
You have but fed on the roses and lain in the lilies of life.   60

V [1]

I

A voice by the cedar tree
In the meadow under the Hall!
She is singing an air that is known to me,
A passionate ballad gallant and gay,
A martial song like a trumpet's call!   5

---

43. At Saïs in the Egyptian Delta there was a statue of Isis with the in-
scription: "No one has lifted my veil."

[1] "He fights against his growing passion" (Tennyson).

Singing alone in the morning of life,
In the happy morning of life and of May,
Singing of men that in battle array,
Ready in heart and ready in hand,
March with banner and bugle and fife   10
To the death, for their native land.

II

Maud with her exquisite face,
And wild voice pealing up to the sunny sky,
And feet like sunny gems on an English green,
Maud in the light of her youth and her grace,   15
Singing of Death, and of Honour that cannot die,
Till I well could weep for a time so sordid and mean,
And myself so languid and base.

III

Silence, beautiful voice!
Be still, for you only trouble the mind   20
With a joy in which I cannot rejoice,
A glory I shall not find.
Still!   I will hear you no more,
For your sweetness hardly leaves me a choice
But to move to the meadow and fall before   25
Her feet on the meadow grass, and adore,
Not her, who is neither courtly nor kind,
Not her, not her, but a voice.

VI [1]

I

Morning arises stormy and pale,
No sun, but a wannish glare
In fold upon fold of hueless cloud,
And the budded peaks of the wood are bow'd
Caught and cuff'd by the gale: 5
I had fancied it would be fair.

---

[1] The hero meets Maud for the first time since her return to the Hall.

II

Whom but Maud should I meet
Last night, when the sunset burn'd
On the blossom'd gable-ends
At the head of the village street,   10
Whom but Maud should I meet?
And she touch'd my hand with a smile so sweet,
She made me divine amends
For a courtesy not return'd.

III

And thus a delicate spark   15
Of glowing and growing light
Thro' the livelong hours of the dark
Kept itself warm in the heart of my dreams,
Ready to burst in a colour'd flame;
Till at last when the morning came   20
In a cloud, it faded, and seems
But an ashen-gray delight.

IV

What if with her sunny hair,
And smile as sunny as cold,
She meant to weave me a snare   25
Of some coquettish deceit,
Cleopatra-like as of old
To entangle me when we met,
To have her lion roll in a silken net
And fawn at a victor's feet.   30

V

Ah, what shall I be at fifty
Should Nature keep me alive,
If I find the world so bitter
When I am but twenty-five?
Yet, if she were not a cheat,   35
If Maud were all that she seem'd,
And her smile were all that I dream'd,
Then the world were not so bitter
But a smile could make it sweet.

VI

What if tho' her eye seem'd full   40
Of a kind intent to me,
What if that dandy-despot, he,
That jewell'd mass of millinery,
That oil'd and curl'd Assyrian Bull
Smelling of musk and of insolence,   45
Her brother, from whom I keep aloof,
Who wants the finer politic sense
To mask, tho' but in his own behoof,
With a glassy smile his brutal scorn —
What if he had told her yestermorn   50
How prettily for his own sweet sake
A face of tenderness might be feign'd,
And a moist mirage in desert eyes,
That so, when the rotten hustings shake
In another month to his brazen lies,   55
A wretched vote may be gain'd.

VII

For a raven ever croaks, at my side,
Keep watch and ward, keep watch and ward,
Or thou wilt prove their tool.
Yea, too, myself from myself I guard,   60
For often a man's own angry pride
Is cap and bells for a fool.

VIII

Perhaps the smile and tender tone
Came out of her pitying womanhood,
For am I not, am I not, here alone   65
So many a summer since she died,
My mother, who was so gentle and good?
Living alone in an empty house,

VI. 42 f. The descriptions of Maud's brother, beringed and bejewelled, remind us of the extravagances of early Victorian masculine costume which we associate with Bulwer and the young Disraeli. Compare I, xiii, 11–13.

44. The image of the Assyrian Bull reflects Tennyson's interest in Sir Austen Henry Layard's excavations at Nineveh. See Layard's *Nineveh and Its Remains,* 1848, and later publications. The great winged bulls had been brought to the British Museum shortly before the composition of "Maud" and had inspired Rossetti's poem "The Burden of Nineveh."

Here half-hid in the gleaming wood,
Where I hear the dead at midday moan,   70
And the shrieking rush of the wainscot mouse,
And my own sad name in corners cried,
When the shiver of dancing leaves is thrown
About its echoing chambers wide,
Till a morbid hate and horror have grown   75
Of a world in which I have hardly mixt,
And a morbid eating lichen fixt
On a heart half-turn'd to stone.

IX

O heart of stone, are you flesh, and caught
By that you swore to withstand?   80
For what was it else within me wrought
But, I fear, the new strong wine of love,
That made my tongue so stammer and trip
When I saw the treasured splendour, her hand
Come sliding out of her sacred glove,   85
And the sunlight broke from her lip?

X

I have play'd with her when a child;
She remembers it now we meet.
Ah well, well, well, I *may* be beguiled
By some coquettish deceit.   90
Yet, if she were not a cheat,
If Maud were all that she seem'd,
And her smile had all that I dream'd,
Then the world were not so bitter
But a smile could make it sweet.   95

VII [1]

I

Did I hear it half in a doze
    Long since, I know not where?
Did I dream it an hour ago,
    When asleep in this arm-chair?

---

[1] The hero remembers that when a child he heard his father and her
father talking shortly before the birth of Maud. They intended that their

II

Men were drinking together,   5
  Drinking and talking of me;
'Well, if it prove a girl, the boy
  Will have plenty: so let it be.'

III

Is it an echo of something
  Read with a boy's delight,   10
Viziers nodding together
  In some Arabian night?

IV

Strange, that I hear two men,
  Somewhere, talking of me;
'Well, if it prove a girl, my boy   15
  Will have plenty: so let it be.'

VIII [1]

She came to the village church,
And sat by a pillar alone;
An angel watching an urn
Wept over her, carved in stone;
And once, but once, she lifted her eyes,   5
And suddenly, sweetly, strangely blush'd
To find they were met by my own;
And suddenly, sweetly, my heart beat stronger
And thicker, until I heard no longer
The snowy-banded, dilettante,   10
Delicate-handed priest intone;
And thought, is it pride, and mused and sigh'd
'No surely, now it cannot be pride.'

---

children should marry one day; and his father assured his friend that the
boy would inherit a fortune. In 1855 the critics were puzzled by this section; and to make the situation clearer Tennyson added in 1856 Part I, section xix.

[1] At I, xix, 63 f. it is explained that before her return home Maud had
been forbidden by her brother to speak to her old friend (the hero).

IX [1]

I was walking a mile,
More than a mile from the shore,
The sun look'd out with a smile
Betwixt the cloud and the moor
And riding at set of day   5
Over the dark moor land,
Rapidly riding far away,
She waved to me with her hand.
There were two at her side,
Something flash'd in the sun,   10
Down by the hill I saw them ride,
In a moment they were gone:
Like a sudden spark
Struck vainly in the night,
Then returns the dark   15
With no more hope of light.

X [2]

I

Sick, am I sick of a jealous dread?
Was not one of the two at her side
This new-made lord, whose splendour plucks
The slavish hat from the villager's head?
Whose old grandfather has lately died,   5
Gone to a blacker pit, for whom
Grimy nakedness dragging his trucks
And laying his trams in a poison'd gloom
Wrought, till he crept from a gutted mine
Master of half a servile shire,   10
And left his coal all turn'd into gold
To a grandson, first of his noble line,
Rich in the grace all women desire,
Strong in the power that all men adore,
And simper and set their voices lower,   15
And soften as if to a girl, and hold

---

[1] One of the figures at Maud's side is her brother, the other, the young lord, her suitor, whom the hero now sees for the first time.

[2] Tennyson left no explanation of this section. The hero's "jealous dread" at the sight of the young lord leads on to a diatribe against society.

Awe-stricken breaths at a work divine,
Seeing his gewgaw castle shine,
New as his title, built last year,
There amid perky larches and pine,   20
And over the sullen-purple moor
(Look at it) pricking a cockney ear.

II

What, has he found my jewel out?
For one of the two that rode at her side
Bound for the Hall, I am sure was he: 25
Bound for the Hall, and I think for a bride.
Blithe would her brother's acceptance be.
Maud could be gracious too, no doubt
To a lord, a captain, a padded shape,
A bought commission, a waxen face,   30
A rabbit mouth that is ever agape —
Bought? what is it he cannot buy?
And therefore splenetic, personal, base,
A wounded thing with a rancorous cry,
At war with myself and a wretched race,   35
Sick, sick to the heart of life, am I.

III

Last week came one to the country town,
To preach our poor little army down,
And play the game of the despot kings,
Tho' the state has done it and thrice as well: 40
This broad-brimm'd hawker of holy things,
Whose ear is cramm'd with his cotton, and rings
Even in dreams to the chink of his pence,
This huckster put down war! can he tell
Whether war be a cause or a consequence?   45
Put down the passions that make earth Hell!
Down with ambition, avarice, pride,
Jealousy, down! cut off from the mind

X. 37 f. This passage was thought to be an attack on John Bright; but
Tennyson said: "I did not even know at the time that he was a Quaker."
The poet's son adds: "It was not against Quakers but against peace-at-all-
price men that the hero fulminates."   The allusion to Quakers in l. 41
seems, however, obvious.

The bitter springs of anger and fear;
Down too, down at your own fireside,   50
With the evil tongue and the evil ear,
For each is at war with mankind.

IV

I wish I could hear again
The chivalrous battle-song
That she warbled alone in her joy!   55
I might persuade myself then
She would not do herself this great wrong,
To take a wanton dissolute boy
For a man and leader of men.

V

Ah God, for a man with heart, head, hand,   60
Like some of the simple great ones gone
For ever and ever by,
One still strong man in a blatant land,
Whatever they call him, what care I,
Aristocrat, democrat, autocrat — one   65
Who can rule and dare not lie.

VI

And ah for a man to arise in me,
That the man I am may cease to be!

XI[1]

I

O let the solid ground
    Not fail beneath my feet
Before my life has found
    What some have found so sweet;
Then let come what come may,   5
What matter if I go mad,
I shall have had my day.

60–6. This passage, with its Carlylean advocacy of the rule of a "still
strong man," is not in the original edition but was added in 1856.

67–8. Not in original edition; added 1856.

[1] Tennyson left no interpretation of this section; nor does it require one.

II

Let the sweet heavens endure,
    Not close and darken above me
Before I am quite quite sure   10
    That there is one to love me;
Then let come what come may
To a life that has been so sad,
I shall have had my day.

XII [1]

I

Birds in the high Hall-garden
    When twilight was falling,
Maud, Maud, Maud, Maud,
    They were crying and calling.

II

Where was Maud? in our wood;   5
    And I, who else, was with her,
Gathering woodland lilies,
    Myriads blow together.

III

Birds in our wood sang
    Ringing thro' the valleys,   10
Maud is here, here, here
    In among the lilies.

IV

I kiss'd her slender hand,
    She took the kiss sedately;
Maud is not seventeen,   15
    But she is tall and stately.

V

I to cry out on pride
    Who have won her favour!

---

[1] A meeting with Maud. "The birds are partisans of the characters: the caw of the rooks in the Hall garden summons Maud to the suitor whom her brother favours; but the little songsters of the lover's woods exult in her presence" (Van Dyke).

O Maud were sure of Heaven
   If lowliness could save her.   20

VI

I know the way she went
   Home with her maiden posy,
For her feet have touch'd the meadows
   And left the daisies rosy.

VII

Birds in the high Hall-garden   25
   Were crying and calling to her,
Where is Maud, Maud, Maud?
   One is come to woo her.

VIII

Look, a horse at the door,
   And little King Charley snarling,   30
Go back, my lord, across the moor,
   You are not her darling.

XIII [1]

I

Scorn'd, to be scorn'd by one that I scorn,
Is that a matter to make me fret?
That a calamity hard to be borne?
Well, he may live to hate me yet.
Fool that I am to be vext with his pride!   5
I past him, I was crossing his lands;
He stood on the path a little aside;
His face, as I grant, in spite of spite,
Has a broad-blown comeliness, red and white,
And six feet two, as I think, he stands;   10

XII, 24. "Because if you tread on the daisy, it turns up a rosy under-
side" — Tennyson's comment upon a characteristically accurate bit of nature-observation. Contrast in Pope's *Pastorals* the "blushing flowers" which
rise where're the lady treads. Pope would have been at a loss to account
for the phenomenon, and would not have felt any necessity to do so.

[1] The morbid forebodings of this section are inspired by a chance meeting with Maud's brother who refuses to recognize him.

But his essences turn'd the live air sick,
And barbarous opulence jewel-thick
Sunn'd itself on his breast and his hands.

II

Who shall call me ungentle, unfair,
I long'd so heartily then and there 15
To give him the grasp of fellowship;
But while I past he was humming an air,
Stopt, and then with a riding whip
Leisurely tapping a glossy boot,
And curving a contumelious lip, 20
Gorgonised me from head to foot
With a stony British stare.

III

Why sits he here in his father's chair?
That old man never comes to his place:
Shall I believe him ashamed to be seen? 25
For only once, in the village street,
Last year, I caught a glimpse of his face,
A gray old wolf and a lean.
Scarcely, now, would I call him a cheat;
For then, perhaps, as a child of deceit, 30
She might by a true descent be untrue;
And Maud is as true as Maud is sweet:
Tho' I fancy her sweetness only due
To the sweeter blood by the other side;
Her mother has been a thing complete, 35
However she came to be so allied.
And fair without, faithful within,
Maud to him is nothing akin:
Some peculiar mystic grace
Made her only the child of her mother, 40
And heap'd the whole inherited sin
On that huge scapegoat of the race,
All, all upon the brother.

IV

Peace, angry spirit, and let him be!
Has not his sister smiled on me? 45

XIV [1]

I

Maud has a garden of roses
And lilies fair on a lawn;
There she walks in her state
And tends upon bed and bower,
And thither I climb'd at dawn   5
And stood by her garden-gate;
A lion ramps at the top,
He is claspt by a passion-flower.

II

Maud's own little oak-room
(Which Maud, like a precious stone   10
Set in the heart of the carven gloom,
Lights with herself, when alone
She sits by her music and books
And her brother lingers late
With a roystering company) looks   15
Upon Maud's own garden-gate:
And I thought as I stood, if a hand, as white
As ocean-foam in the moon, were laid
On the hasp of the window, and my Delight
Had a sudden desire, like a glorious ghost, to   20
     glide,
Like a beam of the seventh Heaven, down to
     my side,
There were but a step to be made.

III

The fancy flatter'd my mind,
And again seem'd overbold;
Now I thought that she cared for me,   25
Now I thought she was kind
Only because she was cold.

IV

I heard no sound where I stood
But the rivulet on from the lawn

---

[1] Tennyson left no comment on this section.

Running down to my own dark wood;   30
Or the voice of the long sea-wave as it swell'd
Now and then in the dim-gray dawn;
But I look'd, and round, all round the house I
    beheld
The death-white curtain drawn;
Felt a horror over me creep,   35
Prickle my skin and catch my breath,
Knew that the death-white curtain meant but
    sleep,
Yet I shudder'd and thought like a fool of the
    sleep of death.

XV[1]

So dark a mind within me dwells,
    And I make myself such evil cheer,
That if *I* be dear to some one else,
    Then some one else may have much to fear;
But if *I* be dear to some one else,   5
    Then I should be to myself more dear.
Shall I not take care of all that I think,
Yea ev'n of wretched meat and drink,
If I be dear,
If I be dear to some one else.   10

XVI[2]

I

This lump of earth has left his estate
The lighter by the loss of his weight;
And so that he find what he went to seek,
And fulsome Pleasure clog him, and drown
His heart in the gross mud-honey of town,   5
He may stay for a year who has gone for a week:
But this is the day when I must speak
And I see my Oread coming down,
O this is the day!
O beautiful creature, what am I   10

---

[1] Tennyson left no comment on this section.
[2] "He will declare his love" (Tennyson).

That I dare to look her way;
Think I may hold dominion sweet,
Lord of the pulse that is lord of her breast,
And dream of her beauty with tender dread,
From the delicate Arab arch of her feet   15
To the grace that, bright and light as the crest
Of a peacock, sits on her shining head,
And she knows it not: O, if she knew it,
To know her beauty might half undo it.
I know it the one bright thing to save   20
My yet young life in the wilds of Time,
Perhaps from madness, perhaps from crime,
Perhaps from a selfish grave.

II

What, if she be fasten'd to this fool lord,
Dare I bid her abide by her word?   25
Should I love her so well if she
Had given her word to a thing so low?
Shall I love her as well if she
Can break her word were it even for me?
I trust that it is not so.   30

III

Catch not my breath, O clamorous heart,
Let not my tongue be a thrall to my eye,
For I must tell her before we part,
I must tell her, or die.

XVII [1]

Go not, happy day,
    From the shining fields,
Go not, happy day,
    Till the maiden yields.
Rosy is the West,   5
    Rosy is the South,
Roses are her cheeks,
    And a rose her mouth

---

[1] "Accepted" (Tennyson).

When the happy Yes
   Falters from her lips,   10
Pass and blush the news
   Over glowing ships;
Over blowing seas,
   Over seas at rest,
Pass the happy news,   15
   Blush it thro' the West;
Till the red man dance
   By his red cedar-tree,
And the red man's babe
   Leap, beyond the sea.   20
Blush from West to East,
   Blush from East to West,
Till the West is East,
   Blush it thro' the West.
Rosy is the West,   25
   Rosy is the South,
Roses are her cheeks,
   And a rose her mouth.

XVIII [1]

I

I have led her home, my love, my only friend.
There is none like her, none.
And never yet so warmly ran my blood
And sweetly, on and on,
Calming itself to the long-wish'd-for end,   5
Full to the banks, close on the promised good.

II

None like her, none.
Just now the dry-tongued laurels' pattering talk
Seem'd her light foot along the garden walk,
And shook my heart to think she comes once more;   10
But even then I heard her close the door,
The gates of Heaven are closed, and she is gone.

---

[1] "Happy. The sigh in the cedar branches seems to chime in with his own yearning" (Tennyson). There was a great Cedar of Lebanon on the lawn at Farringford.

III

There is none like her, none,
Nor will be when our summers have deceased.
O, art thou sighing for Lebanon   15
In the long breeze that streams to thy delicious East,
Sighing for Lebanon,
Dark cedar, tho' thy limbs have here increased
Upon a pastoral slope as fair,
And looking to the South, and fed   20
With honey'd rain and delicate air,
And haunted by the starry head
Of her whose gentle will has changed my fate,
And made my life a perfumed altar-flame;
And over whom thy darkness must have spread   25
With such delight as theirs of old, thy great
Forefathers of the thornless garden, there
Shadowing the snow-limb'd Eve from whom she came.

IV

Here will I lie, while these long branches sway,
And you fair stars that crown a happy day   30
Go in and out as if at merry play,
Who am no more so all forlorn,
As when it seem'd far better to be born
To labour and the mattock-harden'd hand,
Than nursed at ease and brought to understand   35
A sad astrology, the boundless plan
That makes you tyrants in your iron skies,
Innumerable, pitiless, passionless eyes,
Cold fires, yet with power to burn and brand
His nothingness into man.   40

V

But now shine on, and what care I,
Who in this stormy gulf have found a pearl

XVIII. 27. *the thornless garden.* Compare *Paradise Lost*, iv, 256:
            Flow'rs of all hue, and without thorn the rose.

    36. *A sad astrology,* "modern astronomy, for of old astrology was
thought to sympathise with and rule man's fate" (Tennyson). Compare
Lucretius, *De Rerum Natura*, v, 1204 f.

The countercharm of space and hollow sky,
And do accept my madness, and would die
To save from some slight shame one simple girl.   45

VI

Would die; for sullen-seeming Death may give
More life to Love than is or ever was
In our low world, where yet 'tis sweet to live.
Let no one ask me how it came to pass;
It seems that I am happy, that to me   50
A livelier emerald twinkles in the grass,
A purer sapphire melts into the sea.

VII

Not die; but live a life of truest breath,
And teach true life to fight with mortal wrongs.
O, why should Love, like men in drinking-songs,   55
Spice his fair banquet with the dust of death?
Make answer, Maud my bliss,
Maud made my Maud by that long loving kiss,
Life of my life, wilt thou not answer this?
'The dusky strand of Death inwoven here   60
With dear Love's tie, makes Love himself more dear.'

VIII

Is that enchanted moan only the swell
Of the long waves that roll in yonder bay?
And hark the clock within, the silver knell
Of twelve sweet hours that past in bridal white,   65
And died to live, long as my pulses play;
But now by this my love has closed her sight
And given false death her hand, and stol'n away
To dreamful wastes where footless fancies dwell
Among the fragments of the golden day.   70
May nothing there her maiden grace affright!
Dear heart, I feel with thee the drowsy spell.
My bride to be, my evermore delight,
My own heart's heart, my ownest own, farewell; .

---

68. *false death,* sleep.

It is but for a little space I go: 75
And ye meanwhile far over moor and fell
Beat to the noiseless music of the night!
Has our whole earth gone nearer to the glow
Of your soft splendours that you look so bright?
I have climb'd nearer out of lonely Hell.   80
Beat, happy stars, timing with things below,
Beat with my heart more blest than heart can tell,
Blest, but for some dark undercurrent woe
That seems to draw — but it shall not be so:
Let all be well, be well.   85

XIX [1]

I

Her brother is coming back to-night,
Breaking up my dream of delight.

II

My dream? do I dream of bliss?
I have walk'd awake with Truth.
O when did a morning shine   5
So rich in atonement as this
For my dark-dawning youth,
Darken'd watching a mother decline
And that dead man at her heart and mine:
For who was left to watch her but I?   10
Yet so did I let my freshness die.

III

I trust that I did not talk
To gentle Maud in our walk
(For often in lonely wanderings
I have cursed him even to lifeless things)
But I trust that I did not talk,   15
Not touch on her father's sin:
I am sure I did but speak
Of my mother's faded cheek
When it slowly grew so thin,   20

---

[1] This section, added in 1856, elucidates and enriches the story.

That I felt she was slowly dying
Vext with lawyers and harass'd with debt:
For how often I caught her with eyes all wet,
Shaking her head at her son and sighing
A world of trouble within!   25

IV

And Maud too, Maud was moved
To speak of the mother she loved
As one scarce less forlorn,
Dying abroad and it seems apart
From him who had ceased to share her heart,   30
And ever mourning over the feud,
The household Fury sprinkled with blood
By which our houses are torn:
How strange was what she said,
When only Maud and the brother   35
Hung over her dying bed —
That Maud's dark father and mine
Had bound us one to the other,
Betrothed us over their wine,
On the day when Maud was born;   40
Seal'd her mine from her first sweet breath.
Mine, mine by a right, from birth till death.
Mine, mine — our fathers have sworn.

V

But the true blood spilt had in it a heat
To dissolve the precious seal on a bond   45
That, if left uncancell'd, had been so sweet:
And none of us thought of a something beyond,
A desire that awoke in the heart of the child,
As it were a duty done to the tomb,
To be friends for her sake, to be reconciled;   50
And I was cursing them and my doom,
And letting a dangerous thought run wild
While often abroad in the fragrant gloom
Of foreign churches — I see her there,
Bright English lily, breathing a prayer   55
To be friends, to be reconciled!

VI

But then what a flint is he!
Abroad, at Florence, at Rome,
I find whenever she touch'd on me
This brother had laugh'd her down,   60
And at last, when each came home,
He had darken'd into a frown,
Chid her, and forbid her to speak
To me, her friend of the years before;
And this was what had redden'd her cheek   65
When I bow'd to her on the moor.

VII

Yet Maud, altho' not blind
To the faults of his heart and mind,
I see she cannot but love him,
And says he is rough but kind,   70
And wishes me to approve him,
And tells me, when she lay
Sick once, with a fear of worse,
That he left his wine and horses and play,
Sat with her, read to her, night and day,   75
And tended her like a nurse.

VIII

Kind? but the deathbed desire
Spurn'd by this heir of the liar —
Rough but kind? yet I know
He has plotted against me in this,   80
That he plots against me still.
Kind to Maud? that were not amiss.
Well, rough but kind; why let it be so:
For shall not Maud have her will!

IX

For, Maud, so tender and true,   85
As long as my life endures
I feel I shall owe you a debt,
That I never can hope to pay;
And if ever I should forget
That I owe this debt to you   90
And for your sweet sake to yours;

O then, what then shall I say? —
If ever I *should* forget,
May God make me more wretched
Than ever I have been yet!   95

X

So now I have sworn to bury
All this dead body of hate,
I feel so free and so clear
By the loss of that dead weight,
That I should grow light-headed, I fear,   100
Fantastically merry;
But that her brother comes, like a blight
On my fresh hope, to the Hall to-night.

XX [1]

I

Strange, that I felt so gay,
Strange, that *I* tried to-day
To beguile her melancholy;
The Sultan, as we name him, —
She did not wish to blame him —   5
But he vext her and perplext her
With his worldly talk and folly:
Was it gentle to reprove her
For stealing out of view
From a little lazy lover   10
Who but claims her as his due?
Or for chilling his caresses
By the coolness of her manners,
Nay, the plainness of her dresses?
Now I know her but in two,   15
Nor can pronounce upon it
If one should ask me whether
The habit, hat, and feather,
Or the frock and gipsy bonnet
Be the neater and completer;   20

---

[1] Tennyson left no comment on this section. It is simple narrative, preparing the way for the triumphant lyric, section XXII. "The Sultan" of l. 4 is Maud's brother who reproves her for stealing away from the "little lazy lover" (the young lord) of l. 10.

For nothing can be sweeter
Than maiden Maud in either.

II

But to-morrow if we live,
Our ponderous squire will give
A grand political dinner   25
To half the squirelings near;
And Maud will wear her jewels,
And the bird of prey will hover,
And the titmouse hope to win her
With his chirrup at her ear.   30

III

A grand political dinner
To the men of many acres,
A gathering of the Tory,
A dinner and then a dance
For the maids and marriage-makers,   35
And every eye but mine will glance
At Maud in all her glory.

IV

For I am not invited,
But, with the Sultan's pardon,
I am all as well delighted,   40
For I know her own rose-garden,
And mean to linger in it
Till the dancing will be over;
And then, oh then, come out to me
For a minute, but for a minute,   45
Come out to your own true lover,
That your true lover may see
Your glory also, and render
All homage to his own darling,
Queen Maud in all her splendour.   50

XXI [1]

Rivulet crossing my ground,
And bringing me down from the Hall

---

[1] "Before the Ball" (Tennyson) which is to follow the "grand political
dinner." A charmingly conceived introduction to the lyric which follows.

This garden-rose that I found,
  Forgetful of Maud and me,
And lost in trouble and moving round   5
Here at the head of a tinkling fall,
  And trying to pass to the sea;
O Rivulet, born at the Hall,
  My Maud has sent it by thee
(If I read her sweet will right)   10
  On a blushing mission to me,
Saying in odour and colour, 'Ah, be
  Among the roses to-night.'

XXII [1]

I

Come into the garden, Maud,
  For the black bat, night, has flown,
Come into the garden, Maud,
  I am here at the gate alone;
And the woodbine spices are wafted abroad,   5
  And the musk of the rose is blown.

II

For a breeze of morning moves,
  And the planet of Love is on high,
Beginning to faint in the light that she loves
  On a bed of daffodil sky,
To faint in the light of the sun she loves,   10
  To faint in his light, and to die.

III

All night have the roses heard
  The flute, violin, bassoon;
All night has the casement jessamine stirr'd   15
  To the dancers dancing in tune;
Till a silence fell with the waking bird,
  And a hush with the setting moon.

_____

[1] "In the Hall-Garden" (Tennyson). The old _aubades_ were songs of
lovers' partings; but this dawn-song is a song of rapturous expectancy.

IV

I said to the lily, 'There is but one
   With whom she has heart to be gay.   20
When will the dancers leave her alone?
   She is weary of dance and play.'
Now half to the setting moon are gone,
   And half to the rising day;
Low on the sand and loud on the stone   25
   The last wheel echoes away.

V

I said to the rose, 'The brief night goes
   In babble and revel and wine.
O young lord-lover, what sighs are those,
   For one that will never be thine?   30
But mine, but mine,' so I sware to the rose,
   'For ever and ever, mine.'

VI

And the soul of the rose went into my blood,
   As the music clash'd in the hall;
And long by the garden lake I stood,   35
   For I heard your rivulet fall
From the lake to the meadow and on to the wood,
   Our wood, that is dearer than all;

VII

From the meadow your walks have left so sweet
   That whenever a March-wind sighs   40
He sets the jewel-print of your feet
   In violets blue as your eyes,
To the woody hollows in which we meet
   And the valleys of Paradise.

VIII

The slender acacia would not shake   45
   One long milk-bloom on the tree;
The white lake-blossom fell into the lake
   As the pimpernel dozed on the lea;
But the rose was awake all night for your sake,
   Knowing your promise to me;   50

The lilies and roses were all awake,
  They sigh'd for the dawn and thee.

IX

Queen rose of the rosebud garden of girls,
  Come hither, the dances are done,
In gloss of satin and glimmer of pearls,   55
  Queen lily and rose in one;
Shine out, little head, sunning over with curls,
  To the flowers, and be their sun.

X

There has fallen a splendid tear
  From the passion-flower at the gate.   60
She is coming, my dove, my dear;
  She is coming, my life, my fate;
The red rose cries, 'She is near, she is near;'
  And the white rose weeps, 'She is late;'
The larkspur listens, 'I hear, I hear;'   65
  And the lily whispers, 'I wait.'

XI

She is coming, my own, my sweet;
  Were it ever so airy a tread,
My heart would hear her and beat,
  Were it earth in an earthy bed;   70
My dust would hear her and beat,
  Had I lain for a century dead;
Would start and tremble under her feet,
  And blossom in purple and red.

PART II

I [1]

I

'The fault was mine, the fault was mine' —
Why am I sitting here so stunn'd and still,
Plucking the harmless wild-flower on the hill? —
It is this guilty hand! —

---

[1] After the duel with Maud's brother. Tennyson called this section "the Phantom."

And there rises ever a passionate cry   5
From underneath in the darkening land —
What is it that has been done?
O dawn of Eden bright over earth and sky,
The fires of Hell brake out of thy rising sun,
The fires of Hell and of Hate;   10
For she, sweet soul, had hardly spoken a word,
When her brother ran in his rage to the gate,
He came with the babe-faced lord;
Heap'd on her terms of disgrace,
And while she wept, and I strove to be cool,   15
He fiercely gave me the lie,
Till I with as fierce an anger spoke,
And he struck me, madman, over the face,
Struck me before the languid fool,
Who was gaping and grinning by: 20
Struck for himself an evil stroke;
Wrought for his house an irredeemable woe;
For front to front in an hour we stood,
And a million horrible bellowing echoes broke
From the red-ribb'd hollow behind the wood,   25
And thunder'd up into Heaven the Christless code,
That must have life for a blow.
Ever and ever afresh they seem'd to grow.
Was it he lay there with a fading eye?
'The fault was mine,' he whisper'd, 'fly!'   30
Then glided out of the joyous wood
The ghastly Wraith of one that I know;
And there rang on a sudden a passionate cry,
A cry for a brother's blood:
It will ring in my heart and my ears, till I die, till I die. 35

II

Is it gone? my pulses beat —
What was it? a lying trick of the brain?
Yet I thought I saw her stand,
A shadow there at my feet,
High over the shadowy land.   40
It is gone; and the heavens fall in a gentle rain,
When they should burst and drown with deluging storms

The feeble vassals of wine and anger and lust,
The little hearts that know not how to forgive:
Arise, my God, and strike, for we hold Thee just,   45
Strike dead the whole weak race of venomous worms,
That sting each other here in the dust;
We are not worthy to live.

II [1]

I

See what a lovely shell,
Small and pure as a pearl,
Lying close to my foot,
Frail, but a work divine,
Made so fairily well   5
With delicate spire and whorl,
How exquisitely minute,
A miracle of design!

II

What is it? a learned man
Could give it a clumsy name.   10
Let him name it who can,
The beauty would be the same.

III

The tiny cell is forlorn,
Void of the little living will
That made it stir on the shore.   15
Did he stand at the diamond door
Of his house in a rainbow frill?
Did he push, when he was uncurl'd,
A golden foot or a fairy horn
Thro' his dim water-world?   20

IV

Slight, to be crush'd with a tap
Of my finger-nail on the sand,

---

[1] In Brittany. "The shell undestroyed amid the storm perhaps sym-
bolizes to him his own first and highest nature preserved amid the storms
of passion" (Tennyson).

Small, but a work divine,
Frail, but of force to withstand,
Year upon year, the shock   25
Of cataract seas that snap
The three decker's oaken spine
Athwart the ledges of rock,
Here on the Breton strand!

v

Breton, not Briton; here   30
Like a shipwreck'd man on a coast
Of ancient fable and fear —
Plagued with a flitting to and fro,
A disease, a hard mechanic ghost
That never came from on high   35
Nor ever arose from below,
But only moves with the moving eye,
Flying along the land and the main —
Why should it look like Maud?
Am I to be overawed   40
By what I cannot but know
Is a juggle born of the brain?

vi

Back from the Breton coast,
Sick of a nameless fear,
Back to the dark sea-line   45
Looking, thinking of all I have lost;
An old song vexes my ear;
But that of Lamech is mine.

vii

For years, a measureless ill,
For years, for ever, to part —   50
But she, she would love me still;
And as long, O God, as she
Have a grain of love for me,
So long, no doubt, no doubt,

II. 48. Genesis, iv, 23: "I have slain a man to my wounding, and a
young man to my hurt."

Shall I nurse in my dark heart,   55
However weary, a spark of will
Not to be trampled out.

VIII

Strange, that the mind, when fraught
With a passion so intense
One would think that it well   60
Might drown all life in the eye, —
That it should, by being so overwrought,
Suddenly strike on a sharper sense
For a shell, or a flower, little things
Which else would have been past by!   65
And now I remember, I,
When he lay dying there,
I noticed one of his many rings
(For he had many, poor worm) and thought
It is his mother's hair.   70

IX

Who knows if he be dead?
Whether I need have fled?
Am I guilty of blood?
However this may be,
Comfort her, comfort her, all things good,   75
While I am over the sea!
Let me and my passionate love go by,
But speak to her all things holy and high,
Whatever happen to me!
Me and my harmful love go by;   80
But come to her waking, find her asleep,
Powers of the height, Powers of the deep,
And comfort her tho' I die.

III [1]

Courage, poor heart of stone!
I will not ask thee why

---

[1] This section, not in the original edition, was added in 1856. It makes clear what without it can only be surmised, that Maud is dead. "He felt himself going mad" (Tennyson).

Thou canst not understand
That thou art left for ever alone:
Courage, poor stupid heart of stone. —   5
Or if I ask thee why,
Care not thou to reply:
She is but dead, and the time is at hand
When thou shalt more than die.

IV [1]

I

O that 'twere possible
After long grief and pain
To find the arms of my true love
Round me once again!

II

When I was wont to meet her   5
In the silent woody places
By the home that gave me birth,
We stood tranced in long embraces
Mixt with kisses sweeter sweeter
Than anything on earth.   10

III

A shadow flits before me,
Not thou, but like to thee:
Ah Christ, that it were possible
For one short hour to see
The souls we loved, that they might tell us,   15
What and where they be.

---

[1] "Haunted (after Maud's death)" (Tennyson). The principal changes from the version of 1837 are recorded below.

IV. 7. *By the home;* 1837: "Of the land."

13. *Ah Christ;* 1837: "Ah God!"

13 f. Compare John Webster, *The Duchess of Malfi,* IV, ii, 27 f.:

O, that it were possible we might
But hold some two days' conference with the dead!
From them I should learn somewhat, I am sure,
I never shall know here.

IV

It leads me forth at evening,
It lightly winds and steals
In a cold white robe before me,
When all my spirit reels   20
At the shouts, the leagues of lights,
And the roaring of the wheels.

V

Half the night I waste in sighs,
Half in dreams I sorrow after
The delight of early skies;   25
In a wakeful doze I sorrow
For the hand, the lips, the eyes,
For the meeting of the morrow,
The delight of happy laughter,
The delight of low replies.   30

VI

'Tis a morning pure and sweet,
And a dewy splendour falls
On the little flower that clings
To the turrets and the walls;
'Tis a morning pure and sweet,   35
And the light and shadow fleet;
She is walking in the meadow,
And the woodland echo rings;
In a moment we shall meet;
She is singing in the meadow   40
And the rivulet at her feet

24–5. These two lines are not in the version of 1837.

31–55. These two stanzas are new; they are substituted for the following:

> Do I hear the pleasant ditty,
> That I heard her chant of old?
> But I wake — my dream is fled.
> Without knowledge, without pity —
> In the shuddering dawn behold,
> By the curtains of my bed,
> That abiding phantom cold.

Ripples on in light and shadow
To the ballad that she sings.

VII

Do I hear her sing as of old,
My bird with the shining head,   45
My own dove with the tender eye?
But there rings on a sudden a passionate cry,
There is some one dying or dead,
And a sullen thunder is roll'd;
For a tumult shakes the city,   50
And I wake, my dream is fled;
In the shuddering dawn, behold,
Without knowledge, without pity,
By the curtains of my bed
That abiding phantom cold.   55

VIII

Get thee hence, nor come again,
Mix not memory with doubt,
Pass, thou deathlike type of pain,
Pass and cease to move about!
'Tis the blot upon the brain   60
That *will* show itself without.

IX

Then I rise, the eavedrops fall,
And the yellow vapours choke
The great city sounding wide;
The day comes, a dull red ball   65
Wrapt in drifts of lurid smoke
On the misty river-tide.

X

Thro' the hubbub of the market
I steal, a wasted frame,
It crosses here, it crosses there,   70
Thro' all that crowd confused and loud,
The shadow still the same;

56–61. In 1837 this stanza preceded the present stanza xii.

And on my heavy eyelids
My anguish hangs like shame.

XI

Alas for her that met me,   75
That heard me softly call,
Came glimmering thro' the laurels
At the quiet evenfall,
In the garden by the turrets
Of the old manorial hall.   80

XII

Would the happy spirit descend,
From the realms of light and song,
In the chamber or the street,
As she looks among the blest,
Should I fear to greet my friend   85
Or to say, 'Forgive the wrong,'
Or to ask her, 'Take me, sweet,
To the regions of thy rest'?

XIII

But the broad light glares and beats,
And the shadow flits and fleets   90
And will not let me be;
And I loathe the squares and streets,
And the faces that one meets,
Hearts with no love for me:
Always I long to creep   95
Into some still cavern deep,
There to weep, and weep, and weep
My whole soul out to thee.

---

80. After this, in 1837, came the present stanza xiii (with some insignificant variations). Then followed the present stanzas viii and xii,
with the addition of lines 82 and 86.

98. For four stanzas with which the original version of this section con-
cluded and which Tennyson wisely suppressed see *The Tribute*, pp. 248 f.
In the *Works*, Cambridge edition, p. 835, they are incorrectly arranged as
three stanzas.

V [1]

I

Dead, long dead,
Long dead!
And my heart is a handful of dust,
And the wheels go over my head,
And my bones are shaken with pain,   5
For into a shallow grave they are thrust,
Only a yard beneath the street,
And the hoofs of the horses beat, beat,
The hoofs of the horses beat,
Beat into my scalp and my brain,   10
With never an end to the stream of passing feet,
Driving, hurrying, marrying, burying,
Clamour and rumble, and ringing and clatter,
And here beneath it is all as bad,
For I thought the dead had peace, but it is not so;   15
To have no peace in the grave, is that not sad?
But up and down and to and fro,
Ever about me the dead men go;
And then to hear a dead man chatter
Is enough to drive one mad.   20

II

Wretchedest age since Time began,
They cannot even bury a man;
And tho' we paid our tithes in the days that are gone,
Not a bell was rung, not a prayer was read;
It is that which makes us loud in the world of the dead;   25
There is none that does his work, not one;
A touch of their office might have sufficed,
But the churchmen fain would kill their church,
As the churches have kill'd their Christ.

III

See, there is one of us sobbing,   30
No limit to his distress;

---

[1] "In the madhouse" (Tennyson). The poet's success in the delineation of insanity has been much discussed. The contemporary verdict was on the whole favourable; recent criticism is more dubious.

And another, a lord of all things, praying
To his own great self, as I guess;
And another, a statesman there, betraying
His party-secret, fool, to the press;   35
And yonder a vile physician, blabbing
The case of his patient — all for what?
To tickle the maggot born in an empty head,
And wheedle a world that loves him not,
For it is but a world of the dead.   40

IV

Nothing but idiot gabble!
For the prophecy given of old
And then not understood,
Has come to pass as foretold;
Not let any man think for the public good,   45
But babble, merely for babble.
For I never whisper'd a private affair
Within the hearing of cat or mouse,
No, not to myself in the closet alone,
But I heard it shouted at once from the top of the house;   50
Everything came to be known.
Who told *him* we were there?

V

Not that gray old wolf, for he came not back
From the wilderness, full of wolves, where he used to lie;
He has gather'd the bones for his o'ergrown whelp to crack;   55
Crack them now for yourself, and howl, and die.

VI

Prophet, curse me the blabbing lip,
And curse me the British vermin, the rat;
I know not whether he came in the Hanover ship,
But I know that he lies and listens mute   60

V. 52. *him,* the brother.

53. *that old gray wolf,* Maud's father.   See Part I, xiii, 28.

58 f. Tennyson's explanation of these insane babblings is that the
Norwegian rat, which has driven out the old English rat, was brought into
England at the time of the Hanoverian succession and was called by the
Jacobites "the Hanover rat."

In an ancient mansion's crannies and holes:
Arsenic, arsenic, sure, would do it,
Except that now we poison our babes, poor souls!
It is all used up for that.

VII

Tell him now: she is standing here at my head;   65
Not beautiful now, not even kind;
He may take her now; for she never speaks her mind,
But is ever the one thing silent here.
She is not *of* us, as I divine;
She comes from another stiller world of the dead,   70
Stiller, not fairer than mine.

VIII

But I know where a garden grows,
Fairer than aught in the world beside,
All made up of lily and rose
That blow by night, when the season is good,   75
To the sound of dancing music and flutes:
It is only flowers, they had no fruits,
And I almost fear they are not roses, but blood;
For the keeper was one, so full of pride,
He linkt a dead man there to a spectral bride;   80
For he, if he had not been a Sultan of brutes,
Would he have that hole in his side?

IX

But what will the old man say?
He laid a cruel snare in a pit
To catch a friend of mine one stormy day;   85
Yet now I could even weep to think of it;
For what will the old man say?
When he comes to the second corpse in the pit?

---

79. *the keeper*, Maud's brother.

83. *the old man*, Maud's father.

88. *the second corpse*, the corpse of Maud's brother, the first being that
of the protagonist's father, murdered as he thinks by Maud's father.

X

Friend, to be struck by the public foe,
Then to strike him and lay him low,   90
That were a public merit, far,
Whatever the Quaker holds, from sin;
But the red life spilt for a private blow —
I swear to you, lawful and lawless war
Are scarcely even akin.   95

XI

O me, why have they not buried me deep enough?
Is it kind to have made me a grave so rough,
Me, that was never a quiet sleeper?
Maybe still I am but half-dead;
Then I cannot be wholly dumb;   100
I will cry to the steps above my head
And somebody, surely, some kind heart will come
To bury me, bury me
Deeper, ever so little deeper.

PART III[1]

I

My life has crept so long on a broken wing
Thro' cells of madness, haunts of horror and fear,
That I come to be grateful at last for a little thing:
My mood is changed, for it fell at a time of year
When the face of night is fair on the dewy downs,   5
And the shining daffodil dies, and the Charioteer
And starry Gemini hang like glorious crowns
Over Orion's grave low down in the west,
Then like a silent lightning under the stars
She seem'd to divide in a dream from a band of the blest,   10
And spoke of a hope for the world in the coming wars —
'And in that hope, dear soul, let trouble have rest,
Knowing I tarry for thee,' and pointed to Mars
As he glow'd like a ruddy shield on the Lion's breast.

---

[1] "Sane, but shattered. Written when the cannon was heard booming from the battleships in the Solent before the Crimean War" (Tennyson). Tennyson was both attacked and defended for welcoming war as an alternative to a corrupt and inglorious peace.

II

And it was but a dream, yet it yielded a dear delight   15
To have look'd, tho' but in a dream, upon eyes so fair,
That had been in a weary world my one thing bright;
And it was but a dream, yet it lighten'd my despair
When I thought that a war would arise in defence of the right,
That an iron tyranny now should bend or cease,   20
The glory of manhood stand on his ancient height,
Nor Britain's one sole God be the millionaire:
No more shall commerce be all in all, and Peace
Pipe on her pastoral hillock a languid note,
And watch her harvest ripen, her herd increase,   25
Nor the cannon-bullet rust on a slothful shore,
And the cobweb woven across the cannon's throat
Shall shake its threaded tears in the wind no more.

III

And as months ran on and rumour of battle grew,
'It is time, it is time, O passionate heart,' said I   30
(For I cleaved to a cause that I felt to be pure and true),
'It is time, O passionate heart and morbid eye,
That old hysterical mock-disease should die.'
And I stood on a giant deck and mix'd my breath
With a loyal people shouting a battle cry,   35
Till I saw the dreary phantom arise and fly
Far into the North, and battle, and seas of death.

IV

Let it go or stay, so I wake to the higher aims
Of a land that has lost for a little her lust of gold,
And love of a peace that was full of wrongs and shames,   40
Horrible, hateful, monstrous, not to be told;
And hail once more to the banner of battle unroll'd!
Tho' many a light shall darken, and many shall weep
For those that are crush'd in the clash of jarring claims,
Yet God's just wrath shall be wreak'd on a giant liar;   45
And many a darkness into the light shall leap,
And shine in the sudden making of splendid names,
And noble thought be freër under the sun,
And the heart of a people beat with one desire;

For the peace, that I deem'd no peace, is over and done,   50
And now by the side of the Black and the Baltic deep,
And deathful-grinning mouths of the fortress, flames
The blood-red blossom of war with a heart of fire.

V

Let it flame or fade, and the war roll down like a wind,
We have proved we have hearts in a cause, we are noble still, 55
And myself have awaked, as it seems, to the better mind;
It is better to fight for the good than to rail at the ill;
I have felt with my native land, I am one with my kind,
I embrace the purpose of God, and the doom assign'd.

THE CHARGE OF THE LIGHT BRIGADE [1]

I

Half a league, half a league,
Half a league onward,
All in the valley of Death
Rode the six hundred.

---

53. Here the poem ended in 1855. The six lines which follow were added in 1856, perhaps to make the poet's feelings about war clearer.

[1] The charge of the Light Brigade at Balaclava took place on October 25, 1854. On November 14 the *Times* published a report of the disastrous engagement together with an editorial comment on the gallantry of the soldiers who were the victims of "some hideous blunder." Kinglake, the historian of the Crimean War, places the responsibility upon Lord Lucan, the commander of the cavalry division. Tennyson composed his poem very rapidly on December 2, 1854, and it was published in *The Examiner* on December 9. For this original version see *Works*, Cambridge edition, pp. 837 f. Its most notable variation from the final text is that it fixes the responsibility for the order upon a certain Captain Nolan ("'Forward, the Light Brigade! Take the guns,' Nolan said"), who had carried the message from headquarters to Lord Lucan. Ill-advised by some friends, Tennyson revised the poem before reprinting it in *Maud*, 1855. (See *Works*, Cambridge edition, p. 838). In this second version the Light Brigade is not named and the famous phrase "Someone had blundered" does not occur. Ruskin and others protested against these changes; and Tennyson reverted to the original version with some expansions when he had a thousand copies on printed slips sent to the soldiers in the Crimea. (It is perhaps worth remarking that the suggestion that this be done came to the poet from — of all inappropriate organizations — the Society for the Propagation of the Gospel!) This separate version was the final one; it was reprinted in the second edition of *Maud*, 1856.

'Forward, the Light Brigade!   5
Charge for the guns!' he said:
Into the valley of Death
    Rode the six hundred.

II

'Forward, the Light Brigade!'
Was there a man dismay'd?   10
Not tho' the soldier knew
    Some one had blunder'd:
Theirs not to make reply,
Theirs not to reason why,
Theirs but to do and die: 15
Into the valley of Death
    Rode the six hundred.

III

Cannon to right of them,
Cannon to left of them,
Cannon in front of them   20
    Volley'd and thunder'd;
Storm'd at with shot and shell,
Boldly they rode and well,
Into the jaws of Death,
Into the mouth of Hell   25
    Rode the six hundred.

IV

Flash'd all their sabres bare,
Flash'd as they turn'd in air
Sabring the gunners there,
Charging an army, while   30
    All the world wonder'd:
Plunged in the battery-smoke
Right thro' the line they broke;
Cossack and Russian
Reel'd from the sabre-stroke   35
    Shatter'd and sunder'd.
Then they rode back, but not —
    Not the six hundred.

V

Cannon to right of them,
Cannon to left of them,   40
Cannon behind them
    Volley'd and thunder'd;
Storm'd at with shot and shell,
While horse and hero fell,
They that had fought so well   45
Came thro' the jaws of Death,
Back from the mouth of Hell,
All that was left of them,
    Left of six hundred.

VI

When can their glory fade?   50
O the wild charge they made!
    All the world wonder'd.
Honour the charge they made!
Honour the Light Brigade,
    Noble six hundred!   55

ENOCH ARDEN [1]

Long lines of cliff breaking have left a chasm;
And in the chasm are foam and yellow sands;
Beyond, red roofs about a narrow wharf
In cluster; then a moulder'd church; and higher
A long street climbs to one tall-tower'd mill;   5
And high in heaven behind it a gray down
With Danish barrows; and a hazelwood,

---

[1] This poem was written in about a fortnight in the summer of 1862 (*Memoir*, i, 487; ii, 7). It was published in *Enoch Arden, Etc.*, 1864, a volume which immediately won an enormous success, the first edition consisting of sixty thousand copies. The subject was suggested to Tennyson by Thomas Woolner, the sculptor. There are many analogues in folklore and literature, but Tennyson does not seem to have known or made use of them. Browning discussed with Miss Wedgwood how he would have written the poem. See *Robert Browning and Julia Wedgwood*, New York, 1937, especially pp. 56–9.

7. *barrows*, burial-mounds. Some of those in the Isle of Wight, thought to be Danish, are now known to be much older than the Danish invasion.

By autumn nutters haunted, flourishes
Green in a cuplike hollow of the down.

Here on this beach a hundred years ago,   10
Three children of three houses, Annie Lee,
The prettiest little damsel in the port,
And Philip Ray the miller's only son,
And Enoch Arden, a rough sailor's lad
Made orphan by a winter shipwreck, play'd   15
Among the waste and lumber of the shore,
Hard coils of cordage, swarthy fishing-nets,
Anchors of rusty fluke, and boats updrawn;
And built their castles of dissolving sand
To watch them overflow'd, or following up   20
And flying the white breaker, daily left
The little footprint daily wash'd away.

A narrow cave ran in beneath the cliff:
In this the children play'd at keeping house.
Enoch was host one day, Philip the next,   25
While Annie still was mistress; but at times
Enoch would hold possession for a week:
'This is my house and this my little wife.'
'Mine too,' said Philip, 'turn and turn about:'
When, if they quarrell'd, Enoch stronger-made   30
Was master: then would Philip, his blue eyes
All flooded with the helpless wrath of tears,
Shriek out, 'I hate you, Enoch,' and at this
The little wife would weep for company,
And pray them not to quarrel for her sake,   35
And say she would be little wife to both.

But when the dawn of rosy childhood past,
And the new warmth of life's ascending sun
Was felt by either, either fixt his heart
On that one girl; and Enoch spoke his love,   40
But Philip loved in silence; and the girl
Seem'd kinder unto Philip than to him;
But she loved Enoch; tho' she knew it not,
And would if ask'd deny it. Enoch set

A purpose evermore before his eyes,   45
To hoard all savings to the uttermost,
To purchase his own boat, and make a home
For Annie: and so prosper'd that at last
A luckier or a bolder fisherman,
A carefuller in peril, did not breathe   50
For leagues along that breaker-beaten coast
Than Enoch. Likewise had he served a year
On board a merchantman, and made himself
Full sailor; and he thrice had pluck'd a life
From the dread sweep of the down-streaming seas: 55
And all men look'd upon him favourably:
And ere he touch'd his one-and-twentieth May
He purchased his own boat, and made a home
For Annie, neat and nestlike, halfway up
The narrow street that clamber'd toward the mill.   60

   Then, on a golden autumn eventide,
The younger people making holiday,
With bag and sack and basket, great and small,
Went nutting to the hazels. Philip stay'd
(His father lying sick and needing him)   65
An hour behind; but as he climb'd the hill,
Just where the prone edge of the wood began
To feather toward the hollow, saw the pair,
Enoch and Annie, sitting hand-in-hand,
His large gray eyes and weather-beaten face   70
All-kindled by a still and sacred fire,
That burn'd as on an altar. Philip look'd,
And in their eyes and faces read his doom;
Then, as their faces drew together, groan'd,
And slipt aside, and like a wounded life   75
Crept down into the hollows of the wood;
There, while the rest were loud in merry-making,
Had his dark hour unseen, and rose and past
Bearing a lifelong hunger in his heart.

   So these were wed, and merrily rang the bells,   80
And merrily ran the years, seven happy years,
Seven happy years of health and competence,
And mutual love and honourable toil;

With children; first a daughter. In him woke,
With his first babe's first cry, the noble wish   85
To save all earnings to the uttermost,
And give his child a better bringing-up
Than his had been, or hers; a wish renew'd,
When two years after came a boy to be
The rosy idol of her solitudes,   90
While Enoch was abroad on wrathful seas,
Or often journeying landward; for in truth
Enoch's white horse, and Enoch's ocean-spoil
In ocean-smelling osier, and his face,
Rough-redden'd with a thousand winter gales,   95
Not only to the market-cross were known,
But in the leafy lanes behind the down,
Far as the portal-warding lion-whelp,
And peacock-yewtree of the lonely Hall,
Whose Friday fare was Enoch's ministering.   100

    Then came a change, as all things human change.
Ten miles to northward of the narrow port
Open'd a larger haven: thither used
Enoch at times to go by land or sea;
And once when there, and clambering on a mast   105
In harbour, by mischance he slipt and fell:
A limb was broken when they lifted him;
And while he lay recovering there, his wife
Bore him another son, a sickly one:
Another hand crept too across his trade   110
Taking her bread and theirs: and on him fell,
Altho' a grave and staid God-fearing man,
Yet lying thus inactive, doubt and gloom.
He seem'd, as in a nightmare of the night,
To see his children leading evermore   115
Low miserable lives of hand-to-mouth,
And her, he loved, a beggar: then he pray'd
'Save them from this, whatever comes to me.'
And while he pray'd, the master of that ship
Enoch had served in, hearing his mischance,   120
Came, for he knew the man and valued him,

---

99. *peacock-yewtree*, a yew clipped into the shape of a peacock.

Reporting of his vessel China-bound,
And wanting yet a boatswain.   Would he go?
There yet were many weeks before she sail'd,
Sail'd from this port.   Would Enoch have the place?   125
And Enoch all at once assented to it,
Rejoicing at that answer to his prayer.

   So now that shadow of mischance appear'd
No graver than as when some little cloud
Cuts off the fiery highway of the sun,   130
And isles a light in the offing; yet the wife —
When he was gone — the children — what to do?
Then Enoch lay long-pondering on his plans;
To sell the boat — and yet he loved her well —
How many a rough sea had he weather'd in her!   135
He knew her, as a horseman knows his horse —
And yet to sell her — then with what she brought
Buy goods and stores — set Annie forth in trade
With all that seamen needed or their wives —
So might she keep the house while he was gone.   140
Should he not trade himself out yonder? go
This voyage more than once? yea twice or thrice —
As oft as needed — last, returning rich,
Become the master of a larger craft,
With fuller profits lead an easier life,   145
Have all his pretty young ones educated,
And pass his days in peace among his own.

   Thus Enoch in his heart determined all:
Then moving homeward came on Annie pale,
Nursing the sickly babe, her latest-born.   150
Forward she started with a happy cry,
And laid the feeble infant in his arms;
Whom Enoch took, and handled all his limbs,
Appraised his weight and fondled father-like,
But had no heart to break his purposes   155
To Annie, till the morrow, when he spoke.

   Then first since Enoch's golden ring had girt
Her finger, Annie fought against his will:
Yet not with brawling opposition she,

But manifold entreaties, many a tear,   160
Many a sad kiss by day by night renew'd
(Sure that all evil would come out of it)
Besought him, supplicating, if he cared
For her or his dear children, not to go.
He not for his own self caring but her,   165
Her and her children, let her plead in vain;
So grieving held his will, and bore it thro'.

     For Enoch parted with his old sea friend,
Bought Annie goods and stores, and set his hand
To fit their little streetward sitting-room   170
With shelf and corner for the goods and stores.
So all day long till Enoch's last at home,
Shaking their pretty cabin, hammer and axe,
Auger and saw, while Annie seem'd to hear
Her own death-scaffold raising, shrill'd and rang,   175
Till this was ended, and his careful hand, —
The space was narrow, — having order'd all
Almost as neat and close as Nature packs
Her blossom or her seedling, paused; and he,
Who needs would work for Annie to the last,   180
Ascending tired, heavily slept till morn.

     And Enoch faced this morning of farewell
Brightly and boldly.   All his Annie's fears,
Save, as his Annie's, were a laughter to him.
Yet Enoch as a brave God-fearing man   185
Bow'd himself down, and in that mystery
Where God-in-man is one with man-in-God,
Pray'd for a blessing on his wife and babes
Whatever came to him: and then he said:
'Annie, this voyage by the grace of God   190
Will bring fair weather yet to all of us.
Keep a clean hearth and a clear fire for me,
For I'll be back, my girl, before you know it.'
Then lightly rocking baby's cradle, 'and he,
This pretty, puny, weakly little one, —   195
Nay — for I love him all the better for it —
God bless him, he shall sit upon my knees
And I will tell him tales of foreign parts,

And make him merry, when I come home again.
Come, Annie, come, cheer up before I go.'   200

   Him running on thus hopefully she heard,
And almost hoped herself; but when he turn'd
The current of his talk to graver things
In sailor fashion roughly sermonizing
On providence and trust in Heaven, she heard,   205
Heard and not heard him; as the village girl,
Who sets her pitcher underneath the spring,
Musing on him that used to fill it for her,
Hears and not hears, and lets it overflow.

   At length she spoke: 'O Enoch, you are wise;   210
And yet for all your wisdom well know I
That I shall look upon your face no more.'

   'Well then,' said Enoch, 'I shall look on yours.
Annie, the ship I sail in passes here
(He named the day); get you a seaman's glass,   215
Spy out my face, and laugh at all your fears.'
   But when the last of those last moments came,
'Annie, my girl, cheer up, be comforted,
Look to the babes, and till I come again
Keep everything shipshape, for I must go.   220
And fear no more for me; or if you fear
Cast all your cares on God; that anchor holds.
Is He not yonder in those uttermost
Parts of the morning? if I flee to these
Can I go from Him? and the sea is His,   225
The sea is His: He made it.'

             Enoch rose,
Cast his strong arms about his drooping wife,
And kiss'd his wonder-stricken little ones;
But for the third, the sickly one, who slept
After a night of feverous wakefulness,   230
When Annie would have raised him Enoch said,

  222–6. A catena of Biblical passages; see Psalms, xcv, 5 and cxxxix, 9;
Hebrews, vi, 19; 1 Peter, v, 7.

'Wake him not; let him sleep; how should the child
Remember this?' and kiss'd him in his cot.
But Annie from her baby's forehead clipt
A tiny curl, and gave it: this he kept   235
Thro' all his future; but now hastily caught
His bundle, waved his hand, and went his way.

She, when the day, that Enoch mention'd, came,
Borrow'd a glass, but all in vain: perhaps
She could not fix the glass to suit her eye;   240
Perhaps her eye was dim, hand tremulous;
She saw him not: and while he stood on deck
Waving, the moment and the vessel past.

Ev'n to the last dip of the vanishing sail
She watch'd it, and departed weeping for him;   245
Then, tho' she mourn'd his absence as his grave,
Set her sad will no less to chime with his,
But throve not in her trade, not being bred
To barter, nor compensating the want
By shrewdness, neither capable of lies,   250
Nor asking overmuch and taking less,
And still foreboding 'what would Enoch say?'
For more than once, in days of difficulty
And pressure, had she sold her wares for less
Than what she gave in buying what she sold: 255
She fail'd and sadden'd knowing it; and thus,
Expectant of that news which never came,
Gain'd for her own a scanty sustenance,
And lived a life of silent melancholy.

Now the third child was sickly-born and grew   260
Yet sicklier, tho' the mother cared for it
With all a mother's care: nevertheless,
Whether her business often call'd her from it,
Or thro' the want of what it needed most,
Or means to pay the voice who best could tell   265
What most it needed — howsoe'er it was,
After a lingering, — ere she was aware, —
Like the caged bird escaping suddenly,
The little innocent soul flitted away.

In that same week when Annie buried it,   270
Philip's true heart, which hunger'd for her peace
(Since Enoch left he had not look'd upon her),
Smote him, as having kept aloof so long.
'Surely,' said Philip, 'I may see her now,
May be some little comfort;' therefore went,   275
Past thro' the solitary room in front,
Paused for a moment at an inner door,
Then struck it thrice, and, no one opening,
Enter'd; but Annie, seated with her grief,
Fresh from the burial of her little one,   280
Cared not to look on any human face,
But turn'd her own toward the wall and wept.
Then Philip standing up said falteringly,
'Annie, I came to ask a favour of you.'

He spoke; the passion in her moan'd reply,   285
'Favour from one so sad and so forlorn
As I am!' half abash'd him; yet unask'd,
His bashfulness and tenderness at war,
He set himself beside her, saying to her:

'I came to speak to you of what he wish'd,   290
Enoch, your husband: I have ever said
You chose the best among us — a strong man:
For where he fixt his heart he set his hand
To do the thing he will'd, and bore it thro'.
And wherefore did he go this weary way,   295
And leave you lonely? not to see the world —
For pleasure? — nay, but for the wherewithal
To give his babes a better bringing-up
Than his had been, or yours: that was his wish.
And if he come again, vext will he be   300
To find the precious morning hours were lost.
And it would vex him even in his grave,
If he could know his babes were running wild
Like colts about the waste.   So, Annie, now —
Have we not known each other all our lives?   305
I do beseech you by the love you bear
Him and his children not to say me nay —
For, if you will, when Enoch comes again

Why then he shall repay me — if you will,
Annie — for I am rich and well-to-do.   310
Now let me put the boy and girl to school:
This is the favour that I came to ask.'

    Then Annie with her brows against the wall
Answer'd, 'I cannot look you in the face;
I seem so foolish and so broken down.   315
When you came in my sorrow broke me down;
And now I think your kindness breaks me down;
But Enoch lives; that is borne in on me:
He will repay you: money can be repaid;
Not kindness such as yours.'

                    And Philip ask'd   320
'Then you will let me Annie?'

                            There she turn'd,
She rose, and fixt her swimming eyes upon him,
And dwelt a moment on his kindly face,
Then calling down a blessing on his head
Caught at his hand, and wrung it passionately,   325
And past into the little garth beyond.
So lifted up in spirit he moved away.

    Then Philip put the boy and girl to school,
And bought them needful books, and every way,
Like one who does his duty by his own,   330
Made himself theirs; and tho' for Annie's sake,
Fearing the lazy gossip of the port,
He oft denied his heart his dearest wish,
And seldom crost her threshold, yet he sent
Gifts by the children, garden-herbs and fruit,   335
The late and early roses from his wall,
Or conies from the down, and now and then,
With some pretext of fineness in the meal
To save the offence of charitable, flour
From his tall mill that whistled on the waste.   340

    But Philip did not fathom Annie's mind:
Scarce could the woman when he came upon her,

Out of full heart and boundless gratitude
Light on a broken word to thank him with.
But Philip was her children's all-in-all;   345
From distant corners of the street they ran
To greet his hearty welcome heartily;
Lords of his house and of his mill were they;
Worried his passive ear with petty wrongs
Or pleasures, hung upon him, play'd with him   350
And call'd him Father Philip.   Philip gain'd
As Enoch lost; for Enoch seem'd to them
Uncertain as a vision or a dream,
Faint as a figure seen in early dawn
Down at the far end of an avenue,   355
Going we know not where: and so ten years,
Since Enoch left his heart and native land,
Fled forward, and no news of Enoch came.

It chanced one evening Annie's children long'd
To go with others, nutting to the wood,   360
And Annie would go with them; then they begg'd
For Father Philip (as they call'd him) too:
Him, like the working bee in blossom-dust,
Blanch'd with his mill, they found; and saying to him,
'Come with us, Father Philip,' he denied;   365
But when the children pluck'd at him to go,
He laugh'd, and yielded readily to their wish,
For was not Annie with them? and they went.

But after scaling half the weary down,
Just where the prone edge of the wood began   370
To feather toward the hollow, all her force
Fail'd her; and sighing, 'Let me rest' she said:
So Philip rested with her well-content;
While all the younger ones with jubilant cries
Broke from their elders, and tumultuously   375
Down thro' the whitening hazels made a plunge
To the bottom, and dispersed, and bent or broke
The lithe reluctant boughs to tear away
Their tawny clusters, crying to each other
And calling, here and there, about the wood.   380

But Philip sitting at her side forgot
Her presence, and remember'd one dark hour
Here in this wood, when like a wounded life
He crept into the shadow: at last he said,
Lifting his honest forehead, 'Listen, Annie,   385
How merry they are down yonder in the wood.
Tired, Annie?' for she did not speak a word.
'Tired?' but her face had fall'n upon her hands;
At which, as with a kind of anger in him,
'The ship was lost,' he said, 'the ship was lost!   390
No more of that! why should you kill yourself
And make them orphans quite?'   And Annie said,
'I thought not of it: but — I know not why —
Their voices make me feel so solitary.'

    Then Philip coming somewhat closer spoke: 395
'Annie, there is a thing upon my mind,
And it has been upon my mind so long,
That tho' I know not when it first came there,
I know that it will out at last.   O Annie,
It is beyond all hope, against all chance,   400
That he who left you ten long years ago
Should still be living; well then — let me speak:
I grieve to see you poor and wanting help:
I cannot help you as I wish to do
Unless — they say that women are so quick —   405
Perhaps you know what I would have you know —
I wish you for my wife.   I fain would prove
A father to your children: I do think
They love me as a father: I am sure
That I love them as if they were mine own;   410
And I believe, if you were fast my wife,
That after all these sad uncertain years,
We might be still as happy as God grants
To any of his creatures.   Think upon it:
For I am well-to-do — no kin, no care,   415
No burthen, save my care for you and yours:
And we have known each other all our lives,
And I have loved you longer than you know.'

    Then answer'd Annie; tenderly she spoke:
'You have been as God's good angel in our house.   420

God bless you for it, God reward you for it,
Philip, with something happier than myself.
Can one love twice? can you be ever loved
As Enoch was? what is it that you ask?'
'I am content,' he answer'd, 'to be loved   425
A little after Enoch.'   'O,' she cried,
Scared as it were, 'dear Philip, wait a while:
If Enoch comes — but Enoch will not come —
Yet wait a year, a year is not so long:
Surely I shall be wiser in a year: 430
O wait a little!'   Philip sadly said,
'Annie, as I have waited all my life
I well may wait a little.'   'Nay,' she cried,
'I am bound: you have my promise — in a year:
Will you not bide your year as I bide mine?'   435
And Philip answer'd, 'I will bide my year.'

    Here both were mute, till Philip glancing up
Beheld the dead flame of the fallen day
Pass from the Danish barrow overhead;
Then fearing night and chill for Annie, rose   440
And sent his voice beneath him thro' the wood.
Up came the children laden with their spoil;
Then all descended to the port, and there
At Annie's door he paused and gave his hand,
Saying gently, "Annie, when I spoke to you,   445
That was your hour of weakness.   I was wrong,
I am always bound to you, but you are free.'
Then Annie weeping answer'd, 'I am bound.'

    She spoke; and in one moment as it were,
While yet she went about her household ways,   450
Ev'n as she dwelt upon his latest words,
That he had loved her longer than she knew,
That autumn into autumn flash'd again,
And there he stood once more before her face,
Claiming her promise.   'Is it a year?' she ask'd.   455
'Yes, if the nuts,' he said, 'be ripe again:
Come out and see.'   But she — she put him off —
So much to look to — such a change — a month —
Give her a month — she knew that she was bound —

A month — no more. Then Philip with his eyes   460
Full of that lifelong hunger, and his voice
Shaking a little like a drunkard's hand,
'Take your own time, Annie, take your own time.'
And Annie could have wept for pity of him;
And yet she held him on delayingly   465
With many a scarce-believable excuse,
Trying his truth and his long-sufferance,
Till half-another year had slipt away.

   By this the lazy gossips of the port,
Abhorrent of a calculation crost,   470
Began to chafe as at a personal wrong.
Some thought that Philip did but trifle with her;
Some that she but held off to draw him on;
And others laugh'd at her and Philip too,
As simple folk that knew not their own minds,   475
And one, in whom all evil fancies clung
Like serpent eggs together, laughingly
Would hint at worse in either.   Her own son
Was silent, tho' he often look'd his wish;
But evermore the daughter prest upon her   480
To wed the man so dear to all of them
And lift the household out of poverty;
And Philip's rosy face contracting grew
Careworn and wan; and all these things fell on her
Sharp as reproach.

              At last one night it chanced   485
That Annie could not sleep, but earnestly
Pray'd for a sign, 'my Enoch, is he gone?'
Then compass'd round by the blind wall of night
Brook'd not the expectant terror of her heart,
Started from bed, and struck herself a light,   490
Then desperately seized the holy Book,
Suddenly set it wide to find a sign,
Suddenly put her finger on the text,

---

    491 f. This method of divination is called stichomancy. It is the same
as the famous "Sortes Virgilianæ" except that the Bible is substituted for
the *Aeneid*.

'Under the palm-tree.' That was nothing to her:
No meaning there: she closed the Book and slept: 495
When lo! her Enoch sitting on a height,
Under a palm-tree, over him the Sun:
'He is gone,' she thought, 'he is happy, he is singing
Hosanna in the highest: yonder shines
The Sun of Righteousness, and these be palms   500
Whereof the happy people strowing cried
"Hosanna in the highest!"' Here she woke,
Resolved, sent for him and said wildly to him,
'There is no reason why we should not wed.'
'Then for God's sake,' he answer'd, 'both our sakes,   505
So you will wed me, let it be at once.'

     So these were wed and merrily rang the bells,
Merrily rang the bells and they were wed.
But never merrily beat Annie's heart.
A footstep seem'd to fall beside her path,   510
She knew not whence; a whisper on her ear,
She knew not what; nor loved she to be left
Alone at home, nor ventured out alone.
What ail'd her then, that ere she enter'd, often
Her hand dwelt lingeringly on the latch,   515
Fearing to enter: Philip thought he knew:
Such doubts and fears were common to her state,
Being with child: but when her child was born,
Then her new child was as herself renew'd,
Then the new mother came about her heart,   520
Then her good Philip was her all-in-all,
And that mysterious instinct wholly died.

     And where was Enoch? prosperously sail'd
The ship 'Good Fortune,' tho' at setting forth
The Biscay, roughly ridging eastward, shook   525
And almost overwhelm'd her, yet unvext
She slipt across the summer of the world,
Then after a long tumble about the Cape
And frequent interchange of foul and fair,
She passing thro' the summer world again,   530

---

494. Judges, iv, 5.

The breath of heaven came continually
And sent her sweetly by the golden isles,
Till silent in her oriental haven.

There Enoch traded for himself, and bought
Quaint monsters for the market of those times,   535
A gilded dragon, also, for the babes.

Less lucky her home-voyage: at first indeed
Thro' many a fair sea-circle, day by day,
Scarce-rocking, her full-busted figurehead
Stared o'er the ripple feathering from her bows: 540
Then follow'd calms, and then winds variable,
Then baffling, a long course of them; and last
Storm, such as drove her under moonless heavens
Till hard upon the cry of 'breakers' came
The crash of ruin, and the loss of all   545
But Enoch and two others. Half the night,
Buoy'd upon floating tackle and broken spars,
These drifted, stranding on an isle at morn
Rich, but the loneliest in a lonely sea.

No want was there of human sustenance,   550
Soft fruitage, mighty nuts, and nourishing roots;
Nor save for pity was it hard to take
The helpless life so wild that it was tame.
There in a seaward-gazing mountain-gorge
They built, and thatch'd with leaves of palm, a hut,   555
Half hut, half native cavern. So the three,
Set in this Eden of all plenteousness,
Dwelt with eternal summer, ill-content.

For one, the youngest, hardly more than boy,
Hurt in that night of sudden ruin and wreck,   560
Lay lingering out a five-years' death-in-life.
They could not leave him. After he was gone
The two remaining found a fallen stem;
And Enoch's comrade, careless of himself,
Fire-hollowing this in Indian fashion, fell   565

527. That is, the ship passed the Equator.

Sun-stricken, and that other lived alone.
In those two deaths he read God's warning 'wait.'

   The mountain wooded to the peak, the lawns
And winding glades high up like ways to heaven,
The slender coco's drooping crown of plumes,   570
The lightning flash of insect and of bird,
The lustre of the long convolvuluses
That coil'd around the stately stems, and ran
Ev'n to the limit of the land, the glows
And glories of the broad belt of the world,   575
All these he saw; but what he fain had seen
He could not see, the kindly human face,
Nor ever hear a kindly voice, but heard
The myriad shriek of wheeling ocean-fowl,
The league-long roller thundering on the reef,   580
The moving whisper of huge trees that branch'd
And blossom'd in the zenith, or the sweep
Of some precipitous rivulet to the wave,
As down the shore he ranged, or all day long
Sat often in the seaward-gazing gorge,   585
A shipwreck'd sailor, waiting for a sail:
No sail from day to day, but every day
The sunrise broken into scarlet shafts
Among the palms and ferns and precipices;
The blaze upon the waters to the east;   590
The blaze upon his island overhead;
The blaze upon the waters to the west;
Then the great stars that globed themselves in heaven,
The hollower-bellowing ocean, and again
The scarlet shafts of sunrise — but no sail.   595

   There often as he watch'd or seem'd to watch,
So still, the golden lizard on him paused,
A phantom made of many phantoms moved
Before him haunting him, or he himself
Moved haunting people, things and places, known   600
Far in a darker isle beyond the line;
The babes, their babble, Annie, the small house,
The climbing street, the mill, the leafy lanes,
The peacock-yewtree and the lonely Hall,

The horse he drove, the boat he sold, the chill   605
November dawns and dewy-glooming downs,
The gentle shower, the smell of dying leaves,
And the low moan of leaden-colour'd seas.

Once likewise, in the ringing of his ears,
Tho' faintly, merrily — far and far away —   610
He heard the pealing of his parish bells;
Then, tho' he knew not wherefore, started up
Shuddering, and when the beauteous hateful isle
Return'd upon him, had not his poor heart
Spoken with That, which being everywhere   615
Lets none, who speaks with Him, seem all alone,
Surely the man had died of solitude.

Thus over Enoch's early-silvering head
The sunny and rainy seasons came and went
Year after year. His hopes to see his own,   620
And pace the sacred old familiar fields,
Not yet had perish'd, when his lonely doom
Came suddenly to an end. Another ship
(She wanted water) blown by baffling winds,
Like the 'Good Fortune,' from her destined course,   625
Stay'd by this isle, not knowing where she lay:
For since the mate had seen at early dawn
Across a break on the mist-wreathen isle
The silent water slipping from the hills,
They sent a crew that landing burst away   630
In search of stream or fount, and fill'd the shores
With clamour. Downward from his mountain gorge
Stept the long-hair'd long-bearded solitary,
Brown, looking hardly human, strangely clad,
Muttering and mumbling, idiotlike it seem'd,   635
With inarticulate rage, and making signs
They knew not what: and yet he led the way
To where the rivulets of sweet water ran;

---

609 f. A. W. Kinglake told Tennyson that he had heard his own parish
bells in the midst of an eastern desert; having no calendar, he did not know
that it was Sunday when the church-bells would have been ringing at
home (*Memoir,* ii, 8; and compare Kinglake's *Eothen,* chapter xvii).

And ever as he mingled with the crew,
And heard them talking, his long-bounden tongue   640
Was loosen'd, till he made them understand;
Whom, when their casks were fill'd they took aboard:
And there the tale he utter'd brokenly,
Scarce-credited at first but more and more,
Amazed and melted all who listen'd to it: 645
And clothes they gave him and free passage home;
But oft he work'd among the rest and shook
His isolation from him. None of these
Came from his country, or could answer him,
If question'd, aught of what he cared to know.   650
And dull the voyage was with long delays,
The vessel scarce sea-worthy; but evermore
His fancy fled before the lazy wind
Returning, till beneath a clouded moon
He like a lover down thro' all his blood   655
Drew in the dewy meadowy morning-breath
Of England, blown across her ghostly wall:
And that same morning officers and men
Levied a kindly tax upon themselves,
Pitying the lonely man, and gave him it: 660
Then moving up the coast they landed him,
Ev'n in that harbour whence he sail'd before.

   There Enoch spoke no word to any one,
But homeward — home — what home? had he a home?
His home, he walk'd. Bright was that afternoon,   665
Sunny but chill; till drawn thro' either chasm,
Where either haven open'd on the deeps,
Roll'd a sea-haze and whelm'd the world in gray;
Cut off the length of highway on before,
And left but narrow breadth to left and right   670
Of wither'd holt or tilth or pasturage.
On the nigh-naked tree the robin piped
Disconsolate, and thro' the dripping haze
The dead weight of the dead leaf bore it down:
Thicker the drizzle grew, deeper the gloom;   675
Last, as it seem'd, a great mist-blotted light
Flared on him, and he came upon the place.

Then down the long street having slowly stolen,
His heart foreshadowing all calamity,
His eyes upon the stones, he reach'd the home   680
Where Annie lived and loved him, and his babes
In those far-off seven happy years were born;
But finding neither light nor murmur there
(A bill of sale gleam'd thro' the drizzle) crept
Still downward thinking 'dead or dead to me!'   685

Down to the pool and narrow wharf he went,
Seeking a tavern which of old he knew,
A front of timber-crost antiquity,
So propt, worm-eaten, ruinously old,
He thought it must have gone; but he was gone   690
Who kept it; and his widow Miriam Lane,
With daily-dwindling profits held the house;
A haunt of brawling seamen once, but now
Stiller, with yet a bed for wandering men.
There Enoch rested silent many days.   695

But Miriam Lane was good and garrulous,
Nor let him be, but often breaking in,
Told him, with other annals of the port,
Not knowing — Enoch was so brown, so bow'd,
So broken — all the story of his house.   700
His baby's death, her growing poverty,
How Philip put her little ones to school,
And kept them in it, his long wooing her,
Her slow consent, and marriage, and the birth
Of Philip's child: and o'er his countenance   705
No shadow past, nor motion: any one,
Regarding, well had deem'd he felt the tale
Less than the teller: only when she closed,
'Enoch, poor man, was cast away and lost,'
He, shaking his gray head pathetically,   710
Repeated muttering 'cast away and lost;'
Again in deeper inward whispers 'lost!'

But Enoch yearn'd to see her face again;
'If I might look on her sweet face again
And know that she is happy.' So the thought   715

Haunted and harass'd him, and drove him forth,
At evening when the dull November day
Was growing duller twilight, to the hill.
There he sat down gazing on all below;
There did a thousand memories roll upon him,   720
Unspeakable for sadness. By and by
The ruddy square of comfortable light,
Far-blazing from the rear of Philip's house,
Allured him, as the beacon-blaze allures
The bird of passage, till he madly strikes   725
Against it, and beats out his weary life.

For Philip's dwelling fronted on the street,
The latest house to landward; but behind,
With one small gate that open'd on the waste,
Flourish'd a little garden square and wall'd: 730
And in it throve an ancient evergreen,
A yewtree, and all round it ran a walk
Of shingle, and a walk divided it:
But Enoch shunn'd the middle walk and stole
Up by the wall, behind the yew; and thence   735
That which he better might have shunn'd, if griefs
Like his have worse or better, Enoch saw.

For cups and silver on the burnish'd board
Sparkled and shone; so genial was the hearth:
And on the right hand of the hearth he saw   740
Philip, the slighted suitor of old times,
Stout, rosy, with his babe across his knees;
And o'er her second father stoopt a girl,
A later but a loftier Annie Lee,
Fair-hair'd and tall, and from her lifted hand   745
Dangled a length of ribbon and a ring
To tempt the babe, who rear'd his creasy arms,
Caught at and ever miss'd it, and they laugh'd;
And on the left hand of the hearth he saw
The mother glancing often toward her babe,   750
But turning now and then to speak with him,
Her son, who stood beside her tall and strong,
And saying that which pleased him, for he smiled.

Now when the dead man come to life beheld
His wife his wife no more, and saw the babe 755
Hers, yet not his, upon the father's knee,
And all the warmth, the peace, the happiness,
And his own children tall and beautiful,
And him, that other, reigning in his place,
Lord of his rights and of his children's love, — 760
Then he, tho' Miriam Lane had told him all,
Because things seen are mightier than things heard,
Stagger'd and shook, holding the branch, and fear'd
To send abroad a shrill and terrible cry,
Which in one moment, like the blast of doom, 765
Would shatter all the happiness of the hearth.

He therefore turning softly like a thief,
Lest the harsh shingle should grate under foot,
And feeling all along the garden-wall,
Lest he should swoon and tumble and be found, 770
Crept to the gate, and open'd it, and closed,
As lightly as a sick man's chamber-door,
Behind him, and came out upon the waste.

And there he would have knelt, but that his knees
Were feeble, so that falling prone he dug 775
His fingers into the wet earth, and pray'd.

'Too hard to bear! why did they take me thence?
O God Almighty, blessed Saviour, Thou
That didst uphold me on my lonely isle,
Uphold me, Father, in my loneliness 780
A little longer! aid me, give me strength
Not to tell her, never to let her know.
Help me not to break in upon her peace.
My children too! must I not speak to these?
They know me not. I should betray myself. 785
Never: No father's kiss for me — the girl
So like her mother, and the boy, my son.'

There speech and thought and nature fail'd a little,
And he lay tranced; but when he rose and paced
Back toward his solitary home again, 790
All down the long and narrow street he went

Beating it in upon his weary brain,
As tho' it were the burthen of a song,
'Not to tell her, never to let her know.'

   He was not all unhappy. His resolve   795
Upbore him, and firm faith, and evermore
Prayer from a living source within the will,
And beating up thro' all the bitter world,
Like fountains of sweet water in the sea,
Kept him a living soul. 'This miller's wife,'   800
He said to Miriam, 'that you spoke about,
Has she no fear that her first husband lives?'
'Ay, ay, poor soul,' said Miriam, 'fear enow!
If you could tell her you had seen him dead,
Why, that would be her comfort;' and he thought   805
'After the Lord has call'd me she shall know.
I wait His time,' and Enoch set himself,
Scorning an alms, to work whereby to live.
Almost to all things could he turn his hand.
Cooper he was and carpenter, and wrought   810
To make the boatmen fishing-nets, or help'd
At lading and unlading the tall barks,
That brought the stinted commerce of those days;
Thus earn'd a scanty living for himself:
Yet since he did but labour for himself,   815
Work without hope, there was not life in it
Whereby the man could live; and as the year
Roll'd itself round again to meet the day
When Enoch had return'd, a langour came
Upon him, gentle sickness, gradually   820
Weakening the man, till he could do no more,
But kept the house, his chair, and last his bed.
And Enoch bore his weakness cheerfully.
For sure no gladlier does the stranded wreck
See thro' the gray skirts of a lifting squall   825
The boat that bears the hope of life approach
To save the life despair'd of, than he saw
Death dawning on him, and the close of all.

   For thro' that dawning gleam'd a kindlier hope
On Enoch thinking, 'after I am gone,   830
Then may she learn I lov'd her to the last.'

He call'd aloud for Miriam Lane and said,
'Woman, I have a secret — only swear,
Before I tell you — swear upon the book
Not to reveal it, till you see me dead.'   835
'Dead,' clamour'd the good woman, 'hear him talk!
I warrant, man, that we shall bring you round.'
'Swear,' added Enoch sternly, 'on the book.'
And on the book, half-frighted, Miriam swore.
Then Enoch rolling his gray eyes upon her,   840
'Did you know Enoch Arden of this town?'
'Know him?' she said, 'I knew him far away.
Ay, ay, I mind him coming down the street;
Held his head high, and cared for no man, he.'
Slowly and sadly Enoch answer'd her: 845
'His head is low, and no man cares for him.
I think I have not three days more to live;
I am the man.'   At which the woman gave
A half-incredulous, half-hysterical cry.
'You Arden, you! nay, — sure he was a foot   850
Higher than you be.'   Enoch said again,
'My God has bow'd me down to what I am;
My grief and solitude have broken me;
Nevertheless, know you that I am he
Who married — but that name has twice been changed —   855
I married her who married Philip Ray.
Sit, listen.'   Then he told her of his voyage,
His wreck, his lonely life, his coming back,
His gazing in on Annie, his resolve,
And how he kept it.   As the woman heard,   860
Fast flow'd the current of her easy tears,
While in her heart she yearn'd incessantly
To rush abroad all round the little haven,
Proclaiming Enoch Arden and his woes;
But awed and promise-bounden she forbore,   865
Saying only, 'See your bairns before you go!
Eh, let me fetch 'em, Arden,' and arose
Eager to bring them down, for Enoch hung
A moment on her words, but then replied:

'Woman, disturb me not now at the last,   870
But let me hold my purpose till I die.

Sit down again; mark me and understand,
While I have power to speak. I charge you now,
When you shall see her, tell her that I died
Blessing her, praying for her, loving her;   875
Save for the bar between us, loving her
As when she laid her head beside my own.
And tell my daughter Annie, whom I saw
So like her mother, that my latest breath
Was spent in blessing her and praying for her.   880
And tell my son that I died blessing him.
And say to Philip that I blest him too;
He never meant us any thing but good.
But if my children care to see me dead,
Who hardly knew me living, let them come,   885
I am their father; but she must not come,
For my dead face would vex her after-life.
And now there is but one of all my blood
Who will embrace me in the world-to-be.
This hair is his: she cut it off and gave it,   890
And I have borne it with me all these years,
And thought to bear it with me to my grave;
But now my mind is changed, for I shall see him,
My babe in bliss: wherefore when I am gone,
Take, give her this, for it may comfort her: 895
It will moreover be a token to her,
That I am he.'

                He ceased; and Miriam Lane
Made such a voluble answer promising all,
That once again he roll'd his eyes upon her
Repeating all he wish'd, and once again   900
She promised.

                Then the third night after this,
While Enoch slumber'd motionless and pale,
And Miriam watch'd and dozed at intervals,
There came so loud a calling of the sea,
That all the houses in the haven rang.   905

---

904. In the West of England a ground-swell is termed "the calling of
the sea" (Tennyson).

He woke, he rose, he spread his arms abroad
Crying with a loud voice 'A sail! a sail!
I am saved;' and so fell back and spoke no more.

So past the strong heroic soul away.
And when they buried him the little port   910
Had seldom seen a costlier funeral.

NORTHERN FARMER [1]

OLD STYLE

I

WHEER 'asta beän saw long and meä liggin' 'ere aloän?
Noorse? thourt nowt o' a noorse: whoy, Doctor's abeän an'
      agoän:
Says that I moänt 'a naw moor aäle: but I beänt a fool:
Git ma my aäle, fur I beänt a-gawin' to breäk my rule.

II

Doctors, they knaws nowt, fur a says what's nawways true: 5
Naw soort o' koind o' use to saäy the things that a do.
I've 'ed my point o' aäle ivry noight sin' I beän 'ere.
An' I've 'ed my quart ivry market-noight for foorty year.

III

Parson's a beän loikewoise, an' a sittin' 'ere o' my bed.
'The amoighty's a taäkin' o' you to 'issén, my friend,' a said, 10

---

[1] Written in 1861; published in *Enoch Arden, Etc.*, 1864. The poem
was suggested by the dying words of a farm-bailiff of Lincolnshire as reported to Tennyson: "God A'mighty little knows what He's about, a-taking
me. An' Squire will be so mad an' all" (*Memoir*, ii, 9). In subsequent
editions Tennyson greatly altered the spelling of dialect words in the effort to render their sounds more precisely.

1. *'asta beän*, hast thou been; *liggin'*, lying.

2. *noorse*, nurse.

3. *moänt 'a*, may not have.

7. *point*, pint.

10. *'issén*, himself.

An' a towd ma my sins, an's toithe were due, an' I gied it in
    hond;
I done moy duty boy 'um, as I 'a done boy the lond.

IV

Larn'd a ma' beä. I reckons I 'annot sa mooch to larn.
But a cast oop, thot a did, 'bout Bessy Marris's barne.
Thaw a knaws I hallus voäted wi' Squoire an' choorch an'
    staäte,   15
An' i' the woost o' toimes I wur niver agin the raäte.

V

An' I hallus coom'd to 's chooch afoor moy Sally wur deäd,
An' 'eärd 'um a bummin' awaäy loike a buzzard-clock ower my
    'eäd,
An' I niver knaw'd whot a meän'd but I thowt a 'ad summut
    to saäy,
An' I thowt a said whot a owt to 'a said an I coom'd awaäy. 20

VI

Bessy Marris's barne! tha knaws she laäid it to meä.
Mowt a beän, mayhap, for she wur a bad un, sheä.
'Siver, I kep 'um, I kep 'um my lass, tha mun understond;
I done moy duty boy 'um as I 'a done boy the lond.

VII

But Parson a cooms an' a goäs, an' a says it eäsy an' freeä 25
'The amoighty's a taäkin o' you to 'issén, my friend, says 'eä.
I weänt saäy men be loiars, thaw summun said it in aäste:
But 'e reäds wonn sarmin a weeäk, an' I 'a stubb'd Thurnaby
    waäste.

---

11. *towd*, told; *boy*, by.
13. *Larn'd a ma' beä*, learned he may be.
14. *a cast oop*, he brought up against me; *barne*, child.
16. *raäte*, the poor tax.
18. *buzzard-clock*, cockchafer.
23. *'Siver*, however.
27. *summut*, David; see Psalm cxvi, 11.
28. *stubb'd*, ploughed for cultivation.

VIII

D'ya moind the waäste, my lass? naw, naw, tha was not born
    then;
Theer wur a boggle in it, I often 'eärd 'um mysen;   30
Moäst loike a butter-bump, fur I 'eärd 'um about an' about,
But I stubb'd 'um oop wi' the lot, an' raäved an' rembled 'um
    out.

IX

Keäper's it wur; fo' they fun 'um theer a-laäid of 'is faäce
Down i' the woild 'enemies afoor I coom'd to the plaäce.
Noäks or Thimbleby — toäner 'ed shot 'um as deäd as a
    naäil.   35
Noäks wur 'ang'd for it oop at 'soize — but git ma my aäle.

X

Dubbut looök at the waäste: theer warn't not feeäd for a cow;
Nowt at all but bracken an' fuzz, an' looök at it now —
Warnt worth nowt a haäcre, an' now theer's lots o' feeäd,
Fourscoor yows upon it an' some on it down i' seeäd.   40

XI

Nobbut a bit on it's left, an' I meän'd to 'a stubb'd it at fall,
Done it ta-year I meän'd, an runn'd plow thruff it an' all,
If godamoighty an' parson 'ud nobbut let ma aloän,
Meä, wi' haäte hoonderd haäcre o' Squoire's, an' lond o' my
    oän.

---

30. *boggle*, bogie, ghost.
31. *butter-bump*, the bittern or marsh-drum.
32. *raäved an' rembled*, tore up and threw away.
33. *Keäper's it wur*, it was the ghost of the game-keeper.
34. *'enemies*, anemones.
35. *toäner*, one or other.
36. *at 'soize*, at the assizes.
37. *Dubbut*, do but.
40. *yows*, ewes; *seeäd*, clover.
42. *ta-year*, this year; *thruff*, through.
43. *'ud nobbut*, would not.

XII

Do godamoighty knaw what a's doing a-taäkin' o' meä?   45
I beänt wonn as saws 'ere a beän an' yonder a peä;
An' Squoire 'ull be sa mad an' all — a' dear a' dear!
And I 'a managed for Squoire coom Michaelmas thutty year.

XIII

A mowt 'a taäen owd Joänes, as 'ant not a 'aäpoth o' sense,
Or a mowt 'a taäen young Robins — a niver mended a fence: 50
But godamoighty a moost taäke meä an' taäke ma now
Wi' aäf the cows to cauve an' Thurnaby hoälms to plow!

XIV

Looök 'ow quoloty smoiles when they seeäs ma a passin' boy,
Says to thessén naw doubt 'what a man a beä sewer-loy!'
Fur they knaws what I beän to Squoire sin fust a coom'd to the
     'All;   55
I done moy duty by Squoire an' I done moy duty boy hall.

XV

Squoire's i' Lunnon, an' summun I reckon 'ull 'a to wroite,
For whoä's to howd the lond ater meä thot muddles ma quoit;
Sartin-sewer I beä, thot a weänt niver give it to Joänes,
Naw, nor a moänt to Robins — a niver rembles the stoäns. 60

XVI

But summun 'ull come ater meä mayhap wi' 'is kittle o' steäm
Huzzin' an' maäzin' the blessed feälds wi' the Divil's oän teäm.
Sin' I mun doy I mun doy, thaw loife they says is sweet,
But sin' I mun doy I mun doy, for I couldn abeär to see it.

---

48. *Michaelmas*, September 29.

52. *hoälms*, low, flat lands by a stream.

53. *quoloty*, quality, the gentry.

54. *thessén*, themselves; *sewer-loy*, surely.

61. *kittle*, boiler. The steam threshing-machine was introduced into
Lincolnshire in 1848.

62. *Huzzin' an' maäzin'*, worrying and bewildering.

63. *Sin'*, since; *doy*, die.

XVII

What atta stannin' theer fur, an' doesn bring ma the aäle? 65
Doctor's a 'toättler, lass, an a's hallus i' the owd taäle;
I weänt breäk rules fur Doctor, a knaws naw moor nor a floy;
Git ma my aäle I tell tha, an' if I mun doy I mun doy.

NORTHERN FARMER [1]

NEW STYLE

I

Dosn't thou 'ear my 'erse's legs, as they canters awaäy?
Proputty, proputty, proputty — that's what I 'ears 'em saäy.
Proputty, proputty, proputty — Sam, thou's an ass for thy
   paaïns:
Theer's moor sense i' one o' 'is legs nor in all thy braaïns.

II

Woä — theer's a craw to pluck wi' tha, Sam: yon's parson's
   'ouse —   5
Dosn't thou knaw that a man mun be eäther a man or a mouse?
Time to think on it then; for thou'll be twenty to weeäk.
Proputty, proputty — woä then woä — let ma 'ear mysén speäk.

III

Me an' thy muther, Sammy, 'as beän a-talkin' o' thee;
Thou's beän talkin' to muther, an' she beän a tellin' it me. 10
Thou'll not marry for munny — thou's sweet upo' parson's
   lass —
Noä — thou'll marry for luvv — an' we boäth on us thinks tha
   an ass.

---

66. 'toättler, teetotaler.

67. floy, fly.

[1] Published in *The Holy Grail and Other Poems*, 1869. This dramatic
monologue portrays the "new style" independent farmer of large holdings
who succeeded the "old style" farm-bailiff. Tennyson had heard that
the favourite saying of such a farmer was "When I canters my 'erse [horse]
along the ramper [highway] I 'ears proputty, proputty, proputty" (*Memoir*,
ii, 9). The dialect is slightly less broad than that in the companion poem,
perhaps to indicate that it was beginning to die out.

7. *to weeäk*, this week.

IV

Seeäd her todaäy goä by — Saäint's-daäy — they was ringing
the bells.
She's a beauty thou thinks — an' soä is scoors o' gells,
Them as 'as munny an' all — wot's a beauty? — the flower as
blaws.   15
But proputty, proputty sticks, an' proputty, proputty graws.

V

Do'ant be stunt: taäke time: I knaws what maäkes tha sa mad.
Warn't I craäzed fur the lasses mysén when I wur a lad?
But I knaw'd a Quaäker feller as often 'as towd ma this:
'Doänt thou marry for munny, but goä wheer munny is!'   20

VI

An' I went wheer munny war: an' thy muther coom to 'and,
Wi' lots o' munny laaïd by, an' a nicetish bit o' land.
Maäybe she warn't a beauty: — I niver giv it a thowt —
But varn't she as good to cuddle an' kiss as a lass as 'ant nowt?

VII

Parson's lass 'ant nowt, an' she weänt 'a nowt when 'e's deäd, 25
Mun be a guvness, lad, or summut, and addle her breäd:
Why? fur 'e's nobbut a curate, an' weänt niver git hissén cleär,
An' 'e maäde the bed as 'e ligs on afoor 'e coom'd to the shere.

VIII

'An thin 'e coom'd to the parish wi' lots o' Varsity debt,
Stook to his taaïl they did, an' 'e 'ant got shut on 'em yet.   30
An' 'e ligs on 'is back i' the grip, wi' noän to lend 'im a shuvv,
Woorse nor a far-welter'd yowe: fur, Sammy, 'e married fur
luvv.

---

14. *geils*, girls.
17. *stunt*, obstinate.
24. *as 'ant nowt*, that has nothing.
25. *weänt 'a*, will not have.
26. *addle*, earn.
30. *shut on*, clear of.
31. *i' the grip*, in the ditch.
32. *a far-welter'd yowe*, a ewe lying on her back.

IX

Luvv? what's luvv? thou can luvv thy lass an' 'er munny too,
Maakin' 'em goä togither as they've good right to do.
Couldn I luvv thy muther by cause o' 'er munny laaïd by?   35
Naäy — fur I luvv'd 'er a vast sight moor fur it: reäson why.

X

Ay an' thy muther says thou wants to marry the lass,
Cooms of a gentleman burn: an' we boäth on us thinks tha an
     ass.
Woä then, proputty, wiltha? — an ass as near as mays nowt —
Woä then, wiltha? dangtha! — the bees is as fell as owt.   40

XI

Breäk me a bit o' the esh for his 'eäd, lad, out o' the fence!
Gentleman burn! what's gentleman burn? is it shillins an' pence?
Proputty, proputty's ivrything 'ere, an', Sammy, I'm blest
If it isn't the saäme oop yonder, fur them as 'as it's the best.

XII

Tis'n them as 'as munny as breäks into 'ouses an' steäls,   45
Them as 'as coäts to their backs an' taäkes their regular meäls.
Noä, but it's them as niver knaws wheer a meäl's to be 'ad.
Taäke my word for it, Sammy, the poor in a loomp is bad.

XIII

Them or thir feythers, tha sees, mun 'a beän a laäzy lot,
Fur work mun 'a gone to the gittin' whiniver munny was
     got.   50
Feyther 'ad ammost nowt; leästways 'is munny was 'id.
But 'e tued an' moil'd 'issén deäd, an' 'e died a good un, 'e did.

---

38. *burn*, born.
39. *mays nowt*, makes nothing.
40. *the bees is as fell as owt*, the flies are as fierce as anything.
41. *esh*, ash.
52. *tued an' moil'd*, tugged and drudged.

XIV

Looök thou theer wheer Wrigglesby beck cooms out by the 'ill!
Feyther run oop to the farm, an' I runs oop to the mill;
An' I'll run oop to the brig, an' that thou'll live to see;   55
And if thou marries a good un I'll leäve the land to thee.

XV

Thim's my noätions, Sammy, wheerby I means to stick;
But if thou marries a bad un, I'll leäve the land to Dick. —
Coom oop, proputty, proputty — that's what I 'ears 'im saäy —
Proputty, proputty, proputty — canter an' canter awaäy.   60

THE REVENGE

A BALLAD OF THE FLEET[1]

I

At Flores in the Azores Sir Richard Grenville lay,
And a pinnace, like a flutter'd bird, came flying from far away:
'Spanish ships of war at sea! we have sighted fifty-three!'
Then sware Lord Thomas Howard: ' 'Fore God I am no coward;

---

53. *beck*, brook.
54. *Feyther run oop*, father's land ran up.
55. *brig*, bridge.

---

1. The final syllable of both Flores and Azores is pronounced, as in Spanish.

[1] Written in 1873; published in *The Nineteenth Century*, March, 1878; reprinted in *Ballads and Other Poems*, 1880. James Anthony Froude's narrative of the last fight of the *Revenge* is the climax of his article on "England's Forgotten Worthies," published in *The Westminster Review*, July, 1852, and reprinted in the first volume of *Short Studies in Great Subjects*. From the *Memoir* (ii, 142) we learn that the first line of Tennyson's ballad lay on the poet's desk for years; it is possible that it dates from his first reading of Froude's narrative. In 1871 Edward Arber included in his *English Reprints* the three sixteenth-century accounts of the battle, Sir Walter Ralegh's, Gervase Markham's, and Jan Huygen Van Linschoten's. (Of this compilation there is a new edition, 1912). It seems probable that Arber's book stimulated Tennyson's interest in the subject; and it is noteworthy that Arber likens the fight to the charge at Balaclava. Ralegh's *Report of the Truth of the Fight about the Iles of Acores, this last Sommer, betwixt the Revenge, one of her Maiesties Shippes, and an Armada of the*

But I cannot meet them here, for my ships are out of gear,   5
And the half my men are sick. I must fly, but follow quick.
We are six ships of the line; can we fight with fifty-three?'

II

Then spake Sir Richard Grenville: 'I know you are no coward;
You fly them for a moment to fight with them again.
But I've ninety men and more that are lying sick ashore.   10
I should count myself the coward if I left them, my Lord
      Howard,
To these Inquisition dogs and the devildoms of Spain.'

III

So Lord Howard past away with five ships of war that day,
Till he melted like a cloud in the silent summer heaven;
But Sir Richard bore in hand all his sick men from the land   15
Very carefully and slow,
Men of Bideford in Devon,
And we laid them on the ballast down below;
For we brought them all aboard,
And they blest him in their pain, that they were not left to
      Spain,   20
To the thumbscrew and the stake, for the glory of the Lord.

IV

He had only a hundred seamen to work the ship and to fight,
And he sailed away from Flores till the Spaniard came in sight,

---

King of Spaine appeared anonymously in 1591. It was ascribed to Ralegh
when reprinted in the second edition, 1599–1600, of Richard Hakluyt's
*Principal Navigations, Voyages, Traffiques and Discoveries of the English
Nation* (ii, 169 f.; ed. Glasgow, 1904, vii, 38 f.). Gervase Markham's
poem, *The Most Honorable Tragedie of Sir Richard Grinvile, Knight*, 1595,
is desperately mannered and dull. The Dutch traveler Van Linschoten
included a brief account in his *Itinerario* (Amsterdam, 1595–6) which was
translated into English as a *Discours of Voyages into ye Easte and West
Indies*, 1598. This is not the place to discuss afresh the vexed question of
Grenville's motives in refusing to obey the orders of his commanding officer
and in giving battle to an immensely superior force of Spaniards (September
10, 1591). For the latest study of the problem see A. L. Rowse, *Sir
Richard Grenville of the "Revenge,"* London, 1937. See also J. S. Corbett,
Drake and the Tudor Navy, ii, 386 f.

With his huge sea-castles heaving upon the weather bow.
'Shall we fight or shall we fly?   25
Good Sir Richard, tell us now,
For to fight is but to die!
There'll be little of us left by the time this sun be set.'
And Sir Richard said again: 'We be all good English men.
Let us bang these dogs of Seville, the children of the devil,   30
For I never turn'd my back upon Don or devil yet.'

V

Sir Richard spoke and he laugh'd, and we roar'd a hurrah,
    and so
The little Revenge ran on sheer into the heart of the foe,
With her hundred fighters on deck, and her ninety sick below;
For half of their fleet to the right and half to the left were
    seen,   35
And the little Revenge ran on thro' the long sea-lane between.

VI

Thousands of their soldiers look'd down from their decks and
    laugh'd,
Thousands of their seamen made mock at the mad little craft
Running on and on, till delay'd
By their mountain-like San Philip that, of fifteen hundred
    tons,   40
And up-shadowing high above us with her yawning tiers of
    guns,
Took the breath from our sails, and we stay'd.

VII

And while now the great San Philip hung above us like a cloud
Whence the thunderbolt will fall
Long and loud,   45
Four galleons drew away
From the Spanish fleet that day,
And two upon the larboard and two upon the starboard lay,
And the battle-thunder broke from them all.

VIII

But anon the great San Philip, she bethought herself and
    went   50

Having that within her womb that had left her ill content;
And the rest they came aboard us, and they fought us hand to
 hand,
For a dozen times they came with their pikes and musqueteers,
And a dozen times we shook 'em off as a dog that shakes his
 ears
When he leaps from the water to the land.   55

IX

And the sun went down, and the stars came out far over the
 summer sea,
But never a moment ceased the fight of the one and the fifty-
 three.
Ship after ship, the whole night long, their high-built galleons
 came,
Ship after ship, the whole night long, with her battle-thunder
 and flame;
Ship after ship, the whole night long, drew back with her dead
 and her shame.   60
For some were sunk and many were shatter'd, and so could
 fight us no more —
God of battles, was ever a battle like this in the world before?

X

For he said 'Fight on! fight on!'
Tho' his vessel was all but a wreck;
And it chanced that, when half of the short summer night was
 gone,   65
With a grisly wound to be drest he had left the deck,
But a bullet struck him that was dressing it suddenly dead,
And himself he was wounded again in the side and the head,
And he said 'Fight on! fight on!'

XI

And the night went down, and the sun smiled out far over the
 summer sea,   70
And the Spanish fleet with broken sides lay round us all in a
 ring;

---

51. *womb*, the belly of the ship.

But they dared not touch us again, for they fear'd that we still
    could sting,
So they watch'd what the end would be.
And we had not fought them in vain,
But in perilous plight were we,   75
Seeing forty of our poor hundred were slain,
And half of the rest of us maim'd for life
In the crash of the cannonades and the desperate strife;
And the sick men down in the hold were most of them stark
    and cold,
And the pikes were all broken or bent, and the powder was all
    of it spent;   80
And the masts and the rigging were lying over the side;
But Sir Richard cried in his English pride,
'We have fought such a fight for a day and a night
As may never be fought again!
We have won great glory, my men!   85
And a day less or more
At sea or ashore,
We die — does it matter when?
Sink me the ship, Master Gunner — sink her, split her in twain!
Fall into the hands of God, not into the hands of Spain!'   90

XII

And the gunner said 'Ay, ay,' but the seamen made reply:
'We have children, we have wives,
And the Lord hath spared our lives.
We will make the Spaniard promise, if we yield, to let us go;
We shall live to fight again and to strike another blow.'   95
And the lion there lay dying, and they yielded to the foe.

XIII

And the stately Spanish men to their flagship bore him then,
Where they laid him by the mast, old Sir Richard caught at
    last,
And they praised him to his face with their courtly foreign
    grace;
But he rose upon their decks, and he cried: 100
'I have fought for Queen and Faith like a valiant man and true;
I have only done my duty as a man is bound to do:

With a joyful spirit I Sir Richard Grenville die!'
And he fell upon their decks, and he died.

XIV

And they stared at the dead that had been so valiant and
        true,   105
And had holden the power and glory of Spain so cheap
That he dared her with one little ship and his English few;
Was he devil or man?   He was devil for aught they knew,
But they sank his body with honour down into the deep,
And they mann'd the Revenge with a swarthier alien crew, 110
And away she sail'd with her loss and long'd for her own;
When a wind from the lands they had ruin'd awoke from sleep,
And the water began to heave and the weather to moan,
And or ever that evening ended a great gale blew,
And a wave like the wave that is raised by an earthquake
        grew,   115
Till it smote on their hulls and their sails and their masts and
        their flags,
And the whole sea plunged and fell on the shot-shatter'd navy
        of Spain,
And the little Revenge herself went down by the island crags
To be lost evermore in the main.

RIZPAH [1]

17—.

I

WAILING, wailing, wailing, the wind over land and sea —
And Willy's voice in the wind, 'O mother come out to me.'
Why should he call me to-night, when he knows that I cannot
        go?

---

104. Grenville actually died three or four days after the battle, and the
storm in which the *Revenge* went down arose several days thereafter.

[1] Published in *Ballads and Other Poems,* 1880. The incident upon
which this dramatic monologue was founded was brought to Tennyson's
attention by Mary Brotherton, a friend and neighbour at Freshwater. She
communicated to him an article on "Old Brighton" in a penny magazine.
A well-known character at Brighton in Regency days was Phoebe Hessell
who sold gingerbread and apples at a street-corner, was the recipient of a

For the downs are as bright as day, and the full moon stares at
    the snow.

II

We should be seen, my dear; they would spy us out of the
    town.   5
The loud black nights for us, and the storm rushing over the
    down,
When I cannot see my own hand, but am led by the creak of
    the chain,
And grovel and grope for my son till I find myself drenched
    with the rain.

III

Anything fallen again? nay — what was there left to fall?
I have taken them home, I have number'd the bones, I have hid-
    den them all.   10
What am I saying? and what are *you*? do you come as a spy?
Falls? what falls? who knows? As the tree falls so must it lie.

---

small pension from the Prince of Wales, and died in 1821 at the age of 106.
(See Osbert Sitwell and Margaret Barton, *Brighton*, 1935, p. 251). Some
time in the later eighteenth century she lodged information with the author-
ities which led to the arrest and conviction of two mail-robbers, Rooke and
Howell, who were hanged in chains. Rooke's aged mother was seen to go
night after night to the gibbet on the Downs, returning home with something in her apron. It was discovered that as the wind and rain scattered
the bones of the hanging corpse she gathered them up and conveyed them
to her house. When the elements had stripped the gibbet of its burden
she interred the bones in a churchyard. The narrative which Tennyson
read concludes: "What a sad story of a Brighton Rizpah!" For the Biblical analogue see 2 Samuel, xxi, 8 f. — This poem, written at the age of
seventy-one, is the finest in a volume which marks an astonishing rebirth
of Tennyson's powers. Contemporary critics were quick to remark upon
this. The *Edinburgh Review* (October, 1881) said that in "Rizpah" Tennyson "has broken on the world with a new strength and splendour" and
"has achieved a new reputation." Swinburne, forgetting old rancours,
wrote: "Never since the very beginning of all poetry were the twin passions of terror and pity more divinely done into deathless words or set to
more perfect and profound magnificence of music; . . . the poet never
lived on earth whose glory would not be heightened by the attribution of
this poem to his hand"; and so forth ("Tennyson and Musset," *The Fortnightly Review*, February, 1881; reprinted in *Miscellanies*, 1886).
    12. Ecclesiastes, xi, 3.

IV

Who let her in? how long has she been? you — what have you
    heard?
Why did you sit so quiet? you never have spoken a word.
O — to   pray   with   me — yes — a   lady — none   of   their
    spies —   15
But the night has crept into my heart, and begun to darken my
    eyes.

V

Ah — you, that have lived so soft, what should *you* know of the
    night,
The blast and the burning shame and the bitter frost and the
    fright?
I have done it, while you were asleep — you were only made for
    the day.
I have gather'd my baby together — and now you may go your
    way.   20

VI

Nay — for it's kind of you, Madam, to sit by an old dying wife.
But say nothing hard of my boy, I have only an hour of life.
I kiss'd my boy in the prison, before he went out to die.
'They dared me to do it,' he said, and he never has told me a
    lie.
I whipt him for robbing an orchard once when he was but a
    child —   25
'The farmer dared me to do it,' he said; he was always so
    wild —
And idle — and couldn't be idle — my Willy — he never could
    rest.
The King should have made him a soldier, he would have been
    one of his best.

VII

But he lived with a lot of wild mates, and they never would let
    him be good;
They swore that he dare not rob the mail, and he swore that he
    would;   30

And he took no life, but he took one purse, and when all was
    done
He flung it among his fellows — I'll none of it, said my son.

VIII

I came into court to the Judge and the lawyers. I told them
    my tale,
God's own truth — but they kill'd him, they kill'd him for rob-
    bing the mail.
They hang'd him in chains for a show — we had always borne
    a good name —   35
To be hang'd for a thief — and then put away — isn't that
    enough shame?
Dust to dust — low down — let us hide! but they set him so
    high
That all the ships of the world could stare at him, passing by.
God 'ill pardon the hell-black raven and horrible fowls of the
    air,
But not the black heart of the lawyer who kill'd him and hang'd
    him there.   40

IX

And the jailer forced me away. I had bid him my last good-
    bye;
They had fasten'd the door of his cell. 'O mother!' I heard
    him cry.
I couldn't get back tho' I tried, he had something further to
    say,
And now I never shall know it. The jailer forced me away.

X

Then since I couldn't but hear that cry of my boy that was
    dead,   45
They seized me and shut me up: they fasten'd me down on my
    bed.
'Mother, O mother!' — he call'd in the dark to me year after
    year —

---

38. The gibbet on the Downs could be seen from ships in the English Channel.

They beat me for that, they beat me — you know that I couldn't
    but hear;
And then at the last they found I had grown so stupid and still
They let me abroad again — but the creatures had worked their
    will.   50

XI

Flesh of my flesh was gone, but bone of my bone was left —
I stole them all from the lawyers — and you, will you call it a
    theft? —
My baby, the bones that had suck'd me, the bones that had
    laugh'd and had cried —
Theirs?   O no! they are mine — not theirs — they had moved
    in my side.

XII

Do you think I was scared by the bones?   I kiss'd 'em, I
    buried 'em all —   55
I can't dig deep, I am old — in the night by the churchyard
    wall.
My Willy 'ill rise up whole when the trumpet of judgment 'ill
    sound;
But I charge you never to say that I laid him in holy ground.

XIII

They would scratch him up — they would hang him again on
    the cursed tree.
Sin?   O yes — we are sinners, I know — let all that be,   60
And read me a Bible verse of the Lord's good will toward
    men —
'Full of compassion and mercy, the Lord' — let me hear it
    again;
'Full of compassion and mercy — long-suffering.'   Yes, O yes!
For the lawyer is born but to murder — the Saviour lives but to
    bless.
He'll never put on the black cap except for the worst of the
    worst,   65

----

    51. *Flesh of my flesh.* Genesis, xi, 3.
    57. 1 Thessalonians, iv, 16.
    62. Psalms, lxxxvi, 15.

And the first may be last — I have heard it in church — and the
    last may be first.
Suffering — O long-suffering — yes, as the Lord must know,
Year after year in the mist and the wind and the shower and
    the snow.

XIV

Heard, have you? what? they have told you he never repented
    his sin.
How do they know it? are *they* his mother? are *you* of his
    kin?   70
Heard! have you ever heard, when the storm on the downs
    began,
The wind that 'ill wail like a child and the sea that 'ill moan
    like a man?

XV

Election, Election and Reprobation — it's all very well.
But I go to-night to my boy, and I shall not find him in Hell.
For I cared so much for my boy that the Lord has look'd into
    my care,   75
And He means me I'm sure to be happy with Willy, I know
    not where.

XVI

And if *he* be lost — but to save *my* soul, that is all your desire:
Do you think that I care for *my* soul if my boy be gone to the
    fire?
I have been with God in the dark — go, go, you may leave me
    alone —
You never have borne a child — you are just as hard as a
    stone.   80

XVII

Madam, I beg your pardon!   I think that you mean to be kind,
But I cannot hear what you say for my Willy's voice in the
    wind —

---

66. Matthew, xix, 30; etc.

73. *Election and Reprobation,* Calvinistic doctrines, that certain persons are chosen by God for salvation and others excluded therefrom.

The snow and the sky so bright — he used but to call in the
    dark,
And he calls to me now from the church and not from the gib-
    bet — for hark!
Nay — you can hear it yourself — it is coming — shaking the
    walls —   85
Willy — the moon's in a cloud — Goodnight. I am going.
    He calls.

THE VOYAGE OF MAELDUNE

(FOUNDED ON AN IRISH LEGEND A.D. 700.) [1]

I

I was the chief of the race — he had stricken my father dead —
But I gather'd my fellows together, I swore I would strike off
    his head.
Each of them look'd like a king, and was noble in birth as in
    worth,
And each of them boasted he sprang from the oldest race upon
    earth.
Each was as brave in the fight as the bravest hero of song,   5
And each of them liefer had died than have done one another
    a wrong.
He lived on an isle in the ocean — we sail'd on a Friday
    morn —
He that had slain my father the day before I was born.

II

And we came to the isle in the ocean, and there on the shore
    was he.
But a sudden blast blew us out and away thro' a boundless
    sea.   10

---

[1] Written after reading the original story in P. W. Joyce's *Old Celtic
Romances,* 1879; published in *Ballads and Other Poems,* 1880.   Tennyson
took hints from Joyce, but he omitted some incidents and invented others,
changing and, as some readers will think, spoiling the conclusion (see
note on l. 127).   The poem is not mentioned in the *Memoir,* but in a
note in the Eversley edition of the *Works* (iv, 555) the poet's son records
that his father "intended to represent, in his own original way, the Celtic
genius."   There is some vague underlying symbolism which comes to the
surface only in stanza x (see note on l. 105).

III

And we came to the Silent Isle that we never had touch'd at
    before,
Where a silent ocean always broke on a silent shore,
And the brooks glitter'd on in the light without sound, and the
    long waterfalls
Pour'd in a thunderless plunge to the base of the mountain
    walls,
And the poplar and cypress unshaken by storm flourish'd up
    beyond sight,   15
And the pine shot aloft from the crag to an unbelievable height,
And high in the heaven above it there flicker'd a songless lark,
And the cock couldn't crow, and the bull couldn't low, and the
    dog couldn't bark.
And round it we went, and thro' it, but never a murmur, a
    breath —
It was all of it fair as life, it was all of it quiet as death,   20
And we hated the beautiful Isle, for whenever we strove to
    speak
Our voices were thinner and fainter than any flittermouse-
    shriek;
And the men that were mighty of tongue and could raise such
    a battle-cry
That a hundred who heard it would rush on a thousand lances
    and die —
O they to be dumb'd by the charm! — so fluster'd with anger
    were they   25
They almost fell on each other; but after we sail'd away.

IV

And we came to the Isle of Shouting, we landed, a score of wild
    birds
Cried from the topmost summit with human voices and words;
Once in an hour they cried, and whenever their voices peal'd
The steer fell down at the plow and the harvest died from the
    field,   30
And the men dropt dead in the valleys and half of the cattle
    went lame,
And the roof sank in on the hearth, and the dwelling broke into
    flame;

And the shouting of these wild birds ran into the hearts of my crew,
Till they shouted along with the shouting and seized one another and slew;
But I drew them the one from the other; I saw that we could not stay,   35
And we left the dead to the birds and we sail'd with our wounded away.

V

And we came to the Isle of Flowers: their breath met us out on the seas,
For the Spring and the middle Summer sat each on the lap of the breeze;
And the red passion-flower to the cliffs, and the dark-blue clematis, clung,
And starr'd with a myriad blossom the long convolvulus hung;   40
And the topmost spire of the mountain was lilies in lieu of snow,
And the lilies like glaciers winded down, running out below
Thro' the fire of the tulip and poppy, the blaze of gorse, and the blush
Of millions of roses that sprang without leaf or a thorn from the bush;
And the whole isle-side flashing down from the peak without ever a tree   45
Swept like a torrent of gems from the sky to the blue of the sea;
And we roll'd upon capes of crocus and vaunted our kith and our kin,
And we wallow'd in beds of lilies, and chanted the triumph of Finn,
Till each like a golden image was pollen'd from head to feet
And each was as dry as a cricket, with thirst in the middle-day heat.   50
Blossom and blossom, and promise of blossom, but never a fruit!

---

48. *Finn,* the most famous hero of Irish legend. He was the father of Ossian.

And we hated the Flowering Isle, as we hated the isle that was
 mute,
And we tore up the flowers by the million and flung them in
 bight and bay,
And we left but a naked rock, and in anger we sail'd away.

VI

And we came to the Isle of Fruits: all round from the cliffs and
 the capes,   55
Purple or amber, dangled a hundred fathom of grapes,
And the warm melon lay like a little sun on the tawny sand,
And the fig ran up from the beach and rioted over the land,
And the mountain arose like a jewell'd throne thro' the fragrant
 air,
Glowing with all-colour'd plums and with golden masses of
 pear,   60
And the crimson and scarlet of berries that flamed upon bine
 and vine,
But in every berry and fruit was the poisonous pleasure of wine;
And the peak of the mountain was apples, the hugest that ever
 were seen,
And they prest, as they grew, on each other, with hardly a
 leaflet between,
And all of them redder than rosiest health or than utterest
 shame,   65
And setting, when Even descended, the very sunset aflame;
And we stay'd three days, and we gorged and we madden'd, till
 every one drew
His sword on his fellow to slay him, and ever they struck and
 they slew;
And myself, I had eaten but sparely, and fought till I sunder'd
 the fray,
Then I bade them remember my father's death, and we sail'd
 away.   70

VII

And we came to the Isle of Fire: we were lured by the light
 from afar,
For the peak sent up one league of fire to the Northern Star;
Lured by the glare and the blare, but scarcely could stand upright,

For the whole isle shudder'd and shook like a man in a mortal
    affright;
We were giddy besides with the fruits we had gorged, and so
    crazed that at last   75
There were some leap'd into the fire; and away we sail'd, and
    we past
Over that undersea isle, where the water is clearer than air:
Down we look'd: what a garden! O bliss, what a Paradise
    there!
Towers of a happier time, low down in a rainbow deep
Silent palaces, quiet fields of eternal sleep!   80
And three of the gentlest and best of my people, whate'er I
    could say,
Plunged head down in the sea, and the Paradise trembled away.

VIII

And we came to the Bounteous Isle, where the heavens lean low
    on the land,
And ever at dawn from the cloud glitter'd o'er us a sunbright
    hand,
Then it open'd and dropt at the side of each man, as he rose
    from his rest,   85
Bread enough for his need till the labourless day dipt under the
    West;
And we wander'd about it and thro' it. O never was time so
    good!
And we sang of the triumphs of Finn, and the boast of our
    ancient blood,
And we gazed at the wandering wave as we sat by the gurgle
    of springs,
And we chanted the songs of the Bards and the glories of fairy
    kings;   90
But at length we began to be weary, to sigh, and to stretch and
    yawn,
Till we hated the Bounteous Isle and the sunbright hand of the
    dawn,
For there was not an enemy near, but the whole green Isle was
    our own,
And we took to playing at ball, and we took to throwing the
    stone,

And we took to playing at battle, but that was a perilous
   play,   95
For the passion of battle was in us, we slew and we sail'd away.

                                IX

And we past to the Isle of Witches and heard their musical
   cry —
'Come to us, O come, come' in the stormy red of a sky
Dashing the fires and the shadows of dawn on the beautiful
   shapes,
For a wild witch naked as heaven stood on each of the loftiest
   capes,   100
And a hundred ranged on the rock like white sea-birds in a row,
And a hundred gamboll'd and pranced on the wrecks in the
   sand below,
And a hundred splash'd from the ledges, and bosom'd the burst
   of the spray,
But I knew we should fall on each other, and hastily sail'd away.

                                X

And we came in an evil time to the Isle of the Double
   Towers,   105
One was of smooth-cut stone, one carved all over with flowers,
But an earthquake always moved in the hollows under the dells,
And they shock'd on each other and butted each other with
   clashing of bells,
And the daws flew out of the Towers and jangled and wrangled
   in vain,
And the clash and boom of the bells rang into the heart and the
   brain,   110
Till the passion of battle was on us, and all took sides with the
   Towers,
There were some for the clean-cut stone, there were more for
   the carven flowers,
And the wrathful thunder of God peal'd over us all the day,
For the one half slew the other, and after we sail'd away.

—————

   105 f. The visit to the Isle of the Double Towers is wholly Tennyson's
invention. The poet's son explains it as symbolical of the contest between
Roman Catholics and Protestants (*Works,* Eversley edition, iv, 556).

XI

And we came to the Isle of a Saint who had sail'd with St.
    Brendan of yore,   115
He had lived ever since on the Isle and his winters were fifteen
    score,
And his voice was low as from other worlds, and his eyes were
    sweet,
And his white hair sank to his heels and his white beard fell to
    his feet,
And he spake to me, 'O Maeldune, let be this purpose of thine!
Remember the words of the Lord when he told us "Vengeance
    is mine!"   120
His fathers have slain thy fathers in war or in single strife,
Thy fathers have slain his fathers, each taken a life for a life,
Thy father had slain his father, how long shall the murder last?
Go back to the Isle of Finn and suffer the Past to be Past.'
And we kiss'd the fringe of his beard and we pray'd as we heard
    him pray,   125
And the Holy man he assoil'd us, and sadly we sail'd away.

XII

And we came to the Isle we were blown from, and there on the
    shore was he,
The man that had slain my father. I saw him and let him be.
O weary was I of the travel, the trouble, the strife and the sin,
When I landed again, with a tithe of my men, on the Isle of
    Finn.   130

---

115. Saint Brendan, the subject of the famous legendary *Voyage of
Saint Brendan.*

127 f. In the original story Maildun, having been advised by the holy
hermit to forgive his enemy, the slayer of his father, comes to an island
where this enemy dwells. Maildun overhears him talking with his companions at supper. One of them asks him what he would do if Maildun
were to appear; and he answers, "Though we were enemies once, I should
certainly give him a welcome and a kind reception." Whereupon Maildun
enters, is recognized and entertained, and the enemies forgive each other.

"IN MEMORIAM" AND OTHER ELEGIES

TO J. S.[1]

THE wind, that beats the mountain, blows
    More softly round the open wold,
And gently comes the world to those
    That are cast in gentle mould.

And me this knowledge bolder made,   5
    Or else I had not dared to flow
In these words toward you, and invade
    Even with a verse your holy woe.

'Tis strange that those we lean on most,
    Those in whose laps our limbs are nursed,   10
Fall into shadow, soonest lost:
    Those we love first are taken first.

God gives us love. Something to love
    He lends us; but, when love is grown
To ripeness, that on which it throve   15
    Falls off, and love is left alone.

This is the curse of time. Alas!
    In grief I am not all unlearn'd;
Once thro' mine own doors Death did pass;
    One went, who never hath return'd.   20

---

[1] We return now to Tennyson's early years. This poem, addressed to
James Spedding on the death of his brother, Edward Spedding, was pub-
lished in *Poems,* 1832 and, with insignificant changes, reprinted in 1842.
Arthur Henry Hallam commended the lines as "perfect" (*Memoir*, i, 88).
Within a year Hallam's death followed. The grave and tenderly elegiac
mood of the poem makes it a fit prelude to *In Memoriam.*

He will not smile — not speak to me
   Once more. Two years his chair is seen
Empty before us. That was he
   Without whose life I had not been.

Your loss is rarer; for this star   25
   Rose with you thro' a little arc
Of heaven, nor having wander'd far
   Shot on the sudden into dark.

I knew your brother: his mute dust
   I honour and his living worth: 30
A man more pure and bold and just
   Was never born into the earth.

I have not look'd upon you nigh,
   Since that dear soul hath fall'n asleep.
Great Nature is more wise than I: 35
   I will not tell you not to weep.

And tho' mine own eyes fill with dew,
   Drawn from the spirit thro' the brain,
I will not even preach to you,
   'Weep, weeping dulls the inward pain.'   40

Let Grief be her own mistress still.
   She loveth her own anguish deep
More than much pleasure. Let her will
   Be done — to weep or not to weep.

I will not say, 'God's ordinance   45
   Of Death is blown in every wind;'
For that is not a common chance
   That takes away a noble mind.

His memory long will live alone
   In all our hearts, as mournful light   50
That broods above the fallen sun,
   And dwells in heaven half the night.

Vain solace!   Memory standing near
     Cast down her eyes, and in her throat
Her voice seem'd distant, and a tear   55
     Dropt on the letters as I wrote.

I wrote I know not what. In truth,
     How *should* I soothe you anyway,
Who miss the brother of your youth?
     Yet something I did wish to say: 60

For he too was a friend to me:
     Both are my friends, and my true breast
Bleedeth for both; yet it may be
     That only silence suiteth best.

Words weaker than your grief would make   65
     Grief more. 'Twere better I should cease
Although myself could almost take
     The place of him that sleeps in peace.

Sleep sweetly, tender heart, in peace:
     Sleep, holy spirit, blessed soul,   70
While the stars burn, the moons increase,
     And the great ages onward roll.

Sleep till the end, true soul and sweet.
     Nothing comes to thee new or strange.
Sleep full of rest from head to feet;   75
     Lie still, dry dust, secure of change.

"BREAK, BREAK, BREAK"[1]

BREAK, break, break,
     On thy cold gray stones, O Sea!
And I would that my tongue could utter
     The thoughts that arise in me.

---

[1] The date of composition is unknown, though tradition has it that this
poem was one of the earliest expressions of grief after receiving the news
of the death of Arthur Henry Hallam (September 15, 1833). All that
the *Memoir* (i, 190) tells us is that it was "made in a Lincolnshire lane

O well for the fisherman's boy, 5
  That he shouts with his sister at play!
O well for the sailor lad,
  That he sings in his boat on the bay!

And the stately ships go on
  To their haven under the hill; 10
But O for the touch of a vanish'd hand,
  And the sound of a voice that is still!

Break, break, break,
  At the foot of thy crags, O Sea!
But the tender grace of a day that is dead 15
  Will never come back to me.

IN MEMORIAM A. H. H.

OBIIT MDCCCXXXIII

Editor's Note. — The composition of *In Memoriam* covers
the years from 1833, when Hallam died, to 1849, the date
appended by Tennyson to the introductory section. The poem
was published in 1850, anonymously but with no effort to keep
the authorship a secret. In later editions two sections were
added and there were various verbal changes. Of these the
most important are recorded in our notes. — Arthur Henry
Hallam, son of Henry Hallam the historian, was born February
1, 1811. At Trinity College, Cambridge, he and Tennyson
formed an intimate friendship. They travelled together in
Germany and France; each visited the other's home; and Hallam became engaged to the poet's sister Emily. At Vienna,
on September 15, 1833, during a tour on the Continent, he died

---

at five o'clock in the morning between blossoming hedges." It was published in 1842. — Has it been remarked that the metrical movement is
suggestive of the Funeral March in Handel's *Saul?* Compare the beat in
the opening lines of the "Ode on the Death of the Duke of Wellington."
  11. *a vanish'd hand.* Compare *In Memoriam,* vii, 5; x, 19; xiii, 7.

suddenly of apoplexy. Brought by sea from Trieste to England, his body was buried at Clevedon church on the Bristol Channel. The overwhelming nature of this loss to Tennyson is one of the most familiar facts in the history of English poetry. The "earliest jottings" of the poem, at first referred to simply as the "Elegies," date from the autumn of 1833; and it is on record (*Memoir*, i, 109) that the earliest written sections are IX, XXX, XXXI, LXXXV (probably only the first stanza; see note on that section), and XXVIII. External or internal evidence dates more or less closely a few other sections. Thus XCVIII, if it refers to Charles Tennyson's marriage-tour, belongs to 1836; C–CIII refer to the departure from Somersby in 1837: the next two refer to the new home at High Beech; and LXXXVI was probably written in 1839. From the *Memoir* (i, 223) we learn that the sections "about Evolution" were written some years before the appearance of Robert Chambers's *Vestiges of the Natural History of Creation* (1844); but which these sections are is not specified; they probably embrace LV, LVI, CXVIII, and CXXIII. New sections were being added between 1840 and 1845 (*ibid.*, i, 201 f.). A few allusions in the poem are indicative of the late date of the sections in which they occur. Not until nearly all had been written did the thought come to Tennyson to mould these separate "Elegies" into a single poem. An early position does not therefore indicate that a section is necessarily of early date, for there was artistic and logical arrangement, so that the whole became, in Tennyson's famous phrase, "a sort of *Divine Comedy* ending in happiness." This plan was in accordance with the tradition of the elegy, which moved (as in *Lycidas* and *Adonais*) from grief to triumph. The point of transition from the one to the other mood has been sought for in various sections of *In Memoriam;* something may be said for LVII and LXXXV, but the most evident turning-point is LXXVIII. The history of the composition of the poem must not be confused with its internal chronology; the one is a matter of biography, the other of artistic planning. This plan is seasonal (following an old poetic tradition), the poem being built up around three Christmas-tides, two anniversaries of the friend's death, and three recurring springs. A more specific summary is as follows: Autumn after the friend's death (xi); the first Christmas (xxviii f.); Spring (xxxviii f.); the first Anniversary (lxxii); the second Christmas (lxxviii); Spring (lxxxvi and lxxxviii); the second Anniversary (xcix); the third Christmas (civ f.); New Year's Day (cvi); Spring (cxv f.). There are other small indications of the seasons but none occur later than the third Spring.— Tennyson's opinion of Hallam's moral character, personal charm, intellectual ability, and transcendent promise is confirmed by the testimony of all who knew him. "Among his contemporaries he stood supreme," said Gladstone. "Arthur Henry Hallam was a spirit so exceptional that everything with which he was brought into relation . . . came to be, through this contact, glorified by a touch of the ideal. . . . He resembled a passing emanation from some other and less darkly chequered world" (*The Daily Telegraph,* January 5, 1898; quoted by Bradley, *Commentary,* p. 5).— *In Memoriam* has inspired much exegesis (see Bibliography). A. C. Bradley's *Commentary on Tennyson's In Memoriam,* second edition, revised, London, 1907, is especially to be recommended. The notes to the present edition are intended to explain obscurities and to indicate the most important literary parallels in a poem one of whose most delightful characteristics is its range of poetic reminiscence. Little that is novel in the way of comment has been, or for that matter, at this date, can be, added. The problem has been one of selection and condensation.

> Strong Son of God, immortal Love,
>   Whom we, that have not seen thy face,
>   By faith, and faith alone, embrace,
> Believing where we cannot prove;

Prologue. Tennyson attached no title to the introductory stanzas, but it is convenient to refer to them as the "Prologue" and to the final epithalamium as the "Epilogue."

1. *immortal Love.* Tennyson said he used the word "Love" in the same sense as in 1 John, iv (*Memoir,* i, 312).

Thine are these orbs of light and shade;   5
   Thou madest Life in man and brute;
   Thou madest Death; and lo, thy foot
Is on the skull which thou hast made.

Thou wilt not leave us in the dust:
   Thou madest man, he knows not why,   10
   He thinks he was not made to die;
And thou hast made him: thou art just.

Thou seemest human and divine,
   The highest, holiest manhood, thou:
   Our wills are ours, we know not how;   15
Our wills are ours, to make them thine.

Our little systems have their day;
   They have their day and cease to be:
   They are but broken lights of thee,
And thou, O Lord, art more than they.   20

We have but faith: we cannot know;
   For knowledge is of things we see;
   And yet we trust it comes from thee,
A beam in darkness: let it grow.

Let knowledge grow from more to more,   25
   But more of reverence in us dwell;
   That mind and soul, according well,
May make one music as before,

But vaster. We are fools and slight;
   We mock thee when we do not fear: 30
   But help thy foolish ones to bear;
Help thy vain worlds to bear thy light.

---

5. *light and shade,* literally, day and night on such orbs as the earth;
but "light" is intended to suggest Life, and "shade" Death.

19. *broken lights.* Compare Shelley, *Adonais,* lii:

> Life, like a dome of many-coloured glass,
> Stains the white radiance of eternity.

Forgive what seem'd my sin in me;
  What seem'd my worth since I began;
  For merit lives from man to man,   35
And not from man, O Lord, to thee.

Forgive my grief for one removed,
  Thy creature, whom I found so fair.
  I trust he lives in thee, and there
I find him worthier to be loved.   40

Forgive these wild and wandering cries,
  Confusions of a wasted youth;
  Forgive them where they fail in truth,
And in thy wisdom make me wise.

                              1849.

                    I

I HELD it truth, with him who sings
  To one clear harp in divers tones,
  That men may rise on stepping-stones
Of their dead selves to higher things.

But who shall so forecast the years   5
  And find in loss a gain to match?
  Or reach a hand thro' time to catch
The far-off interest of tears?

Let Love clasp Grief lest both be drown'd,
  Let darkness keep her raven gloss: 10
  Ah, sweeter to be drunk with loss,
To dance with death, to beat the ground,

I. 1–2. Tennyson said that he referred to Goethe.

3–4. *stepping-stones.* Compare Longfellow's "Ladder of Saint Augustine" and a passage in Augustine's Sermons (iii): "De vitiis nostris scalam nobis facimus."

10. *raven gloss.* Compare Milton, *Comus,* 1. 251: "The raven down of darkness."

Than that the victor Hours should scorn
    The long result of Love, and boast,
    'Behold the man that loved and lost,   15
But all he was is overworn.'

II

Old Yew, which graspest at the stones
    That name the under-lying dead,
    Thy fibres net the dreamless head,
Thy roots are wrapt about the bones.

The seasons bring the flower again,   5
    And bring the firstling to the flock;
    And in the dusk of thee, the clock
Beats out the little lives of men.

O not for thee the glow, the bloom,
    Who changest not in any gale,   10
    Nor branding summer suns avail
To touch thy thousand years of gloom:

And gazing on thee, sullen tree,
    Sick for thy stubborn hardihood,
    I seem to fail from out my blood   15
And grow incorporate into thee.

III

O Sorrow, cruel fellowship,
    O Priestess in the vaults of Death,
    O sweet and bitter in a breath,
What whispers from thy lying lip?

'The stars,' she whispers, 'blindly run;   5
    A web is wov'n across the sky;
    From out waste places comes a cry,
And murmurs from the dying sun:

---

13. Compare "The Victor Hours" (*Memoir,* i, 307), a suppressed
section of *In Memoriam.*

II. 10. *gale,* breeze, a sense common in our older poetry.

III. 5. Compare Pope, *Essay on Man,* i, 252: "Planets and Suns run
lawless thro' the sky."

8. *the dying sun.* Compare CXVIII, 4.

'And all the phantom, Nature, stands —
   With all the music in her tone,   10
   A hollow echo of my own, —
A hollow form with empty hands.'

And shall I take a thing so blind,
   Embrace her as my natural good;
   Or crush her, like a vice of blood,   15
Upon the threshold of the mind?

IV

To Sleep I give my powers away;
   My will is bondsman to the dark;
   I sit within a helmless bark,
And with my heart I muse and say:

O heart, how fares it with thee now,   5
   That thou should'st fail from thy desire,
   Who scarcely darest to inquire,
'What is it makes me beat so low?'

Something it is which thou hast lost,
   Some pleasure from thine early years.   10
   Break, thou deep vase of chilling tears,
That grief hath shaken into frost!

Such clouds of nameless trouble cross
   All night below the darken'd eyes;
   With morning wakes the will, and cries,   15
'Thou shalt not be the fool of loss.'

V

I sometimes hold it half a sin
   To put in words the grief I feel;
   For words, like Nature, half reveal
And half conceal the Soul within.

---

15. Compare *Othello*, I, iii, 123: "The vices of my blood."

IV. 11–12. The image is from the phenomenon of water that is lowered in temperature below freezing point without solidifying but turns into ice if disturbed.

But, for the unquiet heart and brain,   5
    A use in measured language lies;
    The sad mechanic exercise,
Like dull narcotics, numbing pain.

In words, like weeds, I'll wrap me o'er,
    Like coarsest clothes against the cold: 10
    But that large grief which these enfold
Is given in outline and no more.

VI

One writes, that 'Other friends remain,'
    That 'Loss is common to the race' —
    And common is the commonplace,
And vacant chaff well meant for grain.

That loss is common would not make   5
    My own less bitter, rather more:
    Too common! Never morning wore
To evening, but some heart did break.

O father, wheresoe'er thou be,
    Who pledgest now thy gallant son;   10
    A shot, ere half thy draught be done,
Hath still'd the life that beat from thee.

O mother, praying God will save
    Thy sailor, — while thy head is bow'd,
    His heavy-shotted hammock-shroud   15
Drops in his vast and wandering grave.

VI. 7–8. Compare *Hamlet,* I, ii, 72; and especially the grand lines in
Lucretius *De Rerum Natura,* ii, 578 f.:

    nec nox ulla diem neque noctem aurora secutast [secuta est]
    quae non audierit mixtos vagitibus aegris
    ploratus mortis comites et funeris atri.

W. E. Leonard's rendering is:

    No night a day, no dawn a night hath followed
    That heard not, mingling with the small birth-cries,
    The wild laments, companions old of death
    And the black rites.

16. Compare *Richard III,* I, iv, 39: "The empty, vast and wandering
air."

Ye know no more than I who wrought
　　At that last hour to please him well;
　　Who mused on all I had to tell,
And something written, something thought;　　　20

Expecting still his advent home;
　　And ever met him on his way
　　With wishes, thinking, 'here to-day,'
Or 'here to-morrow will he come.'

O somewhere, meek, unconscious dove,　　　25
　　That sittest ranging golden hair;
　　And glad to find thyself so fair,
Poor child, that waitest for thy love!

For now her father's chimney glows
　　In expectation of a guest;　　　30
　　And thinking, 'this will please him best,'
She takes a riband or a rose;

For he will see them on to-night;
　　And with the thought her colour burns;
　　And, having left the glass, she turns　　　35
Once more to set a ringlet right;

And, even when she turn'd, the curse
　　Had fallen, and her future Lord
　　Was drown'd in passing thro' the ford,
Or kill'd in falling from his horse.　　　40

O what to her shall be the end?
　　And what to me remains of good?
　　To her, perpetual maidenhood,
And unto me no second friend.

VII

Dark house, by which once more I stand
　　Here in the long unlovely street,
　　Doors, where my heart was used to beat
So quickly, waiting for a hand,

VII. 1–2. Hallam had lived with his father at 67, Wimpole Street, near Cavendish Square.

A hand that can be clasp'd no more —   5
  Behold me, for I cannot sleep,
  And like a guilty thing I creep
At earliest morning to the door.

He is not here; but far away
  The noise of life begins again,   10
  And ghastly thro' the drizzling rain
On the bald street breaks the blank day.

VIII

A happy lover who has come
  To look on her that loves him well,
  Who 'lights and rings the gateway bell,
And learns her gone and far from home;

He saddens, all the magic light   5
  Dies off at once from bower and hall,
  And all the place is dark, and all
The chambers emptied of delight:

So find I every pleasant spot
  In which we two were wont to meet,   10
  The field, the chamber and the street,
For all is dark where thou art not.

Yet as that other, wandering there
  In those deserted walks, may find
  A flower beat with rain and wind,   15
Which once she foster'd up with care;

So seems it in my deep regret,
  O my forsaken heart, with thee
  And this poor flower of poesy
Which little cared for fades not yet.   20

But since it pleased a vanish'd eye,
  I go to plant it on his tomb,
  That if it can it there may bloom,
Or dying, there at least may die.

IX

Fair ship, that from the Italian shore
 Sailest the placid ocean-plains
 With my lost Arthur's loved remains,
Spread thy full wings, and waft him o'er.

So draw him home to those that mourn   5
 In vain; a favourable speed
 Ruffle thy mirror'd mast, and lead
Thro' prosperous floods his holy urn.

All night no ruder air perplex
 Thy sliding keel, till Phosphor, bright 10
 As our pure love, thro' early light
Shall glimmer on the dewy decks.

Sphere all your lights around, above;
 Sleep, gentle heavens, before the prow;
 Sleep, gentle winds, as he sleeps now, 15
My friend, the brother of my love;

My Arthur, whom I shall not see
 Till all my widow'd race be run;
 Dear as the mother to the son,
More than my brothers are to me. 20

X

I hear the noise about thy keel;
 I hear the bell struck in the night:
 I see the cabin-window bright;
I see the sailor at the wheel.

Thou bring'st the sailor to his wife, 5
 And travell'd men from foreign lands;
 And letters unto trembling hands;
And, thy dark freight, a vanish'd life.

IX. This section contains many reminiscences of the Latin poets. See
Mustard, *op. cit.*, p. 132.

10. *Phosphor*, the morning star.

So bring him: we have idle dreams:
   This look of quiet flatters thus   10
   Our home-bred fancies: O to us,
The fools of habit, sweeter seems

To rest beneath the clover sod,
   That takes the sunshine and the rains,
   Or where the kneeling hamlet drains   15
The chalice of the grapes of God;

Than if with thee the roaring wells
   Should gulf him fathom-deep in brine;
   And hands so often clasp'd in mine,
Should toss with tangle and with shells.   20

XI

Calm is the morn without a sound,
   Calm as to suit a calmer grief,
   And only thro' the faded leaf
The chestnut pattering to the ground:

Calm and deep peace on this high wold,   5
   And on these dews that drench the furze,
   And all the silvery gossamers
That twinkle into green and gold:

Calm and still light on yon great plain
   That sweeps with all its autumn bowers,   10
   And crowded farms and lessening towers,
To mingle with the bounding main:

Calm and deep peace in this wide air,
   These leaves that redden to the fall;
   And in my heart, if calm at all,   15
If any calm, a calm despair:

X. 17. *wells,* used by Tennyson in the peculiar sense of waters from a well-spring, as in Genesis, vii, 11: "The fountains of the great deep."

20. *tangle,* oarweed, a kind of sea-weed growing at tidal limits.

XI. 5. Tennyson noted that the scene is not at Clevedon churchyard but on a Lincolnshire wold.

Calm on the seas, and silver sleep,
    And waves that sway themselves in rest,
    And dead calm in that noble breast
Which heaves but with the heaving deep.   20

XII

Lo, as a dove when up she springs
    To bear thro' Heaven a tale of woe,
    Some dolorous message knit below
The wild pulsation of her wings;

Like her I go; I cannot stay;   5
    I leave this mortal ark behind,
    A weight of nerves without a mind,
And leave the cliffs, and haste away

O'er ocean-mirrors rounded large,
    And reach the glow of southern skies,   10
    And see the sails at distance rise,
And linger weeping on the marge,

And saying: 'Comes he thus, my friend?
    Is this the end of all my care?'
    And circle moaning in the air: 15
'Is this the end? Is this the end?'

And forward dart again, and play
    About the prow, and back return
    To where the body sits, and learn
That I have been an hour away.   20

---

20. Compare Byron, *The Bride of Abydos,* II, xxvi: "His head heaves with the heaving billow."

XII. 6. *this mortal ark.* Compare "The Two Voices," l. 389: "Who sought'st to wreck my mortal ark," a use of the phrase which, taken in conjunction with the simile of the dove in the present section, shows that Tennyson had in mind the story of the Flood rather than St. Paul's phrase: "Our earthly house of this tabernacle" (2 Corinthians, v, 1).

XIII

Tears of the widower, when he sees
  A late-lost form that sleep reveals,
  And moves his doubtful arms, and feels
Her place is empty, fall like these;

Which weep a loss for ever new,   5
  A void where heart on heart reposed;
  And, where warm hands have prest and closed,
Silence, till I be silent too.

Which weep the comrade of my choice,
  An awful thought, a life removed,   10
  The human-hearted man I loved,
A Spirit, not a breathing voice.

Come Time, and teach me, many years,
  I do not suffer in a dream;
  For now so strange do these things seem,   15
Mine eyes have leisure for their tears;

My fancies time to rise on wing,
  And glance about the approaching sails,
  As tho' they brought but merchants' bales,
And not the burthen that they bring.   20

XIV

If one should bring me this report,
  That thou hadst touch'd the land to-day,
  And I went down unto the quay,
And found thee lying in the port;

And standing, muffled round with woe,   5
  Should see thy passengers in rank
  Come stepping lightly down the plank,
And beckoning unto those they know;

And if along with these should come
  The man I held as half-divine;   10
  Should strike a sudden hand in mine,
And ask a thousand things of home;

And I should tell him all my pain,
  And how my life had droop'd of late,
  And he should sorrow o'er my state   15
And marvel what possess'd my brain;

And I perceived no touch of change,
  No hint of death in all his frame,
  But found him all in all the same,
I should not feel it to be strange.   20

XV

To-night the winds begin to rise
  And roar from yonder dropping day:
  The last red leaf is whirl'd away,
The rooks are blown about the skies;

The forest crack'd, the waters curl'd,   5
  The cattle huddled on the lea;
  And wildly dash'd on tower and tree
The sunbeam strikes along the world:

And but for fancies, which aver
  That all thy motions gently pass   10
  Athwart a plane of molten glass,
I scarce could brook the strain and stir

That makes the barren branches loud;
  And but for fear it is not so,
  The wild unrest that lives in woe   15
Would dote and pore on yonder cloud

That rises upward always higher,
  And onward drags a labouring breast,
  And topples round the dreary west,
A looming bastion fringed with fire.   20

XV. 20. *bastion*. Compare Shelley, "The Witch of Atlas," xlviii:
    The clouds whose moving turrets make
  The bastions of the storm.

XVI

What words are these have fall'n from me?
  Can calm despair and wild unrest
  Be tenants of a single breast,
Or sorrow such a changeling be?

Or doth she only seem to take   5
  The touch of change in calm or storm;
  But knows no more of transient form
In her deep self, than some dead lake

That holds the shadow of a lark
  Hung in the shadow of a heaven?   10
  Or has the shock, so harshly given,
Confused me like the unhappy bark

That strikes by night a craggy shelf,
  And staggers blindly ere she sink?
  And stunn'd me from my power to think   15
And all my knowledge of myself;

And made me that delirious man
  Whose fancy fuses old and new,
  And flashes into false and true,
And mingles all without a plan?   20

XVII

Thou comest, much wept for: such a breeze
  Compell'd thy canvas, and my prayer
  Was as the whisper of an air
To breathe thee over lonely seas.

For I in spirit saw thee move   5
  Thro' circles of the bounding sky,
  Week after week: the days go by:
Come quick, thou bringest all I love.

Henceforth, wherever thou may'st roam,
  My blessing, like a line of light,   10
  Is on the waters day and night,
And like a beacon guards thee home.

So may whatever tempest mars
  Mid-ocean, spare thee, sacred bark;
  And balmy drops in summer dark   15
Slide from the bosom of the stars.

So kind an office hath been done,
  Such precious relics brought by thee;
  The dust of him I shall not see
Till all my widow'd race be run.   20

XVIII

'Tis well; 'tis something; we may stand
  Where he in English earth is laid,
  And from his ashes may be made   .
The violet of his native land.

'Tis little; but it looks in truth   5
  As if the quiet bones were blest
  Among familiar names to rest
And in the places of his youth.

Come then, pure hands, and bear the head
  That sleeps or wears the mask of sleep,   10
  And come, whatever loves to weep,
And hear the ritual of the dead.

Ah yet, ev'n yet, if this might be,
  I, falling on his faithful heart,
  Would breathing thro' his lips impart   15
The life that almost dies in me;

XVIII. 3–4. Compare *Hamlet,* V, i, 262 f.:
             From her fair and unpolluted flesh
         May violets spring;
and Persius, *Satires,* i, 39:
             nunc non e tumulo fortunataque favilla
             nascentur violae?
("Now will not violets spring from his tomb and favoured ashes?").
15–16. Compare 2 Kings, iv, 34.

That dies not, but endures with pain,
    And slowly forms the firmer mind,
    Treasuring the look it cannot find,
The words that are not heard again.   20

XIX

The Danube to the Severn gave
    The darken'd heart that beat no more;
    They laid him by the pleasant shore,
And in the hearing of the wave.

There twice a day the Severn fills;   5
    The salt sea-water passes by,
    And hushes half the babbling Wye,
And makes a silence in the hills.

The Wye is hush'd nor moved along,
    And hush'd my deepest grief of all,   10
    When fill'd with tears that cannot fall,
I brim with sorrow drowning song.

The tide flows down, the wave again
    Is vocal in its wooded walls;
    My deeper anguish also falls   15
And I can speak a little then.

XX

The lesser griefs that may be said,
    That breathe a thousand tender vows,
    Are but as servants in a house
Where lies the master newly dead;

Who speak their feeling as it is,   5
    And weep the fulness from the mind:
    'It will be hard,' they say, 'to find
Another service such as this.'

XIX. This section was written in Tintern Abbey. For the image of
the river silent when the tide is in flood but vocal it ebbs compare *The
Rape of Lucrece*, ll. 1328 f.:

    'Tis but a part of sorrow that we hear:
    Deep sounds make lesser noise than shallow fords,
    And sorrow ebbs, being blown with wind of words.

My lighter moods are like to these,
    That out of words a comfort win;   10
    But there are other griefs within,
And tears that at their fountain freeze;

For by the hearth the children sit
    Cold in that atmosphere of Death,
    And scarce endure to draw the breath,   15
Or like to noiseless phantoms flit:

But open converse is there none,
    So much the vital spirits sink
    To see the vacant chair, and think,
'How good! how kind! and he is gone.'   20

XXI

I sing to him that rests below,
    And, since the grasses round me wave,
    I take the grasses of the grave,
And make them pipes whereon to blow.

The traveller hears me now and then,   5
    And sometimes harshly will he speak:
    'This fellow would make weakness weak,
And melt the waxen hearts of men.'

Another answers, 'Let him be,
    He loves to make parade of pain,   10
    That with his piping he may gain
The praise that comes to constancy.'

A third is wroth: 'Is this an hour
    For private sorrow's barren song,
    When more and more the people throng   15
The chairs and thrones of civil power?

XXI. The convention of the classical pastoral elegy in which the poet
is supposed to be a singing and piping shepherd is employed here and
occasionally elsewhere in *In Memoriam*.

15–16. Possibly a reference to the Chartist movement.

'A time to sicken and to swoon,
    When Science reaches forth her arms
    To feel from world to world, and charms
Her secret from the latest moon?'   20

Behold, ye speak an idle thing:
    Ye never knew the sacred dust:
    I do but sing because I must,
And pipe but as the linnets sing:

And one is glad; her note is gay,   25
    For now her little ones have ranged;
    And one is sad; her note is changed,
Because her brood is stol'n away.

XXII

The path by which we twain did go,
    Which led by tracts that pleased us well,
    Thro' four sweet years arose and fell,
From flower to flower, from snow to snow:

And we with singing cheer'd the way,   5
    And, crown'd with all the season lent,
    From April on to April went,
And glad at heart from May to May:

But where the path we walk'd began
    To slant the fifth autumnal slope,   10
    As we descended following Hope
There sat the Shadow fear'd of man;

18–20. The discovery of the planet Neptune, made possible by calcula-
tions of the irregularities in the motion of Uranus, was confirmed in 1846;
and the two satellites of Uranus were rediscovered in 1847. It has been
objected that if Tennyson alludes to these discoveries the section must be
of very late date; but it may well be one of the parts written shortly
before the poem's publication. The use of the pastoral convention makes
this the more likely.

24. Compare Goethe, the Harper's Song in *Wilhelm Meisters Lehrjahre,*
ii, 11: "Ich singe wie der Vogel singt." (In Carlyle's translation *Vogel*
becomes specifically "linnet").

XXII. This is the first of several sections in which Petrarch's influence seems evident. Compare *In Morte di Madonna Laura,* Sonnet xlvii,
where Death, likened to a black shadow, looms, glaring enviously at the
lovers. But the image of Death as a shadow is a poetic commonplace.

Who broke our fair companionship,
  And spread his mantle dark and cold,
  And wrapt thee formless in the fold,   15
And dull'd the murmur on thy lip,

And bore thee where I could not see
  Nor follow, tho' I walk in haste,
  And think, that somewhere in the waste
The Shadow sits and waits for me.   20

XXIII

Now, sometimes in my sorrow shut,
  Or breaking into song by fits,
  Alone, alone, to where he sits,
The Shadow cloak'd from head to foot,

Who keeps the keys of all the creeds,   5
  I wander, often falling lame,
  And looking back to whence I came,
Or on to where the pathway leads;

And crying, How changed from where it ran
  Thro' lands where not a leaf was dumb;   10
  But all the lavish hills would hum
The murmur of a happy Pan:

When each by turns was guide to each,
  And Fancy light from Fancy caught,
  And Thought leapt out to wed with Thought   15
Ere Thought could wed itself with Speech;

And all we met was fair and good,
  And all was good that Time could bring,
  And all the secret of the Spring
Moved in the chambers of the blood;   20

And many an old philosophy
  On Argive heights divinely sang,
  And round us all the thicket rang
To many a flute of Arcady.

XXIV

And was the day of my delight
  As pure and perfect as I say?
  The very source and fount of Day
Is dash'd with wandering isles of night.

If all was good and fair we met,   5
  This earth had been the Paradise
  It never look'd to human eyes
Since our first Sun arose and set.

And is it that the haze of grief
  Makes former gladness loom so great?   10
  The lowness of the present state,
That sets the past in this relief?

Or that the past will always win
  A glory from its being far;
  And orb into the perfect star   15
We saw not, when we moved therein?

XXV

I know that this was Life, — the track
  Whereon with equal feet we fared;
  And then, as now, the day prepared
The daily burden for the back.

But this it was that made me move   5
  As light as carrier-birds in air;
  I loved the weight I had to bear,
Because it needed help of Love:

Nor could I weary, heart or limb,
  When mighty Love would cleave in twain   10
  The lading of a single pain,
And part it, giving half to him.

XXIV. 4. *isles of night,* sun-spots.

8. 1850: "Since Adam left his garden yet."

14–16. For the theme of a "stellar gauge" of human experience compare Thomas Hardy's sonnet, "At a Lunar Eclipse."

XXVI

Still onward winds the dreary way;
  I with it; for I long to prove
  No lapse of moons can canker Love,
Whatever fickle tongues may say.

And if that eye which watches guilt   5
  And goodness, and hath power to see
  Within the green the moulder'd tree,
And towers fall'n as soon as built —

Oh, if indeed that eye foresee
  Or see (in Him is no before)   10
  In more of life true life no more
And Love the indifference to be,

Then might I find, ere yet the morn
  Breaks hither over Indian seas,
  That Shadow waiting with the keys,   15
To shroud me from my proper scorn.

XXVII

I envy not in any moods
  The captive void of noble rage,
  The linnet born within the cage,
That never knew the summer woods:

I envy not the beast that takes   5
  His license in the field of time,
  Unfetter'd by the sense of crime,
To whom a conscience never wakes;

Nor, what may count itself as blest,
  The heart that never plighted troth   10
  But stagnates in the weeds of sloth;
Nor any want-begotten rest.

I hold it true, whate'er befall;
    I feel it, when I sorrow most;
    'Tis better to have loved and lost   15
Than never to have loved at all.

XXVIII

The time draws near the birth of Christ:
    The moon is hid; the night is still;
    The Christmas bells from hill to hill
Answer each other in the mist.

Four voices of four hamlets round,   5
    From far and near, on mead and moor,
    Swell out and fail, as if a door
Were shut between me and the sound:

Each voice four changes on the wind,
    That now dilate, and now decrease,   10
    Peace and goodwill, goodwill and peace,
Peace and goodwill, to all mankind.

This year I slept and woke with pain,
    I almost wish'd no more to wake,
    And that my hold on life would break   15
Before I heard those bells again;

XXVII. 15–16. Compare Congreve, *The Way of the World,* II, i: 'Tis
better to be left, than never to have been loved.' The close echo in A. H.
Clough's "Peschiera" (1849):

        'Tis better to have fought and lost,
        Than never to have fought at all

is only explicable if Clough had seen part of *In Memoriam* in manuscript.
See note on LXXXV. — With the conviction expressed in the closing lines
of XXVII the poem, as Bradley observes, comes to a break, "as though a
definite stage of advance were reached."

XXVIII. The first Christmas-tide after Hallam's death. "So far the
poet's thoughts have been concentrated on his grief and love, and on the
past. The idea of the continued life of the beloved dead now emerges"
(Bradley).

5. There have been attempts to identify the "four hamlets" near
Somersby; but many churches in the neighbourhood have peals of bells.

13. *This year,* 1833. This is one of the earliest written sections of
the poem.

But they my troubled spirit rule,
    For they controll'd me when a boy;
    They bring me sorrow touch'd with joy,
The merry merry bells of Yule.   20

XXIX

With such compelling cause to grieve
    As daily vexes household peace,
    And chains regret to his decease,
How dare we keep our Christmas-eve;

Which brings no more a welcome guest   5
    To enrich the threshold of the night
    With shower'd largess of delight
In dance and song and game and jest?

Yet go, and while the holly boughs
    Entwine the cold baptismal font,   10
    Make one wreath more for Use and Wont,
That guard the portals of the house;

Old sisters of a day gone by,
    Gray nurses, loving nothing new;
    Why should they miss their yearly due   15
Before their time? They too will die.

XXX

With trembling fingers did we weave
    The holly round the Christmas hearth;
    A rainy cloud possess'd the earth,
And sadly fell our Christmas-eve.

At our old pastimes in the hall   5
    We gamboll'd, making vain pretence
    Of gladness, with an awful sense
Of one mute Shadow watching all.

We paused: the winds were in the beech:
    We heard them sweep the winter land;   10
    And in a circle hand-in-hand
Sat silent, looking each at each.

XXX. 8. *Shadow,* not Death (as in XXII and XXIII) but the dead
friend.

Then echo-like our voices rang;
   We sung, tho' every eye was dim,
   A merry song we sang with him   15
Last year: impetuously we sang:

We ceased: a gentler feeling crept
   Upon us: surely rest is meet:
   'They rest,' we said, 'their sleep is sweet,'
And silence follow'd, and we wept.   20

Our voices took a higher range;
   Once more we sang: 'They do not die
   Nor lose their mortal sympathy,
Nor change to us, altho' they change;

'Rapt from the fickle and the frail   25
   With gather'd power, yet the same,
   Pierces the keen seraphic flame
From orb to orb, from veil to veil.'

Rise, happy morn, rise, holy morn,
   Draw forth the cheerful day from night: 30
   O Father, touch the east, and light
The light that shone when Hope was born.

XXXI

When Lazarus left his charnel-cave,
   And home to Mary's house return'd,
   Was this demanded — if he yearn'd
To hear her weeping by his grave?

'Where wert thou, brother, those four days?'   5
   There lives no record of reply,
   Which telling what it is to die
Had surely added praise to praise.

From every house the neighbours met,
   The streets were fill'd with joyful sound,   10
   A solemn gladness even crown'd
The purple brows of Olivet.

XXXI. John, xi, 1-45.

Behold a man raised up by Christ!
   The rest remaineth unreveal'd;
   He told it not; or something seal'd   15
The lips of that Evangelist.

XXXII

Her eyes are homes of silent prayer,
   Nor other thought her mind admits
   But, he was dead, and there he sits,
And he that brought him back is there.

Then one deep love doth supersede   5
   All other, when her ardent gaze
   Roves from the living brother's face,
And rests upon the Life indeed.

All subtle thought, all curious fears,
   Borne down by gladness so complete,   10
   She bows, she bathes the Saviour's feet
With costly spikenard and with tears.

Thrice blest whose lives are faithful prayers,
   Whose loves in higher love endure;
   What souls possess themselves so pure,   15
Or is there blessedness like theirs?

XXXIII

O thou that after toil and storm
   Mayst seem to have reach'd a purer air,
   Whose faith has centre everywhere,
Nor cares to fix itself to form,

Leave thou thy sister when she prays,   5
   Her early Heaven, her happy views;
   Nor thou with shadow'd hint confuse
A life that leads melodious days.

XXXII. 12–13. John, xii, 3.

XXXIII. 5. *sister.* The relationship was perhaps suggested by, or is intended to suggest, the Mary of the preceding sections; but the brother is
not a counterpart of Lazarus. The contrast in this section is not between
belief and scepticism, as some commentators have held, but between faith
in "truth revealed" and an intellectual faith as further illustrated in the
two sections which follow.

Her faith thro' form is pure as thine,
   Her hands are quicker unto good: 10
   Oh, sacred be the flesh and blood
To which she links a truth divine!

See thou, that countest reason ripe
   In holding by the law within,
   Thou fail not in a world of sin,   15
And ev'n for want of such a type.

XXXIV

My own dim life should teach me this,
   That life shall live for evermore,
   Else earth is darkness at the core,
And dust and ashes all that is;

This round of green, this orb of flame,   5
   Fantastic beauty; such as lurks
   In some wild Poet, when he works
Without a conscience or an aim.

When then were God to such as I?
   'Twere hardly worth my while to choose   10
   Of things all mortal, or to use
A little patience ere I die;

'Twere best at once to sink to peace,
   Like birds the charming serpent draws,
   To drop head-foremost in the jaws   15
Of vacant darkness and to cease.

XXXV

Yet if some voice that man could trust
   Should murmur from the narrow house,
   'The cheeks drop in; the body bows;
Man dies: nor is there hope in dust:'

XXXIV. 7–8. It has been suggested that the "wild Poet" Tennyson had in mind was Thomas Lovell Beddoes who died in 1849 and concerning whom there were various obituary notices just before the publication of *In Memoriam*.

Might I not say: 'Yet even here,   5
   But for one hour, O Love, I strive
   To keep so sweet a thing alive?'
But I should turn mine ears and hear

The moanings of the homeless sea,
   The sound of streams that swift or slow   10
   Draw down Æonian hills, and sow
The dust of continents to be;

And Love would answer with a sigh,
   'The sound of that forgetful shore
   Will change my sweetness more and more,   15
Half-dead to know that I shall die.'

O me, what profits it to put
   An idle case? If Death were seen
   At first as Death, Love had not been,
Or been in narrowest working shut,   20

Mere fellowship of sluggish moods,
   Or in his coarsest Satyr-shape
   Had bruised the herb and crush'd the grape,
And bask'd and batten'd in the woods.

XXXVI

Tho' truths in manhood darkly join,
   Deep-seated in our mystic frame,
   We yield all blessing to the name
Of Him that made them current coin;

XXXV. 11. *Æonian hills,* hills that have lasted for ages.

14. *forgetful shore,* the shore of Lethe, the stream that brings forget-fulness. Compare *Paradise Lost,* ii, 73 f.:

the sleepy drench
Of that forgetful lake.

XXXVI. 1–4. That is, Christ made the truth that man is immortal "current coin." When inquiries came to Tennyson concerning his belief in Christ he was wont to point to this section of *In Memoriam* (*Memoir,* i, 325).

For Wisdom dealt with mortal powers,   5
   Where truth in closest words shall fail,
   When truth embodied in a tale
Shall enter in at lowly doors.

And so the Word had breath, and wrought
   With human hands the creed of creeds   10
   In loveliness of perfect deeds,
More strong than all poetic thought;

Which he may read that binds the sheaf,
   Or builds the house, or digs the grave,
   And those wild eyes that watch the wave   15
In roarings round the coral reef.

XXXVII

Urania speaks with darken'd brow:
   'Thou pratest here where thou art least;
   This faith has many a purer priest,
And many an abler voice than thou.

'Go down beside thy native rill,   5
   On thy Parnassus set thy feet,
   And hear thy laurel whisper sweet
About the ledges of the hill.'

And my Melpomene replies,
   A touch of shame upon her cheek: 10
   'I am not worthy ev'n to speak
Of thy prevailing mysteries;

'For I am but an earthly Muse,
   And owning but a little art
   To lull with song an aching heart,   15
And render human love his dues;

---

9. John, i, 14.

15–16. The Pacific Islanders.

XXXVII. 1. *Urania*, the Muse of Astronomy; conceived by Milton as the goddess of divine poetry. See *Paradise Lost*, vii, 1 f.

9. *Melpomene*, the Muse of Tragedy, conceived by Tennyson as the Muse of elegiac poetry.

'But brooding on the dear one dead,
    And all he said of things divine,
    (And dear to me as sacred wine
To dying lips is all he said),   20

'I murmur'd, as I came along,
    Of comfort clasp'd in truth reveal'd;
    And loiter'd in the master's field,
And darken'd sanctities with song.'

XXXVIII

With weary steps I loiter on,
    Tho' always under alter'd skies
    The purple from the distance dies,
My prospect and horizon gone.

No joy the blowing season gives,   5
    The herald melodies of spring,
    But in the songs I love to sing
A doubtful gleam of solace lives.

If any care for what is here
    Survive in spirits render'd free,   10
    Then are these songs I sing of thee
Not all ungrateful to thine ear.

XXXIX

Old warder of these buried bones,
    And answering now my random stroke
    With fruitful cloud and living smoke,
Dark yew, that graspest at the stones

And dippest toward the dreamless head,   5
    To thee too comes the golden hour
    When flower is feeling after flower;
But Sorrow — fixt upon the dead,

---

19. 1850: "And dear as sacramental wine."

XXXIX. This section, written in 1868, was added in the Miniature edition of the *Works*, 1871.

3. The pollen (hence "fruitful") goes up from the shaken tree like smoke. Compare "The Holy Grail," ll. 13 f.

7. The yew-tree is sometimes bi-sexual.

And darkening the dark graves of men, —
   What whisper'd from her lying lips?   10
   Thy gloom is kindled at the tips,
And passes into gloom again.

XL

Could we forget the widow'd hour
   And look on Spirits breathed away,
   As on a maiden in the day
When first she wears her orange-flower!

When crown'd with blessing she doth rise   5
   To take her latest leave of home,
   And hopes and light regrets that come
Make April of her tender eyes;

And doubtful joys the father move,
   And tears are on the mother's face,   10
   As parting with a long embrace
She enters other realms of love;

Her office there to rear, to teach,
   Becoming as is meet and fit
   A link among the days, to knit   15
The generations each with each;

And, doubtless, unto thee is given
   A life that bears immortal fruit
   In those great offices that suit
The full-grown energies of heaven.   20

Ay me, the difference I discern!
   How often shall her old fireside
   Be cheer'd with tidings of the bride,
How often she herself return,

And tell them all they would have told,   25
   And bring her babe, and make her boast,
   Till even those that miss'd her most
Shall count new things as dear as old:

But thou and I have shaken hands,
　　Till growing winters lay me low;   30
　　My paths are in the fields I know,
And thine in undiscover'd lands.

XLI

Thy spirit ere our fatal loss
　　Did ever rise from high to higher;
　　As mounts the heavenward altar-fire,
As flies the lighter thro' the gross.

But thou art turn'd to something strange,   5
　　And I have lost the links that bound
　　Thy changes; here upon the ground,
No more partaker of thy change.

Deep folly! yet that this could be —
　　That I could wing my will with might   10
　　To leap the grades of life and light,
And flash at once, my friend, to thee.

For tho' my nature rarely yields
　　To that vague fear implied in death;
　　Nor shudders at the gulfs beneath,   15
The howlings from forgotten fields;

Yet oft when sundown skirts the moor
　　An inner trouble I behold,
　　A spectral doubt which makes me cold,
That I shall be thy mate no more,   20

XL. 32. Compare *Hamlet*, III, i, 79: "The undiscovered country."

XLI. 5. An echo of Ariel's "something rich and strange."

15–16. Reminiscent of Dante's *Inferno* (especially of the wailing that meets the poet's ear at the entrance to the City of Dis) and of Virgil's "lugentes campi" (*Aeneid*, vi, 441). The "howlings" suggest, and were probably suggested by, *Hamlet*, V, i, 265, and *Measure for Measure*, III, i, 128. *Forgotten* — not, as has been thought, by the poet, because such tales of horror have almost faded from his mind, but "God-forgotten." Compare the Dedication to "The Palace of Art":

> He that shuts Love out, in turn shall be
> Shut out from Love, and on her threshold lie
> Howling in outer darkness.

Tho' following with an upward mind
   The wonders that have come to thee,
   Thro' all the secular to-be,
But evermore a life behind.

XLII

I vex my heart with fancies dim:
   He still outstript me in the race;
   It was but unity of place
That made me dream I rank'd with him.

And so may Place retain us still,   5
   And he the much-beloved again,
   A lord of large experience, train
To riper growth the mind and will:

And what delights can equal those
   That stir the spirit's inner deeps,   10
   When one that loves but knows not, reaps
A truth from one that loves and knows?

XLIII

If Sleep and Death be truly one,
   And every spirit's folded bloom
   Thro' all its intervital gloom
In some long trance should slumber on;

Unconscious of the sliding hour,   5
   Bare of the body, might it last,
   And silent traces of the past
Be all the colour of the flower:

So then were nothing lost to man;
   So that still garden of the souls   10
   In many a figured leaf enrolls
The total world since life began;

---

   23. *the secular to-be,* the age-long future.   Milton (*Samson Agonistes,*
l. 1711) calls the phœnix "a secular bird."

And love will last as pure and whole
    As when he loved me here in Time,
    And at the spiritual prime   15
Rewaken with the dawning soul.

XLIV

How fares it with the happy dead?
    For here the man is more and more;
    But he forgets the days before
God shut the doorways of his head.

The days have vanish'd, tone and tint,   5
    And yet perhaps the hoarding sense
    Gives out at times (he knows not whence)
A little flash, a mystic hint;

And in the long harmonious years
    (If Death so taste Lethean springs),   10
    May some dim touch of earthly things
Surprise thee ranging with thy peers.

If such a dreamy touch should fall,
    O turn thee round, resolve the doubt;
    My guardian angel will speak out   15
In that high place, and tell thee all.

XLV

The baby new to earth and sky,
    What time his tender palm is prest
    Against the circle of the breast,
Has never thought that 'this is I:'

XLIV. This obscurest section is the subject of ten pages in Bradley's
Commentary, pp. 125 f. All there is room to note here is that it has to
do with the Platonic notion of recollections of pre-existence; see *Phaedo*,
73 A f. and compare Wordsworth's "Ode on Intimations of Immortality."

4. *the doorways of his head,* the sutures of the skull which close after
babyhood.

XLV. The idea that the soul of the individual issues from the "general
Soul" occurs elsewhere in Tennyson: see *In Memoriam*, Epilogue, l. 123;
"De Profundis"; and "Crossing the Bar."

But as he grows he gathers much,   5
   And learns the use of 'I,' and 'me,'
   And finds 'I am not what I see,
And other than the things I touch.'

So rounds he to a separate mind
   From whence clear memory may begin,   10
   As thro' the frame that binds him in
His isolation grows defined.

This use may lie in blood and breath,
   Which else were fruitless of their due,
   Had man to learn himself anew   15
Beyond the second birth of Death.

XLVI

We ranging down this lower track,
   The path we came by, thorn and flower,
   Is shadow'd by the growing hour,
Lest life should fail in looking back.

So be it: there no shade can last   5
   In that deep dawn behind the tomb,
   But clear from marge to marge shall bloom
The eternal landscape of the past;

A lifelong tract of time reveal'd;
   The fruitful hours of still increase;   10
   Days order'd in a wealthy peace,
And those five years its richest field.

O Love, thy province were not large,
   A bounded field, nor stretching far;
   Look also, Love, a brooding star,   15
A rosy warmth from marge to marge.

XLVII

That each, who seems a separate whole,
   Should move his rounds, and fusing all
   The skirts of self again, should fall
Remerging in the general Soul,

Is faith as vague as all unsweet: 5
    Eternal form shall still divide
    The eternal soul from all beside;
And I shall know him when we meet:

And we shall sit at endless feast,
    Enjoying each the other's good: 10
    What vaster dream can hit the mood
Of Love on earth?   He seeks at least

Upon the last and sharpest height,
    Before the spirits fade away,
    Some landing-place, to clasp and say,   15
'Farewell! We lose ourselves in light.'

                    XLVIII

If these brief lays, of Sorrow born,
    Were taken to be such as closed
    Grave doubts and answers here proposed,
Then these were such as men might scorn:

Her care is not to part and prove;   5
    She takes, when harsher moods remit,
    What slender shade of doubt may flit,
And makes it vassal unto love:

And hence, indeed, she sports with words,
    But better serves a wholesome law,   10
    And holds it sin and shame to draw
The deepest measure from the chords:

XLVII. 13. *the last and sharpest height,* the last of many existences
(or "states") before the spirit is absorbed into the general Soul. Compare
XXX, 27 f. and LXXXII, 6: "From state to state the spirit walks."
Tennyson said to his son: "If the absorption into the divine in the after-
life be the creed of some, let them at all events allow us many existences
of individuality before this absorption; since this short-lived individuality
seems to be but too short a preparation for so mighty a union" (*Memoir,*
i, 319).

XLVIII. 8. *vassal unto love.* Compare Shakespeare, *Sonnets,* xxvi:
"Lord of my love, to whom in vassalage," etc.

Nor dare she trust a larger lay,
 But rather loosens from the lip
 Short swallow-flights of song, that dip   15
Their wings in tears, and skim away.

XLIX

From art, from nature, from the schools,
 Let random influences glance,
 Like light in many a shiver'd lance
That breaks about the dappled pools:

The lightest wave of thought shall lisp,   5
 The fancy's tenderest eddy wreathe,
 The slightest air of song shall breathe
To make the sullen surface crisp.

And look thy look, and go thy way,
 But blame not thou the winds that make   10
 The seeming-wanton ripple break,
The tender-pencill'd shadow play.

Beneath all fancied hopes and fears
 Ay me, the sorrow deepens down,
 Whose muffled motions blindly drown   15
The bases of my life in tears.

L

Be near me when my light is low,
 When the blood creeps, and the nerves prick
 And tingle; and the heart is sick,
And all the wheels of Being slow.

Be near me when the sensuous frame   5
 Is rack'd with pangs that conquer trust;
 And Time, a maniac scattering dust,
And Life, a Fury slinging flame.

L. This famous section opens a group extending through LVI in which
the poet expresses his desire for personal and present communion with the
spirit of his friend. This desire is intertwined with meditations upon the
pain and evil of the world which prompt doubts as to the faith that Love
is the universal law and that man is immortal.

Be near me when my faith is dry,
  And men the flies of latter spring,   10
    That lay their eggs, and sting and sing
And weave their petty cells and die.

Be near me when I fade away,
  To point the term of human strife,
    And on the low dark verge of life   15
The twilight of eternal day.

LI

Do we indeed desire the dead
  Should still be near us at our side?
    Is there no baseness we would hide?
No inner vileness that we dread?

Shall he for whose applause I strove,   5
  I had such reverence for his blame,
    See with clear eye some hidden shame
And I be lessen'd in his love?

I wrong the grave with fears untrue:
  Shall love be blamed for want of faith?   10
    There must be wisdom with great Death:
The dead shall look me thro' and thro'.

Be near us when we climb or fall:
  Ye watch, like God, the rolling hours
    With larger other eyes than ours,   15
To make allowance for us all.

LII

I cannot love thee as I ought,
  For love reflects the thing beloved;
    My words are only words, and moved
Upon the topmost froth of thought.

LI. 10. Of several possible interpretations of this line Bradley's seems
best: "Shall I who love my friend be guilty of a want of faith that would
incur his blame."

'Yet blame not thou thy plaintive song,'   5
    The Spirit of true love replied;
    'Thou canst not move me from thy side,
Nor human frailty do me wrong.

'What keeps a spirit wholly true
    To that ideal which he bears?   10
    What record? not the sinless years
That breathed beneath the Syrian blue:

'So fret not, like an idle girl,
    That life is dash'd with flecks of sin.
    Abide: thy wealth is gather'd in,   15
When Time hath sunder'd shell from pearl.'

LIII

How many a father have I seen,
    A sober man, among his boys,
    Whose youth was full of foolish noise,
Who wears his manhood hale and green:

And dare we to this fancy give,   5
    That had the wild oat not been sown,
    The soil, left barren, scarce had grown
The grain by which a man may live?

Or, if we held the doctrine sound
    For life outliving heats of youth,   10
    Yet who would preach it as a truth
To those that eddy round and round?

Hold thou the good: define it well:
    For fear divine Philosophy
    Should push beyond her mark, and be   15
Procuress to the Lords of Hell.

LIII. 5 f. Compare *Measure for Measure*, V, i, 444 f.:
        They say, best men are moulded out of faults,
        And, for the most, become much more the better
        For being a little bad.

LIV

Oh yet we trust that somehow good
  Will be the final goal of ill,
  To pangs of nature, sins of will,
Defects of doubt, and taints of blood;

That nothing walks with aimless feet;   5
  That not one life shall be destroy'd,
  Or cast as rubbish to the void,
When God hath made the pile complete;

That not a worm is cloven in vain;
  That not a moth with vain desire   10
  Is shrivell'd in a fruitless fire,
Or but subserves another's gain.

Behold, we know not anything;
  I can but trust that good shall fall
  At last — far off — at last, to all,   15
And every winter change to spring.

So runs my dream: but what am I?
  An infant crying in the night:
  An infant crying for the light:
And with no language but a cry.   20

LV

The wish, that of the living whole
  No life may fail beyond the grave,
  Derives it not from what we have
The likest God within the soul?

Are God and Nature then at strife,   5
  That Nature lends such evil dreams?
  So careful of the type she seems,
So careless of the single life;

That I, considering everywhere
  Her secret meaning in her deeds,   10
  And finding that of fifty seeds
She often brings but one to bear,

I falter where I firmly trod,
   And falling with my weight of cares
   Upon the great world's altar-stairs   15
That slope thro' darkness up to God,

I stretch lame hands of faith, and grope,
   And gather dust and chaff, and call
   To what I feel is Lord of all,
And faintly trust the larger hope.   20

LVI

'So careful of the type?' but no.
   From scarped cliff and quarried stone
   She cries, 'A thousand types are gone:
I care for nothing, all shall go.

'Thou makest thine appeal to me: 5
   I bring to life, I bring to death:
   The spirit does but mean the breath:
I know no more.' And he, shall he,

Man, her last work, who seem'd so fair,
   Such splendid purpose in his eyes,   10
   Who roll'd the psalm to wintry skies,
Who built him fanes of fruitless prayer,

Who trusted God was love indeed
   And love Creation's final law —
   Tho' Nature, red in tooth and claw   15
With ravine, shriek'd against his creed —

Who loved, who suffer'd countless ills,
   Who battled for the True, the Just,
   Be blown about the desert dust,
Or seal'd within the iron hills?   20

LV. 20. *the larger hope.* By this famous phrase Tennyson meant "that the whole human race would through, perhaps, ages of suffering, be at length purified and saved" (*Memoir*, i, 321 f.).

LVI. 2. *scarped,* cut away perpendicularly or steeply, thus exposing the strata. In such exposed layers fossils are found.

No more?   A monster then, a dream,
    A discord.   Dragons of the prime,
    That tare each other in their slime,
Were mellow music match'd with him.

O life as futile, then, as frail!   25
    O for thy voice to soothe and bless!
    What hope of answer, or redress?
Behind the veil, behind the veil.

                              LVII

Peace; come away: the song of woe
    Is after all an earthly song:
    Peace; come away: we do him wrong
To sing so wildly: let us go.

Come; let us go: your cheeks are pale;   5
    But half my life I leave behind:
    Methinks my friend is richly shrined;
But I shall pass; my work will fail.

Yet in these ears, till hearing dies,
    One set slow bell will seem to toll   10
    The passing of the sweetest soul
That ever look'd with human eyes.

I hear it now, and o'er and o'er,
    Eternal greetings to the dead;
    And 'Ave, Ave, Ave,' said,   15
'Adieu, adieu,' for evermore.

22-3. Compare the "monstrous eft" of *Maud*, I, iv, 31.

28. *the veil.* Is the metaphor of the veil concealing the "holy place"
in the temple (Leviticus, xvi, 2; Hebrews, vi, 19), or of the veiled statue
of Isis (compare *Maud*, I, iv, 43)?

LVII. Compare Shelley, *Adonais*, xxxix.

15-16. Catullus, ci: "Atque in perpetuum, frater, ave atque vale."
The three-fold farewell greeting of Tennyson's line may have been suggested by Virgil's "magna manes ter voce vocavi" (*Aeneid*, vi, 506).

LVIII

In those sad words I took farewell:
   Like echoes in sepulchral halls,
   As drop by drop the water falls
In vaults and catacombs, they fell;

And, falling, idly broke the peace   5
   Of hearts that beat from day to day,
   Half-conscious of their dying clay,
And those cold crypts where they shall cease.

The high Muse answer'd: 'Wherefore grieve
   Thy brethren with a fruitless tear?   10
   Abide a little longer here,
And thou shalt take a nobler leave.'

LIX

O Sorrow, wilt thou live with me
   No casual mistress, but a wife,
   My bosom-friend and half of life;
As I confess it needs must be;

O Sorrow, wilt thou rule my blood,   5
   Be sometimes lovely like a bride,
   And put thy harsher moods aside,
If thou wilt have me wise and good.

My centred passion cannot move,
   Nor will it lessen from to-day;   10
   But I'll have leave at times to play
As with the creature of my love;

And set thee forth, for thou art mine,
   With so much hope for years to come,
   That, howsoe'er I know thee, some   15
Could hardly tell what name were thine.

LVIII. 9. *The high Muse.* Urania is probably intended (compare XXXVII, 1).

LIX. Not in the first edition; added in the fourth edition, 1851. Compare the song "To Sorrow I bade good morrow" in Keats's *Endymion,* canto iv.

LX

He past; a soul of nobler tone:
   My spirit loved and loves him yet,
   Like some poor girl whose heart is set
On one whose rank exceeds her own

He mixing with his proper sphere,   5
   She finds the baseness of her lot,
   Half jealous of she knows not what,
And envying all that meet him there.

The little village looks forlorn;
   She sighs amid her narrow days,   10
   Moving about the household ways,
In that dark house where she was born.

The foolish neighbours come and go,
   And tease her till the day draws by:
   At night she weeps, 'How vain am I!   15
How should he love a thing so low?'

LXI

If, in thy second state sublime,
   Thy ransom'd reason change replies
   With all the circle of the wise,
The perfect flower of human time;

And if thou cast thine eyes below,   5
   How dimly character'd and slight,
   How dwarf'd a growth of cold and night,
How blanch'd with darkness must I grow!

Yet turn thee to the doubtful shore,
   Where thy first form was made a man;   10
   I loved thee, Spirit, and love, nor can
The soul of Shakespeare love thee more.

LX. 1. *nobler,* very noble (a Latinism).

LXI. 12. The Shakespeare of the *Sonnets* is intended, the devoted
lover of a friend.

LXII

Tho' if an eye that's downward cast
    Could make thee somewhat blench or fail,
    Then be my love an idle tale,
And fading legend of the past;

And thou, as one that once declined,   5
    When he was little more than boy,
    On some unworthy heart with joy,
But lives to wed an equal mind;

And breathes a novel world, the while
    His other passion wholly dies,   10
    Or in the light of deeper eyes
Is matter for a flying smile.

LXIII

Yet pity for a horse o'er-driven,
    And love in which my hound has part,
    Can hang no weight upon my heart
In its assumptions up to heaven;

And I am so much more than these,   5
    As thou, perchance, art more than I,
    And yet I spare them sympathy,
And I would set their pains at ease.

So mayst thou watch me where I weep,
    As, unto vaster motions bound,   10
    The circuits of thine orbit round
A higher height, a deeper deep.

LXIV

Dost thou look back on what hath been,
    As some divinely gifted man,
    Whose life in low estate began
And on a simple village green;

LXII. 5. *declined.* See note on "Locksley Hall," ll. 43-4.

Who breaks his birth's invidious bar,   5
  And grasps the skirts of happy chance,
  And breasts the blows of circumstance,
And grapples with his evil star;

Who makes by force his merit known
  And lives to clutch the golden keys,   10
  To mould a mighty state's decrees,
And shape the whisper of the throne;

And moving up from high to higher,
  Becomes on Fortune's crowning slope
  The pillar of a people's hope,   15
The centre of a world's desire;

Yet feels, as in a pensive dream,
  When all his active powers are still,
  A distant dearness in the hill,
A secret sweetness in the stream,   20

The limit of his narrower fate,
  While yet beside its vocal springs
  He play'd at counsellors and kings,
With one that was his earliest mate;

Who ploughs with pain his native lea   25
  And reaps the labour of his hands,
  Or in the furrow musing stands;
'Does my old friend remember me?'

LXV

Sweet soul, do with me as thou wilt;
  I lull a fancy trouble-tost
  With 'Love's too precious to be lost,
A little grain shall not be spilt.'

And in that solace can I sing,   5
  Till out of painful phases wrought
  There flutters up a happy thought,
Self-balanced on a lightsome wing:

LXIV. 10. *the golden keys,* insignia of offices of state.

Since we deserved the name of friends,
   And thine effect so lives in me,   10
   A part of mine may live in thee
And move thee on to noble ends.

LXVI

You thought my heart too far diseased;
   You wonder when my fancies play
   To find me gay among the gay,
Like one with any trifle pleased.

The shade by which my life was crost,   5
   Which makes a desert in the mind,
   Has made me kindly with my kind,
And like to him whose sight is lost;

Whose feet are guided thro' the land,
   Whose jest among his friends is free,   10
   Who takes the children on his knee,
And winds their curls about his hand:

He plays with threads, he beats his chair
   For pastime, dreaming of the sky;
   His inner day can never die,   15
His night of loss is always there.

LXVII

When on my bed the moonlight falls,
   I know that in thy place of rest
   By that broad water of the west,
There comes a glory on the walls:

Thy marble bright in dark appears,   5
   As slowly steals a silver flame
   Along the letters of thy name,
And o'er the number of thy years.

LXVI. 1. *You* is an unnamed friend who has wondered at the change
in the poet.

The mystic glory swims away;
   From off my bed the moonlight dies;   10
   And closing eaves of wearied eyes
I sleep till dusk is dipt in gray:

And then I know the mist is drawn
   A lucid veil from coast to coast,
   And in the dark church like a ghost   15
Thy tablet glimmers to the dawn.

LXVIII

When in the down I sink my head,
   Sleep, Death's twin-brother, times my breath;
   Sleep, Death's twin-brother, knows not Death,
Nor can I dream of thee as dead:

I walk as ere I walk'd forlorn,   5
   When all our path was fresh with dew,
   And all the bugle breezes blew
Reveillée to the breaking morn.

But what is this? I turn about,
   I find a trouble in thine eye,   10
   Which makes me sad I know not why,
Nor can my dream resolve the doubt:

But ere the lark hath left the lea
   I wake, and I discern the truth;
   It is the trouble of my youth   15
That foolish sleep transfers to thee.

LXIX

I dream'd there would be Spring no more,
   That Nature's ancient power was lost:
   The streets were black with smoke and frost,
They chatter'd trifles at the door:

LXVII. 15. *dark church;* 1850 "chancel." Tennyson did not visit
Clevedon till years after the burial of Hallam. He then altered "chancel"
because the memorial tablet is in an aisle of the church.

LXVIII. 2. In the *Iliad* (xiv, 231) Sleep is the brother of Death.
Compare Virgil, *Aeneid,* vi, 278: "consanguineus Leti Sopor"; and the
opening lines of Shelley's *Queen Mab.*

I wander'd from the noisy town,   5
   I found a wood with thorny boughs:
   I took the thorns to bind my brows,
I wore them like a civic crown:

I met with scoffs, I met with scorns
   From youth and babe and hoary hairs: 10
   They call'd me in the public squares
The fool that wears a crown of thorns:

They call'd me fool, they call'd me child:
   I found an angel of the night;
   The voice was low, the look was bright;   15
He look'd upon my crown and smiled:

He reach'd the glory of a hand,
   That seem'd to touch it into leaf:
   The voice was not the voice of grief,
The words were hard to understand.   20

LXX

I cannot see the features right,
   When on the gloom I strive to paint
   The face I know; the hues are faint
And mix with hollow masks of night;

Cloud-towers by ghostly masons wrought,   5
   A gulf that ever shuts and gapes,
   A hand that points, and palled shapes
In shadowy thoroughfares of thought;

And crowds that stream from yawning doors,
   And shoals of pucker'd faces drive;   10
   Dark bulks that tumble half alive,
And lazy lengths on boundless shores;

LXX. 1. Compare Sir Thomas Browne, *Religio Medici,* ii, 6: "Whom
we truly love like our own selves, we forget their looks, nor can our
memory retain the idea of their faces."

Till all at once beyond the will
 I hear a wizard music roll,
 And thro' a lattice on the soul   15
Looks thy fair face and makes it still.

LXXI

Sleep, kinsman thou to death and trance
 And madness, thou hast forged at last
 A night-long Present of the Past
In which we went thro' summer France.

Hadst thou such credit with the soul?   5
 Then bring an opiate trebly strong,
 Drug down the blindfold sense of wrong
That so my pleasure may be whole;

While now we talk as once we talk'd
 Of men and minds, the dust of change,   10
 The days that grow to something strange,
In walking as of old we walk'd

Beside the river's wooded reach,
 The fortress, and the mountain ridge,
 The cataract flashing from the bridge,   15
The breaker breaking on the beach.

LXXII

Risest thou thus, dim dawn, again,
 And howlest, issuing out of night,
 With blasts that blow the poplar white,
And lash with storm the streaming pane?

Day, when my crown'd estate begun   5
 To pine in that reverse of doom,
 Which sicken'd every living bloom,
And blurr'd the splendour of the sun;

LXXI. 4. In the summer of 1830 Tennyson went with Hallam to the
Pyrenees. See "In the Valley of Cauteretz."

LXXII. The first anniversary of Hallam's death.

Who usherest in the dolorous hour
   With thy quick tears that make the rose   10
   Pull sideways, and the daisy close
Her crimson fringes to the shower;

Who might'st have heaved a windless flame
   Up the deep East, or, whispering, play'd
   A chequer-work of beam and shade   15
Along the hills, yet look'd the same.

As wan, as chill, as wild as now;
   Day, mark'd as with some hideous crime,
   When the dark hand struck down thro' time,
And cancell'd nature's best: but thou   20

Lift as thou may'st thy burthen'd brows
   Thro' clouds that drench the morning star,
   And whirl the ungarner'd sheaf afar,
And sow the sky with flying boughs,

And up thy vault with roaring sound   25
   Climb thy thick noon, disastrous day;
   Touch thy dull goal of joyless gray,
And hide thy shame beneath the ground.

LXXIII

So many worlds, so much to do,
   So little done, such things to be,
   How know I what had need of thee,
For thou wert strong as thou wert true?

The fame is quench'd that I foresaw,   5
   The head hath miss'd an earthly wreath:
   I curse not nature, no, nor death;
For nothing is that errs from law.

---

28. So Shakespeare imagines the sun "stealing unseen to west with this disgrace" (*Sonnets*, xxxiii).

LXXIII. The meditations upon Fame in this and the immediately following sections are reminiscent of *Lycidas*.

We pass; the path that each man trod
　　Is dim, or will be dim, with weeds: 10
　　What fame is left for human deeds
In endless age?   It rests with God.

O hollow wraith of dying fame,
　　Fade wholly, while the soul exults,
　　And self-infolds the large results   15
Of force that would have forged a name.

LXXIV

As sometimes in a dead man's face,
　　To those that watch it more and more,
　　A likeness, hardly seen before,
Comes out — to some one of his race:

So, dearest, now thy brows are cold,   5
　　I see thee what thou art, and know
　　Thy likeness to the wise below,
Thy kindred with the great of old.

But there is more than I can see,
　　And what I see I leave unsaid,   10
　　Nor speak it, knowing Death has made
His darkness beautiful with thee.

LXXV

I leave thy praises unexpress'd
　　In verse that brings myself relief,
　　And by the measure of my grief
I leave thy greatness to be guess'd;

What practice howsoe'er expert   5
　　In fitting aptest words to things,
　　Or voice the richest-toned that sings,
Hath power to give thee as thou wert?

LXXIV. 1–4. Sir Thomas Browne had observed this phenomenon
(*Letter to a Friend*).

I care not in these fading days
 To raise a cry that lasts not long,   10
  And round thee with the breeze of song
To stir a little dust of praise.

Thy leaf has perish'd in the green,
 And, while we breathe beneath the sun,
  The world which credits what is done 15
Is cold to all that might have been.

So here shall silence guard thy fame;
 But somewhere, out of human view,
  Whate'er thy hands are set to do
Is wrought with tumult of acclaim.   20

LXXVI

Take wings of fancy, and ascend,
 And in a moment set thy face
  Where all the starry heavens of space
Are sharpen'd to a needle's end;

Take wings of foresight; lighten thro'   5
 The secular abyss to come,
  And lo, thy deepest lays are dumb
Before the mouldering of a yew;

And if the matin songs, that woke
 The darkness of our planet, last,   10
  Thine own shall wither in the vast,
Ere half the lifetime of an oak.

Ere these have clothed their branchy bowers
 With fifty Mays, thy songs are vain;
  And what are they when these remain 15
The ruin'd shells of hollow towers?

LXXV. 11. *the breeze of song.* The phrase is from Pindar, *Pythian Odes,* iv, 5.

LXXVI. 9. *the matin songs.* Tennyson explained this as the writings of the great early poets.

LXXVII

What hope is here for modern rhyme
    To him, who turns a musing eye
    On songs, and deeds, and lives, that lie
Foreshorten'd in the tract of time?

These mortal lullabies of pain   5
    May bind a book, may line a box,
    May serve to curl a maiden's locks;
Or when a thousand moons shall wane

A man upon a stall may find,
    And, passing, turn the page that tells   10
    A grief, then changed to something else,
Sung by a long-forgotten mind.

But what of that? My darken'd ways
    Shall ring with music all the same;
    To breathe my loss is more than fame,   15
To utter love more sweet than praise.

LXXVIII

Again at Christmas did we weave
    The holly round the Christmas hearth;
    The silent snow possess'd the earth,
And calmly fell our Christmas-eve:

The yule-clog sparkled keen with frost,   5
    No wing of wind the region swept,
    But over all things brooding slept
The quiet sense of something lost.

LXXVII. 4. Compare Shelley, *Queen Mab,* iii, 5:
    How many names in the long sweep of time
    That so foreshortens greatness.

LXXVIII. The second Christmas-tide after Hallam's death. Compare XXX.

5. *yule-clog,* yule-log, "clog" being a northern dialect word occurring in Lincolnshire.

As in the winters left behind,
  Again our ancient games had place,   10
  The mimic picture's breathing grace,
And dance and song and hoodman-blind.

Who show'd a token of distress?
  No single tear, no mark of pain:
  O sorrow, then can sorrow wane?   15
O grief, can grief be changed to less?

O last regret, regret can die!
  No — mixt with all this mystic frame,
  Her deep relations are the same,
But with long use her tears are dry.   20

LXXIX

'More than my brothers are to me,' —
  Let this not vex thee, noble heart!
  I know thee of what force thou art
To hold the costliest love in fee.

But thou and I are one in kind,   5
  As moulded like in Nature's mint;
  And hill and wood and field did print
The same sweet forms in either mind.

For us the same cold streamlet curl'd
  Thro' all his eddying coves; the same   10
  All winds that roam the twilight came
In whispers of the beauteous world.

At one dear knee we proffer'd vows,
  One lesson from one book we learn'd,
  Ere childhood's flaxen ringlet turn'd   15
To black and brown on kindred brows.

---

11. tableaux vivants (Tennyson's explanation).

12. *hoodman-blind*, blindman's buff. Compare *Hamlet*, III, iv, 77.

LXXIX. Addressed to one of the poet's brothers. Line 1 refers back
to IX, 20.

4. *in fee*, in possession.

And so my wealth resembles thine,
    But he was rich where I was poor,
    And he supplied my want the more
As his unlikeness fitted mine.   20

LXXX

If any vague desire should rise,
    That holy Death ere Arthur died
    Had moved me kindly from his side,
And dropt the dust on tearless eyes;

Then fancy shapes, as fancy can,   5
    The grief my loss in him had wrought,
    A grief as deep as life or thought,
But stay'd in peace with God and man.

I make a picture in the brain;
    I hear the sentence that he speaks;   10
    He bears the burthen of the weeks
But turns his burthen into gain.

His credit thus shall set me free;
    And, influence-rich to soothe and save,
    Unused example from the grave   15
Reach out dead hands to comfort me.

LXXXI

Could I have said while he was here,
    'My love shall now no further range;
    There cannot come a mellower change,
For now is love mature in ear.'

Love, then, had hope of richer store: 5
    What end is here to my complaint?
    This haunting whisper makes me faint,
'More years had made me love thee more.'

LXXX. 8. *stay'd,* propped and so held fast.

LXXXI. 1. *Could I have said.* Tennyson explained this as meaning
"Would that I could have said." See on this phrase and on the problem
of punctuation in l. 4, *Works,* Eversley edition, ii, 567, and Bradley,
Commentary, pp. 172 f.

But Death returns an answer sweet:
   'My sudden frost was sudden gain,   10
   And gave all ripeness to the grain,
It might have drawn from after-heat.'

LXXXII

I wage not any feud with Death
   For changes wrought on form and face;
   No lower life that earth's embrace
May breed with him, can fright my faith.

Eternal process moving on,   5
   From state to state the spirit walks;
   And these are but the shatter'd stalks,
Or ruin'd chrysalis of one.

Nor blame I Death, because he bare
   The use of virtue out of earth: 10
   I know transplanted human worth
Will bloom to profit, otherwhere.

For this alone on Death I wreak
   The wrath that garners in my heart:
   He put our lives so far apart   15
We cannot hear each other speak.

LXXXIII

Dip down upon the northern shore,
   O sweet new-year delaying long;
   Thou doest expectant nature wrong;
Delaying long, delay no more.

What stays thee from the clouded noons,   5
   Thy sweetness from its proper place?
   Can trouble live with April days,
Or sadness in the summer moons?

LXXXII. 6. See note on XLVII, 13.

14. *garners,* is stored up.   This intransitive use is very rare.

LXXXIII. 2. *O sweet new-year,* not New Year's Day but the spring of
the year, as in "The May Queen."

Bring orchis, bring the foxglove spire,
   The little speedwell's darling blue,   10
   Deep tulips dash'd with fiery dew,
Laburnums, dropping-wells of fire.

O thou new-year, delaying long,
   Delayest the sorrow in my blood,
   That longs to burst a frozen bud   15
And flood a fresher throat with song.

LXXXIV

When I contemplate all alone
   The life that had been thine below,
   And fix my thoughts on all the glow
To which thy crescent would have grown;

I see thee sitting crown'd with good,   5
   A central warmth diffusing bliss
   In glance and smile, and clasp and kiss,
On all the branches of thy blood;

Thy blood, my friend, and partly mine;
   For now the day was drawing on,   10
   When thou should'st link thy life with one
Of mine own house, and boys of thine

Had babbled 'Uncle' on my knee;
   But that remorseless iron hour
   Made cypress of her orange flower,   15
Despair of Hope, and earth of thee.

I seem to meet their least desire,
   To clap their cheeks, to call them mine.
   I see their unborn faces shine
Beside the never-lighted fire.   20

I see myself an honour'd guest,
   Thy partner in the flowery walk
   Of letters, genial table-talk,
Or deep dispute, and graceful jest;

LXXXIV. 11–12. Hallam had been betrothed to the poet's sister
Emily.

While now thy prosperous labour fills   25
  The lips of men with honest praise,
  And sun by sun the happy days
Descend below the golden hills

With promise of a morn as fair;
  And all the train of bounteous hours   30
  Conduct by paths of growing powers,
To reverence and the silver hair;

Till slowly worn her earthly robe,
  Her lavish mission richly wrought,
  Leaving great legacies of thought,   35
Thy spirit should fail from off the globe;

What time mine own might also flee,
  As link'd with thine in love and fate,
  And, hovering o'er the dolorous strait
To the other shore, involved in thee,   40

Arrive at last the blessed goal,
  And He that died in Holy Land
  Would reach us out the shining hand
And take us as a single soul.

What reed was that on which I leant?   45
  Ah, backward fancy, wherefore wake
  The old bitterness again, and break
The low beginnings of content.

LXXXV

This truth came borne with bier and pall,
  I felt it, when I sorrow'd most,
  'Tis better to have loved and lost,
Than never to have loved at all —

LXXXV. According to the *Memoir* (i, 109), this was one of the first
written sections of *In Memoriam;* but it is altogether likely, as Bradley
guesses, that this statement applies to the first stanza only. There is a
definite break after line 4. It is almost inconceivable that so early as
1833 Tennyson would have written ll. 61–2:

           I count it crime
      To mourn for many overmuch.

O true in word, and tried in deed,   5
    Demanding, so to bring relief
    To this which is our common grief,
What kind of life is that I lead;

And whether trust in things above
    Be dimm'd of sorrow, or sustain'd;   10
    And whether love for him have drain'd
My capabilities of love;

Your words have virtue such as draws
    A faithful answer from the breast,
    Thro' light reproaches, half exprest,   15
And loyal unto kindly laws.

My blood an even tenor kept,
    Till on mine ear this message falls,
    That in Vienna's fatal walls
God's finger touch'd him, and he slept.   20

The great Intelligences fair
    That range above our mortal state,
    In circle round the blessed gate,
Received and gave him welcome there;

And led him thro' the blissful climes,   25
    And show'd him in the fountain fresh
    All knowledge that the sons of flesh
Shall gather in the cycled times.

Moreover Tennyson seems not to have known Edmund Lushington (to whom this section is addressed) at all intimately till about 1840. And the tone of the section, apart from the first stanza, is late. If early in any form, it was certainly much revised long afterwards.

21. *The great Intelligences fair,* the spirits who, according to the medieval conception, guide the nine Heavens. Compare Dante, *Paradiso,* ii, 127 f.:

> Lo moto e la virtù de' santi giri, . . .
> Da' beati motor convien che spiri

("The motion and the virtue of the holy spheres must needs be inspired by blessed movers"), and *ibid.,* xxviii, 78: "In ciascun cielo, a sua intelligenza." Compare also Adam addressing Raphael as "pure Intelligence of Heaven" (*Paradise Lost,* viii, 180).

But I remain'd, whose hopes were dim,
  Whose life, whose thoughts were little worth,   30
  To wander on a darken'd earth,
Where all things round me breathed of him.

O friendship, equal-poised control,
  O heart, with kindliest motion warm,
  O sacred essence, other form,   35
O solemn ghost, O crowned soul!

Yet none could better know than I,
  How much of act at human hands
  The sense of human will demands
By which we dare to live or die.   40

Whatever way my days decline,
  I felt and feel, tho' left alone,
  His being working in mine own,
The footsteps of his life in mine;

A life that all the Muses deck'd   45
  With gifts of grace, that might express
  All-comprehensive tenderness,
All-subtilising intellect:

And so my passion hath not swerved
  To works of weakness, but I find   50
  An image comforting the mind,
And in my grief a strength reserved.

Likewise the imaginative woe,
  That loved to handle spiritual strife,
  Diffused the shock thro' all my life,   55
But in the present broke the blow.

My pulses therefore beat again
  For other friends that once I met;
  Nor can it suit me to forget
The mighty hopes that make us men.   60

I woo your love: I count it crime
  To mourn for any overmuch;
  I, the divided half of such
A friendship as had master'd Time;

Which masters Time indeed, and is   65
   Eternal, separate from fears:
   The all-assuming months and years
Can take no part away from this:

But Summer on the steaming floods,
   And Spring that swells the narrow brooks,   70
   And Autumn, with a noise of rooks,
That gather in the waning woods,

And every pulse of wind and wave
   Recalls, in change of light or gloom,
   My old affection of the tomb,   75
And my prime passion in the grave:

My old affection of the tomb,
   A part of stillness, yearns to speak:
   'Arise, and get thee forth and seek
A friendship for the years to come.   80

'I watch thee from the quiet shore;
   Thy spirit up to mine can reach;
   But in dear words of human speech
We two communicate no more.'

And I, 'Can clouds of nature stain   85
   The starry clearness of the free?
   How is it?   Canst thou feel for me
Some painless sympathy with pain?'

And lightly does the whisper fall;
   ' 'Tis hard for thee to fathom this;   90
   I triumph in conclusive bliss,
And that serene result of all.'

So hold I commerce with the dead;
   Or so methinks the dead would say;
   Or so shall grief with symbols play   95
And pining life be fancy-fed.

Now looking to some settled end,
   That these things pass, and I shall prove
   A meeting somewhere, love with love,
I crave your pardon, O my friend;   100

If not so fresh, with love as true,
   I, clasping brother-hands, aver
   I could not, if I would, transfer
The whole I felt for him to you.

For which be they that hold apart   105
   The promise of the golden hours?
   First love, first friendship, equal powers,
That marry with the virgin heart.

Still mine, that cannot but deplore,
   That beats within a lonely place,   110
   That yet remembers his embrace,
But at his footstep leaps no more,

My heart, tho' widow'd, may not rest
   Quite in the love of what is gone,
   But seeks to beat in time with one   115
That warms another living breast.

Ah, take the imperfect gift I bring,
   Knowing the primrose yet is dear,
   The primrose of the later year,
As not unlike to that of Spring.   120

LXXXVI

Sweet after showers, ambrosial air,
   That rollest from the gorgeous gloom
   Of evening over brake and bloom
And meadow, slowly breathing bare

LXXXVI. Written at Barmouth in North Wales, probably in the summer of 1839 (*Memoir*, i, 173, 313). The sunsets on the estuary of the Mawddach are famous.

The round of space, and rapt below   5
    Thro' all the dewy-tassell'd wood,
    And shadowing down the horned flood
In ripples, fan my brows and blow

The fever from my cheek, and sigh
    The full new life that feeds thy breath   10
    Throughout my frame, till Doubt and Death,
Ill brethren, let the fancy fly

From belt to belt of crimson seas
    On leagues of odour streaming far,
    To where in yonder orient star   15
A hundred spirits whisper 'Peace.'

LXXXVII

I past beside the reverend walls
    In which of old I wore the gown;
    I roved at random thro' the town,
And saw the tumult of the halls;

And heard once more in college fanes   5
    The storm their high-built organs make,
    And thunder-music, rolling, shake
The prophet blazon'd on the panes;

And caught once more the distant shout,
    The measured pulse of racing oars   10
    Among the willows; paced the shores
And many a bridge, and all about

The same gray flats again, and felt
    The same, but not the same; and last
    Up that long walk of limes I past   15
To see the rooms in which he dwelt.

---

7. *horned,* winding rather than branching. The phrase is Virgilian (*Aeneid,* viii, 77) and Miltonic (*Paradise Lost,* xi, 831).

LXXXVII. This section records a visit to Cambridge at an uncertain date but evidently some years after Hallam's death.

15. The walk of lime-trees is at Trinity College.

Another name was on the door:
   I linger'd; all within was noise
   Of songs, and clapping hands, and boys
That crash'd the glass and beat the floor;   20

Where once we held debate, a band
   Of youthful friends, on mind and art,
   And labour, and the changing mart,
And all the framework of the land;

When one would aim an arrow fair,   25
   But send it slackly from the string;
   And one would pierce an outer ring,
And one an inner, here and there;

And last the master-bowman, he,
   Would cleave the mark. A willing ear   30
   We lent him. Who, but hung to hear
The rapt oration flowing free

From point to point, with power and grace
   And music in the bounds of law,
   To those conclusions when we saw   35
The God within him light his face,

And seem to lift the form, and glow
   In azure orbits heavenly-wise;
   And over those ethereal eyes
The bar of Michael Angelo.   40

LXXXVIII

Wild bird, whose warble, liquid sweet,
   Rings Eden thro' the budded quicks,
   O tell me where the senses mix,
O tell me where the passions meet,

---

40. *The bar of Michael Angelo.* "These lines," said Tennyson, "I
wrote from what Arthur Hallam said after reading of the prominent ridge
of bone over the eyes of Michael Angelo: 'Alfred, look over my eyes;
surely I have the bar of Michael Angelo!'" (*Memoir*, i, 38).

LXXXVIII. With this section compare Thomas Hardy's "The Darkling
Thrush."

Whence radiate: fierce extremes employ   5
  Thy spirits in the darkening leaf,
  And in the midmost heart of grief
Thy passion clasps a secret joy:

And I — my harp would prelude woe —
  I cannot all command the strings;   10
  The glory of the sum of things
Will flash along the chords and go.

LXXXIX

Witch-elms that counterchange the floor
  Of this flat lawn with dusk and bright;
  And thou, with all thy breadth and height
Of foliage, towering sycamore;

How often, hither wandering down,   5
  My Arthur found your shadows fair,
  And shook to all the liberal air
The dust and din and steam of town:

He brought an eye for all he saw;
  He mixt in all our simple sports;   10
  They pleased him, fresh from brawling courts
And dusty purlieus of the law.

O joy to him in this retreat,
  Immantled in ambrosial dark,
  To drink the cooler air, and mark   15
The landscape winking thro' the heat:

O sound to rout the brood of cares,
  The sweep of scythe in morning dew,
  The gust that round the garden flew,
And tumbled half the mellowing pears!   20

---

11. *the sum of things.* The phrase is used by Milton (*Paradise Lost,* vi. 673) and A. E. Housman ("Epitaph on an Army of Mercenaries").

LXXXIX. Memories of Hallam's visits to Somersby.

1. *counterchange,* chequer.

7. *the liberal air.* Compare Byron, *Manfred,* I, ii, 50: "Pipes in the liberal air."

O bliss, when all in circle drawn
    About him, heart and ear were fed
    To hear him as he lay and read
The Tuscan poets on the lawn:

Or in the all-golden afternoon   25
    A guest, or happy sister, sung,
    Or here she brought the harp and flung
A ballad to the brightening moon:

Nor less it pleased in livelier moods,
    Beyond the bounding hill to stray,   30
    And break the livelong summer day
With banquet in the distant woods;

Whereat we glanced from theme to theme,
    Discuss'd the books to love or hate,
    Or touch'd the changes of the state,   35
Or threaded some Socratic dream;

But if I praised the busy town,
    He loved to rail against it still,
    For 'ground in yonder social mill
We rub each other's angles down,   40

'And merge,' he said, 'in form and gloss
    The picturesque of man and man.'
    We talk'd: the stream beneath us ran,
The wine-flask lying couch'd in moss,

Or cool'd within the glooming wave;   45
    And last, returning from afar,
    Before the crimson-circled star
Had fall'n into her father's grave,

And brushing ankle-deep in flowers,
    We heard behind the woodbine veil   50
    The milk that bubbled in the pail,
And buzzings of the honied hours.

---

    31. *break . . . the day,* a Horatian phrase, "diem . . . fregi," *Odes,*
ii, 3. 6.

    47–8. The periphrasis is far-fetched. The planet Venus, thrown off,
according to the nebular hypothesis, by the sun (which is therefore her
father), sets amid crimson clouds after the sun.

XC

He tasted love with half his mind,
  Nor ever drank the inviolate spring
  Where nighest heaven, who first could fling
This bitter seed among mankind;

That could the dead, whose dying eyes   5
  Were closed with wail, resume their life,
  They would but find in child and wife
An iron welcome when they rise:

'Twas well, indeed, when warm with wine,
  To pledge them with a kindly tear,   10
  To talk them o'er, to wish them here,
To count their memories half divine;

But if they came who past away,
  Behold their brides in other hands;
  The hard heir strides about their lands,   15
And will not yield them for a day.

Yea, tho' their sons were none of these,
  Not less the yet-loved sire would make
  Confusion worse than death, and shake
The pillars of domestic peace.   20

Ah dear, but come thou back to me:
  Whatever change the years have wrought,
  I find not yet one lonely thought
That cries against my wish for thee.

XCI

When rosy plumelets tuft the larch,
  And rarely pipes the mounted thrush;
  Or underneath the barren bush
Flits by the sea-blue bird of March;

XC. 14 f. Compare "The Lotos-Eaters," ll. 71 f.
XCI. 4. *the sea-blue bird of March.* As Tennyson was "walking one

Come, wear the form by which I know   5
   Thy spirit in time among thy peers;
   The hope of unaccomplish'd years
Be large and lucid round thy brow.

When summer's hourly-mellowing change
   May breathe, with many roses sweet,   10
   Upon the thousand waves of wheat,
That ripple round the lonely grange;

Come: not in watches of the night,
   But where the sunbeam broodeth warm,
   Come, beauteous in thine after form,   15
And like a finer light in light.

XCII

If any vision should reveal
   Thy likeness, I might count it vain
   As but the canker of the brain;
Yea, tho' it spake and made appeal

To chances where our lots were cast   5
   Together in the days behind,
   I might but say, I hear a wind
Of memory murmuring the past.

Yea, tho' it spake and bared to view
   A fact within the coming year;   10
   And tho' the months, revolving near,
Should prove the phantom-warning true,

---

day in March by a deep-banked brook . . . he saw the kingfisher flitting
or fleeting underneath him, and there came into his head a fragment of an
old Greek poet" — Alcman (Fragment 8 B.), who describes the halcyon
as the "sea-purple bird of spring." See *Memoir,* ii, 4. The line is thus
an excellent example of nature-observation mingling with classical reminiscence in Tennyson's poetry.

They might not seem thy prophecies,
  But spiritual presentiments,
  And such refraction of events   15
As often rises ere they rise.

XCIII

I shall not see thee. Dare I say
  No spirit ever brake the band
  That stays him from the native land
Where first he walk'd when claspt in clay?

No visual shade of some one lost,   5
  But he, the Spirit himself, may come
  Where all the nerve of sense is numb;
Spirit to Spirit, Ghost to Ghost.

O, therefore from thy sightless range
  With gods in unconjectured bliss,   10
  O, from the distance of the abyss
Of tenfold-complicated change,

Descend, and touch, and enter; hear
  The wish too strong for words to name;
  That in this blindness of the frame   15
My Ghost may feel that thine is near.

XCIV

How pure at heart and sound in head,
  With what divine affections bold
  Should be the man whose thought would hold
An hour's communion with the dead.

XCII. 15–16. *refraction,* as in a mirage. Compare Coleridge's versions
of Schiller's *The Death of Wallenstein*, V, i:

> As the sun
> Ere it is risen, sometimes paints its image
> In the atmosphere, so often do the spirits
> Of great events stride on before the events,
> And in to-day already walks to-morrow.

XCIII. 8. It is possible that this line should end with an interrogation-
mark, the stanza being then a continuation, by contrast, of the line of
thought in the first stanza. See further Bradley, *op. cit.,* p. 188.

9. *thy sightless range,* the place where thou rangest invisible. Compare for this meaning of the adjective the "sightless substances" and
"sightless couriers" of *Macbeth*, I, v, 50, and I, vii, 23.

In vain shalt thou, or any, call   5
   The spirits from their golden day,
   Except, like them, thou too canst say,
My spirit is at peace with all.

They haunt the silence of the breast,
   Imaginations calm and fair,   10
   The memory like a cloudless air,
The conscience as a sea at rest:

But when the heart is full of din,
   And doubt beside the portal waits,
   They can but listen at the gates,   15
And hear the household jar within.

XCV

By night we linger'd on the lawn,
   For underfoot the herb was dry;
   And genial warmth; and o'er the sky
The silvery haze of summer drawn;

And calm that let the tapers burn   5
   Unwavering: not a cricket chirr'd:
   The brook alone far-off was heard,
And on the board the fluttering urn:

And bats went round in fragrant skies,
   And wheel'd or lit the filmy shapes   10
   That haunt the dusk, with ermine capes
And woolly breasts and beaded eyes;

While now we sang old songs that peal'd
   From knoll to knoll, where, couch'd at ease,
   The white kine glimmer'd, and the trees   15
Laid their dark arms about the field.

But when those others, one by one,
   Withdrew themselves from me and night,
   And in the house light after light
Went out, and I was all alone,   20

XCV. See *Memoir*, i, 320, for Tennyson's experiences of trance.

A hunger seized my heart; I read
   Of that glad year which once had been,
   In those fall'n leaves which kept their green,
The noble letters of the dead:

And strangely on the silence broke   25
   The silent-speaking words, and strange
   Was love's dumb cry defying change
To test his worth; and strangely spoke

The faith the vigour, bold to dwell
   On doubts that drive the coward back,   30
   And keen thro' wordy snares to track
Suggestion to her inmost cell.

So word by word, and line by line,
   The dead man touch'd me from the past,
   And all at once it seem'd at last   35
The living soul was flash'd on mine,

And mine in this was wound, and whirl'd
   About empyreal heights of thought,
   And came on that which is, and caught
The deep pulsations of the world,   40

Æonian music measuring out
   The steps of Time — the shocks of Chance —
   The blows of Death. At length my trance
Was cancell'd, stricken thro' with doubt.

Vague words! but ah, how hard to frame   45
   In matter-moulded forms of speech,
   Or ev'n for intellect to reach
Thro' memory that which I became:

36-7. *The living soul . . . mine in this.* 1850: "His living soul . . . mine in his." Tennyson said that his "conscience was troubled" by the original "his" which implied too definitely that the vision was of Hallam's spirit. See Bradley, *op. cit.*, pp. 191 f., note 1.

42-3. Compare Milton, "On Time": "Triumphing over Death and Chance and thee, O Time."

Till now the doubtful dusk reveal'd
   The knolls once more where, couch'd at ease,   50
   The white kine glimmer'd, and the trees
Laid their dark arms about the field:

And suck'd from out the distant gloom
   A breeze began to tremble o'er
   The large leaves of the sycamore,   55
And fluctuate all the still perfume,

And gathering freshlier overhead,
   Rock'd the full-foliaged elms, and swung
   The heavy-folded rose, and flung
The lilies to and fro, and said,   60

'The dawn, the dawn,' and died away;
   And East and West, without a breath,
   Mixt their dim lights, like life and death,
To broaden into boundless day.

XCVI

You say, but with no touch of scorn,
   Sweet-hearted, you, whose light-blue eyes
   Are tender over drowning flies,
You tell me, doubt is Devil-born.

I know not: one indeed I knew   5
   In many a subtle question versed,
   Who touch'd a jarring lyre at first,
But ever strove to make it true:

Perplext in faith, but pure in deeds,
   At last he beat his music out.   10
   There lives more faith in honest doubt,
Believe me, that in half the creeds.

49–64. These four stanzas Bradley rightly calls "one of the most wonderful descriptive passages in all poetry."

XCVI. 5. *one.* Some commentators identify this person with the poet himself — an odd interpretation. Tennyson noted (*Works,* Eversley edition, ii, 573) that he referred to Hallam.

He fought his doubts and gather'd strength,
  He would not make his judgment blind,
  He faced the spectres of the mind   15
And laid them: thus he came at length

To find a stronger faith his own;
  And Power was with him in the night,
  Which makes the darkness and the light,
And dwells not in the light alone,   20

But in the darkness and the cloud,
  As over Sinaï's peaks of old,
  While Israel made their gods of gold,
Altho' the trumpet blew so loud.

XCVII

My love has talk'd with rocks and trees;
  He finds on misty mountain-ground
  His own vast shadow glory-crown'd;
He sees himself in all he sees.

Two partners of a married life —   5
  I look'd on these and thought of thee
  In vastness and in mystery,
And of my spirit as of a wife.

These two — they dwelt with eye on eye,
  Their hearts of old have beat in tune,   10
  Their meetings made December June,
Their every parting was to die.

Their love has never past away;
  The days she never can forget
  Are earnest that he loves her yet,   15
Whate'er the faithless people say.

21–4. Exodus, xix, 16 f. and xxxii.
XCVII. 2–3. The image is suggested by the spectre of the Brocken.

Her life is lone, he sits apart,
   He loves her yet, she will not weep,
   Tho' rapt in matters dark and deep
He seems to slight her simple heart.   20

He thrids the labyrinth of the mind,
   He reads the secret of the star,
   He seems so near and yet so far,
He looks so cold: she thinks him kind.

She keeps the gift of years before,   25
   A wither'd violet is her bliss:
   She knows not what his greatness is,
For that, for all, she loves him more.

For him she plays, to him she sings
   Of early faith and plighted vows;   30
   She knows but matters of the house,
And he, he knows a thousand things.

Her faith is fixt and cannot move,
   She darkly feels him great and wise,
   She dwells on him with faithful eyes,   35
'I cannot understand: I love.'

XCVIII

You leave us: you will see the Rhine,
   And those fair hills I sail'd below,
   When I was there with him; and go
By summer belts of wheat and vine

To where he breathed his latest breath,   5
   That City.   All her splendour seems
   No livelier than the wisp that gleams
On Lethe in the eyes of Death.

XCVIII. 1. *You.* According to the *Memoir* (i, 148) this section is addressed to the poet's brother Charles on the occasion of his bridal-tour in 1836; but in *Works*, Eversley edition, ii, 574, Tennyson is quoted as saying that " 'you' is imaginary."

   7. *wisp*, the ignis-fatuus or will o' the wisp.

Let her great Danube rolling fair
   Enwind her isles, unmark'd of me: 10
   I have not seen, I will not see
Vienna; rather dream that there,

A treble darkness, Evil haunts
   The birth, the bridal; friend from friend
   Is oftener parted, fathers bend   15
Above more graves, a thousand wants

Gnarr at the heels of men, and prey
   By each cold hearth, and sadness flings
   Her shadow on the blaze of kings:
And yet myself have heard him say,   20

That not in any mother town
   With statelier progress to and fro
   The double tides of chariots flow
By park and suburb under brown

Of lustier leaves; nor more content,   25
   He told me, lives in any crowd,
   When all is gay with lamps, and loud
With sport and song, in booth and tent,

Imperial halls, or open plain,
   And wheels the circled dance, and breaks   30
   The rocket molten into flakes
Of crimson or in emerald rain.

XCIX

Risest thou thus, dim dawn, again,
   So loud with voices of the birds,
   So thick with lowings of the herds,
Day, when I lost the flower of men;

---

17. *gnarr*, snarl, a word used by Spenser and Shakespeare.
21. *mother town*, metropolis.
XCIX. The second anniversary of Hallam's death. Compare LXXII.

Who tremblest thro' thy darkling red   5
　On yon swoll'n brook that bubbles fast
　By meadows breathing of the past,
And woodlands holy to the dead;

Who murmurest in the foliaged eaves
　A song that slights the coming care,   10
　And Autumn laying here and there
A fiery finger on the leaves;

Who wakenest with thy balmy breath
　To myriads on the genial earth,
　Memories of bridal, or of birth,   15
And unto myriads more, of death.

O wheresoever those may be,
　Betwixt the slumber of the poles,
　To-day they count as kindred souls;
They know me not, but mourn with me.   20

C

I climb the hill: from end to end
　Of all the landscape underneath,
　I find no place that does not breathe
Some gracious memory of my friend;

No gray old grange, or lonely fold,   5
　Or low morass and whispering reed,
　Or simple stile from mead to mead,
Or sheepwalk up the windy wold;

Nor hoary knoll of ash and haw
　That hears the latest linnet trill,   10
　Nor quarry trenched along the hill
And haunted by the wrangling daw;

---

18. *the slumber of the poles.* "The ends of the axis of the earth,
which move so slowly that they seem not to move, but slumber" (Tennyson). Compare Marlowe, *Doctor Faustus,* I, i, 57: "All things that
move between the quiet poles."

C. This section and the next three have to do with the removal of the
Tennyson family from Somersby in 1837.

Nor runlet tinkling from the rock;
　　Nor pastoral rivulet that swerves
　　To left and right thro' meadowy curves,   15
That feed the mothers of the flock;

But each has pleased a kindred eye,
　　And each reflects a kindlier day;
　　And, leaving these, to pass away,
I think once more he seems to die.   20

CI

Unwatch'd, the garden bough shall sway,
　　The tender blossom flutter down,
　　Unloved, that beech will gather brown,
This maple burn itself away;

Unloved, the sun-flower, shining fair,   5
　　Ray round with flames her disk of seed,
　　And many a rose-carnation feed
With summer spice the humming air;

Unloved, by many a sandy bar,
　　The brook shall babble down the plain,   10
　　At noon or when the lesser wain
Is twisting round the polar star;

Uncared for, gird the windy grove,
　　And flood the haunts of hern and crake;
　　Or into silver arrows break   15
The sailing moon in creek and cove;

Till from the garden and the wild
　　A fresh association blow,
　　And year by year the landscape grow
Familiar to the stranger's child;   20

As year by year the labourer tills
　　His wonted glebe, or lops the glades;
　　And year by year our memory fades
From all the circle of the hills.

　　CI. 11-12. *the lesser wain,* the constellation of Ursa Minor which circles close to the Pole-star and contains it.

CII

We leave the well-beloved place
  Where first we gazed upon the sky;
  The roofs, that heard our earliest cry,
Will shelter one of stranger race.

We go, but ere we go from home,   5
  As down the garden-walks I move,
  Two spirits of a diverse love
Contend for loving masterdom.

One whispers, 'Here thy boyhood sung
  Long since its matin song, and heard   10
  The low love-language of the bird
In native hazels tassel-hung.'

The other answers, 'Yea, but here
  Thy feet have stray'd in after hours
  With thy lost friend among the bowers,   15
And this hath made them trebly dear.'

These two have striven half the day,
  And each prefers his separate claim,
  Poor rivals in a losing game,
That will not yield each other way.   20

I turn to go: my feet are set
  To leave the pleasant fields and farms;
  They mix in one another's arms
To one pure image of regret.

CIII

On that last night before we went
  From out the doors where I was bred,
  I dream'd a vision of the dead,
Which left my after-morn content.

CIII. The narrative of a dream would be less convincing if the allegory
were wholly consistent. Tennyson's own notes supply as much interpretation as is necessary (*Works,* Eversley edition, ii, 576 f.): the maidens
(l. 5) are "the Muses, poetry, arts — all that made life beautiful here,

Methought I dwelt within a hall,   5
   And maidens with me: distant hills
   From hidden summits fed with rills
A river sliding by the wall.

The hall with harp and carol rang.
   They sang of what is wise and good   10
   And graceful. In the centre stood
A statue veil'd, to which they sang;

And which, tho' veil'd, was known to me,
   The shape of him I loved, and love
   For ever: then flew in a dove   15
And brought a summons from the sea:

And when they learnt that I must go
   They wept and wail'd, but led the way
   To where a little shallop lay
At anchor in the flood below;   20

And on by many a level mead,
   And shadowing bluff that made the banks,
   We glided winding under ranks
Of iris, and the golden reed;

And still as vaster grew the shore   25
   And rolled the floods in grander space,
   The maidens gather'd strength and grace
And presence, lordlier than before;

And I myself, who sat apart
   And watch'd them, wax'd in every limb;   30
   I felt the thews of Anakim,
The pulses of a Titan's heart;

which we hope will pass with us beyond the grave"; the hidden summits
(l. 6) represent "the divine" which feeds the river of life on earth (l. 7)
which flows into the sea of eternity (l. 16). "The progress of the Age"
is suggested in ll. 25–8, and "the great hopes of humanity and science"
in ll. 33–6. For a more detailed interpretation see Bradley, op. cit.,
pp. 198 f.

15–16. Compare the last line of "Vastness."

As one would sing the death of war,
    And one would chant the history
    Of that great race, which is to be,   35
And one the shaping of a star;

Until the forward-creeping tides
    Began to foam, and we to draw
    From deep to deep, to where we saw
A great ship lift her shining sides.   40

The man we loved was there on deck,
    But thrice as large as man he bent
    To greet us. Up the side I went,
And fell in silence on his neck:

Whereat those maidens with one mind   45
    Bewail'd their lot; I did them wrong:
    'We served thee here,' they said, 'so long,
And wilt thou leave us now behind?'

So rapt I was, they could not win
    An answer from my lips, but he   50
    Replying, 'Enter likewise ye
And go with us:' they enter'd in.

And while the wind began to sweep
    A music out of sheet and shroud,
    We steer'd her toward a crimson cloud   55
That landlike slept along the deep.

CIV

The time draws near the birth of Christ;
    The moon is hid, the night is still;
    A single church below the hill
Is pealing, folded in the mist.

CIV. The third Christmas (compare XXVIII–XXX and LXXVIII) is passed in an unfamiliar place, High Beech, Epping Forest, Essex, to which the Tennysons moved from Somersby in 1837 (*Memoir*, i, 150).

    3. *A single church*, Waltham Abbey.

A single peal of bells below,   5
  That wakens at this hour of rest
  A single murmur in the breast,
That these are not the bells I know.

Like strangers' voices here they sound,
  In lands where not a memory strays,   10
  Nor landmark breathes of other days,
But all is new unhallow'd ground.

CV

To-night ungather'd let us leave
  This laurel, let this holly stand:
  We live within the stranger's land,
And strangely falls our Christmas-eve.

Our father's dust is left alone   5
  And silent under other snows:
  There in due time the woodbine blows,
The violet comes, but we are gone.

No more shall wayward grief abuse
  The genial hour with mask and mime;   10
  For change of place, like growth of time,
Has broke the bond of dying use.

Let cares that petty shadows cast,
  By which our lives are chiefly proved,
  A little spare the night I loved,   15
And hold it solemn to the past.

But let no footstep beat the floor,
  Nor bowl of wassail mantle warm;
  For who would keep an ancient form
Thro' which the spirit breathes no more?   20

Be neither song, nor game, nor feast;
  Nor harp be touch'd, nor flute be blown;
  No dance, no motion, save alone
What lightens in the lucid east

Of rising worlds by yonder wood.   25
   Long sleeps the summer in the seed;
   Run out your measured arcs, and lead
The closing cycle rich in good.

CVI

Ring out, wild bells, to the wild sky,
   The flying cloud, the frosty light:
   The year is dying in the night;
Ring out, wild bells, and let him die.

Ring out the old, ring in the new,   5
   Ring, happy bells, across the snow:
   The year is going, let him go;
Ring out the false, ring in the true.

Ring out the grief that saps the mind,
   For those that here we see no more;   10
   Ring out the feud of rich and poor,
Ring in redress to all mankind.

Ring out a slowly dying cause,
   And ancient forms of party strife;
   Ring in the nobler modes of life,   15
With sweeter manners, purer laws.

Ring out the want, the care, the sin,
   The faithless coldness of the times;
   Ring out, ring out my mournful rhymes,
But ring the fuller minstrel in.   20

Ring out false pride in place and blood,
   The civic slander and the spite;
   Ring in the love of truth and right,
Ring in the common love of good.

CV. 28. *The closing cycle.* Virgil's "ultima . . . aetas" (*Eclogues,*
iv, 4). In the Sibylline Books Time was divided into cycles or periods;
Virgil imagines that the Golden Age returns with the final cycle. Compare the final chorus of Shelley's *Hellas:*

    The world's great age begins anew,
    The golden years return.

Ring out old shapes of foul disease;   25
   Ring out the narrowing lust of gold;
   Ring out the thousand wars of old,
Ring in the thousand years of peace.

Ring in the valiant man and free,
   The larger heart, the kindlier hand;   30
   Ring out the darkness of the land,
Ring in the Christ that is to be.

CVII

It is the day when he was born,
   A bitter day that early sank
   Behind a purple-frosty bank
Of vapour, leaving night forlorn.

The time admits not flowers or leaves   5
   To deck the banquet. Fiercely flies
   The blast of North and East, and ice
Makes daggers at the sharpen'd eaves,

And bristles all the brakes and thorns
   To yon hard crescent, as she hangs   10
   Above the wood which grides and clangs
Its leafless ribs and iron horns

Together, in the drifts that pass
   To darken on the rolling brine
   That breaks the coast. But fetch the wine,   15
Arrange the board and brim the glass;

CVI. 32. Tennyson was convinced that "the forms of Christian religion would alter, but that the spirit of Christ would still grow from more to more . . . Christianity without bigotry will triumph when the controversies of creeds shall have vanished" (*Memoir*, i, 325 f.).

CVII. Hallam's birthday (February 1).

5. *The time*. The winter scene which is described may have been modelled after Fragment 34 of Alcaeus and upon Horace, *Odes*, i, 9. See Mustard, *op. cit.*, p. 22.

11–13. *grides . . . together*, makes grate together. A Shelleyan word.

Bring in great logs and let them lie,
　To make a solid core of heat;
　Be cheerful-minded, talk and treat
Of all things ev'n as he were by;   20

We keep the day. With festal cheer,
　With books and music, surely we
　Will drink to him, whate'er he be,
And sing the songs he loved to hear.

CVIII

I will not shut me from my kind,
　And, lest I stiffen into stone,
　I will not eat my heart alone,
Nor feed with sighs a passing wind:

What profit lies in barren faith,   5
　And vacant yearning, tho' with might
　To scale the heaven's highest height,
Or dive below the wells of Death?

What find I in the highest place,
　But mine own phantom chanting hymns?   10
　And on the depths of death there swims
The reflex of a human face.

I'll rather take what fruit may be
　Of sorrow under human skies:
　'Tis held that sorrow makes us wise,   15
Whatever wisdom sleep with thee.

CIX

Heart-affluence in discursive talk
　From household fountains never dry;
　The critic clearness of an eye,
That saw thro' all the Muses' walk;

CVIII. 3. *eat my heart.* The figure is classical; see Mustard, *op. cit.,*
p. 145. Compare Spenser, *The Faerie Queene,* I, ii, 6: "He . . . did his
stout heart eat."

Seraphic intellect and force   5
    To seize and throw the doubts of man;
    Impassion'd logic, which outran
The hearer in its fiery course;

High nature amorous of the good,
    But touch'd with no ascetic gloom;   10
    And passion pure in snowy bloom
Thro' all the years of April blood;

A love of freedom rarely felt,
    Of freedom in her regal seat
    Of England; not the schoolboy heat,   15
The blind hysterics of the Celt;

And manhood fused with female grace
    In such a sort, the child would twine
    A trustful hand, unask'd, in thine,
And find his comfort in thy face;   20

All these have been, and thee mine eyes
    Have look'd on: if they look'd in vain,
    My shame is greater who remain,
Nor let thy wisdom make me wise.

                              CX

Thy converse drew us with delight,
    The men of rathe and riper years:
    The feeble soul, a haunt of fears,
Forgot his weakness in thy sight.

CIX. 16. Compare CXXVII, 7, and the "Conclusion" of *The Princess*
where Tennyson contrasts Britain, a nation having a sense of duty, a
reverence for laws, patient force and civic manhood, with France:

> But yonder, whiff! there comes a sudden heat,
> The gravest citizen seems to lose his head,
> The king is scared, the soldier will not fight,
> The little boys begin to shoot and stab,
> A kingdom topples over with a shriek
> Like an old woman, and down rolls the world
> In mock heroics —

and so on, in the poet's most complacently British manner.

CX. 2. *rathe,* early.

On thee the loyal-hearted hung,   5
   The proud was half disarm'd of pride,
   Nor cared the serpent at thy side
To flicker with his double tongue.

The stern were mild when thou wert by,
   The flippant put himself to school   10
   And heard thee, and the brazen fool
Was soften'd, and he knew not why;

While I, thy nearest, sat apart,
   And felt thy triumph was as mine;
   And loved them more, that they were thine,   15
The graceful tact, the Christian art;

Nor mine the sweetness or the skill,
   But mine the love that will not tire,
   And, born of love, the vague desire
That spurs an imitative will.   20

CXI

The churl in spirit, up or down
   Along the scale of ranks, thro' all,
   To him who grasps a golden ball,
By blood a king, at heart a clown;

The churl in spirit, howe'er he veil   5
   His want in forms for fashion's sake,
   Will let his coltish nature break
At seasons thro' the gilded pale:

For who can always act? but he,
   To whom a thousand memories call,   ·   10
   Not being less but more than all
The gentleness he seem'd to be,

Best seem'd the thing he was, and join'd
   Each office of the social hour
   To noble manners, as the flower   15
And native growth of noble mind;

---

   8. *double tongue.* 1850: "triple tongue," a reading further from nature but nearer Virgil's "linguis . . . trisulcis" (*Georgics,* iii, 439, and *Aeneid,* ii, 475).

Nor ever narrowness or spite,
    Or villain fancy fleeting by,
    Drew in the expression of an eye,
Where God and Nature met in light;   20

And thus he bore without abuse
    The grand old name of gentleman,
    Defamed by every charlatan,
And soil'd with all ignoble use.

CXII

High wisdom holds my wisdom less,
    That I, who gaze with temperate eyes
    On glorious insufficiencies,
Set light by narrower perfectness.

But thou, that fillest all the room   5
    Of all my love, art reason why
    I seem to cast a careless eye
On souls, the lesser lords of doom.

For what wert thou? some novel power
    Sprang up for ever at a touch,   10
    And hope could never hope too much,
In watching thee from hour to hour,

Large elements in order brought,
    And tracts of calm from tempest made,
    And world-wide fluctuation sway'd   15
In vassal tides that follow'd thought.

CXIII

'Tis held that sorrow makes us wise;
    Yet how much wisdom sleeps with thee
    Which not alone had guided me,
But served the seasons that may rise!

CXII. Bradley's interpretation (*op. cit.,* pp. 207 f.) of this obscure poem is the most convincing. The poet rejects both "glorious insufficiencies" (men of splendid but unevenly developed powers) and "narrower perfectness" (men of smaller powers but fully developed), because his friend had the virtues of each and the defects of neither type.

For can I doubt, who knew thee keen   5
   In intellect, with force and skill
   To strive, to fashion, to fulfil? —
I doubt not what thou wouldst have been:

A life in civic action warm,
   A soul on highest mission sent,   10
   A potent voice of Parliament,
A pillar steadfast in the storm,

Should licensed boldness gather force,
   Becoming, when the time has birth,
   A lever to uplift the earth   15
And roll it in another course,

With thousand shocks that come and go,
   With agonies, with energies,
   With overthrowings, and with cries,
And undulations to and fro.   20

CXIV

Who loves not Knowledge?   Who shall rail
   Against her beauty?   May she mix
   With men and prosper!   Who shall fix
Her pillars?   Let her work prevail.

But on her forehead sits a fire: 5
   She sets her forward countenance
   And leaps into the future chance,
Submitting all things to desire.

Half-grown as yet, a child, and vain —
   She cannot fight the fear of death.   10
   What is she, cut from love and faith,
But some wild Pallas from the brain

CXIV. 4. *pillars.* The commentators derive the image from the
Pillars of Hercules (*i.e.,* boundaries, limits); but Tennyson himself
(*Works,* Eversley edition, ii, 581) cited Proverbs, ix, 1: "Wisdom hath
builded her house, she hath hewn out her seven pillars."

Of Demons? fiery-hot to burst
  All barriers in her onward race
  For power. Let her know her place;   15
She is the second, not the first.

A higher hand must make her mild,
  If all be not in vain; and guide
  Her footsteps, moving side by side
With Wisdom, like the younger child: 20

For she is earthly of the mind,
  But Wisdom heavenly of the soul.
  O friend, who camest to thy goal
So early, leaving me behind,

I would the great world grew like thee,   25
  Who grewest not alone in power
  And knowledge, but by year and hour
In reverence and in charity.

CXV

Now fades the last long streak of snow,
  Now burgeons every maze of quick
  About the flowering squares, and thick
By ashen roots the violets blow.

Now rings the woodland loud and long,   5
  The distance takes a lovelier hue,
  And drown'd in yonder living blue
The lark becomes a sightless song.

Now dance the lights on lawn and lea,
  The flocks are whiter down the vale,   10
  And milkier every milky sail
On winding stream or distant sea;

21–2. Compare the distinction between knowledge and Wisdom expounded by Raphael to Adam, *Paradise Lost,* vii, 126 f. Compare also "Locksley Hall," l. 141: "Knowledge comes, but Wisdom lingers."

CXV. 8. *a sightless song.* Compare Wordsworth, "To a Skylark": "A privacy of glorious light is thine." So Goethe describes the lark as "in dem blauen Raum verloren" ("An die Entfernte").

Where now the seamew pipes, or dives
  In yonder greening gleam, and fly
  The happy birds, that change their sky   15
To build and brood; that live their lives

From land to land; and in my breast
  Spring wakens too; and my regret
  Becomes an April violet,
And buds and blossoms like the rest.   20

CXVI

Is it, then, regret for buried time
  That keenlier in sweet April wakes,
  And meets the year, and gives and takes
The colours of the crescent prime?

Not all: the songs, the stirring air,   5
  The life re-orient out of dust,
  Cry thro' the sense to hearten trust
In that which made the world so fair.

Not all regret: the face will shine
  Upon me, while I muse alone;   10
  And that dear voice, I once have known,
Still speak to me of me and mine:

Yet less of sorrow lives in me
  For days of happy commune dead;
  Less yearning for the friendship fled,   15
Than some strong bond which is to be.

CXVII

O days and hours, your work is this,
  To hold me from my proper place,
  A little while from his embrace,
For fuller gain of after bliss:

---

15. *change their sky.* Compare Horace, *Epodes,* I, xi, 27: "Coelum
. . . mutant."

  CXVI.   11–12.   1850:

      The dear, dear voice that I have known
      Will speak . . .

That out of distance might ensue   5
  Desire of nearness doubly sweet;
  And unto meeting when we meet,
Delight a hundredfold accrue,

For every grain of sand that runs,
  And every span of shade that steals,   10
  And every kiss of toothed wheels,
And all the courses of the suns.

CXVIII

Contemplate all this work of Time,
  The giant labouring in his youth;
  Nor dream of human love and truth,
As dying Nature's earth and lime;

But trust that those we call the dead   5
  Are breathers of an ampler day
  For ever nobler ends. They say,
The solid earth whereon we tread

In tracts of fluent heat began,
  And grew to seeming-random forms,   10
  The seeming prey of cyclic storms,
Till at the last arose the man;

Who throve and branch'd from clime to clime,
  The herald of a higher race,
  And of himself in higher place,   15
If so he type this work of time

CXVII. 10. Compare Shakespeare, *Sonnets,* lxxvii: "Thy dial's shady stealth." There are reminiscences of *Sonnets,* lvi and lix in this section.

CXVIII. 6. *an ampler day.* Compare Wordsworth, *Laodamia:* "An ampler ether, a diviner air." Both phrases are reminiscent of Virgil's "largior aether," *Aeneid,* vi, 640.

9. The nebular hypothesis.

11. *cyclic storms,* periodic cataclysms. Tennyson perhaps had in mind Cuvier's Theory of Catastrophes.

16. *type,* represent.

Within himself, from more to more;
  Or, crown'd with attributes of woe
  Like glories, move his course, and show
That life is not as idle ore,   20

But iron dug from central gloom,
  And heated hot with burning fears,
  And dipt in baths of hissing tears,
And batter'd with the shocks of doom

To shape and use. Arise and fly   25
  The reeling Faun, the sensual feast;
  Move upward, working out the beast
And let the ape and tiger die.

CXIX

Doors, where my heart was used to beat
  So quickly, not as one that weeps
  I come once more; the city sleeps;
I smell the meadow in the street;

I hear a chirp of birds; I see   5
  Betwixt the black fronts long-withdrawn
  A light-blue lane of early dawn,
And think of early days and thee,

And bless thee, for thy lips are bland,
  And bright the friendship of thine eye;   10
  And in my thoughts with scarce a sigh
I take the pressure of thine hand.

CXX

I trust I have not wasted breath:
  I think we are not wholly brain,
  Magnetic mockeries; not in vain,
Like Paul with beasts, I fought with Death;

CXIX. Another visit to the house in Wimpole Street. Contrast VII.

4. Farmers bringing their produce to the London markets in the early morning.

CXX. 4. 1 Corinthians, xv, 32.

Not only cunning casts in clay: 5
    Let Science prove we are, and then
    What matters Science unto men,
At least to me? I would not stay.

Let him, the wiser man who springs
    Hereafter, up from childhood shape   10
    His action like the greater ape,
But I was *born* to other things.

CXXI

Sad Hesper o'er the buried sun
    And ready, thou, to die with him,
    Thou watchest all things ever dim
And dimmer, and a glory done:

The team is loosen'd from the wain,   5
    The boat is drawn upon the shore;
    Thou listenest to the closing door,
And life is darken'd in the brain.

Bright Phosphor, fresher for the night,
    By thee the world's great work is heard   10
    Beginning, and the wakeful bird;
Behind thee comes the greater light:

The market boat is on the stream,
    And voices hail it from the brink;
    Thou hear'st the village hammer clink,   15
And see'st the moving of the team.

Sweet Hesper-Phosphor, double name
    For what is one, the first, the last,
    Thou, like my present and my past,
Thy place is changed; thou art the same.   20

---

12. *born*. In the early editions the word was not italicized. It is not
clear why Tennyson laid special emphasis upon it. See Bradley, *op. cit.,*
p. 217.

CXXI. Compare Shelley's translation of the epigram attributed to
Plato: "Thou wert the morning star among the living."

CXXII

Oh, wast thou with me, dearest, then,
    While I rose up against my doom,
    And yearn'd to burst the folded gloom,
To bare the eternal Heavens again,

To feel once more, in placid awe,   5
    The strong imagination roll
    A sphere of stars about my soul,
In all her motion one with law;

If thou wert with me, and the grave
    Divide us not, be with me now,   10
    And enter in at breast and brow
Till all my blood, a fuller wave,

Be quicken'd with a livelier breath,
    And like an inconsiderate boy,
    As in the former flash of joy,   15
I slip the thoughts of life and death;

And all the breeze of Fancy blows,
    And every dew-drop paints a bow,
    The wizard lightnings deeply glow,
And every thought breaks out a rose.   20

CXXIII

There rolls the deep where grew the tree.
    O earth, what changes hast thou seen!
    There where the long street roars hath been
The stillness of the central sea.

CXXII. The problem of the identification of the occasions here referred
to when the poet was conscious of the presence of the spirit of his friend
occupies seven pages of Bradley's *Commentary*. Compare LXXXVI and
XCV.

CXXIII. Compare Job, xiv, 11, 18, 19; and 2 *Henry IV*, III, i, 45 f.
But Tennyson's interest in geology and his own observation of the en-
croachments of the sea along the east coast of England (compare Swinburne's "By the North Sea") have influenced this section quite as much
as literary reminiscences.

The hills are shadows, and they flow   5
     From form to form, and nothing stands;
     They melt like mist, the solid lands,
Like clouds they shape themselves and go.

But in my spirit will I dwell,
     And dream my dream, and hold it true;   10
     For tho' my lips may breathe adieu,
I cannot think the thing farewell.

CXXIV

That which we dare invoke to bless;
     Our dearest faith; our ghastliest doubt;
     He, They, One, All; within, without;
The Power in darkness whom we guess;

I found Him not in world or sun,   5
     Or eagle's wing, or insect's eye;
     Nor thro' the questions men may try,
The petty cobwebs we have spun:

If e'er when faith had fall'n asleep,
     I heard a voice, 'Believe no more'   10
     And heard an ever-breaking shore
That tumbled in the Godless deep;

A warmth within the breast would melt
     The freezing reason's colder part,
     And like a man in wrath the heart   15
Stood up and answer'd, 'I have felt.'

No, like a child in doubt and fear:
     But that blind clamour made me wise;
     Then was I as a child that cries,
But, crying, knows his father near;   20

CXXIV. With this section, which most readers will probably consider the most impressive in the poem, compare "Akbar's Dream" and "The Ancient Sage."

17–20. Compare George Herbert, "The Collar":

     But as I raved and grew more fierce and wild
         At every word,
     Methought I heard one calling 'Child':
         And I replied, 'My Lord.'

And what I am beheld again
　　What is, and no man understands;
　　And out of darkness came the hands
That reach thro' nature, moulding men.

CXXV

Whatever I have said or sung,
　　Some bitter notes my harp would give,
　　Yea, tho' there often seem'd to live
A contradiction on the tongue,

Yet Hope had never lost her youth;   5
　　She did but look through dimmer eyes;
　　Or Love but play'd with gracious lies,
Because he felt so fix'd in truth:

And if the song were full of care,
　　He breathed the spirit of the song;   10
　　And if the words were sweet and strong
He set his royal signet there;

Abiding with me till I sail
　　To seek thee on the mystic deeps,
　　And this electric force, that keeps   15
A thousand pulses dancing, fail.

CXXVI

Love is and was my Lord and King,
　　And in his presence I attend
　　To hear the tidings of my friend,
Which every hour his couriers bring.

Love is and was my King and Lord,   5
　　And will be, tho' as yet I keep
　　Within his court on earth, and sleep
Encompass'd by his faithful guard,

CXXVI. 3–4. Compare George Herbert, "Holy Communion":
　　　Those to spirits refined at door attend
　　　Despatches from their friend.

And hear at times a sentinel
　　Who moves about from place to place,　　　　10
　　And whispers to the worlds of space,
In the deep night, that all is well.

CXXVII

And all is well, tho' faith and form
　　Be sunder'd in the night of fear;
　　Well roars the storm to those that hear
A deeper voice across the storm,

Proclaiming social truth shall spread,　　　　5
　　And justice, ev'n tho' thrice again
　　The red fool-fury of the Seine
Should pile her barricades with dead.

But ill for him that wears a crown,
　　And him, the lazar, in his rags:　　　　10
　　They tremble, the sustaining crags;
The spires of ice are toppled down,

And molten up, and roar in flood;
　　The fortress crashes from on high,
　　The brute earth lightens to the sky,　　　　15
And the great Æon sinks in blood,

And compass'd by the fires of Hell;
　　While thou, dear spirit, happy star,
　　O'erlook'st the tumult from afar,
And smilest, knowing all is well.　　　　20

CXXVII. 6–8. Tennyson said that these lines did not refer to the Revolution of 1848 for they were "probably written long before." But "probably" indicates some uncertainty; and the phrase "thrice again" suggests the revolutionary years 1789, 1830, and 1848. See note on CIX, 16.

15. *brute earth.* Horace's "bruta tellus," *Odes,* I, xxxiv, 9.

CXXVIII

The love that rose on stronger wings,
    Unpalsied when he met with Death,
    Is comrade of the lesser faith
That sees the course of human things.

No doubt vast eddies in the flood   5
    Of onward time shall yet be made,
    And throned races may degrade;
Yet O ye mysteries of good,

Wild Hours that fly with Hope and Fear,
    If all your office had to do   10
    With old results that look like new;
If this were all your mission here,

To draw, to sheathe a useless sword,
    To fool the crowd with glorious lies,
    To cleave a creed in sects and cries,   15
To change the bearing of a word,

To shift an arbitrary power,
    To cramp the student at his desk,
    To make old bareness picturesque,
And tuft with grass a feudal tower;   20

Why then my scorn might well descend
    On you and yours. I see in part
    That all, as in some piece of art,
Is toil coöperant to an end.

CXXIX

Dear friend, far off, my lost desire,
    So far, so near in woe and weal;
    O loved the most, when most I feel
There is a lower and a higher;

CXXVIII. 3. *lesser*. Faith in human progress is "lesser" than faith in immortality because it contends with no obstacle so formidable as death.

5–7. Compare "Locksley Hall Sixty Years After":

Forward then, but still remember how the course of Time will swerve,
Crook and turn upon itself in many a backward streaming curve.

Known and unknown; human, divine;   5
  Sweet human hand and lips and eye;
  Dear heavenly friend that canst not die,
Mine, mine, for ever, ever mine;

Strange friend, past, present, and to be;
  Loved deeplier, darklier understood;   10
  Behold, I dream a dream of good,
And mingle all the world with thee.

CXXX

Thy voice is on the rolling air;
  I hear thee where the waters run;
  Thou standest in the rising sun,
And in the setting thou art fair.

What art thou then?   I cannot guess;   5
  But tho' I seem in star and flower
  To feel thee some diffusive power,
I do not therefore love thee less:

My love involves the love before;
  My love is vaster passion now;   10
  Tho' mix'd with God and Nature thou,
I seem to love thee more and more.

Far off thou art, but ever nigh;
  I have thee still, and I rejoice;
  I prosper, circled with thy voice;   15
I shall not lose thee tho' I die.

CXXXI

O living will that shalt endure
  When all that seems shall suffer shock,
  Rise in the spiritual rock,
Flow thro' our deeds and make them pure,

CXXX. Compare and contrast Shelley, *Adonais,* xlii and xliii. But Tennyson does not express the pantheism of Shelley, for the spirit of Hallam remains individual and the object of a personal affection.

CXXXI. 1. *O living will.* Not, Tennyson explained (*Memoir,* i, 319), the Divine Will but "that which we know as Free-will, the higher and enduring part of man." But compare *Memoir,* i, 316, and the poem "Will."

That we may lift from out of dust   5
    A voice as unto him that hears,
    A cry above the conquer'd years
To one that with us works, and trust,

With faith that comes of self-control,
    The truths that never can be proved   10
    Until we close with all we loved,
And all we flow from, soul in soul.

———

O true and tried, so well and long,
    Demand not thou a marriage lay;
    In that it is thy marriage day
Is music more than any song.

Nor have I felt so much of bliss   5
    Since first he told me that he loved
    A daughter of our house; nor proved
Since that dark day a day like this;

Tho' I since then have number'd o'er
    Some thrice three years: they went and came,   10
    Remade the blood and changed the frame,
And yet is love not less, but more;

No longer caring to embalm
    In dying songs a dead regret,
    But like a statue solid-set,   15
And moulded in colossal calm.

———

5. *the spiritual rock.* I Corinthians, x, 4.

Epilogue. This epithalamium was written on the occasion of the marriage of Edmund Lushington to the poet's sister Cecilia, October 10, 1842. Its appropriateness here has been questioned, some critics holding that *In Memoriam* is brought to a perfect conclusion with CXXXI. But Tennyson pointed out that the poem was "a sort of *Divine Comedy,* ending in happiness," beginning with a funeral and ending with a marriage. The union of his sister and his friend is the type of hope of that higher race of man foreshadowed in Hallam.

9–10. The nine years from 1833 to 1842.

Regret is dead, but love is more
  Than in the summers that are flown,
  For I myself with these have grown
To something greater than before;   20

Which makes appear the songs I made
  As echoes out of weaker times,
  As half but idle brawling rhymes,
The sport of random sun and shade.

But where is she, the bridal flower,   25
  That must be made a wife ere noon?
  She enters, glowing like the moon
Of Eden on its bridal bower:

On me she bends her blissful eyes
  And then on thee; they meet thy look   30
  And brighten like the star that shook
Betwixt the palms of paradise.

O when her life was yet in bud,
  He too foretold the perfect rose.
  For thee she grew, for thee she grows   35
For ever, and as fair as good.

And thou art worthy; full of power;
  As gentle; liberal-minded, great,
  Consistent; wearing all that weight
Of learning lightly like a flower.   40

But now set out: the noon is near,
  And I must give away the bride;
  She fears not, or with thee beside
And me behind her will not fear:

For I that danced her on my knee,   45
  That watch'd her on her nurse's arm,
  That shielded all her life from harm
At last must part with her to thee;

Now waiting to be made a wife,
    Her feet, my darling, on the dead;   50
    Their pensive tablets round her head,
And the most living words of life

Breathed in her ear.   The ring is on,
    The 'wilt thou' answer'd, and again
    The 'wilt thou' ask'd, till out of twain   55
Her sweet 'I will' has made you one.

Now sign your names, which shall be read,
    Mute symbols of a joyful morn,
    By village eyes as yet unborn;
The names are sign'd, and overhead   60

Begins the clash and clang that tells
    The joy to every wandering breeze;
    The blind wall rocks, and on the trees
The dead leaf trembles to the bells.

O happy hour, and happier hours   65
    Await them.   Many a merry face
    Salutes them — maidens of the place,
That pelt us in the porch with flowers.

O happy hour, behold the bride
    With him to whom her hand I gave.   70
    They leave the porch, they pass the grave
That has to-day its sunny side.

To-day the grave is bright for me,
    For them the light of life increased,
    Who stay to share the morning feast,   75
Who rest to-night beside the sea.

Let all my genial spirits advance
    To meet and greet a whiter sun;
    My drooping memory will not shun
The foaming grape of eastern France.   80

_____

52. The words of the Marriage Service.
78. *a whiter sun.* Catullus, viii, 3: "candidi . . . soles."

It circles round, and fancy plays,
    And hearts are warm'd and faces bloom,
    As drinking health to bride and groom
We wish them store of happy days.

Nor count me all to blame if I   85
    Conjecture of a stiller guest,
    Perchance, perchance, among the rest,
And, tho' in silence, wishing joy.

But they must go, the time draws on,
    And those white-favour'd horses wait;   90
    They rise, but linger; it is late;
Farewell, we kiss, and they are gone.

A shade falls on us like the dark
    From little cloudlets on the grass,
    But sweeps away as out we pass   95
To range the woods, to roam the park,

Discussing how their courtship grew,
    And talk of others that are wed,
    And how she look'd, and what he said,
And back we come at fall of dew.   100

Again the feast, the speech, the glee,
    The shade of passing thought, the wealth
    Of words and wit, the double health,
The crowning cup, the three-times-three,

And last the dance; — till I retire: 105
    Dumb is that tower which spake so loud,
    And high in heaven the streaming cloud,
And on the downs a rising fire:

And rise, O moon, from yonder down,
    Till over down and over dale   110
    All night the shining vapour sail
And pass the silent-lighted town,

The white-faced halls, the glancing rills,
  And catch at every mountain head,
  And o'er the friths that branch and spread   115
Their sleeping silver thro' the hills;

And touch with shade the bridal doors,
  With tender gloom the roof, the wall;
  And breaking let the splendour fall
To spangle all the happy shores   120

By which they rest, and ocean sounds,
  And, star and system rolling past,
  A soul shall draw from out the vast
And strike his being into bounds,

And, moved thro' life of lower phase,   125
  Result in man, be born and think,
  And act and love, a closer link
Betwixt us and the crowning race

Of those that, eye to eye, shall look
  On knowledge; under whose command   130
  Is Earth and Earth's, and in their hand
Is Nature like an open book;

No longer half-akin to brute,
  For all we thought and loved and did,
  And hoped, and suffer'd, is but seed   135
Of what in them is flower and fruit;

Whereof the man, that with me trod
  This planet, was a noble type
  Appearing ere the times were ripe,
That friend of mine who lives in God,   140

That God, which ever lives and loves,
  One God, one law, one element,
  And one far-off divine event,
To which the whole creation moves.

---

125. The image is drawn from the phenomenon of "recapitulation,"
the stages of life in the embryo which appear to represent lower forms of
animal life.

IN THE VALLEY OF CAUTERETZ[1]

ALL along the valley, stream that flashest white,
Deepening thy voice with the deepening of the night,
All along the valley, where thy waters flow,
I walk'd with one I loved two and thirty years ago.
All along the valley, while I walk'd to-day,   5
The two and thirty years were a mist that rolls away;
For all along the valley, down thy rocky bed,
Thy living voice to me was as the voice of the dead,
And all along the valley, by rock and cave and tree,
The voice of the dead was a living voice to me.   10

ODE ON THE DEATH OF THE DUKE OF WELLINGTON[1]

I

BURY the Great Duke,
  With an empire's lamentation,
Let us bury the Great Duke
  To the noise of the mourning of a mighty nation,
Mourning when their leaders fall,   5
Warriors carry the warrior's pall,
And sorrow darkens hamlet and hall.

---

[1] Tennyson, who had visited Cauteretz in the Pyrenees with Arthur Hallam in 1830, revisited it for the first time in the summer of 1861; and after hearing the torrent rushing over its rocky bed and falling in cataracts, he wrote this lyric in memory of his earlier visit (*Memoir*, i, 474). It was published in the *Enoch Arden* volume, 1864.

6. Actually it had been thirty-one years before; but Tennyson, though characteristically rendered uneasy by this small inaccuracy, refrained, probably for the sake of euphony, from altering the line.

---

[1] The Duke of Wellington died on September 14, 1852; the state funeral did not take place till November 18. In the meantime Tennyson composed his "Ode" which was published in pamphlet form on the day of the funeral. Considerably revised, it reappeared as another pamphlet in 1853; and it was somewhat retouched before the final version was published in the *Maud* volume of 1855. The chief variants are noted below. Compare Rossetti's poem, "Wellington's Funeral." For a description of the funeral, written in an appropriately flamboyant style, see Philip Guedalla, *Wellington*, 1931, pp. 477 f.

1. Here, as in "Break, Break, Break," there is an audible echo of the rhythm of the Dead March in *Saul*. See line 267.

5. 1852: "When laurel-garlanded leaders fall."

II

Where shall we lay the man whom we deplore?
Here, in streaming London's central roar.
Let the sound of those he wrought for,   10
And the feet of those he fought for,
Echo round his bones for evermore.

III

Lead out the pageant: sad and slow,
As fits an universal woe,
Let the long long procession go,   15
And let the sorrowing crowd about it grow,
And let the mournful martial music blow;
The last great Englishman is low.

IV

Mourn, for to us he seems the last,
Remembering all his greatness in the Past.   20
No more in soldier fashion will he greet
With lifted hand the gazer in the street.
O friends, our chief state-oracle is mute:
Mourn for the man of long-enduring blood,
The statesman-warrior, moderate, resolute,   25
Whole in himself, a common good.
Mourn for the man of amplest influence,
Yet clearest of ambitious crime,
Our greatest yet with least pretence,
Great in council and great in war,   30
Foremost captain of his time,
Rich in saving common-sense,
And, as the greatest only are,
In his simplicity sublime.

---

8. After this line in 1853: "He died on Walmer's lonely shore."
Walmer Castle, on the Kentish coast, was Wellington's residence as Lord
Warden of the Cinque Ports.

9. This line was added in 1853.

20. 1852: "Our sorrow draws but on the golden Past."

21-2. Not in 1852; added 1853.

26. *Whole in himself.* Compare Horace, *Satires,* ii, 7, 78: "In se ipso
totus."

O good gray head which all men knew,   35
O voice from which their omens all men drew,
O iron nerve to true occasion true,
O fall'n at length that tower of strength
Which stood four-square to all the winds that blew!
Such was he whom we deplore.   40
The long self-sacrifice of life is o'er.
The great World-victor's victor will be seen no more.

                                  v

All is over and done:
Render thanks to the Giver,
England, for thy son.
Let the bell be toll'd.   45
Render thanks to the Giver,
And render him to the mould.
Under the cross of gold
That shines over city and river,   50
There he shall rest for ever
Among the wise and the bold.
Let the bell be toll'd:
And a reverent people behold
The towering car, the sable steeds: 55
Bright let it be with its blazon'd deeds,
Dark in its funeral fold.
Let the bell be toll'd:
And a deeper knell in the heart be knoll'd;

---

35. This "echo" of Claudian, *De Bello Gothico,* 459 f., had been quoted by Disraeli in a tribute to the Duke of Wellington in the House of Commons, November 15, 1852. This speech, because of a charge of plagiarism, was widely discussed and Tennyson doubtless read it. It seems unlikely, however, that Tennyson borrowed the quotation from Disraeli, for the "Ode" was published only two days after the speech had been reported in the press.

38. For the classical and Biblical parallels see Mustard, *op. cit.,* p. 139.

42. *World-victor,* Napoleon.

49. The cross of St. Paul's Cathedral.

55. *The towering car.* For a description of this "sublime vehicle," "twenty-seven feet of assorted allegory," see Guedalla, *op. cit.,* p. 478. Wellington's victories were inscribed in gold letters on the car.

59. Not in 1852; added 1853.

And the sound of the sorrowing anthem roll'd   60
Thro' the dome of the golden cross;
And the volleying cannon thunder his loss;
He knew their voices of old.
For many a time in many a clime
His captain's-ear has heard them boom   65
Bellowing victory, bellowing doom:
When he with those deep voices wrought,
Guarding realms and kings from shame;
With those deep voices our dead captain taught
The tyrant, and asserts his claim   70
In that dread sound to the great name,
Which he has worn so pure of blame,
In praise and in dispraise the same,
A man of well-temper'd frame.
O civic muse, to such a name,   75
To such a name for ages long,
To such a name,
Preserve a broad approach of fame,
And ever-echoing avenues of song.

VI

Who is he that cometh, like an honour'd guest,   80
With banner and with music, with soldier and with priest,
With a nation weeping, and breaking on my rest?
Mighty Seaman, this is he
Was great by land as thou by sea.
Thine island loves thee well, thou famous man,   85
The greatest sailor since our world began.
Now, to the roll of muffled drums,
To thee the greatest soldier comes;
For this is he
Was great by land as thou by sea;   90
His foes were thine; he kept us free;
O give him welcome, this is he

80–2. The question is asked by Lord Nelson, buried in the crypt of
St. Paul's.

91–113. This passage was heavily revised in the second edition, 1853.
For the version of 1852 see *Works,* Cambridge edition, p. 837.

Worthy of our gorgeous rites,
And worthy to be laid by thee;
For this is England's greatest son,   95
He that gain'd a hundred fights,
Nor ever lost an English gun;
This is he that far away
Against the myriads of Assaye
Clash'd with his fiery few and won;   100
And underneath another sun,
Warring on a later day,
Round affrighted Lisbon drew
The treble works, the vast designs
Of his labour'd rampart-lines,   105
Where he greatly stood at bay,
Whence he issued forth anew,
And ever great and greater grew,
Beating from the wasted vines
Back to France her banded swarms,   110
Back to France with countless blows,
Till o'er the hills her eagles flew
Beyond the Pyrenean pines,
Follow'd up in valley and glen
With blare of bugle, clamour of men,   115
Roll of cannon and clash of arms,
And England pouring on her foes.
Such a war had such a close.
Again their ravening eagle rose
In anger, wheel'd on Europe-shadowing wings,   120
And barking for the thrones of kings;
Till one that sought but Duty's iron crown

96–7. In the speech referred to in the note on l. 35 Disraeli said:
"During that period that can be said of him which can be said of no
other captain — that he captured 3,000 cannon from the enemy, and never
lost a single gun."

99. For Wellington's defeat of the Mahrattas at Assaye, in northern
British India, September 23, 1803, see Guedalla, *op. cit.*, p. 110. Five
thousand Englishmen defeated forty thousand Mahrattas.

104. *The treble works.* The lines of Torres Vedras constructed
around Lisbon in 1809–10.

118. After this line, 1852 and 1853 have a line afterwards suppressed:
"He withdrew to brief repose."

On that loud sabbath shook the spoiler down;
A day of onsets of despair!
Dash'd on every rocky square   125
Their surging charges foam'd themselves away;
Last, the Prussian trumpet blew;
Thro' the long-tormented air
Heaven flash'd a sudden jubilant ray,
And down we swept and charged and overthrew.   130
So great a soldier taught us there,
What long-enduring hearts could do
In that world-earthquake, Waterloo!
Mighty Seaman, tender and true,
And pure as he from taint of craven guile,   135
O saviour of the silver-coasted isle,
O shaker of the Baltic and the Nile,
If aught of things that here befall
Touch a spirit among things divine,
If love of country move thee there at all,   140
Be glad, because his bones are laid by thine!
And thro' the centuries let a people's voice
In full acclaim,
A people's voice,
The proof and echo of all human fame,   145
A people's voice, when they rejoice
At civic revel and pomp and game,
Attest their great commander's claim
With honour, honour, honour, honour to him,
Eternal honour to his name.   150

VII

A people's voice! we are a people yet.
Tho' all men else their nobler dreams forget,
Confused by brainless mobs and lawless Powers;
Thank Him who isled us here, and roughly set
His Briton in blown seas and storming showers,   155
We have a voice, with which to pay the debt
Of boundless love and reverence and regret

---

123. *that loud sabbath.* The battle of Waterloo was fought on Sunday, June 18, 1815.

154-5. Not in 1852; added (with "Saxon" for "Briton") in 1853.

To those great men who fought, and kept it ours.
And keep it ours, O God, from brute control;
O Statesmen, guard us, guard the eye, the soul   160
Of Europe, keep our noble England whole,
And save the one true seed of freedom sown
Betwixt a people and their ancient throne,
That sober freedom out of which there springs
Our loyal passion for our temperate kings;   165
For, saving that, ye help to save mankind
Till public wrong be crumbled into dust,
And drill the raw world for the march of mind,
Till crowds at length be sane and crowns be just.
But wink no more in slothful overtrust.   170
Remember him who led your hosts;
He bade you guard the sacred coasts.
Your cannons moulder on the seaward wall;
His voice is silent in your council-hall
For ever; and whatever tempests lour   175
For ever silent; even if they broke
In thunder, silent; yet remember all
He spoke among you, and the Man who spoke;
Who never sold the truth to serve the hour,
Nor palter'd with Eternal God for power;   180
Who let the turbid streams of rumour flow
Thro' either babbling world of high and low;
Whose life was work, whose language rife
With rugged maxims hewn from life;
Who never spoke against a foe;   185
Whose eighty winters freeze with one rebuke
All great self-seekers trampling on the right:

---

170. After this line 1852 has the following, afterwards suppressed:
        Perchance our greatness will increase;
        Perchance a darkening future yields
        Some reverse from worse to worse,
        The blood of men in quiet fields,
        And sprinkled on the sheaves of peace.

172. For Wellington's opinions on national defence see Guedalla, *op. cit.*, p. 462.

181–2. Not in 1852 or 1853; added 1855.

183–4. Not in 1852; added 1853.

185. Not in 1852 or 1853; added 1855.

Truth-teller was our England's Alfred named;
Truth-lover was our English Duke;
Whatever record leap to light   190
He never shall be shamed.

VIII

Lo, the leader in these glorious wars
Now to glorious burial slowly borne,
Follow'd by the brave of other lands,
He, on whom from both her open hands   195
Lavish Honour shower'd all her stars,
And affluent Fortune emptied all her horn.
Yea, let all good things await
Him who cares not to be great,
But as he saves or serves the state.   200
Not once or twice in our rough island-story,
The path of duty was the way to glory:
He that walks it, only thirsting
For the right, and learns to deaden
Love of self, before his journey closes,   205
He shall find the stubborn thistle bursting
Into glossy purples, which outredden
All voluptuous garden-roses.
Not once or twice in our fair island-story,
The path of duty was the way to glory: 210
He, that ever following her commands,
On with toil of heart and knees and hands,
Thro' the long gorge to the far light has won
His path upward, and prevail'd,
Shall find the toppling crags of Duty scaled   215
Are close upon the shining table-lands
To which our God Himself is moon and sun.
Such was he: his work is done.
But while the races of mankind endure,
Let his great example stand   220
Colossal, seen of every land,

188. "Ælfredus veridicus" in old annals.

215. *crags of Duty.* Compare *Hamlet,* I, iii, 48: "The steep and
thorny way to heaven" and see Mustard, *op. cit.,* pp. 22 f. for classical
parallels.

And keep the soldier firm, the statesman pure:
Till in all lands and thro' all human story
The path of duty be the way to glory:
And let the land whose hearths he saved from shame   225
For many and many an age proclaim
At civic revel and pomp and game,
And when the long-illumined cities flame,
Their ever-loyal iron leader's fame,
With honour, honour, honour, honour to him,   230
Eternal honour to his name.

IX

Peace, his triumph will be sung
By some yet unmoulded tongue
Far on in summers that we shall not see:
Peace, it is a day of pain   235
For one about whose patriarchal knee
Late the little children clung:
O peace, it is a day of pain
For one, upon whose hand and heart and brain
Once the weight and fate of Europe hung.   240
Ours the pain, be his the gain!
More than is of man's degree
Must be with us, watching here
At this, our great solemnity.
Whom we see not we revere;   245
We revere, and we refrain
From talk of battles loud and vain,
And brawling memories all too free
For such a wise humility
As befits a solemn fane: 250
We revere, and while we hear
The tides of Music's golden sea
Setting toward eternity,
Uplifted high in heart and hope are we,
Until we doubt not that for one so true   255
There must be other nobler work to do
Than when he fought at Waterloo,

241. Not in 1852; added 1853.

And Victor he must ever be.
For tho' the Giant Ages heave the hill
And break the shore, and evermore   260
Make and break, and work their will;
Tho' world on world in myriad myriads roll
Round us, each with different powers,
And other forms of life than ours,
What know we greater than the soul?   265
On God and Godlike men we build our trust.
Hush, the Dead March wails in the people's ears:
The dark crowd moves, and there are sobs and tears:
The black earth yawns: the mortal disappears;
Ashes to ashes, dust to dust;   270
He is gone who seem'd so great. —
Gone; but nothing can bereave him
Of the force he made his own
Being here, and we believe him
Something far advanced in State,   275
And that he wears a truer crown
Than any wreath that man can weave him.
Speak no more of his renown,
Lay your earthly fancies down,
And in the vast cathedral leave him,   280
God accept him, Christ receive him.

266–70. Not in 1852; the finest of the additions in 1853.

VIII

PERSONAL AND MEDITATIVE POEMS

THE TWO VOICES[1]

A STILL small voice spake unto me,
'Thou art so full of misery,
Were it not better not to be?'

Then to the still small voice I said:
'Let me not cast in endless shade   5
What is so wonderfully made.'

To which the voice did urge reply:
'To-day I saw the dragon-fly
Come from the wells where he did lie.

'An inner impulse rent the veil   10
Of his old husk: from head to tail
Came out clear plates of sapphire mail.

'He dried his wings: like gauze they grew;
Thro' crofts and pastures wet with dew
A living flash of light he flew.'   15

I said, 'When first the world began,
Young Nature thro' five cycles ran,
And in the sixth she moulded man.

---

[1] Composed in the autumn of 1833 shortly after the death of Hallam, but not published till 1842. In this poem "we have a definite and disturbing picture of Tennyson's panic-stricken bewilderment at the blow that had fallen; . . . a picture of a lonely, frightened spirit crouched broodingly over thoughts of death" (Harold Nicolson). See the detailed analysis and appreciation in Nicolson's *Tennyson*, pp. 125-9.

'She gave him mind, the lordliest
Proportion, and, above the rest,   20
Dominion in the head and breast.'

Thereto the silent voice replied:
'Self-blinded are you by your pride:
Look up thro' night: the world is wide.

'This truth within thy mind rehearse,   25
That in a boundless universe
Is boundless better, boundless worse.

'Think you this mould of hopes and fears
Could find no statelier than his peers
In yonder hundred million spheres?'   30

It spake, moreover, in my mind:
'Tho' thou wert scatter'd to the wind,
Yet is there plenty of the kind.'

Then did my response clearer fall:
'No compound of this earthly ball   35
Is like another, all in all.'

To which he answer'd scoffingly:
'Good soul! suppose I grant it thee,
Who'll weep for thy deficiency?

'Or will one beam be less intense,   40
When thy peculiar difference
Is cancell'd in the world of sense?'

I would have said, 'Thou canst not know,'
But my full heart, that work'd below,
Rain'd thro' my sight its overflow.   45

Again the voice spake unto me:
'Thou art so steep'd in misery,
Surely 'twere better not to be.

---

39. *for thy deficiency*, for want of thee.

'Thine anguish will not let thee sleep,
Nor any train of reason keep: 50
Thou canst not think, but thou wilt weep.'

I said, 'The years with change advance:
If I make dark my countenance,
I shut my life from happier chance.

'Some turn this sickness yet might take,   55
Ev'n yet.' But he: 'What drug can make
A wither'd palsy cease to shake?'

I wept, 'Tho' I should die, I know
That all about the thorn will blow
In tufts of rosy-tinted snow;   60

'And men, thro' novel spheres of thought
Still moving after truth long sought,
Will learn new things when I am not.'

'Yet,' said the secret voice, 'some time,
Sooner or later, will gray prime   65
Make thy grass hoar with early rime.

'Not less swift souls that yearn for light,
Rapt after heaven's starry flight,
Would sweep the tracts of day and night.

'Not less the bee would range her cells,   70
The furzy prickle fire the dells,
The foxglove cluster dappled bells.'

I said that 'all the years invent;
Each month is various to present
The world with some development.   75

'Were this not well, to bide mine hour,
Tho' watching from a ruin'd tower
How grows the day of human power?'

'The highest-mounted mind,' he said,
'Still sees the sacred morning spread   80
The silent summit overhead.

'Will thirty seasons render plain
Those lonely lights that still remain,
Just breaking over land and main?

'Or make that morn, from his cold crown   85
And crystal silence creeping down,
Flood with full daylight glebe and town?

'Forerun thy peers, thy time, and let
Thy feet, millenniums hence, be set
In midst of knowledge, dream'd not yet.   90

'Thou hast not gain'd a real height,
Nor art thou nearer to the light,
Because the scale is infinite.

' 'Twere better not to breathe or speak,
Than cry for strength, remaining weak,   95
And seem to find, but still to seek.

'Moreover, but to seem to find
Asks what thou lackest, thought resign'd,
A healthy frame, a quiet mind.'

I said, 'When I am gone away,   100
"He dared not tarry," men will say,
Doing dishonour to my clay.'

'This is more vile,' he made reply,
'To breathe and loathe, to live and sigh,
Than once from dread of pain to die.   105

'Sick art thou — a divided will
Still heaping on the fear of ill
The fear of men, a coward still.

'Do men love thee?   Art thou so bound
To men, that how thy name may sound   110
Will vex thee lying underground?

'The memory of the wither'd leaf
In endless time is scarce more brief
Than of the garner'd Autumn-sheaf.

'Go, vexed Spirit, sleep in trust;   115
The right ear, that is fill'd with dust,
Hears little of the false or just.'

'Hard task, to pluck resolve,' I cried,
'From emptiness and the waste wide
Of that abyss, or scornful pride!   120

'Nay — rather yet that I could raise
One hope that warm'd me in the days
While still I yearn'd for human praise.

'When, wide in soul and bold of tongue,
Among the tents I paused and sung,   125
The distant battle flash'd and rung.

'I sung the joyful Pæan clear,
And, sitting, burnish'd without fear
The brand, the buckler, and the spear —

'Waiting to strive a happy strife,   130
To war with falsehood to the knife,
And not to lose the good of life —

'Some hidden principle to move,
To put together, part and prove,
And mete the bounds of hate and love —   135

'As far as might be, to carve out
Free space for every human doubt,
That the whole mind might orb about —

'To search thro' all I felt or saw,
The springs of life, the depths of awe,   140
And reach the law within the law:

'At least, not rotting like a weed,
But, having sown some generous seed,
Fruitful of further thought and deed,

'To pass, when Life her light withdraws,   145
Not void of righteous self-applause,
Nor merely in a selfish cause —

'In some good cause, not in mine own,
To perish, wept for, honour'd, known,
And like a warrior overthrown;   150

'Whose eyes are dim with glorious tears,
When soil'd with noble dust, he hears
His country's war-song thrill his ears:

'Then dying of a mortal stroke,
What time the foeman's line is broke,   155
And all the war is roll'd in smoke.'

'Yea!' said the voice, 'thy dream was good,
While thou abodest in the bud.
It was the stirring of the blood.

'If Nature put not forth her power   160
About the opening of the flower,
Who is it that could live an hour?

'Then comes the check, the change, the fall,
Pain rises up, old pleasures pall.
There is one remedy for all.   165

'Yet hadst thou, thro' enduring pain,
Link'd month to month with such a chain
Of knitted purport, all were vain.

'Thou hadst not between death and birth
Dissolved the riddle of the earth.   170
So were thy labour little-worth.

'That men with knowledge merely play'd
I told thee — hardly nigher made,
Tho' scaling slow from grade to grade;

'Much less this dreamer, deaf and blind,   175
Named man, may hope some truth to find,
That bears relation to the mind.

'For every worm beneath the moon
Draws different threads, and late and soon
Spins, toiling out his own cocoon.   180

'Cry, faint not: either Truth is born
Beyond the polar gleam forlorn,
Or in the gateways of the morn.

'Cry, faint not, climb: the summits slope
Beyond the furthest flights of hope,   185
Wrapt in dense cloud from base to cope.

'Sometimes a little corner shines,
As over rainy mist inclines
A gleaming crag with belts of pines.

'I will go forward, sayest thou,   190
I shall not fail to find her now.
Look up, the fold is on her brow.

'If straight thy track, or if oblique,
Thou know'st not. Shadows thou dost strike,
Embracing cloud, Ixion-like;   195

'And owning but a little more
Than beasts, abidest lame and poor,
Calling thyself a little lower

---

192. *the fold.* Tennyson explained that he meant the cloud.
195. Ixion, hoping to embrace a goddess, embraced a cloud.

'Than angels. Cease to wail and brawl!
Why inch by inch to darkness crawl?   200
There is one remedy for all.'

'O dull, one-sided voice,' said I,
'Wilt thou make everything a lie,
To flatter me that I may die?

'I knew that age to age succeeds,   205
Blowing a noise of tongues and deeds,
A dust of systems and of creeds.

'I cannot hide that some have striven,
Achieving calm, to whom was given
The joy that mixes man with Heaven: 210

'Who, rowing hard against the stream,
Saw distant gates of Eden gleam,
And did not dream it was a dream;

'But heard, by secret transport led,
Ev'n in the charnels of the dead,   215
The murmur of the fountain-head —

'Which did accomplish their desire,
Bore and forebore, and did not tire,
Like Stephen, an unquenched fire.

'He heeded not reviling tones,   220
Nor sold his heart to idle moans,
Tho' cursed and scorn'd, and bruised with stones:

'But looking upward, full of grace,
He pray'd, and from a happy place
God's glory smote him on the face.'   225

The sullen answer slid betwixt:
'Not that the grounds of hope were fix'd,
The elements were kindlier mix'd.'

228. Tennyson paraphrased this line: "Some have happier disposi-
tions."

I said, 'I toil beneath the curse,
But, knowing not the universe,   230
I fear to slide from bad to worse.

'And that, in seeking to undo
One riddle, and to find the true,
I knit a hundred others new:

'Or that this anguish fleeting hence,   235
Unmanacled from bonds of sense,
Be fix'd and froz'n to permanence:

'For I go, weak from suffering here:
Naked I go, and void of cheer:
What is it that I may not fear?'   240

'Consider well,' the voice replied,
'His face, that two hours since hath died;
Wilt thou find passion, pain or pride?

'Will he obey when one commands?
Or answer should one press his hands   245
He answers not, nor understands.

'His palms are folded on his breast:
There is no other thing express'd
But long disquiet merged in rest.

'His lips are very mild and meek: 250
Tho' one should smite him on the cheek,
And on the mouth, he will not speak.

'His little daughter, whose sweet face
He kiss'd, taking his last embrace,
Becomes dishonour to her race —   255

'His sons grow up that bear his name,
Some grow to honour, some to shame, —
But he is chill to praise or blame.

'He will not hear the north-wind rave,
Nor, moaning, household shelter crave   260
From winter rains that beat his grave.

'High up the vapours fold and swim:
About him broods the twilight dim:
The place he knew forgetteth him.'

'If all be dark, vague voice,' I said,   265
'These things are wrapt in doubt and dread,
Nor canst thou show the dead are dead.

'The sap dries up; the plant declines.
A deeper tale my heart divines.
Know I not Death? the outward signs?   270

'I found him when my years were few;
A shadow on the graves I knew,
And darkness in the village yew.

'From grave to grave the shadow crept:
In her still place the morning wept: 275
Touch'd by his feet the daisy slept.

'The simple senses crown'd his head:
"Omega! thou art Lord," they said,
"We find no motion in the dead."

'Why, if man rot in dreamless ease,   280
Should that plain fact, as taught by these,
Not make him sure that he shall cease?

'Who forged that other influence,
That heat of inward evidence,
By which he doubts against the sense?   285

'He owns the fatal gift of eyes,
That read his spirit blindly wise,
Not simple as a thing that dies.

277. Tennyson paraphrased this line: "The simple senses made death a king."

'Here sits he shaping wings to fly:
His heart forebodes a mystery: 290
He names the name Eternity.

'That type of Perfect in his mind
In Nature can he nowhere find.
He sows himself on every wind.

'He seems to hear a Heavenly Friend,   295
And thro' thick veils to apprehend
A labour working to an end.

'The end and the beginning vex
His reason: many things perplex,
With motions, checks, and counterchecks. 300

'He knows a baseness in his blood
At such strange war with something good,
He may not do the thing he would.

'Heaven opens inward, chasms yawn,
Vast images in glimmering dawn,   305
Half shown, are broken and withdrawn.

'Ah! sure within him and without,
Could his dark wisdom find it out,
There must be answer to his doubt,

'But thou canst answer not again.   310
With thine own weapon art thou slain,
Or thou wilt answer but in vain.

'The doubt would rest, I dare not solve.
In the same circle we revolve.
Assurance only breeds resolve.'   315

As when a billow, blown against,
Falls back, the voice with which I fenced
A little ceased, but recommenced.

'Where wert thou when thy father play'd
In his free field, and pastime made,   320
A merry boy in sun and shade?

'A merry boy they call'd him then,
He sat upon the knees of men
In days that never come again.

'Before the little ducts began   325
To feed thy bones with lime, and ran
Their course, till thou wert also man:

'Who took a wife, who rear'd his race,
Whose wrinkles gather'd on his face,
Whose troubles number with his days: 330

'A life of nothings, nothing-worth,
From that first nothing ere his birth
To that last nothing under earth!'

'These words,' I said, 'are like the rest;
No certain clearness, but at best   335
A vague suspicion of the breast:

'But if I grant, thou might'st defend
The thesis which thy words intend —
That to begin implies to end;

'Yet how should I for certain hold,   340
Because my memory is so cold,
That I first was in human mould?

'I cannot make this matter plain,
But I would shoot, howe'er in vain,
A random arrow from the brain.   345

'It may be that no life is found,
Which only to one engine bound
Falls off, but cycles always round.

325-6. The process of ossification of the cartilage of the embryo.

'As old mythologies relate,
Some draught of Lethe might await   350
The slipping thro' from state to state.

'As here we find in trances, men
Forget the dream that happens then,
Until they fall in trance again,

'So might we, if our state were such   355
As one before, remember much,
For those two likes might meet and touch.

'But, if I lapsed from nobler place,
Some legend of a fallen race
Alone might hint of my disgrace;   360

'Some vague emotion of delight
In gazing up an Alpine height,
Some yearning toward the lamps of night;

'Or if thro' lower lives I came —
Tho' all experience past became   365
Consolidate in mind and frame —

'I might forget my weaker lot;
For is not our first year forgot?
The haunts of memory echo not.

'And men, whose reason long was blind,   370
From cells of madness unconfined,
Oft lose whole years of darker mind.

'Much more, if first I floated free,
As naked essence, must I be
Incompetent of memory: 375

'For memory dealing but with time,
And he with matter, could she climb
Beyond her own material prime?

'Moreover, something is or seems,
That touches me with mystic gleams,   380
Like glimpses of forgotten dreams —

'Of something felt, like something here;
Of something done, I know not where;
Such as no language may declare.'

The still voice laugh'd.   'I talk,' said he,   385
'Not with thy dreams.   Suffice it thee
Thy pain is a reality.'

'But thou,' said I, 'hast missed thy mark,
Who sought'st to wreck my mortal ark,
By making all the horizon dark.   390

'Why not set forth, if I should do
This rashness, that which might ensue
With this old soul in organs new?

'Whatever crazy sorrow saith,
No life that breathes with human breath   395
Has ever truly long'd for death.

' 'Tis life, whereof our nerves are scant,
Oh life, not death, for which we pant;
More life, and fuller, that I want.'

I ceased, and sat as one forlorn.   400
Then said the voice, in quiet scorn,
'Behold, it is the Sabbath morn.'

And I arose, and I released
The casement, and the light increased
With freshness in the dawning east.   405

397–9. Compare "Ulysses," ll. 24–32.

Like soften'd airs that blowing steal,
When meres begin to uncongeal,
The sweet church bells began to peal.

On to God's house the people prest:
Passing the place where each must rest,   410
Each enter'd like a welcome guest.

One walk'd between his wife and child,
With measured footfall firm and mild,
And now and then he gravely smiled.

The prudent partner of his blood   415
Lean'd on him, faithful, gentle, good,
Wearing the rose of womanhood.

And in their double love secure,
The little maiden walk'd demure,
Pacing with downward eyelids pure.   420

These three made unity so sweet,
My frozen heart began to beat,
Remembering its ancient heat.

I blest them, and they wander'd on:
I spoke, but answer came there none: 425
The dull and bitter voice was gone.

A second voice was at mine ear,
A little whisper silver-clear,
A murmur, 'Be of better cheer.'

As from some blissful neighbourhood,   430
A notice faintly understood,
'I see the end, and know the good.'

A little hint to solace woe,
A hint, a whisper breathing low,
'I may not speak of what I know.'   435

Like an Æolian harp that wakes
No certain air, but overtakes
Far thought with music that it makes:

Such seem'd the whisper at my side:
'What is it thou knowest, sweet voice?' I cried.   440
'A hidden hope,' the voice replied:

So heavenly-toned, that in that hour
From out my sullen heart a power
Broke, like the rainbow from the shower,

To feel, altho' no tongue can prove,   445
That every cloud, that spreads above
And veileth love, itself is love.

And forth into the fields I went,
And Nature's living motion lent
The pulse of hope to discontent.   450

I wonder'd at the bounteous hours,
The slow result of winter showers:
You scarce could see the grass for flowers.

I wonder'd, while I paced along:
The woods were fill'd so full with song,   455
There seem'd no room for sense of wrong;

And all so variously wrought,
I marvell'd how the mind was brought
To anchor by one gloomy thought;

And wherefore rather I made choice   460
To commune with that barren voice,
Than him that said, 'Rejoice! Rejoice!'

THE DAISY

WRITTEN AT EDINBURGH[1]

O LOVE, what hours were thine and mine,
In lands of palm and southern pine;
   In lands of palm, of orange-blossom,
Of olive, aloe, and maize and vine.

What Roman strength Turbìa show'd   5
In ruin, by the mountain road;
   How like a gem, beneath, the city
Of little Monaco, basking, glow'd.

How richly down the rocky dell
The torrent vineyard streaming fell   10
   To meet the sun and sunny waters,
That only heaved with a summer swell.

What slender campanili grew
By bays, the peacock's neck in hue;
   Where, here and there, on sandy beaches   15
A milky-bell'd amaryllis blew.

How young Columbus seem'd to rove,
Yet present in his natal grove,
   Now watching high on mountain cornice,
And steering, now, from a purple cove,   20

---

[1] The tour of northern Italy celebrated in this charming poem was undertaken in the summer of 1851 (*Memoir*, i, 340 f.); the poem was written at Edinburgh in the summer of 1853; and it was published with *Maud* in 1855. Tennyson considered the metre one of the most successful of his inventions and called it "a far-off echo of the Horatian Alcaic." This echo is audible in the feminine ending to the third line of each stanza and in the substitution of a trisyllabic for a disyllabic foot in the third measure of the fourth line.

1. *O Love,* the poet's wife.

5. *Turbia,* or La Turbie, a village two miles from, and fifteen hundred feet above, Monte Carlo, where may be seen the ruins of the "Trophaea Augusti" or "Tower of Augustus," commemorating the subjugation of the Ligurians.

Now pacing mute by ocean's rim;
Till, in a narrow street and dim,
    I stay'd the wheels at Cogoletto,
And drank, and loyally drank to him.

Nor knew we well what pleased us most,   25
Not the clipt palm of which they boast;
    But distant colour, happy hamlet,
A moulder'd citadel on the coast,

Or tower, or high hill-convent, seen
A light amid its olives green;   30
    Or olive-hoary cape in ocean;
Or rosy blossom in hot ravine,

Where oleanders flush'd the bed
Of silent torrents, gravel-spread;
    And, crossing, oft we saw the glisten   35
Of ice, far up on a mountain head.

We loved that hall, tho' white and cold,
Those niched shapes of noble mould,
    A princely people's awful princes,
The grave, severe Genovese of old.   40

At Florence too what golden hours,
In those long galleries, were ours;
    What drives about the fresh Cascinè,
Or walks in Boboli's ducal bowers.

---

23. *Cogoletto,* Cogoleto, a village on the Riviera di Ponente fifteen miles west of Genoa. The tradition that Columbus was born there is erroneous.

37. *that hall,* said by Palgrave (probably on the authority of Tennyson) to refer to the hall of the Palazzo Ducale; but, as Rolfe suggested, the poet's memory may have been confused, for the large hall of the Palazzo di San Giorgio is adorned with twenty-one marble statues of famous Genovese.

43. *Cascine,* the park on the right bank of the Arno on the outskirts of Florence.

44. *Boboli's ducal bowers,* the gardens in the rear of the Pitti Palace.

In bright vignettes, and each complete,   45
Of tower or duomo, sunny-sweet,
   Or palace, how the city glitter'd,
Thro' cypress avenues, at our feet.

But when we crost the Lombard plain
Remember what a plague of rain;   50
   Of rain at Reggio, rain at Parma;
At Lodi, rain, Piacenza, rain.

And stern and sad (so rare the smiles
Of sunlight) look'd the Lombard piles;
   Porch-pillars on the lion resting,   55
And sombre, old, colonnaded aisles.

O Milan, O the chanting quires,
The giant windows' blazon'd fires,
   The height, the space, the gloom, the glory!
A mount of marble, a hundred spires!   60

I climb'd the roofs at break of day
Sun-smitten Alps before me lay.
   I stood among the silent statues,
And statued pinnacles, mute as they.

How faintly-flush'd, how phantom-fair,   65
Was Monte Rosa, hanging there
   A thousand shadowy-pencill'd valleys
And snowy dells in a golden air.

Remember how we came at last
To Como; shower and storm and blast   70
   Had blown the lake beyond his limit,
And all was flooded; and how we past

---

55. As at Modena, Parma, Piacenza, and, most notably, San Zeno at Verona.

57 f. The cathedral at Milan.

From Como, when the light was gray,
And in my head, for half the day,
   The rich Virgilian rustic measure   75
Of Lari Maxume, all the way,

Like ballad-burthen music, kept,
As on the Lariano crept
   To that fair port below the castle
Of Queen Theodolind, where we slept;   80

Or hardly slept, but watch'd awake
A cypress in the moonlight shake,
   The moonlight touching o'er a terrace
One tall Agavè above the lake.

What more? we took our last adieu,   85
And up the snowy Splugen drew,
   But ere we reach'd the highest summit
I pluck'd a daisy, I gave it you.

It told of England then to me,
And now it tells of Italy.   90
   O love, we two shall go no longer
To lands of summer across the sea;

75–6. Lacus Larius was the Latin name for Lake Como (hence the
name "Lariano" of the steamboat, l. 77). The "rustic measure" is that
of the *Georgics*. See ii, 159 f.:

    Anne lacus tantos; te, Lari Maxume, teque
    fluctibus et fremitu adsurgens, Benace, marino

("or [shall I speak] of those mighty lakes; of thee, Larius, the greatest,
and thee, Benacus, heaving with the swell and the roar of the ocean?")

79–80. *that fair port*, Varenna, on the eastern bank of the upper part
of Lake Como. On the heights behind the town is a ruined castle, the
Torre di Vezio, associated in popular tradition with Theodolinda, Queen
of the Lombards (died 628 A.D.). For her story see Gibbon, *Decline
and Fall of the Roman Empire*, Chapter xlv, and compare George Meredith,
"The Song of Queen Theodolinda."

84. *Agavè*, the century-plant.

86. *the Splugen*, an Alpine pass from Chiavenna, north of Lake Como,
to Splügen, in the Rheinwaldthal, Switzerland.

So dear a life your arms enfold
Whose crying is a cry for gold:
   Yet here to-night in this dark city,   95
When ill and weary, alone and cold,

I found, tho' crush'd to hard and dry,
This nurseling of another sky
   Still in the little book you lent me,
And where you tenderly laid it by: 100

And I forgot the clouded Forth,
The gloom that saddens Heaven and Earth,
   The bitter east, the misty summer
And gray metropolis of the North.

Perchance, to lull the throbs of pain,   105
Perchance, to charm a vacant brain,
   Perchance, to dream you still beside me,
My fancy fled to the South again.

THE SAILOR BOY [1]

HE ROSE at dawn and, fired with hope,
   Shot o'er the seething harbour-bar,
And reach'd the ship and caught the rope,
   And whistled to the morning star.

And while he whistled long and loud   5
   He heard a fierce mermaiden cry,
'O boy, tho' thou art young and proud,
   I see the place where thou wilt lie.

---

93. The poet's son Hallam was born August 11, 1852.

104. *gray metropolis of the North*, Edinburgh.

[1] Published in *The Victoria Regia, A Christmas Miscellany*, edited by
Adelaide A. Procter and published by Emily Faithful, 1861. Miss Faithful
had founded a printing establishment in London in which only female
compositors were employed. Thackeray and Lowell were also contribu-
tors to this volume. The poem, somewhat altered, was reprinted in
Enoch Arden, Etc., 1864.

'The sands and yeasty surges mix
    In caves about the dreary bay,   10
And on thy ribs the limpet sticks,
    And in thy heart the scrawl shall play.'

'Fool,' he answer'd, 'death is sure
    To those that stay and those that roam,
But I will nevermore endure   15
    To sit with empty hands at home.

'My mother clings about my neck,
    My sisters crying, "Stay for shame;"
My father raves of death and wreck,
    They are all to blame, they are all to blame.   20

'God help me! save I take my part
    Of danger on the roaring sea,
A devil rises in my heart,
    Far worse than any death to me.'

THE VOYAGE[1]

I

WE LEFT behind the painted buoy
    That tosses at the harbour-mouth;
And madly danced our hearts with joy,
    As fast we fleeted to the South:
How fresh was every sight and sound   5
    On open main or winding shore!
We knew the merry world was round,
    And we might sail for evermore.

II

Warm broke the breeze against the brow,
    Dry sang the tackle, sang the sail: 10
The Lady's-head upon the prow
    Caught the shrill salt, and sheer'd the gale.

---

12. *scrawl*, the young of the dog-crab (Lincolnshire dialect).

[1] Published in *Enoch Arden, Etc.*, 1864. The allegorical intention, barely discernible in "The Sailor Boy," is here obvious. Tennyson summarized it as: "Life is the search after the Ideal."

The broad seas swell'd to meet the keel,
   And swept behind; so quick the run,
We felt the good ship shake and reel,   15
   We seem'd to sail into the Sun!

III

How oft we saw the Sun retire,
   And burn the threshold of the night,
Fall from his Ocean-lane of fire,
   And sleep beneath his pillar'd light!   20
How oft the purple-skirted robe
   Of twilight slowly downward drawn,
As thro' the slumber of the globe
   Again we dash'd into the dawn!

IV

New stars all night above the brim   25
   Of waters lighten'd into view;
They climb'd as quickly, for the rim
   Changed every moment as we flew.
Far ran the naked moon across
   The houseless ocean's heaving field,   30
Or flying shone, the silver boss
   Of her own halo's dusky shield;

V

The peaky islet shifted shapes,
   High towns on hills were dimly seen,
We past long lines of Northern capes   35
   And dewy Northern meadows green.
We came to warmer waves, and deep
   Across the boundless east we drove,
Where those long swells of breaker sweep
   The nutmeg rocks and isles of clove.   40

VI

By peaks that flamed, or, all in shade,
   Gloom'd the low coast and quivering brine
With ashy rains, that spreading made
   Fantastic plume or sable pine;

By sands and steaming flats, and floods   45
   Of mighty mouth, we scudded fast,
And hills and scarlet-mingled woods
   Glow'd for a moment as we past.

VII

O hundred shores of happy climes,
   How swiftly stream'd ye by the bark!   50
At times the whole sea burn'd, at times
   With wakes of fire we tore the dark;
At times a carven craft would shoot
   From havens hid in fairy bowers,
With naked limbs and flowers and fruit,   55
   But we nor paused for fruit nor flowers.

VIII

For one fair Vision ever fled
   Down the waste waters day and night,
And still we follow'd where she led,
   In hope to gain upon her flight.   60
Her face was evermore unseen,
   And fixt upon the far sea-line;
But each man murmur'd, 'O my Queen,
   I follow till I make thee mine.'

IX

And now we lost her, now she gleam'd   65
   Like Fancy made of golden air,
Now nearer to the prow she seem'd
   Like Virtue firm, like Knowledge fair,
Now high on waves that idly burst
   Like Heavenly Hope she crown'd the sea,   70
And now, the bloodless point reversed,
   She bore the blade of Liberty.

X

And only one among us — him
   We pleased not — he was seldom pleased:
He saw not far: his eyes were dim: 75
   But ours he swore were all diseased.

---

51. *the whole sea burn'd,* that is, with phosphorescence.
73 f. The allusion in this stanza is perhaps to Carlyle.

'A ship of fools,' he shriek'd in spite,
    'A ship of fools,' he sneer'd and wept.
And overboard one stormy night
    He cast his body, and on we swept.   80

XI

And never sail of ours was furl'd,
    Nor anchor dropt at eve or morn;
We lov'd the glories of the world,
    But laws of nature were our scorn.
For blasts would rise and rave and cease,   85
    But whence were those that drove the sail
Across the whirlwind's heart of peace,
    And to and thro' the counter gale?

XII

Again to colder climes we came,
    For still we follow'd where she led: 90
Now mate is blind and captain lame,
    And half the crew are sick or dead;
But, blind or lame or sick or sound,
    We follow that which flies before:
We know the merry world is round,   95
    And we may sail for evermore.

"FLOWER IN THE CRANNIED WALL"[1]

FLOWER in the crannied wall,
I pluck you out of the crannies,
I hold you here, root and all, in my hand,
Little flower — but *if* I could understand
What you are, root and all, and all in all,   5
I should know what God and man is.

---

77. *'A ship of fools.'* Sebastian Brandt's satire, *Das Narrenschiff*, was translated into English by Alexander Barclay as *The Ship of Folys of the Worlde*, 1509.

84. That is, the free will of man is not controlled by the laws which govern the material universe.

87. "The calm centre of the whirlwind" (Tennyson).

[1] Written on Hindhead, a hill near Tennyson's home, Aldworth, in Surrey. Published in *The Holy Grail and Other Poems*, 1869.

THE HIGHER PANTHEISM [1]

THE sun, the moon, the stars, the seas, the hills and the plains —
Are not these, O Soul, the Vision of Him who reigns?

Is not the Vision He? tho' He be not that which He seems?
Dreams are true while they last, and do we not live in dreams?

Earth, these solid stars, this weight of body and limb,   5
Are they not sign and symbol of thy division from Him?

Dark is the world to thee: thyself art the reason why;
For is He not all but that which has power to feel 'I am I'?

Glory about thee, without thee; and thou fulfillest thy doom
Making Him broken gleams, and a stifled splendour and
     gloom.   10

Speak to Him thou for He hears, and Spirit with Spirit can
     meet —
Closer is He than breathing, and nearer than hands and feet.

God is law, say the wise; O Soul, and let us rejoice,
For if He thunder by law the thunder is yet His voice.

---

[1] Written in 1867; read at the first meeting of the Metaphysical Society, 1869; and published in the *Holy Grail* volume in the same year. — The distinction Tennyson attempts to draw between his "higher" pantheism and pantheism in the ordinary sense seems to be that while both doctrines teach that God is in the phenomenal universe, the former denies whereas the latter teaches that the phenomenal universe expresses the whole of God. What the Metaphysical Society made of this is not on record; Tennyson was not present at the meeting at which the poem was read. In *The Heptalogia, or the Seven Against Sense*, 1880, Swinburne parodied the obscure and, it must be admitted, somewhat pretentious style in which the poem is written:

One, who is not, we see: but one, whom we see not, is:
Surely this is not that: but that is assuredly this.

What, and wherefore, and whence? for under is over and under:
If thunder could be without lightning, lightning could be without thunder.

Doubt is faith in the main: but faith, on the whole, is doubt:
We cannot believe by proof: but could we believe without?

And so forth. (*Works*, Bonchurch edition, v, 247 f.).

Law is God, say some: no God at all, says the fool;   15
For all we have power to see is a straight staff bent in a pool;

And the ear of man cannot hear, and the eye of man cannot see;
But if we could see and hear, this Vision — were it not He?

VASTNESS [1]

I

MANY a hearth upon our dark globe sighs after many a vanish'd
    face,
Many a planet by many a sun may roll with the dust of a
    vanish'd race.

II

Raving politics, never at rest — as this poor earth's pale history
    runs, —
What is it all but a trouble of ants in the gleam of a million
    million of suns?

III

Lies upon this side, lies upon that side, truthless violence
    mourn'd by the Wise,   5
Thousands of voices drowning his own in a popular torrent
    of lies upon lies;

IV

Stately purposes, valour in battle, glorious annals of army and
    fleet,
Death for the right cause, death for the wrong cause, trumpets
    of victory, groans of defeat;

V

Innocence seethed in her mother's milk, and Charity setting the
    martyr aflame;
Thraldom who walks with the banner of Freedom, and recks
    not to ruin a realm in her name.   10

---

15. *says the fool,* as in Psalms, xiv, 1.

17. I Corinthians, ii, 9.

[1] Published in *Macmillan's Magazine,* November, 1885; reprinted in
expanded form in *Demeter and Other Poems,* 1889.

9. Exodus, xxiii, 19; xxxiv, 26.

VI

Faith at her zenith, or all but lost in the gloom of doubts that
    darken the schools;
Craft with a bunch of all-heal in her hand, follow'd up by her
    vassal legion of fools;

VII

Trade flying over a thousand seas with her spice and her vintage,
    her silk and her corn;
Desolate offing, sailorless harbours, famishing populace, wharves
    forlorn;

VIII

Star of the morning, Hope in the sunrise; gloom of the evening,
    Life at a close;   15
Pleasure who flaunts on her wide downway with her flying
    robe and her poison'd rose;

IX

Pain, that has crawl'd from the corpse of Pleasure, a worm
    which writhes all day, and at night
Stirs up again in the heart of the sleeper, and stings him back
    to the curse of the light;

X

Wealth with his wines and his wedded harlots; honest Poverty,
    bare to the bone;
Opulent Avarice, lean as Poverty; Flattery gilding the rift in
    a throne;   20

XI

Fame blowing out from her golden trumpet a jubilant challenge
    to Time and to Fate;
Slander, her shadow, sowing the nettle on all the laurel'd
    graves of the Great;

13–16. Not in 1885; added 1889.

XII

Love for the maiden, crown'd with marriage, no regrets for
aught that has been,
Household happiness, gracious children, debtless competence,
golden mean;

XIII

National hatreds of whole generations, and pigmy spites of the
village spire;   25
Vows that will last to the last death-ruckle, and vows that are
snapt in a moment of fire;

XIV

He that has lived for the lust of the minute, and died in the
doing it, flesh without mind;
He that has nail'd all flesh to the Cross, till Self died out in
the love of his kind;

XV

Spring and Summer and Autumn and Winter, and all these
old revolutions of earth;
All new-old revolutions of Empire — change of the tide —
what is all of it worth?   30

XVI

What the philosophies, all the sciences, poesy, varying voices
of prayer?
All that is noblest, all that is basest, all that is filthy with all
that is fair?

XVII

What is it all, if we all of us end but in being our own corpse-
coffins at last,
Swallow'd in Vastness, lost in Silence, drown'd in the deeps of
a meaningless Past?

---

24. *golden mean.* Horace's "aurea mediocritas," *Odes,* ii, 10, 5.

XVIII

What but a murmur of gnats in the gloom, or a moment's
    anger of bees in their hive? —   35

*   *   *   *

Peace, let it be! for I loved him, and love him for ever: the
    dead are not dead but alive.

BY AN EVOLUTIONIST[1]

THE Lord let the house of a brute to the soul of a man,
    And the man said, 'Am I your debtor?'
And the Lord — 'Not yet: but make it as clean as you can,
    And then I will let you a better.'

I

If my body come from brutes, my soul uncertain, or a fable, 5
    Why not bask amid the senses while the sun of morning
        shines,
I, the finer brute rejoicing in my hounds, and in my stable,
    Youth and Health, and birth and wealth, and choice of
        women and of wines?

II

What hast thou done for me, grim Old Age, save breaking my
    bones on the rack?
    Would I had past in the morning that looks so bright from
        afar!   10

OLD AGE

Done for thee? starved the wild beast that was linkt with thee
    eighty years back.
    Less weight now for the ladder-of-heaven that hangs on a
        star.

---

36. There is disagreement among the commentators as to whether a
new voice speaks here or the old one in revulsion of feeling. Tennyson's
manuscript annotation is: "What matters anything in this world without
full faith in the Immortality of the Soul and of Love?" (*Memoir*, ii, 343).
Compare his letter to Mrs. Elmhirst on the death of her son (*ibid.*, ii,
105) and Queen Victoria's record of a conversation with the poet in 1883
(*ibid.*, ii, 457). The reference in this last line is almost certainly to
Arthur Hallam. Compare *In Memoriam*, CIII, 15 f.

[1] Published in *Demeter and Other Poems*, 1889.

I

If my body come from brutes, tho' somewhat finer than their
    own,
  I am heir, and this my kingdom. Shall the royal voice be
    mute?
No, but if the rebel subject seek to drag me from the throne, 15
  Hold the sceptre, Human Soul, and rule thy Province of the
    brute.

II

I have climb'd to the snows of Age, and I gaze at a field in the
    Past,
  Where I sank with the body at times in the sloughs of a
    low desire,
But I hear no yelp of the beast, and the Man is quiet at last
  As he stands on the heights of his life with a glimpse of a
    height that is higher.   20

MERLIN AND THE GLEAM[1]

I

O young Mariner,
You from the haven
Under the sea-cliff,
You that are watching
The gray Magician   5
With eyes of wonder,
I am Merlin,
And *I* am dying,
I am Merlin
Who follow The Gleam.   10

---

[1] Published in *Demeter and Other Poems*, 1889. Tennyson's son notes:
"He thought that 'Merlin and the Gleam' would probably be enough of
biography for those friends who urged him to write about himself"
(*Works*, Eversley edition, iv, 598; and see analysis of the poem, *ibid.*,
iv, 594 f.). He had read somewhere that in the legend of Merlin and
Nimuë, Nimuë means the Gleam, which in his poem signifies "the higher
poetic imagination" (*Memoir*, ii, 366).

II

Mighty the Wizard
Who found me at sunrise
Sleeping, and woke me
And learn'd me Magic!
Great the Master,   15
And sweet the Magic,
When over the valley,
In early summers,
Over the mountain,
On human faces,   20
And all around me,
Moving to melody,
Floated The Gleam.

III

Once at the croak of a Raven
    who crost it,
A barbarous people,   25
Blind to the magic,
And deaf to the melody,
Snarl'd at and cursed me.
A demon vext me,
The light retreated,   30
The landskip darken'd,
The melody deaden'd,
The Master whisper'd,
'Follow The Gleam.'

IV

Then to the melody,   35
Over a wilderness

---

16 f. The poems of Tennyson's youth.

25 f. The "barbarous people" who snarl'd at and cursed the poet
represent not only "the harsh voice of those who were unsympathetic"
but more particularly such reviewers as John Wilson and J. W. Croker.

30 f. The almost entire silence of ten years following the ill reception
of the *Poems* of 1832.

35 f. The poems of Tennyson's early maturity, especially those in
which he indulged his "romantic fancy."

Gliding, and glancing at
Elf of the woodland,
Gnome of the cavern,
Griffin and Giant,   40
And dancing of Fairies
In desolate hollows,
And wraiths of the mountain,
And rolling of dragons
By warble of water,   45
Or cataract music
Of falling torrents,
Flitted The Gleam.

v

Down from the mountain
And over the level,   50
And streaming and shining on
Silent river,
Silvery willow,
Pasture and plowland,
Innocent maidens,   55
Garrulous children,
Homestead and harvest,
Reaper and gleaner,
And rough-ruddy faces
Of lowly labour,   60
Slided The Gleam —

vi

Then, with a melody
Stronger and statelier,
Led me at length
To the city and palace   65
Of Arthur the king;
Touch'd at the golden
Cross of the churches,

---

49 f. The English Idyls and other similar poems of country life.
63 f. *The Idylls of the King.*

Flash'd on the Tournament,
Flicker'd and bicker'd   70
From helmet to helmet,
And last on the forehead
Of Arthur the blameless
Rested The Gleam.

VII

Clouds and darkness   75
Closed upon Camelot;
Arthur had vanish'd
I knew not whither,
The king who loved me,
And cannot die;   80
For out of the darkness
Silent and slowly
The Gleam, that had waned
        to a wintry glimmer
On icy fallow
And faded forest,   85
Drew to the valley
Named of the shadow,
And slowly brightening
Out of the glimmer,
And slowly moving again to
        a melody   90
Yearningly tender,
Fell on the shadow,
No longer a shadow,
But clothed with The Gleam.

---

75 f. From the commentary by the poet's son we know that the
"clouds and darkness" were caused by the death of Arthur Hallam with
"the consequent darkening of the whole world for him"; but the
chronology appears to be disarranged, for Hallam's death occurred long
before the publication of the *Idylls*. The meaning is that the loss of his
friend made him almost fail in his early intention to write an Arthurian
epic. The Arthur who had "vanish'd" (l. 77) is not only the legendary
king but Arthur Hallam.

VIII

And broader and brighter   95
The Gleam flying onward,
Wed to the melody,
Sang thro' the world;
And slower and fainter,
Old and weary,   100
But eager to follow,
I saw, whenever
In passing it glanced upon
Hamlet or city,
That under the Crosses   105
The dead man's garden,
The mortal hillock,
Would break into blossom
And so to the land's
Last limit I came ——   110
And can no longer,
But die rejoicing,
For thro' the Magic
Of Him the Mighty,
Who taught me in childhood,   115
There on the border
Of boundless Ocean,
And all but in Heaven
Hovers The Gleam.

IX

Not of the sunlight,   120
Not of the moonlight,
Not of the starlight!
O young Mariner,
Down to the haven,
Call your companions,   125
Launch your vessel,
And crowd your canvas,
And, ere it vanishes
Over the margin,
After it, follow it,   130
Follow The Gleam.

---

95 f. The triumph of Faith over Doubt, as recorded in *In Memoriam*.

THE SILENT VOICES [1]

WHEN the dumb Hour, clothed in black,
Brings the Dreams about my bed,
Call me not so often back,
Silent Voices of the dead,
Toward the lowland ways behind me,   5
And the sunlight that is gone!
Call me rather, silent voices,
Forward to the starry track
Glimmering up the heights beyond me
On, and always on!   10

CROSSING THE BAR [1]

SUNSET and evening star,
  And one clear call for me!
And may there be no moaning of the bar,
  When I put out to sea,

But such a tide as moving seems asleep,   5
  Too full for sound and foam,
When that which drew from out the boundless deep
  Turns again home.

---

[1] This poem, set to a melody in F minor by Lady Tennyson, was sung at the poet's funeral in Westminster Abbey, October 12, 1892, and was printed in the "Order of Service at Lord Tennyson's Funeral." Later in the year it reappeared in the posthumous volume, *The Death of Œnone, Akbar's Dream, and Other Poems.* (It is reprinted here from Tennyson's *Poetical Works,* Globe Edition, by permission of The Macmillan Company.)

---

[1] "Written in my father's eighty-first year, on a day in October [1889] when we came from Aldworth to Farringford. Before reaching Farringford he had the Moaning of the Bar in his mind, and after dinner he showed me this poem written out. I said, 'That is the crown of your life's work.' He answered, 'It came in a moment.' . . . A few days before my father's death he said to me: 'Mind you put "Crossing the Bar" at the end of all editions of my poems' " (*Memoir,* ii, 366 f.). The poem was published in the *Demeter* volume of 1889.

Twilight and evening bell,
  And after that the dark!   10
And may there be no sadness of farewell,
  When I embark;

For tho' from out our bourne of Time and Place
  The flood may bear me far,
I hope to see my Pilot face to face   15
  When I have crost the bar.

APPENDICES

APPENDIX I

JUVENILIA [1]

ANTONY TO CLEOPATRA [2]

O, CLEOPATRA! fare thee well,
    We two can meet no more;
This breaking heart alone can tell
    The love to thee I bore.
But wear not thou the conqueror's chain   5
    Upon thy race and thee;
And though we ne'er can meet again,
    Yet still be true to me:
For I for thee have lost a throne,
To wear the crown of love alone.   10

Fair daughter of a regal line!
    To thraldom bow not tame;
My every wish on earth was thine,
    My every hope the same.

---

[1] In the collected edition of 1884 Tennyson grouped together under this heading some poems from the volumes of 1830 and 1832 (some of which had been suppressed in 1842) together with a few other pieces that had not hitherto been printed in any authorized edition. In the present appendix the term "Juvenilia" is used to embrace some of those so styled by the poet and also a few of the pieces published in 1827 which he never reprinted. For other specimens of his immature adolescent work see *Early Unpublished Poems of Alfred Tennyson,* edited by Charles Tennyson, 1931.

[2] Published in *Poems by Two Brothers,* 1827. When this volume was reprinted by Hallam, Lord Tennyson, in 1893, the editor made use of manuscript notes by his uncle Frederick, assigning, so far as memory served, the different poems to their three (not "two") authors. This address of Antony to Cleopatra is faintly Byronic in tone.

And I have mov'd within thy sphere,   15
    And liv'd within thy light;
And oh! thou wert to me so dear,
    I breath'd but in thy sight!
A subject world I lost for thee,
For thou wert all my world to me!   20

Then when the shriekings of the dying
    Were heard along the wave,
Soul of my soul! I saw thee flying;
    I follow'd thee, to save.
The thunder of the brazen prows   25
    O'er Actium's ocean rung;
Fame's garland faded from my brows,
    Her wreath away I flung.
I sought, I saw, I heard but thee:
For what to love was victory?   30

Thine on the earth, and on the throne,
    And in the grave, am I;
And, dying, still I am thine own,
    Thy bleeding Antony.
How shall my spirit joy to hear   35
    That thou art ever true!
Nay — weep not — dry that burning tear,
    That bathes thine eyes' dark hue.
Shades of my fathers! lo! I come;
I hear your voices from the tomb!   40

HERO TO LEANDER [1]

O go not yet, my love!
    The night is dark and vast;
The white moon is hid in her heaven above,
    And the waves climb high and fast.

---

[1] Published in *Poems, Chiefly Lyrical*, 1830, and afterwards suppressed.
The cadences are Shelleyan rather than Byronic. The poem was perhaps
suggested by Thomas Hood's *Hero and Leander;* it apparently owes nothing to Marlowe's and Leigh Hunt's versions of the story. In form it is
an *aubade* or "dawn song."

O, kiss me, kiss me, once again,   5
 Lest thy kiss should be the last!
O kiss me ere we part;
Grow closer to my heart!
My heart is warmer surely than the bosom of the main.
O joy! O bliss of blisses!   10
 My heart of hearts art thou.
Come bathe me with thy kisses,
 My eyelids and my brow.
Hark how the wild rain hisses,
 And the loud sea roars below.   15

Thy heart beats through thy rosy limbs,
 So gladly doth it stir;
Thine eye in drops of gladness swims.
 I have bathed thee with the pleasant myrrh;
Thy locks are dripping balm;   20
Thou shalt not wander hence tonight,
 I'll stay thee with my kisses.
To-night the roaring brine
 Will rend thy golden tresses;
The ocean with the morrow light   25
Will be both blue and calm;
And the billow will embrace thee with a kiss as soft as mine.
No Western odors wander
 On the black and moaning sea,
And when thou art dead, Leander,   30
 My soul must follow thee!
O go not yet, my love!
 Thy voice is sweet and low;
The deep salt wave breaks in above
 Those marble steps below.   35
The turret-stairs are wet
 That lead into the sea.
Leander! go not yet.
The pleasant stars have set:
O, go not, go not yet,   40
 Or will I follow thee!

ON SUBLIMITY [1]

'The sublime always dwells on great objects and terrible.'

BURKE. [2]

O TELL me not of vales in tenderest green,
    The poplar's shade, the plantane's graceful tree;
Give me the wild cascade, the rugged scene,
    The loud surge bursting o'er the purple sea:
On such sad views my soul delights to pore,   5
    By Teneriffe's peak, or Kilda's giant height,
Or dark Loffoden's melancholy shore,
    What time grey eve is fading into night;
When by that twilight beam I scarce descry
The mingled shades of earth and sea and sky.   10

Give me to wander at midnight alone,
    Through some august cathedral, where, from high,
The cold, clear moon on the mosaic stone
    Comes glancing in gay colours gloriously,
Through windows rich with gorgeous blazonry,   15
    Gilding the niches dim, where, side by side,
Stand antique mitred prelates, whose bones lie
    Beneath the pavement, where their deeds of pride
Were graven, but long since are worn away
By constant feet of ages day by day.   20

Then, as Imagination aids, I hear
    Wild heavenly voices sounding from the quoir,
And more than mortal music meets mine ear,
    Whose long, long notes among the tombs expire,
With solemn rustling of cherubic wings,   25
    Round those vast columns which the roof upbear;

---

[1] Published in *Poems by Two Brothers*, 1827. "The ode to Sublimity
is a cataract of tropical and hyperborean evocation" (Harold Nicolson).

[2] *A Philosophical Inquiry into the Origin of Our Ideas of the Sublime
and Beautiful*, 1756. See especially Part II, Sections ii and vii. But
Burke holds that whatever is terrible is sublime "whether this cause of
terror be endued with greatness of dimensions or not."

While sad and undistinguishable things
    Do flit athwart the moonlit windows there;
And my blood curdles at the chilling sound
Of lone, unearthly steps, that pace the hallow'd ground!   30

I love the starry spangled heav'n, resembling
    A canopy with fiery gems o'erspread,
When the wide loch with silvery sheen is trembling,
    Far stretch'd beneath the mountain's hoary head.
But most I love that sky, when, dark with storms,   35
    It frowns terrific o'er this wilder'd earth,
While the black clouds, in strange and uncouth forms,
    Come hurrying onward in their ruinous wrath;
And shrouding in their deep and gloomy robe
The burning eyes of heav'n and Dian's lucid globe!   40

I love your voice, ye echoing winds, that sweep
    Thro' the wide womb of midnight, when the veil
Of darkness rests upon the mighty deep,
    The labouring vessel, and the shatter'd sail —
Save when the forked bolts of lightning leap   45
    On flashing pinions, and the mariner pale
Raises his eyes to heaven. Oh! who would sleep
    What time the rushing of the angry gale
Is loud upon the waters? — Hail, all hail!
Tempest and clouds and night and thunder's rending peal!   50

All hail, Sublimity! thou lofty one,
    For thou dost walk upon the blast, and gird
Thy majesty with terrors, and thy throne
    Is on the whirlwind, and thy voice is heard
In thunders and in shakings: thy delight   55
    Is in the secret wood, the blasted heath,
The ruin'd fortress, and the dizzy height,
    The grave, the ghastly charnel-house of death,
In vaults, in cloisters, and in gloomy piles,
Long corridors and towers and solitary aisles!   60

Thy joy is in obscurity, and plain
    Is nought with thee; and on thy steps attend
Shadows but half-distinguish'd; the thin train
    Of hovering spirits round thy pathway bend,

With their low tremulous voice and airy tread,   65
    What time the tomb above them yawns and gapes:
For thou dost hold communion with the dead
    Phantoms and phantasies and grisly shapes;
And shades and headless spectres of Saint Mark,
Seen by a lurid light, formless and still and dark!   70

What joy to view the varied rainbow smile
    On Niagara's flood of matchless might,
Where all around the melancholy isle
    The billows sparkle with their hues of light!
While, as the restless surges roar and rave,   75
    The arrowy stream descends with awful sound,
Wheeling and whirling with each breathless wave,
    Immense, sublime, magnificent, profound!
If thou hast seen all this, and could'st not feel,
Then know, thine heart is fram'd of marble or of steel.   80

The hurricane fair earth to darkness changing,
    Kentucky's chambers of eternal gloom,
The swift-pac'd columns of the desert ranging
    Th' uneven waste, the violent Simoom,
Thy snow-clad peaks, stupendous Gungotree!   85
    Whence springs the hallow'd Jumna's echoing tide,

---

65. "According to Burke, a low tremulous intermitted sound is con-
ducive to the sublime" (Tennyson's note). See *ibid.*, Part II, Section xix.

69. "It is a received opinion, that on St. Mark's Eve all the persons
who are to die in the following year make their appearances without
their heads in the churches of their respective parishes. — See Dr. Langhorne's *Notes to Collins*" (Tennyson's note). The reference is to
J. Langhorne's edition of the *Poetical Works* of William Collins, 1765;
reprinted 1804. Compare Keats's "The Eve of St. Mark" and James
Montgomery, "St. Mark's Eve." See also Chambers's *Book of Days, sub*
April 25.

73. *the melancholy isle.* "This island, on both sides of which the
waters rush with astonishing swiftness, is 900 or 800 feet long, and its
lower edge is just at the perpendicular edge of the fall" (Tennyson's note).

77. "'Undis Phlegethon perlustrat anhelis.' — Claudian" (Tennyson's
note).

82. "See Dr. Nahum Ward's account of the great Kentucky Cavern,
in the *Monthly Magazine*, October, 1816" (Tennyson's note).

Hoar Cotopaxi's cloud-capt majesty,
   Enormous Chimborazo's naked pride,
The dizzy Cape of winds that cleaves the sky,
Whence we look down into eternity,   90

The pillar'd cave of Morven's giant king,
   The Yanar, and the Geyser's boiling fountain,
The deep volcano's inward murmuring,
   The shadowy Colossus of the mountain;
Antiparos, where sun-beams never enter;   95
   Loud Stromboli, amid the quaking isles;
The terrible Maelstroom, around his centre
   Wheeling his circuit of unnumber'd miles:
These, these are sights and sounds that freeze the blood,
Yet charm the awe-struck soul which doats on solitude.   100

Blest be the bard, whose willing feet rejoice
   To tread the emerald green of Fancy's vales,
Who hears the music of her heavenly voice,
   And breathes the rapture of her nectar'd gales!
Blest be the bard, whom golden Fancy loves,   105
   He strays for ever thro' her blooming bowers,
Amid the rich profusion of her groves,
   And wreathes his forehead with her spicy flowers
Of sunny radiance; but how blest is he
Who feels the genuine force of high Sublimity!   110

TIME: AN ODE[1]

I SEE the chariot, where,
Throughout the purple air,
   The forelock'd monarch rides:
Arm'd like some antique vehicle for war,
Time, hoary Time! I see thy scythed car,   5
In voiceless majesty,

---

89. "In the Ukraine" (Tennyson's note).
91. "Fingal's Cave in the Island of Staffa" (Tennyson's note).
92. *The Yanar*, "or, perpetual fire" (Tennyson's note).
94. "Alias, the Spectre of the Brocken" (Tennyson's note).
[1] Published in *Poems by Two Brothers*, 1827.

Cleaving the clouds of ages that float by,
  And change their many-colour'd sides,
    Now dark, now dun, now richly bright,
    In an ever-varying light.   10
  The great, the lowly, and the brave
    Bow down before the rushing force
    Of thine unconquerable course;
Thy wheels are noiseless as the grave,
Yet fleet as Heaven's red bolt they hurry on,   15
They pass above us, and are gone!

Clear is the track which thou hast past;
    Strew'd with the wrecks of frail renown,
    Robe, sceptre, banner, wreath, and crown,
      The pathway that before thee lies,   20
An undistinguishable waste,
    Invisible to human eyes,
  Which fain would scan the various shapes which glide
    In dusky cavalcade,
  Imperfectly descried,   25
    Through that intense, impenetrable shade.

Four grey steeds thy chariot draw;
In th'obdurate, tameless jaw
  Their rusted iron bits they sternly champ;
    Ye may not hear the echoing tramp   30
    Of their light-bounding, windy feet,
    Upon that cloudy pavement beat.
Four wings have each, which, far outspread,
  Receive the many blasts of heav'n,
As with unwearied speed,   35
  Throughout the long extent of ether driven,
Onward they rush for ever and for aye:
    Thy voice, thou mighty Charioteer!
    Always sounding in their ear,
Throughout the gloom of night and heat of day.   40

Fast behind thee follows Death,
  Thro' the ranks of wan and weeping,
That yield their miserable breath,
  On with his pallid courser proudly sweeping.

Arm'd is he in full mail,   45
    Bright breast-plate and high crest,
        Nor is the trenchant falchion wanting:
So fiercely does he ride the gale,
    On Time's dark car, before him, rest
        The dew-drops of his charger's panting.   50

On, on they go along the boundless skies,
    All human grandeur fades away
Before their flashing, fiery, hollow eyes;
        Beneath the terrible control
            Of those vast armed orbs, which roll   55
    Oblivion on the creatures of a day.
Those splendid monuments alone he spares,
    Which, to her deathless votaries,
Bright Fame, with glowing hand, uprears
Amid the waste of countless years.   60

'Live ye!' to these he crieth; 'live!
To ye eternity I give —
Ye, upon whose blessed birth
    The noblest star of heaven hath shone;
Live, when the ponderous pyramids of earth   65
    Are crumbling in oblivion!
Live, when, wrapt in sullen shade,
The golden hosts of heaven shall fade;
Live, when yon gorgeous sun on high
Shall veil the sparkling of his eye!   70
Live, when imperial Time and Death himself shall die!'

NATIONAL SONG[1]

THERE is no land like England
    Where'er the light of day be;
There are no hearts like English hearts
    Such hearts of oak as they be.

---

45. "I am indebted for the idea of Death's Armour to that famous
Chorus in *Caractacus* beginning with 'Hark! heard ye not that footstep
dread?'" (Tennyson's note). The reference is to William Mason's
quasi-historical tragedy *Caractacus*, 1759.

[1] Published in *Poems, Chiefly Lyrical*, 1830. With new choruses (see

There is no land like England   5
  Where'er the light of day be;
There are no men like Englishmen
  So tall and bold as they be.

Chorus. — For the French the Pope may shrive 'em,
  For the devil a whit we heed 'em: 10
As for the French, God speed 'em
    Unto their heart's desire,
And the merry devil drive 'em
    Through the water and the fire.

Full Ch. — Our glory is our freedom,   15
    We lord it o'er the sea;
  We are the sons of freedom,
    We are free.

There is no land like England
  Where'er the light of day be;
There are no wives like English wives   20
  So fair and chaste as they be.
There is no land like England
  Where'er the light of day be;
There are no maids like English maids   25
  So beautiful as they be.

Chorus. — For the French, &c.

———

above) this Song reappeared in *The Foresters,* Act II, Scene i, a play
written in 1881 but not produced or published till 1892.

  9–18. In place of these choruses *The Foresters* has:

    And these will strike for England
    And man and maid be free
    To foil and spoil the tyrant
    Beneath the greenwood tree.

  27. For this *The Foresters* substitutes:

    And these shall wed with freemen,
    And all their sons be free,
    To sing the songs of England
    Beneath the greenwood tree.

O DARLING ROOM[1]

I

O DARLING room, my heart's delight,
Dear room, the apple of my sight,
With thy two couches soft and white,
There is no room so exquisite,
No little room so warm and bright,   5
Wherein to read, wherein to write.

II

For I the Nonnenwerth have seen,
And Oberwinter's vineyards green,
Musical Lurlei; and between
The hills to Bingen have I been,   10
Bingen in Darmstadt, where the Rhene
Curves toward Mentz, a woody scene.

III

Yet never did there meet my sight,
In any town to left or right,
A little room so exquisite,   15
With two such couches soft and white,
Not any room so warm and bright,
Wherein to read, wherein to write.

---

[1] Published in 1832; afterwards suppressed — wisely. This is one of the poems ridiculed by J. W. Croker in his review of the *Poems* of 1832 in *Blackwood's,* April, 1833. See T. R. Lounsbury, *The Life and Times of Tennyson,* pp. 321 f. Though suppressed, the poem remained in hostile memories to plague Tennyson. To the attack upon him in Bulwer-Lytton's *The New Timon* (Part ii, 1846) there is a footnote in which the piece is quoted in part, with the comment: "The whole of this *Poem* (!!!) is worth reading, in order to see to what depth of silliness the human intellect can descend."

7. Tennyson had just returned from a tour of the Rhineland which he made in the summer of 1832 with Hallam.

CLARIBEL

A MELODY[1]

I

WHERE Claribel low-lieth
  The breezes pause and die,
    Letting the rose-leaves fall:
But the solemn oak-tree sigheth,
    Thick-leaved, ambrosial,   5
  With an ancient melody
  Of an inward agony,
Where Claribel low-lieth.

II

At eve the beetle boometh
  Athwart the thicket lone: 10
At noon the wild bee hummeth
  About the moss'd headstone:
At midnight the moon cometh,
  And looketh down alone.
Her song the lintwhite swelleth,   15
The clear-voiced mavis dwelleth,
  The callow throstle lispeth,
The slumbrous wave outwelleth,
  The babbling runnel crispeth,
The hollow grot replieth   20
  Where Claribel low-lieth.

---

[1] The opening piece in *Poems, Chiefly Lyrical*, 1830, a position of
honour which it retains in all collected editions of Tennyson's *Works*.
— "The king's fair daughter" in *The Tempest* (II, i, 70) is named Claribel.
Compare also Spenser, *The Faerie Queene*, II, iv, 26 f.

15. *the lintwhite,* the linnet.

17. *callow.* 1830 (and till 1851): "fledgling."

19. *runnel,* a small stream.

MARGARET[1]

I

O sweet pale Margaret,
  O rare pale Margaret,
What lit your eyes with tearful power,
Like moonlight on a falling shower?
Who lent you, love, your mortal dower   5
    Of pensive thought and aspect pale,
    Your melancholy sweet and frail
As perfume of the cuckoo-flower?
From the westward-winding flood,
From the evening-lighted wood,   10
    From all things outward you have won
A tearful grace, as tho' you stood
    Between the rainbow and the sun.
The very smile before you speak,
    That dimples your transparent cheek,   15
    Encircles all the heart, and feedeth
The senses with a still delight
    Of dainty sorrow without sound,
    Like the tender amber round,
    Which the moon about her spreadeth,   20
Moving thro' a fleecy night.

II

You love, remaining peacefully,
    To hear the murmur of the strife,
    But enter not the toil of life.
Your spirit is the calmed sea,   25
    Laid by the tumult of the fight.
You are the evening star, alway
    Remaining betwixt dark and bright:
Lull'd echoes of laborious day
    Come to you, gleams of mellow light   30
    Float by you on the verge of night.

---

[1] Published 1830; reprinted with a few changes, 1842.

III

What can it matter, Margaret,
   What songs below the waning stars
The lion-heart, Plantagenet,
      Sang looking thro' his prison bars?   35
        Exquisite Margaret, who can tell
The last wild thought of Chatelet,
    Just ere the falling axe did part
    The burning brain from the true heart,
      Even in her sight he loved so well?   40

IV

A fairy shield your Genius made
   And gave you on your natal day.
Your sorrow, only sorrow's shade,
   Keeps real sorrow far away.
You move not in such solitudes,   45
   You are not less divine,
But more human in your moods,
   Than your twin-sister, Adeline.
Your hair is darker, and your eyes
    Touch'd with a somewhat darker hue,   50
   And less aërially blue,
   But ever trembling thro' the dew
Of dainty-woeful sympathies.

V

   O sweet pale Margaret,
   O rare pale Margaret,   55
Come down, come down, and hear me speak:
Tie up the ringlets on your cheek:
   The sun is just about to set,

---

34. *The lion-heart.* 1830: "the lion-souled."

37. *Chatelet.* Florent-Louis-Marie, duc de Châtelet-Lomont, was executed during the Reign of Terror in 1793. See his *Mémoires*, 1808.

51. *less.* 1830: "more."

The arching limes are tall and shady,
 And faint rainy lights are seen,   60
  Moving in the leavy beech.
Rise from the feast of sorrow, lady,
  Where all day long you sit between
  Joy and woe, and whisper each.

Or only look across the lawn,   65
 Look out below your bower-eaves,
Look down, and let your blue eyes dawn
 Upon me thro' the jasmine-leaves.

"MY LIFE IS FULL OF WEARY DAYS" [1]

I

My LIFE is full of weary days,
 But good things have not kept aloof,
Nor wander'd into other ways:
 I have not lack'd thy mild reproof,
Nor golden largess of thy praise.   5

And now shake hands across the brink
 Of that deep grave to which I go:
Shake hands once more: I cannot sink
 So far — far down, but I shall know
Thy voice, and answer from below.   10

II

When in the darkness over me
 The four-handed mole shall scrape,
Plant thou no dusky cypress-tree,
 Nor wreathe thy cap with doleful crape,
 But pledge me in the flowing grape.   15

And when the sappy field and wood
 Grow green beneath the showery gray,
And rugged barks begin to bud,
 And thro' damp holts new-flush'd with May,
 Ring sudden scritches of the jay,   20

---

[1] Published in 1830; much altered and improved in 1842. "A sort of prevision of *In Memoriam*, of which it is in some sense the germ" (J. W. Mackail, *Studies of English Poets*, p. 236).

Then let wise Nature work her will,
  And on my clay her darnel grow;
Come only, when the days are still,
  And at my headstone whisper low,
  And tell me if the woodbines blow.   25

MARIANA [1]

'Mariana in the moated grange.'

Measure for Measure.

WITH blackest moss the flower-plots
  Were thickly crusted, one and all:
The rusted nails fell from the knots
  That held the pear to the gable-wall.
The broken sheds look'd sad and strange: 5
  Unlifted was the clinking latch;
  Weeded and worn the ancient thatch
Upon the lonely moated grange.
    She only said, 'My life is dreary,
      He cometh not,' she said;   10
    She said, 'I am aweary, aweary,
      I would that I were dead!'

Her tears fell with the dews at even;
  Her tears fell ere the dews were dried;
She could not look on the sweet heaven,   15
  Either at morn or eventide.
After the flitting of the bats,
  When thickest dark did trance the sky,
  She drew her casement curtain by,
And glanced athwart the glooming flats.   20
    She only said, 'The night is dreary,
      He cometh not,' she said;
    She said, 'I am aweary, aweary,
      I would that I were dead!'

---

[1] Published in 1830; reprinted in 1842. "The moated grange was no particular grange, but one which rose to the music of Shakespeare's words: 'There, at the moated grange, resides this dejected Mariana' " (Tennyson). See *Measure for Measure*, III, i, and compare IV, i.

4. Until 1860 this line read "That held the peach to the garden-wall." Tennyson altered it because, as he said, "peach" spoiled the desolation of the picture. It was "not characteristic of the scenery I had in mind."

Upon the middle of the night,   25
  Waking she heard the night-fowl crow:
The cock sung out an hour ere light:
  From the dark fen the oxen's low
Came to her: without hope of change,
  In sleep she seem'd to walk forlorn,   30
Till cold winds woke the gray-eyed morn
  About the lonely moated grange.
     She only said, 'The day is dreary,
      He cometh not,' she said;
     She said, 'I am aweary, aweary,   35
      I would that I were dead!'

About a stone-cast from the wall
  A sluice with blacken'd waters slept,
And o'er it many, round and small,
  The cluster'd marish-mosses crept.   40
Hard by a poplar shook alway,
  All silver-green with gnarled bark:
For leagues no other tree did mark
  The level waste, the rounding gray.
     She only said, 'My life is dreary,   45
      He cometh not,' she said;
     She said, 'I am aweary, aweary,
      I would that I were dead!'

And ever when the moon was low,
  And the shrill winds were up and away,   50
In the white curtain, to and fro,
  She saw the gusty shadow sway.
But when the moon was very low,
  And wild winds bound within their cell,
The shadow of the poplar fell   55
Upon her bed, across her brow.
     She only said, 'The night is dreary,
      He cometh not,' she said;
     She said, 'I am aweary, aweary,
      I would that I were dead!'   60

---

43. *mark*. 1830–1842: "dark."

All day within the dreamy house,
    The doors upon their hinges creak'd;
The blue fly sung in the pane; the mouse
    Behind the mouldering wainscot shriek'd,
Or from the crevice peer'd about.   65
    Old faces glimmer'd thro' the doors,
    Old footsteps trod the upper floors,
Old voices called her from without.
        She only said, 'My life is dreary,
            He cometh not,' she said;   70
        She said, 'I am aweary, aweary,
            I would that I were dead!'

The sparrow's chirrup on the roof,
    The slow clock ticking, and the sound
Which to the wooing wind aloof   75
    The poplar made, did all confound
Her sense; but most she loathed the hour
    When the thick-moted sunbeam lay
    Athwart the chambers, and the day
Was sloping toward his western bower.   80
        Then, said she, 'I am very dreary,
            He will not come,' she said;
        She wept, 'I am aweary, aweary,
            Oh God, that I were dead!'

RECOLLECTIONS OF THE ARABIAN NIGHTS[1]

WHEN the breeze of a joyful dawn blew free
In the silken sail of infancy,
The tide of time flow'd back with me,
    The forward-flowing tide of time;
And many a sheeny summer-morn,   5
Adown the Tigris I was borne,

80. 1830: "Downsloped was westering to his bower."

[1] Published 1830; reprinted with slight alterations, 1842. The version, inaccurate and incomplete, of the *Arabian Nights* (*The Thousand Nights and a Night*) known to Tennyson was based upon Galland's French rendering (1704–1717). E. W. Lane's translation, the first important version in English, did not begin to appear till nine years after this poem was published. The "Golden Prime" of the Abbasid dynasty at Baghdad

By Bagdat's shrines of fretted gold,
High-walled gardens green and old;
True Mussulman was I and sworn,
    For it was in the golden prime   10
      Of good Haroun Alraschid.

Anight my shallop, rustling thro'
The low and bloomed foliage, drove
The fragrant, glistening deeps, and clove
The citron-shadows in the blue: 15
By garden porches on the brim,
The costly doors flung open wide,
Gold glittering thro' lamplight dim,
And broider'd sofas on each side:
    In sooth it was a goodly time,   20
    For it was in the golden prime
      Of good Haroun Alraschid.

Often, where clear-stemm'd platans guard
The outlet, did I turn away
The boat-head down a broad canal   25
From the main river sluiced, where all
The sloping of the moon-lit sward
Was damask-work, and deep inlay
Of braided blooms unmown, which crept
Adown to where the water slept   30
    A goodly place, a goodly time,
    For it was in the golden prime
      Of good Haroun Alraschid.

A motion from the river won
Ridged the smooth level, bearing on   35
My shallop thro' the star-strown calm,
Until another night in night
I enter'd, from the clearer light,

was during the caliphate of Harun al-Rashid (786–809). Two centuries later, when the *Nights* were coming into form, legends and anecdotes of his court provided many humorous anecdotes and amorous romances. See P. K. Hitti, *History of the Arabs,* 1937, pp. 301 f. and 404 f. The fascination which the Orient exerted upon the youthful Tennyson is exemplified in several poems in *Poems by Two Brothers.* It provides a link between him and the two most popular poets of the previous generation, Byron and Thomas Moore.

Imbower'd vaults of pillar'd palm,
Imprisoning sweets, which, as they clomb   40
Heavenward, were stay'd beneath the dome
  Of hollow boughs. — A goodly time,
   For it was in the golden prime
    Of good Haroun Alraschid.

Still onward; and the clear canal   45
Is rounded to as clear a lake.
From the green rivage many a fall
Of diamond rillets musical,
Thro' little crystal arches low
Down from the central fountain's flow   50
Fall'n silver-chiming, seemed to shake
The sparkling flints beneath the prow.
  A goodly place, a goodly time,
   For it was in the golden prime
    Of good Haroun Alraschid.   55

Above thro' many a bowery turn
A walk with vary-colour'd shells
Wander'd engrain'd. On either side
All round about the fragrant marge
From fluted vase, and brazen urn   60
In order, eastern flowers large,
Some dropping low their crimson bells
Half-closed, and others studded wide
  With disks and tiars, fed the time
   With odour in the golden prime   65
    Of good Haroun Alraschid.

Far off, and where the lemon grove
In closest coverture upsprung,
The living airs of middle night
Died round the bulbul as he sung;   70
Not he: but something which possess'd
The darkness of the world, delight,
Life, anguish, death, immortal love,
Ceasing not, mingled, unrepress'd,
  Apart from place, withholding time,   75
   But flattering the golden prime
    Of good Haroun Alraschid.

Black the garden-bowers and grots
Slumber'd: the solemn palms were ranged
Above, unwoo'd of summer wind: 80
A sudden splendour from behind
Flush'd all the leaves with rich gold-green,
And, flowing rapidly between
Their interspaces, counterchanged
The level lake with diamond-plots   85
   Of dark and bright.   A lovely time,
    For it was in the golden prime
      Of good Haroun Alraschid.

Dark-blue the deep sphere overhead,
Distinct with vivid stars inlaid,
Grew darker from that under-flame: 90
So, leaping lightly from the boat,
With silver anchor left afloat,
In marvel whence that glory came
Upon me, as in sleep I sank   95
In cool soft turf upon the bank,
   Entranced with that place and time,
    So worthy of the golden prime
      Of good Haroun Alraschid.

Thence thro' the garden I was drawn —   100
A realm of pleasance, many a mound,
And many a shadow-chequer'd lawn
Full of the city's stilly sound,
And deep myrrh-thickets blowing round
The stately cedar, tamarisks,   105
Thick rosaries of scented thorn,
Tall orient shrubs, and obelisks
   Graven with emblems of the time,
    In honour of the golden prime
      Of good Haroun Alraschid.   110

With dazed vision unawares
From the long alley's latticed shade
Emerged, I came upon the great
Pavilion of the Caliphat.

Right to the carven cedarn doors,   115
Flung inward over spangled floors,
Broad-based flights of marble stairs
Ran up with golden balustrade,
   After the fashion of the time,
    And humour of the golden prime   120
     Of good Haroun Alraschid.

The fourscore windows all alight
As with the quintessence of flame,
A million tapers flaring bright
From twisted silvers look'd to shame   125
The hollow-vaulted dark, and stream'd
Upon the mooned domes aloof
In inmost Bagdat, till there seem'd
Hundreds of crescents on the roof
   Of night new-risen, that marvellous time   130
    To celebrate the golden prime
     Of good Haroun Alraschid.

Then stole I up, and trancedly
Gazed on the Persian girl alone,
Serene with argent-lidded eyes   135
Amorous, and lashes like to rays
Of darkness, and a brow of pearl
Tressed with redolent ebony,
In many a dark delicious curl,
Flowing beneath her rose-hued zone;   140
   The sweetest lady of the time,
    Well worthy of the golden prime
     Of good Haroun Alraschid.

Six columns, three on either side,
Pure silver, underpropt a rich   145
Throne of the massive ore, from which
Down-droop'd, in many a floating fold,
Engarlanded and diaper'd
With inwrought flowers, a cloth of gold.
Thereon, his deep eye laughter-stirr'd   150

With merriment of kingly pride,
    Sole star of all that place and time,
    I saw him — in his golden prime,
    THE GOOD HAROUN ALRASCHID.

THE BALLAD OF ORIANA [1]

MY HEART is wasted with my woe,
    Oriana.
There is no rest for me below,
    Oriana.
When the long dun wolds are ribb'd with snow,
And loud the Norland whirlwinds blow,
    Oriana,
Alone I wander to and fro,
    Oriana.   5

Ere the light on dark was growing,
    Oriana,
At midnight the cock was crowing,
    Oriana:
Winds were blowing, waters flowing,
We heard the steeds to battle going,
    Oriana;
Aloud the hollow bugle blowing,
    Oriana.   10

In the yew-wood black as night,
    Oriana,
Ere I rode into the fight,
    Oriana,
While blissful tears blinded my sight
By star-shine and by moonlight,
    Oriana,
I to thee my troth did plight,
    Oriana.   15

---

[1] Published 1830; reprinted 1842. This poem was much admired by
Rossetti and his circle and had a strong influence upon Pre-Raphaelite
poetry.

She stood upon the castle wall,
>> Oriana:
She watch'd my crest among them all,
>> Oriana:
She saw me fight, she heard me call,
When forth there stept a foeman tall,
>> Oriana,
Atween me and the castle wall,
>> Oriana.   20

The bitter arrow went aside,
>> Oriana:
The false, false arrow went aside,
>> Oriana:
The damned arrow glanced aside,
And pierced thy heart, my love, my bride,
>> Oriana!
Thy heart, my life, my love, my bride,
>> Oriana!   25

Oh! narrow, narrow was the space,
>> Oriana.
Loud, loud rung out the bugle's brays,
>> Oriana.
Oh! deathful stabs were dealt apace,
The battle deepen'd in its place,
>> Oriana;
But I was down upon my face,
>> Oriana.   30

They should have stabb'd me where I lay,
>> Oriana!
How could I rise and come away,
>> Oriana?
How could I look upon the day?
They should have stabb'd me where I lay,
>> Oriana —
They should have trod me into clay,
>> Oriana.   35

O breaking heart that will not break,
          Oriana!
O pale, pale face so sweet and meek,
          Oriana!
Thou smilest, but thou dost not speak,
And then the tears run down my cheek,
        · Oriana:
What wantest thou? whom dost thou seek,
          Oriana?   40

I cry aloud: none hear my cries,
          Oriana.
Thou comest atween me and the skies,
          Oriana.
I feel the tears of blood arise
Up from my heart unto my eyes,
          Oriana.
Within thy heart my arrow lies,
          Oriana.   45

O cursed hand! O cursed blow!
          Oriana!
O happy thou that liest low,
          Oriana!
All night the silence seems to flow
Beside me in my utter woe,
          Oriana.
A weary, weary way I go,
          Oriana.   50

When Norland winds pipe down the sea,
          Oriana,
I walk, I dare not think of thee,
          Oriana.
Thou liest beneath the greenwood tree,
I dare not die and come to thee,
          Oriana.
I hear the roaring of the sea,
          Oriana.   55

THE MERMAN[1]

I

Who would be
A merman bold,
Sitting alone,
Singing alone
Under the sea,   5
With a crown of gold,
On a throne?

II

I would be a merman bold,
I would sit and sing the whole of the day;
I would fill the sea-halls with a voice of power;   10
But at night I would roam abroad and play
With the mermaids in and out of the rocks,
Dressing their hair with the white sea-flower;
And holding them back by their flowing locks
I would kiss them often under the sea,   15
And kiss them again till they kiss'd me
        Laughingly, laughingly;
And then we would wander away, away
To the pale-green sea-groves straight and high,
        Chasing each other merrily.   20

III

There would be neither moon nor star;
But the wave would make music above us afar —
Low thunder and light in the magic night —
        Neither moon nor star.
We would call aloud in the dreamy dells,   25
Call to each other and whoop and cry
        All night, merrily, merrily;
They would pelt me with starry spangles and shells,
Laughing and clapping their hands between,
        All night, merrily, merrily: 30

_____
[1] Published 1830; reprinted 1842.

But I would throw to them back in mine
Turkis and agate and almondine:
Then leaping out upon them unseen
I would kiss them often under the sea,
And kiss them again till they kiss'd me 35
  Laughingly, laughingly.
Oh! what a happy life were mine
Under the hollow-hung ocean green!
Soft are the moss-beds under the sea;
We would live merrily, merrily. 40

THE MERMAID [1]

I

Who would be
A mermaid fair,
Singing alone,
Combing her hair
Under the sea, 5
In a golden curl
With a comb of pearl,
On a throne?

II

I would be a mermaid fair;
I would sing to myself the whole of the day; 10
With a comb of pearl I would comb my hair;
And still as I comb'd I would sing and say,
'Who is it loves me? who loves not me?'
I would comb my hair till my ringlets would fall
  Low adown, low adown, 15
From under my starry sea-bud crown
  Low adown and around,
And I should look like a fountain of gold

---

32. *Turkis,* turquoise. Tennyson had the authority of Milton for the form "turkis" and objected to the "ugly nasal sound in the *oi* diphthong." — *almondine,* a kind of garnet.

[1] Published 1830; reprinted 1842.

Springing alone
With a shrill inner sound,   20
  Over the throne
  In the midst of the hall;
Till that great sea-snake under the sea
From his coiled sleeps in the central deeps
Would slowly trail himself sevenfold   25
Round the hall where I sate, and look in at the gate
With his large calm eyes for the love of me.
And all the mermen under the sea
Would feel their immortality
Die in their hearts for the love of me.   30

III

But at night I would wander away away,
  I would fling on each side my low-flowing locks,
And lightly vault from the throne and play
  With the mermen in and out of the rocks;
We would run to and fro, and hide and seek,   35
  On the broad sea-wolds in the crimson shells,
  Whose silvery spikes are nighest the sea.
But if any came near I would call, and shriek,
And adown the steep like a wave I would leap
  From the diamond-ledges that jut from the dells;   40
For I would not be kiss'd by all who would list,
Of the bold merry mermen under the sea;
They would sue me, and woo me, and flatter me,
In the purple twilights under the sea;
But the king of them all would carry me,   45
Woo me, and win me, and marry me,
In the branching jaspers under the sea;
Then all the dry pied things that be
In the hueless mosses under the sea
Would curl round my silver feet silently,   50
All looking up for the love of me.
And if I should carol aloud, from aloft
All things that are forked, and horned, and soft
Would lean out from the hollow sphere of the sea,
All looking down for the love of me.   55

---

54. *the hollow sphere of the sea.* "An underworld of which the sea
is the heaven" (Tennyson).

THE DYING SWAN[1]

I

THE plain was grassy, wild and bare,
Wide, wild, and open to the air,
Which had built up everywhere
   An under-roof of doleful gray.
With an inner voice the river ran,   5
Adown it floated a dying swan,
     And loudly did lament.
   It was the middle of the day.
Ever the weary wind went on,
     And took the reed-tops as it went.   10

II

Some blue peaks in the distance rose,
And white against the cold-white sky,
Shone out their crowning snows.
   One willow over the river wept,
And shook the wave as the wind did sigh;   15
Above in the wind was the swallow,
     Chasing itself at its own wild will,
     And far thro' the marish green and still
     The tangled water-courses slept,
Shot over with purple, and green, and yellow.   20

III

The wild swan's death-hymn took the soul
Of that waste place with joy
Hidden in sorrow: at first to the ear
The warble was low, and full and clear;
And floating about the under-sky,   25

---

[1] Published in 1830. The belief that the swan sings just before its death is a commonplace of mythology and poetic imagery.

18. *marish,* marsh.

21. *took,* captivated, charmed. Compare *Comus,* l. 256: "Who, as they sung, would take the prison'd soul."

Prevailing in weakness, the coronach stole
Sometimes afar, and sometimes anear
But anon her awful jubilant voice,
With a music strange and manifold,
Flow'd forth on a carol free and bold   30
As when a mighty people rejoice
With shawms, and with cymbals, and harps of gold,
And the tumult of their acclaim is roll'd
Thro' the open gates of the city afar,
To the shepherd who watcheth the evening star.   35
And the creeping mosses and clambering weeds,
And the willow-branches hoar and dank,
And the wavy swell of the soughing reeds,
And the wave-worn horns of the echoing bank,
And the silvery marish-flowers that throng   40
The desolate creeks and pools among,
Were flooded over with eddying song.

THE SEA–FAIRIES [1]

Slow sail'd the weary mariners and saw,
Betwixt the green brink and the running foam,
Sweet faces, rounded arms, and bosoms prest
To little harps of gold; and while they mused
Whispering to each other half in fear,   5
Shrill music reach'd them on the middle sea.

Whither away, whither away, whither away? fly no more.
Whither away from the high green field, and the happy blos-
    soming shore?
Day and night to the billow the fountain calls:

---

26. *coronach*, a Gaelic word for a lamentation for the dead.

33. Compare *In Memoriam*, LXXV, 20.

39. *horns*, projections and indentations. Compare *Paradise Lost*, xi,
831: "the horned flood."

[1] Published in 1830; then suppressed till *Poems*, eighth edition, 1853,
wherein it reappeared with many alterations. The original version is
reprinted in *Works*, Cambridge edition, pp. 786 f. The chief interest of
the piece lies in the fact that it appears to be a preliminary study for
"The Lotos-Eaters."

Down shower the gambolling waterfalls   10
From wandering over the lea:
Out of the live-green heart of the dells
They freshen the silvery-crimson shells,
And thick with white bells the clover-hill swells
High over the full-toned sea: 15
O hither, come hither and furl your sails,
Come hither to me and to me:
Hither, come hither and frolic and play;
Here it is only the mew that wails;
We will sing to you all the day: 20
Mariner, mariner, furl your sails,
For here are the blissful downs and dales,
And merrily, merrily carol the gales,
And the spangle dances in bight and bay,
And the rainbow forms and flies on the land   25
Over the islands free;
And the rainbow lives in the curve of the sand;
Hither, come hither and see;
And the rainbow hangs on the poising wave,
And sweet is the colour of cove and cave,   30
And sweet shall your welcome be:
O hither, come hither, and be our lords,
For merry brides are we:
We will kiss sweet kisses, and speak sweet words:
O listen, listen, your eyes shall glisten   35
With pleasure and love and jubilee:
O listen, listen, your eyes shall glisten
When the sharp clear twang of the golden chords
Runs up the ridged sea.
Who can light on as happy a shore   40
All the world o'er, all the world o'er?
Whither away? listen and stay: mariner, mariner, fly no more.

THE HESPERIDES[1]

Hesperus and his daughters three
That sing about the golden tree. *Comus*.[2]

The North wind fall'n, in the new-starred night
Zidonian Hanno, wandering beyond
The hoary promontory of Soloë,
Past Thymiaterion in calmed bays
Between the southern and the western Horn,   5
Heard neither warbling of the nightingale,
Nor melody of the Libyan Lotus-flute
Blown seaward from the shore; but from a slope
That ran bloom-bright into the Atlantic blue,
Beneath a highland leaning down a weight   10
Of cliffs, and zoned below with cedar-shade,
Came voices like the voices in a dream
Continuous; till he reach'd the outer sea: —

---

[1] Published in 1832; afterwards suppressed. In consequence of Tennyson's expression of regret that he had not included it among his "Juvenilia," the poet's son reprinted it in the *Memoir*, i, 61 f. Hesiod (*Theogony*, ll. 215–6) tells of the Hesperides who guard their apples and the trees that bear the precious fruit "beyond the waters of Ocean." "The purest piece of magic and mystery, and perhaps the only piece of myth-making, that Tennyson ever wrote" (Douglas Bush, *Mythology and the Romantic Tradition in English Poetry*, p. 200). Compare the Song of the Hesperides in William Morris's *The Life and Death of Jason*, xiv, 607 f.

[2] ll. 982–3.

2. *Zidonian Hanno*. Hanno the Carthaginian explorer and colonist, the author of the *Periplus* (a Greek version of the lost Punic original). His voyage beyond the Pillars of Hercules and down the coast of Africa took place *c.* 500 B.C. Though doubts were formerly cast upon not only his veracity but the authenticity of the narrative which goes by his name, historians of geography are now in agreement that the voyage occurred and the account of it is genuine. See Sir Edward Bunbury, *History of Ancient Geography*, i, chapter ix; M. Cary and E. H. Warmington, *The Ancient Explorers*, pp. 47 f., and the English translation of *The Periplus of Hanno* by W. H. Schoff, Philadelphia, 1912. Hanno, however, says nothing about the Hesperides; the association of the daughters of Hesper with him is Tennyson's invention.

3–5. The promontory of Soloë, Thymiaterion, the Horn of the West, and the Horn of the South are all mentioned by Hanno and have been identified by modern scholars with localities on the coast of Africa.

SONG OF THE THREE SISTERS [1]

I

The Golden Apple, the Golden Apple, the hallow'd fruit,
Guard it well, guard it warily,   15
Singing airily,
Standing about the charmed root.
Round about all is mute,
As the snowfield on the mountain-peaks,
As the sandfield at the mountain-foot.   20
Crocodiles in briny creeks
Sleep and stir not: all is mute.
If ye sing not, if ye make false measure,
We shall lose eternal pleasure,
Worth eternal want of rest.   25
Laugh not loudly: watch the treasure
Of the wisdom of the West.
In a corner wisdom whispers. Five and three
(Let it not be preach'd abroad) make an awful mystery:
For the blossom unto threefold music bloweth;   30
Evermore it is born anew,
And the sap to threefold music floweth,
From the root,
Drawn in the dark,
Up to the fruit,   35
Creeping under the fragrant bark,
Liquid gold, honeysweet thro and thro.
Keen-eyed Sisters, singing airily,
Looking warily
Every way,   40
Guard the apple night and day,
Lest one from the East come and take it away.

II

Father Hesper, Father Hesper, Watch, watch, ever and aye,
Looking under silver hair with a silver eye.
Father, twinkle not thy stedfast sight: 45
Kingdoms lapse, and climates change, and races die;

---

[1] The number of the sisters differs in different classical authors, some
saying that there were three, some seven.

Honour comes with mystery;
Hoarded wisdom brings delight.
Number, tell them over, and number
How many the mystic fruit-tree holds,   50
Lest the red-comb'd dragon slumber
Roll'd together in purple folds.
Look to him, father, lest he wink, and the golden apple be stol'n
    away,
For his ancient heart is drunk with over-watchings night and
    day
Round about the hallow'd fruit-tree curl'd —   55
Sing away, sing aloud evermore in the wind without stop,
Lest his sealed eyelid drop,
For he is older than the world.
If he waken, we waken,
Rapidly levelling eager eyes.   60
If he sleep, we sleep,
Dropping the eyelid over our eyes.
If the golden apple be taken
The world will be overwise.
Five links, a golden chain are we,   65
Hesper, the Dragon, and Sisters three
Bound about the golden tree.

III

Father Hesper, Father Hesper, Watch, watch, night and day,
Lest the old wound of the world be healed,
The glory unsealed,   70
The golden apple stol'n away,
And the ancient secret revealed.
Look from West to East along:
Father, old Himala weakens, Caucasus is bold and strong.
Wandering waters unto wandering waters call;   75
Let them clash together, foam and fall.
Out of watchings, out of wiles,
Comes the bliss of secret smiles.
All things are not told to all,
Half-round the mantling night is drawn.   80
Purplefringed with even and dawn
Hesper hateth Phosphor, evening hateth morn.

IV

Every flower and every fruit the redolent breath
  Of the warm seawind ripeneth,
    Arching the billow in his sleep: 85
  But the land-wind wandereth,
    Broken by the highland steep,
    Two streams upon the violet deep.
  For the Western Sun, and the Western Star,
  And the low west-wind, breathing afar,   90
    The end of day and beginning of night,
    Keep the apple Holy and Bright;
Holy and Bright, round and full, bright and blest,
    Mellow'd in a land of rest:
    Watch it warily night and day;   95
    All good things are in the West.
Till mid-noon the cool East light
Is shut out by the round of the tall hill brow,
  But, when the full-faced Sunset yellowly
  Stays on the flowerful arch of the bough,   100
  The luscious fruitage clustereth mellowly,
    Golden-kernell'd, Golden-cored,
  Sunset-ripen'd above on the tree.
  The world is wasted with fire and sword,
  But the Apple of gold hangs over the Sea!   105
  Five links — a Golden chain are we —
  Hesper, the Dragon, and Sisters three,
             Daughters three,
             Round about,
             All round about   110
  The gnarl'd bole of the charmed tree.
The Golden Apple, The Golden Apple,
    The hallow'd fruit,
      Guard it well,
      Guard it warily,   115
      Watch it warily,
      Singing airily,
  Standing about the charmed root.

APPENDIX II

LITERARY SQUABBLES[1]

TO CHRISTOPHER NORTH[2]

You did late review my lays,
    Crusty Christopher;
You did mingle blame and praise,
    Rusty Christopher.
When I learnt from whom it came,   5
I forgave you all the blame,
    Musty Christopher;
I could *not* forgive the praise,
    Fusty Christopher.

---

[1] Here are collected half a dozen short pieces that make up Tennyson's scanty contribution to satiric verse, as distinct from invective and diatribe. The general title we have given them is that bestowed as an after-thought by the poet upon the verses originally called "After-thoughts."

[2] In the "Noctes Ambrosianae" in *Blackwood's Magazine*, February, 1832, John Wilson ("Christopher North") is represented as saying: "I have good hopes of Alfred Tennyson. But the Cockneys are doing what they may to spoil him. . . . I should be sorry for it. . . . He has a fine ear for melody and harmony too — and rich and rare glimpses of imagination. He has — *genius.*" In the same periodical for the following May, Wilson returned to the subject of Tennyson, publishing what was the first attempt at a discriminating review of *Poems, Chiefly Lyrical.* In this he mingled what he called "gentle chastisement" with warm praise of what he called "well-chosen specimens of his fine faculties." The epigram or squib "To Christopher North" was the poet's response, published in 1832 and thereafter suppressed. For further details consult T. R. Lounsbury, *The Life and Times of Tennyson*, especially chapter viii.

THE NEW TIMON AND THE POETS[1]

WE KNOW him, out of SHAKESPEARE's art,
  And those fine curses which he spoke;
The old TIMON, with his noble heart,
  That, strongly loathing, greatly broke.

So died the Old: here comes the New.   5
  Regard him: a familiar face:
I *thought* we knew him: What, it's you,
  The padded man — that wears the stays —

Who killed the girls and thrilled the boys
  With dandy pathos when you wrote!   10
A Lion, you, that made a noise,
  And shook a mane *en papillotes*.

And once you tried the Muses too;
  You failed, Sir: therefore now you turn,
To fall on those who are to you   15
  As Captain is to Subaltern.

---

[1] In December, 1845, there appeared an anonymous poem entitled *The New Timon;* in January, 1846, a second part, in which the author, while celebrating his own severity of taste, expresses his disdain of the meretriciousness of "School-Miss Alfred" who vents
                                            her chaste delight
    On "darling little rooms so warm and bright"
and who with "jingling medley of purloin'd conceits" sings a "modish tune,"
        Outbabying Wordsworth and outglittering Keats.
Sir Robert Peel, the Prime Minister, is upbraided for pensioning Tennyson and leaving James Sheridan Knowles, the dramatist, to starve. Further offensive comment upon Tennyson was made in the notes to the poem. It was soon generally known that Edward Bulwer-Lytton was the author of the poem, and he did not for long trouble to deny it. In *Punch* (x, February 28, 1846, 103) Tennyson replied, over the signature "Alcibiades." These powerful lines he seems not to have intended for publication; they were sent to *Punch* by John Forster. (See note on "Literary Squabbles.") Tennyson never republished the lines and they do not appear in the *Memoir.* In the fourth edition of *The New Timon* Bulwer-Lytton suppressed the attack on Tennyson. For further details see Lounsbury, *op. cit.,* pp. 518 f.

But men of long-enduring hopes,
  And careless what this hour may bring,
Can pardon little would-be POPES
  And BRUMMELS, when they try to sting.   20

An Artist, Sir, should rest in Art,
  And waive a little of his claim;
To have the deep Poetic heart
  Is more than all poetic fame.

But you, Sir, you are hard to please;   25
  You never look but half content;
Nor like a gentleman at ease,
  With moral breadth of temperament.

And what with spites and what with fears,
  You cannot let a body be: 30
It's always ringing in your ears,
  'They call this man as good as *me.*'

What profits now to understand
  The merits of a spotless shirt —
A dapper boot — a little hand —   35
  If half the little soul is dirt?

You talk of tinsel! why, we see
  The old mark of rouge upon your cheeks.
You prate of Nature! you are he
  That spilt his life about the cliques.   40

A TIMON you! Nay, nay, for shame:
  It looks too arrogant a jest —
The fierce old man — to take his name,
  You bandbox. Off, and let him rest.

LITERARY SQUABBLES [1]

AH GOD! the petty fools of rhyme
  That shriek and sweat in pigmy wars
Before the stony face of Time,
  And look'd at by the silent stars:

---

[1] Published, with the title "After-thought" and over the signature

Who hate each other for a song,   5
   And do their little best to bite
And pinch their brethren in the throng,
   And scratch the very dead for spite:

And strain to make an inch of room
   For their sweet selves, and cannot hear   10
The sullen Lethe rolling doom
   On them and theirs and all things here:

When one small touch of Charity
   Could lift them nearer God-like state
Than if the crowded Orb should cry   15
   Like those who cried Diana great:

And I too, talk, and lose the touch
   I talk of.   Surely, after all,
The noblest answer unto such
   Is perfect stillness when they brawl.   20

HENDECASYLLABICS [1]

O you chorus of indolent reviewers,
Irresponsible, indolent reviewers,
Look, I come to the test, a tiny poem
All composed in a metre of Catullus,
All in quantity, careful of my motion,   5
Like the skater on ice that hardly bears him,
Lest I fall unawares before the people,
Waking laughter in indolent reviewers.
Should I flounder awhile without a tumble
Thro' this metrification of Catullus,   10
They should speak to me not without a welcome,
All that chorus of indolent reviewers.
Hard, hard, hard is it, only not to tumble,
So fantastical is the dainty metre.
Wherefore slight me not wholly, nor believe me   15
Too presumptuous, indolent reviewers.

"Alcibiades," in *Punch* (x, March 7, 1846, 106). Reprinted with the present title in the Library edition of the *Poems*, 1872–3.

[1] This is one of three "Experiments in Quantity" published in the *Cornhill Magazine*, December, 1863.

O blatant Magazines, regard me rather —
Since I blush to belaud myself a moment —
As some rare little rose, a piece of inmost
Horticultural art, or half conquette-like   20
Maiden, not to be greeted unbenignly.

TO ——,

AFTER READING A LIFE AND LETTERS[1]

'Cursed be he that moves my bones.'
Shakespeare's Epitaph

You might have won the Poet's name,
   If such be worth the winning now,
   And gain'd a laurel for your brow
Of sounder leaf than I can claim;

But you have made the wiser choice,   5
   A life that moves to gracious ends
   Thro' troops of unrecording friends,
A deedful life, a silent voice:

And you have miss'd the irreverent doom
   Of those that wear the Poet's crown;   10
   Hereafter, neither knave nor clown
Shall hold their orgies at your tomb.

---

19 f. The simile is a humorous echo of Catullus, lxxii, 39 f. See Mustard, *op. cit.*, pp. 96 f.

[1] Published in *The Examiner*, March 24, 1849; reprinted in the sixth edition of the *Poems*, 1850. The explanatory sub-title was added in the eighth edition, 1853. The person addressed is generally believed to be the poet's brother Charles Tennyson-Turner. William Michael Rossetti recorded that Tennyson told him that the lines were "written in a fit of intense disgust after reading Medwin's book about Byron" (*Praeraphaelite Diaries*, 1900, p. 239, under date December, 1849). But Medwin's book was not a biography; it included no letters by Byron; it was a record of conversations; and moreover it had been published a quarter of a century before Tennyson's poem was written. Undoubtedly the book referred to was Richard Monckton Milnes's *Life, Letters and Literary Remains of John Keats*, 1848. Tennyson's son admitted that he "was indignant that Keats's wild love-letters should have been published," but he disclaimed the idea that he had Milnes's volume in mind. The disclaimer and (if Rossetti remembered correctly) the reference to Medwin were due to the desire not to seem to attack Milnes, who was a personal friend.

For now the Poet cannot die,
   Nor leave his music as of old,
   But round him ere he scarce be cold   15
Begins the scandal and the cry:

'Proclaim the faults he would not show:
   Break lock and seal: betray the trust:
   Keep nothing sacred: 'tis but just
The many-headed beast should know.   20

Ah shameless! for he did but sing
   A song that pleased us from its worth;
   No public life was his on earth,
No blazon'd statesman he, nor king.

He gave the people of his best: 25
   His worst he kept, his best he gave.
   My Shakespeare's curse on clown and knave
Who will not let his ashes rest!

Who make it seem more sweet to be
   The little life of bank and brier,   30
   The bird that pipes his lone desire
And dies unheard within his tree,

Than he that warbles long and loud
   And drops at Glory's temple-gates,
   For whom the carrion vulture waits   35
To tear his heart before the crowd!

POETS AND THEIR BIBLIOGRAPHIES[1]

OLD poets foster'd under friendlier skies,
   Old Virgil who would write ten lines, they say,
   At dawn, and lavish all the golden day
To make them wealthier in his readers' eyes;

---

[1] Published in *Tiresias and Other Poems,* 1885; the title, however, was not added till 1889. The bibliographer particularly in question was Richard Herne Shepherd, who in a succession of volumes had reprinted pieces the poet would willingly have let die and against whom he had to bring suit for piracy.

And you, old popular Horace, you the wise   5
   Adviser of the nine-years-ponder'd lay
   And you, that wear a wreath of sweeter bay,
Catullus whose dead songster never dies;
If, glancing downward on the kindly sphere
   That once had roll'd you round and round the Sun,   10
   You see your Art still shrined in human shelves,
You should be jubilant that you flourish'd here
   Before the Love of Letters, overdone,
Had swampt the sacred poets with themselves.

---

6. *Ars Poetica*, l. 388: "Nonumque prematur in annum."
8. Lesbia's sparrow in Catullus, iii.

APPENDIX III

POEMS BY THE POET'S TWO BROTHERS

Frederick Tennyson [1]

THE SKYLARK [2]

I

How the blithe Lark runs up the golden stair
　　That leans thro' cloudy gates from Heaven to Earth;
And all alone in the empyreal air
　　Fills it with jubilant sweet songs of mirth;
　　　　How far he seems, how far　　　　　　　　　　5
　　　　　With the light upon his wings,
　　　　Is it a bird, or star
　　　　　That shines, and sings?

---

[1] Frederick Tennyson (1807–1898), the elder brother of the Poet Laureate, is today best remembered as the friend and correspondent of Edward FitzGerald. The scantiness of his contribution (four pieces) to the joint volume of 1827 accounts for the fact that its title is *Poems by Two* [not Three] *Brothers,* the second brother being Charles. He lived for many years in Italy where, in Florence, he was intimate with the Brownings. In later life he lived in Jersey. In 1854 he published *Days and Hours,* a volume of verse. Discouraged by its reception, he published no more till the last decade of his long life when three more volumes appeared. They won very little attention; but in 1897 Francis Turner Palgrave included four of his poems in *The Golden Treasury,* Second Series. Browning said of him that he had in him much of the Tennysonian poetry in solution, but that it somehow failed to crystallize. In one poem, however, "The Phantom" — strangely overlooked by Palgrave — the "solution" has crystallized into genuine poetry. The four pieces here reprinted are all from *Days and Hours;* the later volumes are pathetically negligible.

[2] This is one of the poems reprinted by Palgrave.

II

What matter if the days be dark and frore,
  That sunbeam tells of other days to be,   10
And singing in the light that floods him o'er
  In joy he overtakes Futurity;
    Under cloud-arches vast
      He peeps, and sees behind
      Great Summer coming fast   15
    Adown the wind!

III

And now he dives into a rainbow's rivers,
  In streams of gold and purple he is drown'd,
Shrilly the arrows of his song he shivers,
  As tho' the stormy drops were turn'd to sound;   20
    And now he issues thro',
      He scales a cloudy tower,
    Faintly, like falling dew,
      His fast notes shower.

IV

Let every wind be hush'd, that I may hear   25
  The wondrous things he tells the World below,
Things that we dream of he is watching near,
  Hopes that we never dream'd he would bestow;
    Alas! the storm hath roll'd
      Back the gold gates again,   30
    Or surely he had told
      All Heaven to men!

V

So the victorious Poet sings alone,
  And fills with light his solitary home,
And thro' that glory sees new worlds foreshown,   35
  And hears high songs, and triumphs yet to come;
    He waves the air of Time
      With thrills of golden chords,
    And makes the world to climb
      On linked words.   40

VI

What if his hair be gray, his eyes be dim,
  If wealth forsake him, and if friends be cold,
Wonder unbars her thousand gates to him,
  Truth never fails, nor Beauty waxeth old;
    More than he tells his eyes   45
      Behold, his spirit hears,
    Of grief, and joy, and sighs
      'Twixt joy and tears.

VII

Blest is the man who with the sound of song
  Can charm away the heartache, and forget   50
The frost of Penury, and the stings of Wrong,
  And drown the fatal whisper of Regret!
    Darker are the abodes
      Of Kings, tho' his be poor,
    While Fancies, like the Gods,   55
      Pass thro' his door.

VIII

Singing thou scalest Heaven upon thy wings,
  Thou liftest a glad heart into the skies;
He maketh his own sunrise, while he sings,
  And turns the dusty Earth to Paradise;   60
    I see thee sail along
      Far up the sunny streams,
    Unseen, I hear his song,
      I see his dreams.

THE GLORY OF NATURE[1]

I

If only once the chariot of the Morn
  Had scatter'd from its wheels the twilight dun,
  But once the unimaginable Sun
Flash'd godlike thro' perennial clouds forlorn,
And shown us Beauty for a moment born;   5

---

[1] Reprinted by Palgrave.

II

If only once blind eyes had seen the Spring,
  Waking amid the triumphs of midnoon;
  But once had seen the lovely Summer boon
Pass by in state like a full-robed King,
The waters dance, the woodlands laugh and sing;   10

III

If only once deaf ears had heard the joy
  Of the wild birds, or morning breezes blowing,
  Or silver fountains from their caverns flowing,
Or the deep-voiced rivers rolling by;
Then Night eternal fallen from the sky;   15

IV

If only once weird Time had rent asunder
  The curtain of the Clouds, and shown us Night
  Climbing into the awful Infinite
Those stairs whose steps are worlds, above and under,
Glory on glory, wonder upon wonder!   20

V

The Lightnings lit the Earthquake on his way;
  The sovran Thunder spoken to the World;
  The realm-wide banners of the Wind unfurl'd;
Earth-prison'd Fires broke loose into the day;
Or the great Seas awoke — then slept for aye!   25

VI

Ah! sure the heart of Man, too strongly tried
  By Godlike Presences so vast and fair,
  Withering with dread, or sick with love's despair,
Had wept for ever, and to Heaven cried,
Or struck with lightnings of delight had died.   30

VII

But He, though heir of Immortality,
  With mortal dust too feeble for the sight,
  Draws thro' a veil God's overwhelming light;
Use arms the Soul — anon there moveth by
A more majestic Angel — and we die!   35

THE VINE

ON CRAGGY summits which the lightnings score
   And noonday beams, thou, curly-headed Vine,
   Fill'st thy brave heart with warmth and purple wine,
And in thy strength increasest more and more,
And beauty, till the fiery days are o'er,   5
   And sun-brown Autumn from thy tresses wrings
   Drops for the golden chalices of Kings,
And brims the earthen vessels of the poor:

So doth the Poet in his days of prime
   From pains, and passions that afflict his heart,   10
From joy, and sorrow, and the storms of time,
   Draw the clear nectar of almighty Art,
And sheds his heartdrops in a gracious dew
That heals all other hearts it passeth thro'.

The earth is thirsty, yet thy veins are full;   15
   The herb is shrivell'd, yet thy leaves are green;
   The chaff lies withering where the grain hath been,
Ere yet thy clusters they begin to cull;
The latest fruits when they have ceased to pull
   The red grape dances in the breeze of heaven,   20
   And laugheth in the light of morn and even
With amber leaves, when summer flowers are dull.

So doth the Poet in his latter time
   Feel God within when other hearts are cold;
When Avarice cannot delve, Ambition climb,   25
   His step is onward, and his heart is bold;
And when his hair is white with many years,
His eye is full of hope, and unshed tears.

And when thy leaves that were so large and fair
   Are whirl'd away before the rushing wind,   30
   And in the wintry vineyard none may find
One haggard cluster out of all that were,

When hill and dale are desolate and bare;
  Thy ruddy dews are sparkling in the light
  Of the illumined hearth, and festal night,   35
Thy golden wave brings back the summer air!

So doth the Poet, from the earth departed,
  Out of the darkness of Oblivion pass,
And to the happy, and the broken-hearted
  Sings of his joys and sorrows — all he was;   40
Till his pale spectre is of vaster span
Than he — the Memory nobler than the Man!

THE PHANTOM

Last even, when the sun was low,
I walk'd, where those bright waters flow,
Where we two wander'd long ago;

With sad, slow steps I linger'd o'er
The ancient woods, the river-shore,   5
Where thou, alas! art found no more;

The winds that shook the dying flowers,
The echoes stirring in the bowers,
Seem'd as the voices of those hours;

With raptured eyes I pierced the gloom,   10
With tears that might have thaw'd the tomb
I cried unto thy Spirit 'Come,'

'Come forth,' I cried, 'twixt hope and fear,
'It is the hour when none are near,
Oh! come, beloved, meet me here.'   15

The sere leaves flitting in the dell
Whisper'd scornfully, as they fell,
'Death is Death, immutable.

'Thou that wouldst with impious haste
Call the Spirit from the vast   20
Of Nature, and recall the past;

Can thy love unlock the earth?
Canst thou bid dry bones come forth,
And give dead dust another birth?

Relume the flowers that fallen be,   25
Bring back the odors as they flee,
Or set the sere leaf on the tree?

If the soul might come to-day,
And with its old companions stay,
And tell them what the Angels say;   30

Such converse couldst thou live and bear,
That deep-eyed presence standing there
Love, even Love would never dare:

Weep not the past, but hope instead;
Mourn not, nor be discomforted,   35
The Living cannot love the Dead.'

The low winds murmur'd, as they went
'Sigh not, weep not, be content,
Death is Death, can he relent?'

Still I cried, 'twixt hope and fear,   40
'It is even, none are here,
Awake, beloved — come anear.'

Was it sad fancy's dreaming eyes,
Or an answer to my sighs?
Methought I saw a shadow rise.   45

Slowly it pass'd into the gray,
With mournful eyes half turn'd away;
And I heard a pale voice say,

In tones beyond imaginings,
As when the wind with tangled wings   50
Is fluttering amid tuneful strings,

'The Living cannot know the Dead,
But the Spirit that is fled
In good things past is perfected:

The bliss of life it felt before   55
Thrills the Spirit o'er and o'er,
Love increaseth more and more;

Never sorrow, never fear;
I am near thee, ever near,
Wakeful, more than eye or ear;   60

Sometime, dearest, we shall greet
Each other in this valley sweet —
The Future and the Past shall meet;

Sometime, we shall linger o'er
These ancient woods, this river-shore,   65
These walks where I am found no more;

Sometime, when the sun is low,
We shall wander, well I know,
Where we two wander'd long ago.

Charles Tennyson-Turner [1]

TO THE LARK

AND am I up with thee, light-hearted minion!
Who never dost thine early flight forego,
Catching for aye upon thy gamesome pinion
What was to fill some lily's cup below,
The matin dew-fall? what is half so thrilling   5
As thy glad voice i' th' argent prime of light?
Whether, in grassy nest, when thou art billing,
Or thus aloft and mocking human sight?

[1] Charles Tennyson (1808–1879), who in 1835 took the surname Turner, after contributing to *Poems by Two Brothers* (1827), published in 1830 a slender volume of *Sonnets and Fugitive Pieces*. This won the praise of Samuel Taylor Coleridge, perhaps because the sonnets reminded him of those by the master of his own youth, William L. Bowles. Further collections, mostly in the sonnet form, appeared in 1864, 1868, and 1873; and in 1880 a posthumous volume of *Collected Sonnets, Old and New* contained more than three hundred pieces in this form. The dozen

Peace dwells with thee for ever, not the peace
Of cool reflection, but redundant glee,   10
And with such vocal token of wild ease
Thou dost reveal thy proud immunity
From mortal care, that thou perforce must please:
Fair fall thy rapid song, sweet bird, and thee!

ON SEEING A CHILD BLUSH ON HIS
FIRST VIEW OF A CORPSE

'Tis good our earliest sympathies to trace,
And I would muse upon a little thing —
What brought the blush into that infant's face
When first confronted with the rueful king?
He boldly came, what made his courage less?   5
A signal for the heart to beat less free
Are all imperial presences, and he
Was aw'd by Death's consummate kingliness! —
And by the high and peerless front he bore —
No thought of dying armies crost the lad,   10
He fear'd the stranger, tho' he knew no more:
Surmising and surpris'd, but most, afraid,
As Crusoe wandering on the desert shore
Saw but an alien footmark and was sad!

TO A. H. H.[1]

When youth is passing from my hoary head,
And life's decline steals brightness from thine eye —
But *that* it cannot soon, nor quench the red
Upon thy cheek that hath so rich a dye —
Then of what crowns of fame may thou and I   5

___

specimens selected by Palgrave for *The Golden Treasury,* Second Series,
present the poet chiefly as the gently mournful memorializer of deceased
children. Three of the four sonnets reprinted in the present volume are
from the volume of 1830; "Letty's Globe," which is of later date, is
given because its somewhat surprising inclusion in *The Oxford Book of
English Verse* has made it, to modern readers, the most familiarly
known of the poems by the Poet's two brothers.

[1] Arthur Henry Hallam.

Avow ourselves the gainers? with what balm
Of christian hope, devotionally calm,
Shall I be then anointed? will this sigh,
Born of distempered feeling, still come forth
As thus, unjoyous? or be left to die   10
Before the rapid and unpausing birth
Of joyous thoughts succeeding momently?
What would not such recoil of bliss be worth,
Replacing in our age this early loss of joy?

LETTY'S GLOBE

WHEN Letty had scarce pass'd her third glad year,
And her young artless words began to flow,
One day we gave the child a colour'd sphere
Of the wide earth, that she might mark and know,
By tint and outline, all its sea and land.   5
She patted all the world; old empires peep'd
Between her baby fingers; her soft hand
Was welcome at all frontiers. How she leap'd,
And laugh'd and prattled in her world-wide bliss;
But when we turn'd her sweet unlearnèd eye   10
On our own isle, she raised a joyous cry —
'Oh! yes, I see it, Letty's home is there!'
And while she hid all England with a kiss,
Bright over Europe fell her golden hair.

INDEX OF FIRST LINES

For the sections of *In Memoriam* see separate index.

The poems by Frederick Tennyson and Charles Tennyson-Turner (in Appendix III) are not included in this index.

511

INDEX TO *IN MEMORIAM* (Pages 306–409)

The references are to sections, not pages.

INDEX OF TITLES

POEMS BY FREDERICK TENNYSON

POEMS BY CHARLES TENNYSON-TURNER

INDEX TO THE NOTES

For notes on the date and circumstances of composition of individual poems see the Index of First Lines and the Index of Titles.

DATE DUE